Social Policy and Citizenship

International Policy Exchange Series

Published in collaboration with the
Center for International Policy Exchanges
University of Maryland

Series Editors
Douglas J. Besharov
Neil Gilbert

SCHOOL of
PUBLIC POLICY

SOCIAL POLICY AND CITIZENSHIP

The Changing Landscape

Edited by

ADALBERT EVERS
ANNE-MARIE GUILLEMARD

OXFORD
UNIVERSITY PRESS

OXFORD
UNIVERSITY PRESS

Oxford University Press is a department of the University of Oxford. It furthers the University's objective
of excellence in research, scholarship, and education by publishing worldwide.

Oxford   New York
Auckland   Cape Town   Dar es Salaam   Hong Kong   Karachi
Kuala Lumpur   Madrid   Melbourne   Mexico City   Nairobi
New Delhi   Shanghai   Taipei   Toronto

With offices in
Argentina   Austria   Brazil   Chile   Czech Republic   France   Greece
Guatemala   Hungary   Italy   Japan   Poland   Portugal   Singapore
South Korea   Switzerland   Thailand   Turkey   Ukraine   Vietnam

Oxford is a registered trademark of Oxford University Press in the UK and certain other countries.

Published in the United States of America by
Oxford University Press
198 Madison Avenue, New York, NY 10016

Copyright © 2013 by Oxford University Press

Library of Congress Cataloging-in-Publication Data
Social policy and citizenship : the changing landscape / edited by Adalbert Evers, Anne-Marie Guillemard.
   p. cm. – (International policy exchange series)
   Includes bibliographical references and index.
   ISBN 978–0–19–975404–5
   1. Europe – Social policy – Case studies.   2. Social service – Europe – Case studies.   3. Manpower
policy – Europe – Case studies.   I. Evers, Adalbert.   II. Guillemard, Anne Marie.
   HN373.5.S6273 2012
   303.3094 – dc23
   2012007070

CONTENTS

CONTRIBUTORS

JEAN-CLAUDE BARBIER
CNRS-MATISSE and University
   Paris 1
Paris, France

INGO BODE
University of Kassel
Kassel, Germany

ADALBERT EVERS
Justus-Liebig-University
Gießen, Germany

VALERIA FARGION
University of Florence
Florence, Italy

NEIL GILBERT
University of California, Berkeley
Berkeley, California

ANNE-MARIE GUILLEMARD
University Paris Descartes Sorbonne
Paris, France

BJØRN HVINDEN
Norwegian University of Science and
   Technology
Trondheim, Norway

JANE JENSON
University of Montreal
Montreal, Canada

HÅKAN JOHANSSON
Lund University
Lund, Sweden

RUTH LISTER
Loughborough University
Leicestershire, United Kingdom

MARTIN POTŮČEK
Charles University
Prague, Czech Republic

MAREK RYMSZA
University of Warsaw
Warsaw, Poland

Tomáš Sirovátka
Masaryk University
Brno, Czech Republic

Julia Szalaï
Hungarian Academy of Sciences
Budapest, Hungary

Lars Svedberg
Ersta Sköndal University College
Stockholm, Sweden

Lars Trägårdh
Ersta Sköndal University College
Stockholm, Sweden

PART I

GENERAL

1

INTRODUCTION: MARSHALL'S CONCEPT OF CITIZENSHIP AND CONTEMPORARY WELFARE RECONFIGURATION

Adalbert Evers and Anne-Marie Guillemard

This book aims to shed light on issues related to the future of the welfare state. It brings together existing knowledge of the complex changes that have been under way in various social policy fields over the past two decades and tries to highlight their consequences on citizenship. The question of how economic, societal, and welfare changes have affected social citizenship and entitlements has received contrasting, even contradictory, responses because of its complexity and also because it is a major concern and interest for individuals and social groups. This debate will linger, and the international financial crisis, budget debts linked to it, as well as what is called the "Euro crisis" will push it further on. This book is contributing to the debate. And even though its chapters have been completed before this international crisis broke out, we claim that the insights and arguments presented here have not lost their validity.

Our introduction to this volume is serving four major aims.

First of all we will outline our theoretical point of reference: the concept of citizenship, as conceptualized by T. H. Marshall over half a century ago, and the major debates and criticisms that have developed during the subsequent decades.

The second step will be to take up the other basic concern of this volume: developments in social policy. We will argue that the changes of the past decades call for more than simply a debate about the reduction or extension of social rights; in fact, they imply qualitative changes, and not only in social rights but also extending to civil and democratic rights. This book is thus about social policy and citizenship rather than just social policy and social rights.

The third part of this introduction presents those simultaneous changes in societies, social policies, and citizenship that we, as the editors of this volume, view as especially important. We will not deal with "the condition of citizenship" (Steenbergen 1994) in modernity at large but rather with the more limited terrain of the changing landscape of linkages between citizenship and social policy. Among the social and institutional changes we refer to are issues such as labor market changes, the expansion of the consumer sphere, pluralization and migration, and finally Europeanization—the way in which citizenship is getting a supranational dimension in Europe. We will then turn to two fundamental changes in the whole approach to social policies and their effects on citizenship: the turn to policies of social investment alongside the upgrading of economic concerns and the increasing impact of policies of activation, accentuating the role of duties and incentives in social policies. The third part ends with some reflections on the wider frame for citizenship in terms of written legal rights— the underlying notions of the divisions of rights and responsibilities between the realms of the state, the market, the third sector and the family, and the respective roles that individuals have there.

The fourth and final part of this introduction will explain the structure of the remainder of the book. For all too long, theoretical reasoning on changes in citizenship and social policy approaches on the one hand and debates on concrete aspects and details of welfare state change on the other hand have been at a distance. This book seeks to bring them closer together by presenting contributions that link the overarching topics of citizenship and social policy change with the analysis of concrete changes in fields of national welfare policies.

CITIZENSHIP, PAST AND PRESENT

Welfare systems embody the principles of solidarity and interdependence that social bonds are based on, especially in western European societies. As we know, one distinctive characteristic of these societies is their relatively generous social model, in comparison with the American one. The welfare system is the necessary condition for building a society in which each person participates fully. It has done much to mold the modern, independent, free citizen as an individual. Marshall adopted this perspective in his well-known essay *Citizenship and Social Class* (1964), which was first published in 1950—at the beginning of the long period of prosperity that followed World War II.

According to Marshall, citizenship in England became institutionalized in a sequence of three stages. It first took the form of civil rights—that is to say, the legal protections provided to individuals and the private sphere under a constitutional monarchy. As democracy developed, political rights, such as the right to vote and to assemble and associate, were added to civil rights. Finally, alongside open, equal, universal access to civil and political rights for all, the concept of citizenship was expanded to include social rights, which have been shaped through the welfare state. Social citizenship has developed hand in hand with social security, redistributive benefits, cash entitlements, and social services.

As we know, Marshall's starting point for thinking about citizenship is the question of how to reconcile the status of the citizen—who, as such, is recognized as a member of a single community and as being equal in terms of rights and obligations to other citizens—with the inequality observed in a class-based society. Universal entitlements do not eradicate inequality entirely but they do mitigate it, as class divisions take on the character of status differences and as, in a democracy, social policy presents opportunities to advance toward equality. For Marshall, civil, political, and social rights and freedoms are interdependent and reinforce one another. Democracy must be built on individual civil rights; it requires social rights, and in turn, welfare arrangements help to stabilize democracy.

Clearly, then, the extension of citizenship, while inconceivable without the establishment of rights, should nevertheless not be confused with a set of rights. Taking the English example, Marshall pictures a historical process involving conflicting agents and the progressive renegotiation of compromises and shared convictions. Citizenship rights rely on citizens and civic practices to some degree, and conversely, enshrining citizenship in guaranteed rights may help to strengthen a culture of civility and "civicness." Thus, what is required from the citizen is "that his acts should be inspired by a lively sense of responsibility towards the welfare of the community" (Marshall, 1964, 123). Marshall's conception presupposes, then, a balance between the rights and entitlements that citizens are granted, to ensure that they are integrated into the community and that they meet the duties and obligations that, in return, every individual has toward the community (see Chapter 2).

This perspective on "active citizenship"—as the counterpart of "passive citizenship" linked to rights and entitlements—leaves much room for interpretation. What is clear, however, is that according to Marshall, rights give rise to citizenship only when citizens—in their interrelationships and their attitude towards a democratic state—can to some extent overcome indifference, egotism, and "clientelism." Among sociologists and political scientists, this perspective on building citizenship has provided an internationally applicable analytical tool. In many countries, its underlying ideas have shaped public discourses on welfare.

Since the 1980s, when the "Welfare State Crisis" erupted (OECD, 1981) and the workings of the welfare state became the subject of political debate, Marshall's explanations have been the subject of increasing debate. One area of debate has been how to interpret the concept properly; another has been its validity.

With regard to an appropriate understanding of Marshall's concept, two major interpretations have been rejected. The first one, as expounded in the early writings of Esping-Andersen (1990, 21–23) for example, suggested that social rights based on citizenship and granted to all would de-commodify wage labor to the extent that individuals could maintain a livelihood without being reliant on the market. However, as Powell (2002) has shown, Marshall's perspective was more modest—namely, bringing about a much looser correlation between the (labor) market situation of an individual and his or her social citizenship rights, rather than doing away with this correlation entirely. Citizenship rights should not replace the market, but moderate its impact.

According to the second, more radical interpretation, which was later widely rejected, the universal right to entitlements in cash or in kind (as services) is fulfilled only once access to these entitlements is linked with no or only minimal conditions. However, although Marshall's vision of universalism was unconditional in the fields of health and education services, he was fully aware that other social rights may be extended conditionally, and that entitlement criteria such as prior contributions, age, or means may be added. Provided this does not lead to a bifurcated service system (the ills of which are discussed in Chapter 12), in which provisions for special groups lead to stigmatization, the sum of these benefits and services—some being more and others less selective—would still contribute towards a more equal citizenry overall (see again Powell, 2002). However, status and de-commodification are also important for a second central aim in Marshall's concept: as well as enhancing equality and inclusion, it is to give a degree of security and protection. Social rights in health, at the workplace, and on provisions for the elderly cannot eradicate risks, but they can mitigate them and provide some degree of security for citizens trying to develop coping strategies. Marshall's far-reaching—yet finite—aims can best be summarized in his often-quoted assertion that "social rights in their modern form imply an invasion of contract by status, the subordination of market price to social justice, the replacement of the free bargain by the declaration of right" (1964, 111).

The debate that surrounds the validity of Marshall's idea of citizenship concerns three main points.

The first one is a possible lack of analytical accuracy in his concept. Two recurring questions here are to what degree the concept can be generalized, and whether or not the foundational sequence of civil, democratic, and social rights is discernable in countries other than England (on such controversies see Bulmer & Rees, 1996; Crouch et al., 2001; Rees, 1996; on the far-ranging consequences of such a sequence missing, see Chapter 8).

But there are also criticisms that reflect various normative and ideological strands of thinking. Basically, due to its "lib-lab" orientation that builds on liberal and social-democratic convictions, the perspective implicit in Marshall's concept has enjoyed much support in academic and public debates. Yet especially from the liberal side there are criticisms concerning—for example—his basic idea of putting social rights on an equal footing with political and civil rights. Traditionally, liberals have prioritized civil rights—which protect people from state intervention—over social rights. Social rights, rather than being seen as complementary to civil and democratic rights, are seen as being in tension with them (for a debate on the tension between civil and social rights as this has accompanied welfare state development and recent changes in Sweden, see Chapter 10). Republican political thinking, on the other hand, is critical of the fact that Marshall takes a more relaxed view on issues such as active citizenship through membership of social movements, political participation, and so on. Once again, from a communitarian point of view the role of social networks, bonds, and certified rights below the level of the nation-state may be seen as critical (see the debate on such positions in Hvinden & Johansson, 2007; Isin, 2000; and Chapter 2).

The third point of debate on the validity of Marshall's concept concerns the degree to which it remains valid when seeking to understand and cope with the various challenges that characterize the social realities of today. Questions have arisen about how relevant Marshall's concept is to contemporary economies and societies and the cultures of living, politics, and welfare that have taken shape since Marshall's time. Three examples of such radical change spring easily to mind: women play a very different role today compared to 50 years ago; people today follow a very different life course, with flexibility and de-standardization replacing the old tripartite division between education for the young, work for adults, and retirement for old age; and today's state must take account of the processes of globalization and decentralization (Crouch et al., 2001; Dwyer, 2010; Giddens, 1996; Guillemard, 2005, Lister, 1990; Powell, 2002). The question of whether new realities require a new and different "post-Marshallian" concept of citizenship, or whether citizenship can by and large still be founded on Marshall's earlier explanations, is the subject of much debate. The editors of this book do not take a particular view on that question. Part of the difficulty of this question stems from the fact that on some much-debated points, Marshall has provided only hints rather than clear positions. In fact, while he discusses the link between rights and responsibilities, his attention to responsibilities is limited. Likewise, it is not clear where to place his analysis between the polar positions of a thorough-going quest for "equality" and the more modest aim of the social inclusion of all society's members. And while Marshall is fully aware that active citizens are required to make citizenship real, his emphasis is more on citizenship rights or "passive citizenship," as one might call it, rather than active citizenship (on these points, see Powell, 2002).

However, the debate about how far Marshall's concept of citizenship is still valid also depends on the perspective one takes when it comes to the character of changes in welfare as they have occurred or as they have been deemed necessary. At issue are the "packages" and "patterns" of rights provided at a time when the risks to be covered and the methods of protection are in flux and controversial.

During the 1980s, debates on social policy centered on reductions in social spending. They sparked mass movements to defend social security. These mainly quantitative debates raised questions about the level of social benefits and the scope of entitlements, and whether the welfare state should be scaled back or expanded further. Since 2000, a more qualitative line of thought has arisen about risks and how to protect citizens from them. Some analyses claim that even if welfare spending is maintained at the same level, it will still be impossible to cope effectively with the challenges and risks of today. A new image of a more active welfare state has appeared that is based on "social investments." As a consequence, trends in welfare reform are more ambivalent and harder to interpret. We can no longer deal with them only in terms of a reduction in social services and entitlements, or a decline in social citizenship. They also have to do with new ways of conceiving of, and safeguarding, people's security in a post-industrial world that requires more mobility, autonomy, and responsibility on the part of the individual. The interest aroused everywhere in Europe by "flexicurity" and by policies for "securing" life-course trajectories is evidence that security is being re-examined in the light of the new risks that stem from the global knowledge-based economy and significant demographic change (an aging population, a declining birth rate, and increased life expectancy). The terms of the debate, then, have shifted. Simply maintaining the welfare states that were established after World War II can no longer fully guarantee the social security of individuals. Since 2000, the quantitative and qualitative orientations have existed side by side. The Euro crisis and the signals that are given by those politicians who actually speak for the EU as well as the debate in the United States may actually have changed the balance once again. The complicated issue of reconfiguring welfare is vanishing over and again behind the seemingly clear and simple advices to cut welfare spending wherever this is possible by few drastic measures that show immediate results (e.g., by reducing the level of pensions, lengthening working life, and tightening all kind of benefits). While the need—and the will—to curb social spending has remained and gets once again more vigor, the new figure of an activist state ready to make social investments is however alive as well, even though this investment depends on social policies that differ significantly from country to country.

BACKGROUND AND CONTEXT: CHANGING WELFARE STATES AND CHANGING METHODS OF ANALYSIS

The 1990s: The Quantitative Debate About Expanding or Curbing the Welfare State

During the 1990s, Europe was characterized by the determination of public authorities to reduce social spending—and indeed public expenditure as a whole—in an effort to control budgets. A macroeconomic orthodoxy circulated that broke with the Keynesian principles of supporting demand—principles on which Europe's welfare states had been built—and turned instead toward supply-side action. The evolution of the EU, particularly through directives passed after the adoption of the Maastricht Treaty (1993), led to increasingly vociferous criticism of social spending. Such expenditure was no longer seen as favorable to economic growth and regulation but as a cost factor, undermining competitiveness and productivity and causing rising unemployment and dependence on social protection. But this change cannot be interpreted simply as an overwhelming move toward neoliberalism, with its focus on controlling and reducing social spending. Analyses of these changes that conceive of them purely in terms of cuts and a turn to residualism—such as the early analysis of Pierson (1994)—have proven insufficient.

An approach that looked only at spending reductions came from a narrow vision of the welfare state that took into account only the level of expenditure and the level of benefits. This may lead us to overlook the qualitative aspects of changes in welfare. As we know, however, it is possible to spend less but better by acting on the specific ways in which social entitlements are designed, without modifying their scope. The disability insurance reform that was undertaken in the Netherlands in 1998 illustrates this point rather well. It made employers responsible by involving them in managing the worker's compensation fund, something that is in line with changes made to Dutch health insurance in 1994 (Guillemard, 2002). As we also know, a risk-prevention strategy can be a more effective form of public intervention than providing compensation once a risk has become a reality.

The quantitative approach also proved to be reductive in a second sense, insofar as it sought to explain trends in welfare reform through variations in spending alone. To use Marshall's terms, by linking social citizenship with a given set of social rights, the debate centered mainly on increasing or decreasing benefits and services, partly by changing the terms of access (such as revised criteria in terms of age, or means testing). This explains some of the simplistic interpretations of the history of the welfare state since World War II. These interpretations summarily account for welfare trends in relation to the universalistic, redistributive welfare state that reached its zenith during the 30-year period of economic growth that followed the war and then quickly declined as new economic and demographic factors emerged, along with a "neoliberal" strategy for adjusting to them.

The preference for macro-social explanations led analysts to overlook the effect of new rules and eligibility requirements on both beneficiaries and the practices of social service agencies. Moreover, such analyses have failed to take account of the quite limited success of cost-containment policies. The cost-containment policies adopted by the Reagan and Thatcher governments, as well as those of many other OECD countries during the 1980s, did not lead to the dismantling of public welfare programs. The attempts to curb social spending met with strong resistance from social groups, which defended their entitlements and vested interests. Furthermore, well-established welfare systems displayed remarkable inertia, even in the face of the most radical reforms. They seemed to be "immovable objects" (Pierson, 2001). This resistance to change was attributed to a double barrier erected by welfare institutions to reforms. First of all, welfare programs generate, in reaction, sundry coalitions of interests among beneficiaries, who watchfully defend their social programs and benefits. This has political implications for the social programs to be designed and implemented and for the broader will to reform welfare. Secondly, the same options that were chosen when building welfare systems continue to weigh heavily when making choices about implementing reforms. According to a key principle of path dependency in the neo-institutionalist approach, all change depends on choices made earlier when building the system. In hindsight, one can actually say that global levels of spending were in fact the weakest indicators for welfare changes.

The points outlined above will help us avoid too narrow an interpretation of the changes now under way. Invoking the "neoliberal turn" taken by Europe (Jobert, 1994) is not sufficient to explain why the expansion of welfare came to a halt and why its underlying principles came to be reviewed. According to this explanation, there is a general trend among European welfare systems towards contraction, the end result of which will be a more "residual" form of social protection, as already exists in the United States with its welfare "safety net" based mainly on assistance. Under this vision, universal public services will be drastically curbed and the market's role in welfare significantly enhanced. However, in *The New Politics of the Welfare State*, Pierson (2001) proposed a quantitative and qualitative grid with which to analyze welfare reforms. He interpreted them in relation to three main points: (1) the re-commodification of needs; (2) cost containment; and (3) the reconfiguration of welfare. This third point represented a first step towards drawing attention to the qualitative dimension.

In summary, any conclusion about how welfare reforms in the 1990s amputated social citizenship must include an assessment of changes in the logics of welfare, how the programs were justified, how they were redesigned, and the impact of these changes on beneficiaries. And even though in the face of the present financial crisis and high household debts the politics of cost containment may be in the foreground, this will not marginalize the challenge to answer those structural weaknesses of welfare arrangements already visible now for decades. Therefore, a methodological shift is urgently needed. We must break with an analysis and practices that focus exclusively on changes in overall spending, or on welfare institutions and their formal rules. For this reason, our book will refer— as will be explained later—to specific cases in specific countries. The aim is an in-depth analysis of how changes in welfare policies as they have taken shape in the past two decades affect the level of social security provided to individuals and ultimately social citizenship.

Since 2000: A More Qualitative Debate on an Active Welfare State

In 2001, a new perspective emerged on changes in welfare. It was evidence of a growing awareness of the limits of the quantitative approach to cost containment that had prevailed during the preceding decade. The first decade of the new millennium has witnessed fundamental changes in both "security" and the policies pursued. The debate has shifted from a quantitative approach to a qualitative explanation of how effective welfare is in satisfying needs. A more critical stance has been adopted vis-à-vis the operation of welfare states. The welfare systems established during the industrial era, with their lists of recognized risks and corresponding entitlements, no longer seem capable of providing coverage for the new kinds of social risks that have emerged in a globalized society based on information, networks, and knowledge. It is necessary to innovate in response to new social security needs, since it is no longer enough to defend the systems set up after World War II. The quantitative debate on expanding or curbing protection is giving way to a qualitative debate on how to redeploy welfare to remedy its main dysfunctions and restore its effectiveness in postindustrial society. This shift is leading to a new philosophy for protecting individuals that is redesigning the very foundations of the postwar welfare state.

The major conclusion to be drawn about social citizenship in 1999 seemed clear: the triad of civic, political, and social rights seemed threatened by what some commentators called the neoliberal revolution. Most debates on citizenship focused on the tensions between social policies (which tended to seek to expand social rights) and economic policies (in favor of free enterprise). However, during the first decade of this new millennium, "third ways" have developed for thinking about social policy, not only in "New Labour" circles in the UK but also among social democrats in Scandinavia. Consequently, across the political spectrum the debate has become less "either-or" in nature (state vs. market, economic vs. social objectives). New blends and balances have emerged (see Chapters 3 and 6).

There is, first of all, broad acceptance of the need to find new ways to reconcile the economy with welfare, which has had a detrimental effect on employment levels. This has led to a search for compromises that avoid the traditional "either-or" choice between Keynesianism and supply-side orthodoxies. Secondly, there is a search for a new balance between the role attached to the welfare state and other actors, especially the agency of the individual citizens. There may be disagreements about the respective share of responsibility on both sides, but there is also increasing agreement that both sides do have to contribute to welfare arrangements. Both points are leading to a new conception of an active welfare state that is primarily concerned with social investment. The mainly redistributive role of the past is being replaced by a state that gives priority to a social investment strategy (Esping-Andersen, 2002, and Chapter 3) and an "enabling state" (Gilbert & Gilbert, 1989, and Chapter 4). This has implications not only for the level but also for the nature and design of social rights, and furthermore it calls for a simultaneous look at the other—civil and democratic—dimensions of citizenship. This book is therefore not only about social policy and social rights, but also about social policy and citizenship.

Every change in the direction outlined above hinges on changes to be made in governance, especially the governance of welfare policies. The implementation of a new "active" welfare state depends on a new "responsibility mix" that emphasizes partnerships and interconnections and complementarity between actors. The new welfare state is tending to establish new forms of solidarity, mixing public and private sources and coordinating them to provide a closer, more individualized form of protection for beneficiaries. The welfare state's shift toward investing in people involves contributing to their "empowerment." Most intervention should be preventive, so as to limit the loss of autonomy and capabilities by individuals. This calls for innovations in policy instruments. What are now being called "life-course social policies" are the principal means by which welfare states will make social investment in order to grant certain rights to all individuals, providing them with the resources and services to enable them to become the authors of their own lives.

It is important to understand that changing ideas about welfare governance, which are reflected in references to an "activating" or "enabling" welfare state, imply changes in social citizenship but equally in those dimensions of citizenship that are associated with individual autonomy and participation rights. Once we move from the "passive" citizenship of rights towards an active citizenship that includes both rights and responsibilities, we will require a participative and inclusive framework in which this more active social citizenship can be cultivated. Such activation may stem from people's concerns or from "top-down" programs, but in either case, and for better or worse, welfare reforms have implications not only for social citizenship but for civil and political citizenship too. To date, social policy debates on citizenship have seldom mentioned this (see as an exception Bussemaker, 1999), but this volume will include this key aspect.

Methodological Considerations for Analyzing Changes in Citizenship

In line with our earlier argument, we now need to clarify the methodology adopted in this book in order to analyze changes in citizenship. In recent years, there has been renewed interest in the subject of citizenship in the literature. This can probably be attributed to the orientation towards an "active social state" that was advocated at the Lisbon Summit in 2000 as part of the EU's strategy for "modernizing the European social model by investing in people and building an active welfare state." Consideration has primarily been devoted to the concept of citizenship and the relevance of Marshall's model to understanding the changes currently under way in social policy and how they affect social citizenship (see Chapter 2 for a review of this literature).

This literature has involved a wide-ranging overview of social policy changes but has not provided any grassroots-level analysis. The studies have sought to outline the new philosophy for protecting individuals that has inspired welfare reforms. As discussions of the "social investment strategy" have shown, this strategy implies redesigning the very foundations of postwar welfare states. Unfortunately, there has been little empirical research into the effects of such changes on beneficiaries. Studies have been limited to analyzing changes in the formal rules, regulations, and eligibility requirements governing welfare arrangements, without considering how these rules are actually applied by social services and their staff in relation to their "clients." Likewise, one knows little about how they affect beneficiaries' entitlements and access to them in reality.

We would like to break free from this abstract treatment of the question of links between social policy changes and changes in citizenship. The chapters in this volume, while they do not neglect changes in rules, regulations, and eligibility requirements, also seek to reveal the implications of these changes all the way down to the level of beneficiaries, so that the impact of welfare reforms on entitlements and social citizenship can be assessed.

We have tried to avoid the pitfalls of the decontextualized, generalized approach that has often led comparative studies to end by drawing normative conclusions. This happened, for example, in the theoretical debates relating to new policies for the "activation of social protection" in Europe. Criticism of this activation model was based on establishing a similarity with what was called "workfare" in the United States under President Richard Nixon. They criticized the proposals as coercive, even punitive, because they were alleged to subordinate eligibility for welfare to a speedy return to the labor market while stigmatizing beneficiaries who have become too estranged from the world of work to be able to return there. Because of the failure to take into consideration the various concrete forms taken by "welfare activation" in European countries, these analyses are unable to account for the different degrees and ways of transformation of citizenship that these policies have fostered in various contexts.

To expand further on the example of the Anglo-American model of "workfare" or "welfare to work"—under which the obligation to work is systematically augmented along with the social control associated with this conception of welfare being conditional upon the efforts of the beneficiary—the actual arrangements that have resulted from the application of this principle have not been identical in every societal context. In particular, the means of sanctioning beneficiaries who do not comply with prescribed obligations differ widely from country to country. Jean-Claude Barbier (2005) (also see Chapter 7 on the application of this activation strategy in France) points out two ways to implement this new principle, each with very distinct consequences for individuals and social citizenship. Barbier distinguishes between two poles of "social activation" in Europe: one liberal and the other social democratic. Both models set out to align welfare better with the labor market in order to avoid the major "pathologies" described by Esping-Andersen (1996a), such as the "welfare state without work" that characterizes continental welfare states. The search for a better balance between citizens' rights and obligations has led to attempts to bring beneficiaries toward the world of work. Accordingly, a job is considered to be the best way to ensure the autonomy of the individual and prevent people from being caught in "poverty traps" and "welfare dependency"—the major pathologies that affected the postwar welfare states.

The implementation of these new obligations differs widely under the two models mentioned above, however. Based on the principle of "work first," the liberal model emphasizes the obligation of a quick return to the labor market in its current form. Eligibility for welfare depends strictly on fulfilling this condition, and all responsibility for doing so rests with the individual. Under the social democratic model, by contrast, coverage is provided through a wide range of services and benefits that draw individuals toward employment and equip them with the resources necessary to rejoin the labor market according to their potential. Social services and their staff thus share the beneficiary's responsibility to return to work. This obligation is proportionate to the beneficiary's capacity and is paired with a set of graduated sanctions.

As this example shows, we must move beyond analyzing changes in welfare principles and rules and try to uncover their impact on social entitlements and citizenship. We are thus led to adopt a strategy of contextualized analysis. This should be founded on empirically based evidence on how these rules and principles have been implemented in the past decade at the grassroots level through the practices of social services and their staff. Moreover, we should investigate the actual consequences on beneficiaries. By focusing on what people receive from welfare and on how they claim their entitlements, we can detect how the various layers of reforms have altogether remolded social citizenship. They go on to do so irrespective of the fact that in face of the threads of the financial crisis and the debts of many public households, they may mingle more than before with traditional cost-containment policies.

The need for contextualization was a basic criterion when designing this book, both in choosing national case studies and placing them in a comparative perspective. Despite the Europeanization of welfare (a process that has arisen from the construction of the EU), social policies remain firmly national. They fit into a national history and a coherent set of national institutions, and we must be aware of this context in order to interpret them accurately. This book is therefore based on a "societal analysis" (Maurice, Sellier, & Sylvestre, 1982), which gives a key place in comparative studies to the effect of the combination of institutional arrangements specific to each national context. Such an approach represents more than the concept of neo-institutionalism, since it takes into account the effect of composition or institutional arrangements.

Likewise, the national context affects the very concept of citizenship itself, as can be seen in the parts devoted to the contrasts between eastern and western Europe. The societal context forms a cognitive framework within which the classificatory forms and value judgments associated with welfare arrangements must be interpreted, as the cognitive sociology of social policy has shown (Muller, 2000; Schmidt, 2000). Over the past two decades social policy and social citizenship have also been developing in central and eastern Europe, a region that this book will not overlook. However, it will show how these concepts have, in this different context, assumed a different meaning in comparison with western Europe.

Given this concern for contextualizing the analysis of social policy reforms and their impact on citizenship, we have not chosen to compare throughout the same sectors of welfare in the countries presented. Rather, the social policy domains, institutions and reforms retained for a country are those that are most relevant and significant with respect to the overarching theme of the link between social policy and citizenship changes in the country's institutions and reforms. Depending on the country, social policies for "activation," health, or family support are examined—whatever sector best illustrates how social citizenship is being remolded in that country.

CONSEQUENCES FOR CITIZENSHIP

Citizenship and Social Change—A Traditional Concept Meets New Realities

It has been over half a century since Marshall wrote his essay *Citizenship and Social Class*, and much has changed in the societies where social policies were implemented. What, then, are the most significant changes to have taken place when it comes to defending the perspective that Marshall once took? We would choose four changes: (a) the new character of labor markets in our societies; (b) the extended role of consumer markets and of individuals as consumers; (c) pluralization and migration; and (d) Europeanization. Let us begin, then, by addressing labor markets and waged labor in relation to citizenship.

Changing Labor Markets

Marshall's essay on social class and citizenship talked of social rights mainly with reference to public services such as education and health. In these areas, Marshall called not only for a minimal level of rights, but actually for extended social rights for all, independent of socioeconomic position or participation in labor markets. The English National Health Service (NHS) is a good example of a concept of "rights," where the only condition for access was membership of the nation-state. However, only a very small number of rights in the modern welfare state have such a universal and unconditional character, dependent only on membership of the citizenry. Most rights are also conditional on wage-earner status and, as such, are built around the citizen-worker. More specifically, they rely on the concept of a male breadwinner with a "standard" employment history. The level of many of the social entitlements thus came to depend on the individual's employment history. Arguably, about 80% of all social spending goes into entitlements and services that are meant for wage-earner citizens—the vast majority of citizens who participate or have participated in the labor market. In this social sector, rights are shaping living and working conditions, many of the social services, and the mechanisms of horizontal redistribution among the wage-earner citizens and along their life course. The other part goes as a kind of vertical redistribution and through special services and cash benefits for social assistance into systems outside the aforementioned sector to those groups in need that have never been in or fallen out of the system of wage-earner citizenship (Taylor-Gooby, 2009, 8).

To the extent that societies were able to integrate steadily increasing numbers of men and women into paid jobs, the distinction between the vast domain of inclusive, purely citizenship-based rights (such as education) and work-based rights (such as retirement pensions) on the one hand, and the more conditional and restricted rights of nonworkers on the other hand (such as social assistance or antipoverty programs) made little difference. However, in today's context of partial, temporary, or unstable integration into the labor market, the work-centeredness of social rights has become problematic (see the exemplary discussion of this point in Chapter 9). It is not only the increasing hierarchies and varying degrees of labor market participation—with ever-more-frequent interruptions—that undermine joint wage-earner citizenship status. Rising numbers of citizens never participate in the labor market, because they are long-term unemployed for example, and have to contend with the entirely different regime of rights and duties that stems from the social assistance tradition. A kind of dualism is emerging under which some citizens are deprived of rights that are normal for workers or retired workers, such as pension plans. While it is often becoming increasingly difficult to enter the labor market and remain there, the link between rights and wage-earnership is becoming ever tighter (look in this respect to the right to draw an old-age pension, for example), and many of the special entitlements for nonworkers and the unemployed are being reshaped by a workfare logic (on this point, see Chapter 11 on the Czech Republic and Chapter 12 on Hungary). It can be imagined that the segregation and decreasing degrees of labor market integration and the rising problem of labor market exclusion could lead to the "erosion of citizenship" (Turner, 2001), both through a reduced level of security and protection and the emergence of an "underclass" or groups of "second-class" citizens. The more new selective and targeted services, programs, and entitlements center on employability, the more welfare states run the risk of moving from de-commodification to re-commodification (Pierson, 2001).

However, the word "risk" reminds us not to draw such a clear-cut conclusion too hastily. Depending on the profile of more recent policies for occupational and social inclusion, it is also possible to find targeted measures and programs that may work within an inclusive, universalistic perspective—such as schemes that give lone and unemployed parents immediate access to childcare facilities, which could also be seen as a kind of positive discrimination (on the ambiguities of inclusion, see Chapter 7). Nevertheless, in the face of declining labor market inclusion, it becomes increasingly difficult for work-centered social policies to maintain a universalistic and inclusive perspective.

The notion of the flexible life course (Guillemard, 2005) could be another way to overcome the exclusion caused by the traditional wage-earner citizenship without adopting the somewhat utopian perspective of unconditional rights. If we adopt a flexible life-course perspective, the challenge for social citizenship could be formulated as follows: which rights do people need in order to guarantee their income throughout a working life fraught with interruptions and transitions and also to bring work and family life together while maintaining their employability despite repeated career breaks? In more abstract terms, one could say that patterns of rights are needed, which, unlike in the past, overcome rather than reinforce the dualism between the status of workers and nonworkers in the traditional wage-based models of social citizenship rights.

In conclusion, one can argue that instead of securing jobs, the emphasis should be on securing the multiple transitions that now exist throughout the work lives of citizens. The challenge is no longer simply to compensate for risks; it is to provide active support for continuity in flexible biographical trajectories. In line with this new challenge, various proposals in recent years have sought to reconfigure welfare by combining security with flexibility. Whether we talk of "social investments" (Esping-Andersen, 1996b), "social drawing rights" (Supiot, 2001) or "transitional labor markets" (Schmid & Gazier, 2002), all these aim to redefine the paradigm that underlies the welfare systems as it has been inherited from the industrial era and the corresponding set of social entitlements.

The Expansion of the Consumer Sphere

Another major trend that has implications for patterns of citizenship rights is the vast expansion of the consumer sphere (Soper & Trentmann, 2008). It was not a matter of social policy and citizenship when Marshall wrote his essay. In fact, this expansion brings together two developments: the increased *de facto* and symbolic role of consumer markets in a society where people have much greater spending power than half a century ago, and the fact that they are now addressed as consumers even in the sector of social services such as health, social care, education, and training. The question of citizenship rights for consumers raises issues of consumer protection, advice, and advocacy and creates a role for consumer organizations.

However, issues of the rights of citizens as consumers have become important as well in the field that Marshall concentrated on—public social services. Since they have been transformed into state-regulated service markets, the challenge now is how to balance security and protection on the one hand and the right to choice—for example, between the provider, time, and types of the measures—on the other hand. The complicated challenge is how the liberal element in the citizenship triad—civil rights in terms of the right on individual choice and on protection from state intervention—can be balanced against the social rights element in terms of guaranteed services and professional advice and decisions (on this point, see Chapter 10). Here, once again, new solutions are needed (such as by granting a disabled person a budget to spend and some advice on how to use it best, rather than offering prescribed services). A new "lib-lab" compromise could mean taking account of people's agency and will to co-produce service arrangements, not only through choice but also by strengthening their voice, for example by introducing elements of decentralization and participation into service systems and by allowing individuals more scope to negotiate care packages. This could be a way to complement Marshall's concern for the wage-earner citizen with the concern of how to define the rights and status of a "consumer-citizen" (Clarke et al., 2007).

Pluralization and Migration

Let us move now to the third fundamental change that leads us to reassess the assumptions on which Marshall's concepts were based. The title of his famous essay quite deliberately linked citizenship with social class. Inequality was, by and large, identical with the inequalities that separated the working class from the better-off strata of society. Giving to the working class what the others already had (access to health and education, for example) was a step toward their cultural and political integration, toward a "mainstreaming" of basic patterns of work, life, behavior, and expectations. These "universal" rights would promote social integration and bring about shared interests, concerns, and cultural patterns. However, as a result of the growing pluralism and diversity that have come about through immigration and multiculturalism, new cleavages have appeared in contemporary societies. Today, two issues are at stake.

Firstly, with respect to migrants, all countries have developed scales of reduced membership of the citizenry and partial access to citizenship rights. Some groups enjoy full social rights as foreign workers but with no (or limited) political rights, such as the right to vote in local elections only (see Bauböck, 1994). It is still unclear how to deal with the patterns of rights one increasingly encounters today, which are represented by differentiated sets of regulations in shades of grey that differ from the once-simple, clear-cut, black-and-white distinction between "them" (with almost no rights) and "us" (with full citizenship status).

Similarly challenging is the fact that, unlike in Marshall's time, the role of the state as nation-state—where statehood and membership are underpinned by a continual process of cultural homogenization—continues to diminish. In some cases, this is because the processes of state building were interrupted by authoritarian communist rule, and the ethnic cleavages of the past have now surfaced once again and with remarkable intensity. What is at stake these days is the recognition of different identities, cultural orientations, and forms of community (Fraser, 2003). Inequality is not only about variations in levels of the same resources and needs fulfilled. Policies also need to tackle inequalities that have a strong cultural and sometimes ethnic dimension, and this involves more than simple redistribution. As mentioned above, discrimination and a lack of recognition goes beyond social citizenship, touching on issues of civil and democratic rights (see Chapter 12, which focuses on postcommunist Hungary and its Roma community).

Given the failure to recognize the fragmented and heterogeneous nature of today's societies, the recourse to *universal* rights remains important but is incomplete. Certain cultural groups may demand special group rights and welcome selective, targeted measures that discriminate positively in their favor, enabling them to achieve the same rights as the majority of citizens. However, the challenge of creating variable patterns of rights is taking place under conditions where the agenda has shifted from passive to active citizenship and from rights to responsibilities (Kymlicka & Norman, 1994). To what extent should immigrants be obliged to learn their host country's language, for example, in order to attain the same citizenship status as nationals through a sometimes difficult assimilation process? And to what extent should they, in the context of "multicultural citizenship" (Kymlicka, 1995), be allowed to live within and cultivate their own communities? The practice of according special cultural and social rights to specific groups—whether by allowing their members to wear veils in public schools or by enforcing affirmative action programs—has become more widespread. But this can fuel divisive conflicts instead of fostering integration. On the political right, native citizens from the lower social strata may envy the extra support provided to groups of migrants. On the left, meanwhile, committed liberals may fear that granting special rights to traditional communities that restrict the individual rights of their members could undermine the existing consensus on the importance of individual freedoms, on which liberal societies are founded (Walzer, 2004).

Europeanization

The Europeanization of welfare policies has also called into question the concept of citizenship as defined by Marshall. As Ferrera (2005) has shown, the process of European unification has brought about tensions in the inherited construction of citizenship, which used to be strictly confined to the territory of the nation-state. The building of a large EU domestic market and the adoption of the principle of the free circulation of merchandise, people, capital, and services are undermining the welfare state's mechanisms for redistributing income and services. Under national welfare programs, benefits are provided within the boundaries of a nation-state to citizens who are endowed with civic, political, and social rights. The development of a supranational level may mean that social security entitlements risk being recalibrated in line with the market and competition. The result of this trend might be, as suggested by Ferrera (2005), either the gloomy scenario of residual social protection or a less grim scenario that would reconcile the marketplace with social solidarity. At this moment it is impossible to see clearly to what degree the present measures on the EU level will result in absorbing better the shocks and threads of the Euro crisis and the public debts and to what degree they will contribute to a mere increase of the uneven distribution of the loads of the crisis and the social policy measures triggered by it, and how much solidarity it entails between nations and classes. Anyway, the heightened level of economic and financial and regulative interventions will accelerate the challenges that result from the fact that the nation-state is no longer the exclusive foundation on which to build citizenship.

Summarizing our discussion of four basic long-term trends concerning labor markets, the consumer sphere, pluralization and migration, and finally Europeanization, we are witnessing the emergence of challenges that exemplify not only "new social risks" (Armingeon & Bonoli, 2006; Guillemard, 2005) but also new cultural and political challenges that demand collective choices. Social citizenship now implies more than an answer to the classic question of how much protection and security to provide for the lower classes. It involves questions about what is to be secured and entitled: What kind of life course? Which policies can both recognize cultural diversity and insist on the duty to integrate and assimilate, and construct access rights to benefits and services from both these perspectives? These issues concern citizenship in general. They are not confined to social rights but extend to civic rights and democracy, as we can see in discussions about immigration policy. In fact, these issues are so wide-ranging that it often appears that the label of "human rights" covers this range of issues better than the phrase "citizenship rights"—even more so since some of these challenges require not only national but also transnational, international, and supranational action.

Citizenship and the Interplay of Welfare and Economic Development—What Is the Possible Impact of a Turn to Social Investment Policies?

There are signs that a consensus is forming that breaks with the situation of the postwar years, especially in western Europe. Social programs and rights are increasingly coming to be seen as part of a broader model of social development that addresses social and economic issues, well-being and productivity, quality of life, and competitiveness simultaneously.

This new framework may support social policy in that it implies abandoning the old idea that welfare equals a kind of consumptive spending that must be subtracted from economic production. Instead, social policies are to be seen as an investment in a society's future. A healthier, better-educated population will promote economic productivity and growth. Giddens (1998, 117) has mentioned the need to turn welfare states into "social investment states" geared to "investment in human capital wherever possible, rather than direct provision of economic maintenance." According to Midgley (1999), social investments are the central element of what he calls "developmental social policies" that should entail a combination of social and economic goals and rationales. Similarly, Jenson and Saint-Martin (2003) have debated possibilities of intertwining economic and social goals. In this vein, Esping-Andersen (2002, 9) has called for more child-centered investment (education, childcare) in an effort to make dual-earner families the norm rather than the exception. Public investment in female human capital would provide larger returns. Accordingly, elements of social policy in local, regional, national, and international development may create wealth and improve welfare more effectively than the traditional stimuli administered to the private economy. Increased resources for health or education services would strengthen and stimulate likewise economic performance and social citizenship. This new perspective does, however, not focus just on quantifiable questions of degree; it also changes the nature of social rights. For example, the debate on "flexicurity" raises questions about how to create rights and regulations that allow for more flexibility in economic matters while also maintaining a degree of security.

At first glance a perspective on social policies as investments that are complementing private investments could be seen as filling the gap between concerns with social rights and concerns with the economy as it is to be found in Marshall's concept of social citizenship rights. There, policies for extending social rights figure very much as a concept in its own right. They were obviously not to harm economic development but as well were not conceived as a means for stimulating it. Yet, an investment perspective that looks in each and every case at the interplay of stating social rights and economic effects is deeply ambivalent.

Such a new framework for social policy could also jeopardize social rights in various ways. For one thing, replacing protective rights with investment in human capital could exacerbate inequality rather than reducing it. For example, to the degree that a social objective such as improving the population's health would be implemented increasingly through investments in people's health literacy instead of using traditional measures of health protection, the main beneficiaries would be the better off who learn more easily. Secondly, the balance between social goals as ends in themselves and as means to economic ends (Sen, 2001) could come undone. This would happen as soon as the economic side effects of measures could become the primary criteria of assessing social policies, especially if the pressure from international competition increases. Social policies with little or no positive economic impact could be neglected or overlooked. This could be the fate of the issue of equality, and thus of redistributive social policies and questions about what degree of income variation is deemed tolerable or fair—irrespective of the constraints that derive from that for the economy. The same could happen to coverage provided to tasks such as care for the frail elderly once they are seen as merely "consumptive" (in contrast to childcare: Lister, 2003).

To summarize, investment-oriented social policies and concepts that see welfare and social entitlements as part of a wider notion of "social development" (Midgley, 1999) could provide new opportunities to argue for entitlements and increases in funding, since social rights are presented as useful both to the recipients and for the economy. But they could, equally, lead to social programs being subsumed by economic development policies. Depending on the balance that is reached between economic and social concerns, the compromises to be struck (concerning flexibility and security, for example) may result in a net loss of social rights, especially if these rights are granted selectively on the basis of economic criteria (for a debate of this ambiguity in a concrete setting, see Lunt, 2008).

Citizenship and Welfare Policies of Activation—From Rights to Duties and Incentives?

The concept of citizenship that is grounded on personal, democratic, and social rights has always been based on the implicit assumption that these rights entail responsibilities, obligations, or even duties. Marshall did not forget about duties when he argued for an extension of citizenship rights. In his essay, he states that "if citizenship is invoked in the defense of rights, the corresponding duties of citizenship cannot be ignored. These do not require a man to sacrifice his individual liberty or to submit without question to every demand made by government. But they do require that his acts should be inspired by a lively sense of responsibility towards the welfare of the community" (1964, 117–118). Yet this classical conception of rights, although being conscious of the impact of a sense of responsibilities, seldom discussed them because these were taken for granted as part of the common culture. Furthermore, the notion of a duty, obligation, or sense of responsibility was not, at that time, seen as endangered.

On this point, once again, changes can be observed. Over the past decade, there has been much discussion about how to design rights and entitlements so that they promote a sense of responsibility. With an eye on citizenship rights, such debates have had an impact at two levels. Some of them address citizens in general, while others are much more targeted, directed at the beneficiaries of social programs, the long-term unemployed and minorities excluded from the worlds of labor who are suspected of being too passive or even immoral or "work-shy."

Concerning the citizenry at large, Giddens' slogan of "no rights without responsibilities" (1998, 65) is a telling sign of the times. However, much depends on how it is interpreted. On the one hand it could mean that the classical assumptions about a sense of responsibility as a cultural given no longer hold true and that today there is a new need to talk specifically of duties or responsibilities as a counterpart to rights. Modern conceptions of welfare and of the "activating" or "enabling state" (Gilbert & Gilbert, 1989) need cooperative citizens who will act as co-producers in health and education.

On the other hand, a stricter and more controversial interpretation of Giddens' phrase is also possible—namely, that each and every right granted should come with an equivalent duty as its counterpart. That would mean, for example, that the entitlement to healthcare presupposes an obligation to undertake specific measures to live healthily; employment security would presuppose the constant duty of the addressees to ensure their own employability or the obligation to achieve certain results in training programs.

One might argue that such trends are merely an increase in conditionality as it is already known in Marshall's concept of social citizenship, because this as well rested not only on entitlements free for all citizens (health and education) but also on a differentiated set of rights that, though they may have been targeted and conditional, also had an inclusive and equalizing effect insofar as they added to the common status of citizenship enjoyed by everyone. Conditionality and selectivity based on age, means, or time limits thus have many facets and a long history (see Goodin, 2002).

Yet what is critical and makes a difference to this past is what we would call "educational conditionality." Under this label we would place those measures where a service or benefit is dependent on certain achievements, actions, or types of behavior expected while it is being given, something that often implies a more or less formalized contract on the mutual obligations being drawn up at the outset. This type of conditionality (analyzed in detail in Chapter 6) does indeed transform rights into an individualized contract that entails conditions.

Of course, most social policies and programs are less harsh and have not yet set out individuals' social rights as items in a contract that are linked to behavioral expectations. However, many smaller changes towards a kind of "educational conditionality" have taken place through government interventions that have involved various groups of the citizenry. Such changes have had their origins in the pressure on governments to ensure that investments and entitlements are effective and lead to the envisaged results. From that point of view, it may simply seem more efficient to give service vouchers to children in families dependent on social assistance rather than additional cash to the families, since in the latter case the money may never reach the children; similar measures turning "open" cash benefits into directive benefits in kind are often observed when groups with a weak citizenship status are involved, such as immigrants. But there is also a second motive. In addition to the aim of gaining greater control, many (mainly politicians and administrators) feel that people need to learn new skills in order to cope better and that public services and entitlements should encourage them to do this. Entitlements are coming to be viewed as incentives. Giddens (1994), for instance, has referred to this "educational" aspect of public policies by calling for a "positive welfare" that not only reduces risks but also qualifies people to cope with them and helps them to lead a satisfying life—his ideas about "a good life" and "good behavior" refer to healthy lifestyles or "active aging."

One way to operationalize new, positive patterns of welfare and well-being would be to continue in the welfare tradition of better services in general, such as investing in an education that will not only provide skills and competences but also increase people's "capabilities" (Sen, 2001). When including additional services for certain target groups that are more disadvantaged than others, this could be a way to reinvigorate the pole position that was already enjoyed by educational and health services under Marshall's concept. But the aim of achieving assured, measurable results in a short time may lead policymakers and administrators to set up quite different measures and programs with less open and more controlling tendencies. In some countries, parents are obliged to send their children for regular health checkups to qualify for family allowances, and now there is intense debate about whether to provide coverage for health problems related to questionable or risky behaviors.

The implication of all this for personal, political, and social rights is that active citizenship and "positive freedoms" are becoming more important. The citizen's behavior and involvement as a "co-responsible" are becoming critical determinants of success. Policies that involve the "co-production" of certain patterns of a "good life" and of coping with the adversities of change do not simply "blame the victim." Rather, they create shared responsibilities, designing and using these measures as well as working incentives, that should ensure that the desired behavior will pay off for citizens. This obviously raises questions about the very idea of social rights, since under these circumstances, entitlements and benefits depend on citizens' cooperation, including their readiness to change their lifestyle. In the current debate about "governmentality," with its references to Foucault (1991), public policies are thus presented as networks of power that conduct to self-conduct, creating the conditions under which the subjects themselves will see to it that they are in line with the government's priorities (Newman et al., 2008).

The second and most debated aspect of public statements about citizens' duties has arisen in the context of the labor market policies of a "welfare-to-work" nature (see Chapters 5, 11, and 12). When expressed in explicitly contractual terms (Handler, 2004), the linkage between what is given and what is expected, between *fördern* and *fordern* ("support" and "demand" in German), has tightened. As social service professionals know, these services are more effective when an interactive partnership develops so that both the professional and the beneficiary are willing to mobilize their resources. However, in service relations of this sort in the field of labor market integration services, a very thin line separates an enabling, empowering approach from one under which, given the imbalance of power between the professional and the client, the latter is forced into a contracted set of actions and obligations. And in that case, what should be done when the long-term unemployed are no longer willing to follow the rules or adopt certain behavior patterns? Should negative sanctions be applied? What kinds of sanction, and in which cases?

When it comes to the legitimacy of policies of activation, one should after all not forget that such changes should be set in a historical context. As long as progress could be seen (as in Marshall's time) as a continuous expansion of rights, since policies tried to meet citizens' expectations and were able to build on a solid economic base as well as on citizens willing to work hard since they knew it would finally pay off, there was little need to talk about appropriate incentives, or to stipulate duties. In part, present activation policies must be seen as arising from profound changes in society, as fault lines and differences have widened and integrative forces have weakened. They have revived questions similar to those raised when modern capitalism was being born. Then, too, public debate and state policies centered on questions of which patterns of behavior ought to be promoted, supported, or rejected and on rights and duties. But to what extent can a "civil society" with responsible, active citizens be "activated" today by directive governments and state-led programs?

Striving for Social Rights and Maintaining Citizenship—Interrelated but Not Equivalent Issues

A strong citizenship status—such as would exist in a society where people see each other, despite differences in wealth, occupation, and family background, as equals—obviously depends on the existence of a political community that is democratic and able to guarantee basic civil rights to all its members. This depends on social rights that reduce inequality and help to include all, which is the focus of this book and this introduction.

However, as stated at the beginning of this introduction, it was never Marshall's intention that unconditional rights should be used to make all members of society equal, or to bring about de-commodification to such an extent that the market would no longer have a role in people's lives and people's status. Instead, by establishing and strengthening citizenship status, the impact of the market on people's chances and expectations would be both moderated and legitimized. Consequently, as has been shown, in many instances one finds what we can call wage-earner citizenship. This combines both sectors—the market and the state. Both the roles of individuals—as citizen and as wage laborer—stay interdependent.

But what has been argued here on the subject of Marshall's aim of strengthening, rather than totalizing, people's status as citizens concerns not only the market but the differentiated society as a whole. It affects not only people's roles as citizens and workers but also their roles as family members and members of communities and associations. The quality of a society rests on a wider system, including state-based provisions and market incomes, the contribution of families and various organizations in the third sector made up by local communities and nonprofit and voluntary organizations. Social rights, government action, and the status of social citizenship have to be seen as developing within a "welfare mix" (Evers, 1993) or a "mixed economy" (Johnson, 1999) of welfare.

Under such a system, notions of the rights and duties of the state, of the individual, of families, voluntary associations, and market organizations, have to be restated and renegotiated. They concern as well people's roles and identities (Andersen, 2005) as citizens, workers, and members of families and associations. As a result, one finds in society a set of notions of rights and duties that are mainly unwritten. These settings frame the issue of what should be enshrined as a state-guaranteed (social) right. They should not be reduced, as they often are, to a debate about the issue of individual versus state-based responsibilities (on this point, see Chapter 3).

Of course, as has been shown in the debate on this wider issue, there have been transfers of material tasks and responsibilities to the market system on the one hand and to states, as emergent welfare states, on the other hand. Nevertheless, not all the rights claimed are addressed to the state and not all the resources to which people feel they are entitled are forthcoming from the welfare state or take the form of statutory social rights. Marshall himself spoke of four different levels of rights, ranging from the "precisely defined and legally enforceable rights" over to "generally accepted standards" and "legitimate expectations" (Marshall, 1981, 96–98).

This would indicate that in political democracies, civil society and its public sphere are central both to state policies on social rights and citizenship and to people's opinions on what they can legitimately expect from each other and from their welfare state. People's habits and the processes of opinion-building and participation are essential. Building and strengthening citizenship status requires not only state action and statutory rights, but also channels of opinion building, dialogue, and participation—a culture of civility and civicness (Evers, 2010; on this point, see Chapter 14 on the role of the Civic Forum in the Czech Republic). And beyond such forms of participation through dialogue, it also requires a degree of readiness to engage in self-organized mutual help and support, and "civic solidarities" (Ignatieff, 1995) that go beyond written rights and duties. These must be anchored across the sectors of social systems, not only in state policies but also in the third sector with its associational life and in families and working life.

Given this picture of the wider system in which social policy and citizenship have their impact, we can formulate three conclusions.

First of all, *in view of the wider mixed and plural social and welfare system, one should be aware of the limitations of what can be achieved through "legally enforceable rights."* It was never Marshall's intention to make people completely independent of the impact of the market, and likewise he respected the societal roles of the voluntary sector and the family. The concept of citizenship status is central to seeing each other as equal and for inclusion. However, citizenship is not meant to replace the resources, restraints, the bonds of responsibility, and the room for personal decision making that are associated with the other subsystems and the roles that individuals have within those as members of associations and communities, as wage earners, consumers, or family members. We have already illustrated this point in relation to consumerism—the increasing effect of rights on choice within public services. Another—less liberal, more communitarian—aspect of this issue of limits of the possible impact of citizenship can be seen by looking at elderly care services, for example. While an entitlement to professional care services is essential, the question of levels of support and rights is as well related to the level of ongoing help given by relatives and the neighborhood. It would be a questionable utopia if, for example, full citizenship status for women (and men) was defined as the creation of entitlements that develop a "right not to rely on the family" (Finch, 1996, 206), so that family-based entitlements are granted whether or not the family itself can help out. Under such an approach, the family would effectively not count at all (much like the market does not count under the perspective of total de-commodification). All in all, this means that citizenship status has a central yet limited impact for people who continue to acknowledge their other roles in society and the sectors, institutions, freedoms, and bonds that go with them.

Secondly, *a strategy that seeks to extend citizenship status will always have to be conscious of the kind of rights to be created; different welfare strategies point to different rights with different effects on the division of roles and responsibilities in the welfare system at large, its public and private parts.* Concrete social and civil rights may restrict the roles of markets, families, and voluntary organizations, but equally they can be used to reinforce the impact of these institutions. For example, social investment policies may strengthen kinds of social rights that support the market economy. Similarly, it could be asked which rights are needed to achieve a better balance between the family and working life. It is currently widely assumed that the work–life balance of men and women should be brought into line. One way for developing new rights in this respect is to guarantee care services for children and frail elderly people. Such rights to care constitute the extension of Marshall's "rights to services" (health and education) into a new sector. However, viewed from another angle, a better work–life balance calls for more rights on "time to care"— the right of both men and women to devote time to caring activities for their next of kin. This latter perspective places the accent on the kinds of rights that are supporting the family as an institution—on reforming regulations concerning "care leave" to reduce the impact of the rigidity and risks of wage labor on people's lives and family arrangements. In many European countries, however, family policies are blending these different types of "rights to care", rights on services substituting family tasks and rights on support that gives more acknowledgement to the role of the family itself (Ostner & Schmitt, 2008) in an often unclear mixture.

Thirdly and finally, *if one aims to ensure a positive link between social rights and citizenship, it is important to be aware of the role of participatory democratic politics.* Until the 1980s, the long history of strengthening social rights and moving toward equality rested in most democracies and welfare states on the constant interplay between social movements on the one hand and state policymaking on the other hand. This process enabled mainstream public opinion to coalesce around equality and inclusion and also created trust in state policymaking. Given this background, one needs to take a second look at what is really meant and done when there are calls for social policies to "activate" citizens. We might well wonder in what role people are really supposed to be activated. Very often, it is their role as workers that is prioritized, rather than as active citizens, and activation relates mainly to lifelong learning in order to enhance employability rather than democratic competence.

Besides that, politicians often have been tempted to buy social and political support by an increase of social rights that may be better described as a strategy of bribery. Welfare policies with attitudes described as "buying survival at a cost" (Taylor-Gooby, 2009, 190), however, ultimately undermine the sense of solidarity and the trust that public policies for citizenship must rely on. A negative spiral begins to take hold: citizens who mistrust their government, both when it gives and when it takes, simply end up defending what is "theirs"—for example, by referring to existing social rights. A large part of the debate on changing or safeguarding existing pension plans is marked by this use of the rhetoric of rights and solidarity to defend partial interests and privileges (on this point, see Chapters 8 and 12). Another example of the often opaque and ambivalent relationship between social rights and citizenship are the plans of many governments to encourage a more important role for nonprofits and voluntary organizations. While this is promoted as the revival of a strong tradition of civic republican citizenship, it can also be seen as a way to privatize and amputate the social dimension of the citizenship status.

The recourse to citizenship as the expression of civil solidarity has all too often been used to veil policies that actually facilitate what is sold to the public as the inevitable result of economic pressures. The loss of historical reserves of political trust that has already occurred and the damages it brings for citizenship is making itself felt today, when governments in the face of the banking crisis and large household debts try to make an appeal to their citizens for being ready to make sacrifices today in order to win back prosperity tomorrow.

In a nutshell, extending legal social rights and strengthening citizenship are two different issues. As has been shown, the interrelations between these two issues are complex and difficult to understand, sometimes even contradictory. Judgments on strategies for social rights involve questions that concern the underlying concept of the division of responsibilities in the welfare mix. Only within a healthy civic culture and political life can it be assumed that the call for greater social rights reflects aspirations for strengthening citizenship at large.

HOW THIS BOOK IS ORGANIZED

The preceding pages have given an outline of the background to this book. Its central message is that the changes under way affect not only the "level" of social rights but also the social, civil, and political dimensions of citizenship itself. It is thus necessary to develop a "post-Marshallian" conception of citizenship. Accordingly, this introduction and the following three chapters will focus on changes in public policies, especially welfare policies and their consequences for citizenship, particularly social citizenship. They place these changes in the broader social and policy context, which will validate our reference to a "post-Marshallian" citizenship. At this level of generalization, the context will be international.

Most of the papers selected for this book are studies conducted at the national level, however. In our view, the national level continues to be central for citizenship and its social dimension. Chapter 5, on the role of the EU, supports this view. References to elements of EU policy will also be mentioned in the chapters devoted to individual country studies.

The national studies to be presented in the book refer to a particular set of countries. Most international collections of articles on welfare and democracy concern western Europe and North America. In our book, the formerly communist countries of central and eastern Europe have also been included. Papers will cover welfare developments not only in England, France, Germany, Italy, and Sweden but also in the Czech Republic, Hungary, and Poland—countries that do not share the same recent history as western Europe. In central and eastern Europe, we will endeavor to show how new welfare arrangements raise issues related to social citizenship, democracy, and personal rights.

Care has been taken to safeguard both the comparability and individuality of national developments. All country studies will have a similar structure. First of all, debates about citizenship are explained along with how they relate to Marshall's concepts. But one should bear in mind that although Marshall's triad of citizenship rights has become an international reference in academia, it has had a much more limited impact on public debates. The discussion of rights, and in particular social rights, has in all countries been shaped by national traditions. Changes in social policy and their consequences for citizenship are therefore analyzed in each case by referring to these national traditions and assessing how Marshall's ideas might serve as a theoretical framework. Each country chapter either refers to several policy fields or highlights a single, characteristic field. The main fields of focus will be social security, labor market policies, and social services.

To analyze how changes in welfare state interventions affect citizenship, all these contributions address four questions:

—Which welfare state reforms make changes in citizenship rights visible?
— What are the characteristics of these changes?
— How do they alter the scope of entitlements and rights delivered to beneficiaries?
— What are the consequences, in the country, on the conception and definition of citizenship and especially in terms of social rights?

Given the wide selection of countries and the reference to both citizenship and social rights, we have decided not to borrow the often-used "welfare regime" framework. Esping-Andersen's (1990) "worlds of capitalism," with its classification of liberal, conservative, and social democratic regimes, focuses narrowly on the development of social citizenship. The shift to citizenship in general, including civil and democratic rights, complicates the picture considerably and makes it more varied than the "welfare regime" concept suggests. Although Scandinavia, for instance, has a stronger tradition of social rights than other European countries or the United States, the same cannot be said about citizenship in general (Hvinden & Johansson, 2007). Furthermore, by looking at the situation in formerly communist countries—with a history that was different from western Europe's for 50 years—we discover realities for which the welfare regime framework is not prepared. The communist legacy includes several "social rights," whereas civil and democratic rights were limited by the authoritarian governments of countries in central and eastern Europe. For this reason, social rights have a different connotation in those countries—not with democracy but with state oppression or with corrupt governments that upheld their power by corrupting people with populist social gratifications. Given this background, many intellectuals in these countries are still suspicious of calls for new social rights, unlike in the West, where these rights have a positive association with democracy (see the chapters about the post-communist countries). For this reason, each country study begins with a short description of how citizenship and social rights should be understood in the national setting.

The book's concluding chapter will sum up the findings from the country studies and discuss them in light of the conceptual and theoretical points raised in the introduction and the first three chapters. Issues not raised there but mentioned in the country studies will receive special attention.

ACKNOWLEDGMENT

The volume has been made possible through the support of the EU-funded Network of Excellence CINEFOGO, the acronym for "Civil Society and New Forms of Governance in Europe—The Making of European Citizenship" (www. cinefogo.com).

REFERENCES

Andersen, J. G. (2005). Citizenship, unemployment and welfare policy. In J. G. Andersen, A. M. Guillemard, P. Jensen, & B. Pfau-Effinger (Eds.), *The changing face of welfare. Consequences and outcomes from citizenship perspective* (pp. 75–92). Bristol: Policy Press.

Armingeon, K., & G. Bonoli (Eds.) (2006). *The politics of post-industrial welfare states: Adapting post-war social policies to new social risks.* London/New York: Routlege.

Barbier, J. C. (2005). Citizenship and the activation of social protection: a comparative approach. In J. G. Andersen, A-M. Guillemard, P. H. Jensen, & B. Pfau-Effinger (Eds.), *The new face of welfare. Social policy, marginalization and citizenship* (pp. 113–134). Bristol: Policy Press.

Barbier J.-C. (2012) *The Road to Social Europe, A contemporary approach to political cultures and diversity in Europe.* Abingdon: Routledge.

Bauböck, R. (1994). *Transnational citizenship: Membership and rights in international migration.* Cheltenham: Edward Elgar.

Bulmer, M., & A. M. Rees (Eds.) (1996). *Citizenship today: The contemporary relevance of T. H. Marshall.* London: UCL Press.

Bussemaker, J. (Ed.) (1999). *Citizenship and welfare state reform in Europe.* London and New York: Routledge.

Clarke, J., J. Newman, N. Smith, E. Vidler, & L. Westmarland (2007). *Creating citizen-consumers: Changing publics and changing public services.* London: Sage.

Crouch, C., K. Eder, & D. Tambini (2001). Introduction—The dilemmas of citizenship. In C. Crouch, K. Eder, & D. Tambini (Eds.), *Citizenship, markets, and the state* (pp. 1–19). Oxford/New York: Oxford University Press.

Dwyer, P. (2010). *Understanding Social Citizenship.* Bristol: Policy Press.

Esping-Andersen, G. (1990). *The three worlds of welfare capitalism.* Cambridge: Polity Press.

Esping-Andersen, G. (1996b). Positive-sum solutions in a world of trade offs? In G. Esping-Andersen (Ed.), *Welfare states in transition: National adaptations in global economies.* (pp. 256–267), London: Sage Publications.

Esping-Andersen, G. (1996a). Welfare State without Work. The impasse of Labour Shading and Familiarism in Continental European Social Policy in G. Esping-Andersen (ED), *Welfare states in transition: National adaptations in global economies.* (pp. 66–87), London: Sage Publications.

Esping-Andersen, G. (2002). *Why we need a new welfare state.* Oxford: Oxford University Press.

Evers, A. (1993). The welfare mix approach. Understanding the pluralism of welfare systems. In A. Evers & I. Svetlik (Eds.), *Balancing pluralism. New welfare mixes in care for the elderly* (pp. 3–31). Aldershot: Avebury.

Evers, A. (2010). Civicness, civility and their meanings for social services. In T. Brandsen, P. Dekker, & A. Evers (Eds.), *Civicness in the governance and delivery of social services* (pp. 41–66). Baden-Baden: Nomos.

Ferrera, M. (2005). *The boundaries of welfare, European integration and the new spatial politics of social solidarity.* Oxford University Press.

Finch, J. (1996). Family responsibilities and rights. In M. Bulmer & A. M. Rees (Eds.), *Citizenship today: The contemporary relevance of T. H. Marshall* (pp. 193–208). London: UCL Press.

Foucault, M. (1991). Governmentality. In G. Burchell, C. Gordon, & P. Miller (Eds.), *The Foucault effect: Studies in governmentality* (pp. 87–104). London: Harvester Wheatsheaf.

Fraser, N. (2003). Social justice in the age of identity politics. In N. Fraser & A. Honneth (Eds.), *Redistribution or recognition? A political-philosophical exchange* (pp. 7–109). London: Verso.

Giddens, A. (1994). *Beyond left and right: The future of radical politics.* Cambridge: Polity Press.

Giddens, A. (1996). T. H. Marshall, the state and democracy. In M. Bulmer & A. M. Rees (Eds.), *Citizenship today: The contemporary relevance of T. H. Marshall* (pp. 65–80). London: UCL Press.

Giddens, A. (1998). *The third way: The renewal of social democracy.* Cambridge: Polity Press.

Gilbert, N., & B. Gilbert (1989). *The enabling state.* New York: Oxford University Press.

Goodin, R. E. (2002). Structures of mutual obligation. *Journal of Social Policy, 31*(4), 579–596.

Guillemard, A. M. (2002). L'Europe continentale face à la retraite anticipée. Barrières institutionnelles et innovations en matière de réforme. *Revue Française de Sociologie, 42,* 333–368.

Guillemard, A. M. (2005). The advent of a flexible life course and the reconfigurations of welfare. In J. G. Andersen, A. M. Guillemard, P. Jensen, & B. Pfau-Effinger (Eds.), *The changing face of welfare. Consequences and outcomes from citizenship perspective* (pp. 55–73). Bristol: Policy Press.

Handler, J. (2004). *Social citizenship and workfare in the United States and western Europe: The paradox of inclusion.* Cambridge: Cambridge University Press.

Hvinden, B., & H. Johansson (Eds.) (2007). *Citizenship in Nordic welfare states: Dynamics of choice, duties and participation in a changing Europe.* London/New York: Routledge.

Ignatieff, M. (1995). The myth of citizenship. In R. Beiner (Ed.), *Theorizing citizenship* (pp. 53–77). Albany: SUNY Press.

Isin, E. (2000). Introduction: democracy, citizenship and the city. in E. Isin (Ed.), *Democracy, citizenship and the global city* (pp. 1–22). London: Routledge.

Jenson, J., & D. Saint-Martin (2003). New routes to social cohesion? Citizenship and the social investment state. *Canadian Journal of Sociology, 28*(1), 77–99.

Jobert, B. (1994). *Le tournant néo-libéral en Europe.* Paris: L'Harmattan.

Johnson, N. (1999). *Mixed economies of welfare. A comparative perspective.* London: Prentice Hall Europe.

Kymlicka, W. (1995) *Multicultural citizenship.* Oxford: Clarendon Press.

Kymlicka, W., & W. Norman (1994). Return of the citizen: A survey of recent work on citizenship theory. *Ethics, 104*(2), 352–381.

Lister, R. (1990). Women, economic dependency and citizenship. *Journal of Social Policy, 19,* 445–467.

Lister, R. (2003). Investing in the citizen-workers of the future: Transformations in citizenship and the state under New Labour. *Social Policy and Administration, 37*(5), 427–443.

Lunt, N. (2008). From welfare state to social development: Winning the war of words in New Zealand. *Social Policy and Society, 7*(4), 405–418.

Marshall, T. H. (1950/1964). *Class, citizenship and social development.* Chicago: University of Chicago Press.

Marshall, T. H. (1981). Afterthought on "The Right to Welfare." In T. H. Marshall (Ed.), *The right to welfare and other essays* (pp. 95–103). London/Edinburgh/Melbourne: The Free Press.

Maurice M., F. Sellier, & J. J. Silvestre (1982). Politique d'éducation et organisation industrielle en France et en Allemagne. Paris: Presses Universitaires de France.

Midgley, J. (1999). Growth, redistribution and welfare: Toward social investment. *Social Service Review, 73*(1), 3–21.

Muller, P. (April 2000). L'analyse cognitive des politiques publiques: vers une sociologie politique de l'action publique. *Revue Française de Science Politique (numéro spécial: Les approches cognitives des politiques publiques), 50*(2), 189–207.

Newman, J., C. Glendinning, & M. Hughes (2008). Beyond modernisation? Social care and the transformation of welfare governance. *Journal of Social Policy, 37*(4), 531–558.

OECD (1981). *The welfare state in crisis.* Paris: OECD.

Ostner, I., & C. Schmitt (Eds.) (2008). *Family policies in the context of family change: The Nordic countries in a comparative perspective.* Wiesbaden: VS Verlag.

Palier, B. (2001). Reshaping the social policy making framework: France from the 1980s to 2000. In P. Taylor-Gooby (Ed.), *Welfare state under pressure* (pp. 52–74). London: Sage.

Pierson, P. (1994). *Dismantling the welfare state? Reagan, Thatcher, and the politics of retrenchment.* Cambridge/New York/Melbourne: Cambridge University Press.

Pierson, P. (1998). Irresistible forces, immovable objects. *Journal of European Public Policy, 5*(4), 539–560.

Pierson, P. (2001). *The new politics of the welfare state.* Oxford: Oxford University Press.

Powell, M. (2002). The hidden history of social citizenship. *Citizen Studies, 6*(3), 229–244.

Rees, A. M. (1996). T. H. Marshall and the progress of citizenship. In M. Bulmer & A. M. Rees (Eds.), *Citizenship today: The contemporary relevance of T. H. Marshall* (pp. 1–23). London: UCL Press.

Schmid, G., & B. Gazier (Eds.). (2002). *The dynamics of full employment. Social integration by transitional labour markets.* Cheltenham: Edward Elgar.

Schmidt, V. (2000). Values and discourse in the politics of adjustment. In F. W. Scharpf & V. Schmidt (Eds.), *Welfare and work in the open economy* (vol. 1, pp. 229–309). Oxford University Press.

Sen, A. (2001). *Development as freedom.* Oxford: Oxford University Press.

Soper, K., & F. Trentmann (Eds.) (2008). *Citizenship and consumption.* Basingstoke, Hampshire: Palgrave Macmillan

Steenbergen, B. v. (Ed.) (1994). *The condition of citizenship.* Newbury Park, CA: Sage Publications.

Supiot, A. (2001). *Beyond employment, changes in work and the future of labour law in Europe.* Oxford University Press.

Taylor-Gooby, P. (2009). *Reframing social citizenship.* Oxford: Oxford University Press.

Turner, B. S. (2001). The erosion of citizenship. *British Journal of Sociology, 52*(2), 189–209.

Walzer, M. (2004). Cultural rights. In M. Walzer (Ed.), *Politics and passion. Toward a more egalitarian liberalism* (pp. 44–65). New Haven/London: Yale University Press.

2

TOWARDS A POST-MARSHALLIAN FRAMEWORK FOR THE ANALYSIS OF SOCIAL CITIZENSHIP

Håkan Johansson and Bjørn Hvinden

INTRODUCTION

In recent years, an increasing amount of theoretical literature has been produced on the subject of citizenship (Hvinden & Johansson, 2007; Isin & Turner, 2007; Somers, 2008; Taylor-Gooby, 2008). This literature can, to a great extent, be viewed as an attempt to make sense of the effects of the substantial societal changes witnessed in various parts of the world. In Europe, these changes include greater economic openness to and scope for cross-border mobility, a shift in the role of government from redistribution to the social regulation of markets, neo-liberalism and individualization, the increasing prominence of human rights and anti-discrimination, and new transnational channels for participation (e.g., Rieger & Leibfried, 2003). Some of these developments have originated from the policy agendas and programs initiated by the European Union (EU), while others are more nationally embedded or have even come about through the activities and involvement of citizens and groups of citizens.

While many important contributions have been made, the literature on citizenship remains somewhat fragmented, as individual contributions have tended to focus on particular aspects or dimensions of citizenship. This chapter aims to present an analytical model that will build upon, and go beyond, existing models of social citizenship. Our attempt to construct a "post-Marshallian" analytical framework for the understanding of social citizenship draws on David Miller's threefold conceptualization of citizenship (Miller, 2000). Citizenship in a *Socio-Liberal* sense sees the relationship between the individual and the state as involving encompassing sets of mutual rights and obligations. Citizenship in a *Libertarian* sense casts the relationship between state and individual more narrowly, with the emphasis on the self-responsibility and autonomy of the individual in combination with very limited activity on the part of the state. Citizenship in a (Civic) *Republican* sense focuses on the citizen's participation in the affairs of his or her community, and the expectation that the individual will be committed to acknowledging and promoting the well-being of the community as a whole. Miller's models bear a resemblance to T. H. Marshall's original understanding of citizenship as dividable into civil, political, and social elements (Marshall, 1950/1965).

However, considering the challenges facing contemporary welfare states, there is a need for greater analytical pluralism that can enable an analysis of the ways in which different models of citizenship interact, contradict, or reinforce each other. Scholars have even argued that we are entering a stage of hybridization of citizenship models (Stasiulis, 2004). Although much current reasoning on social citizenship has—appropriately—focused on the Socio-Liberal or social redistribution element, we propose a relational and unified approach to citizenship encompassing issues of rights and duties, self-responsibility and choice, participation and self-government *at the same time*. In our view, this encompassing conceptualization is necessary if we are to capture the ways in which civil, political, and social citizenship are becoming intertwined in new and sometimes unexpected ways in contemporary societies.

The challenges facing contemporary welfare states have sparked intensive debates over just how "active" citizens ought to be. These debates have focused predominantly on notions of conditionality within Socio-Liberal citizenship, as expressed in slogans like "no rights without responsibilities," for example. Yet, we can detect similar tendencies to separate or demarcate active citizenship from passive citizenship with regard to the other two models of citizenship. Arguably, there is a need for analytical pluralism to incorporate and clarify this active/passive divide, as citizens are currently being encouraged to become more active citizens, which is understood either as shouldering more responsibilities, exercising more choice, or engaging more actively in the public sphere, deliberation, or alternatively in self-organized or voluntary efforts for the benefit of others.

A "post-Marshallian" analytical framework of citizenship must therefore meet two criteria. Firstly, it must address the ways in which aspects of civil, political, and social citizenship are intertwined, in new and sometimes unexpected ways. Secondly, it must move beyond a rigid separation between the passive and active dimensions of citizenship. The last section of this chapter presents an attempt to construct just such a model.

WHY DO WE NEED A NEW ANALYTICAL FRAMEWORK?

We will briefly review some of the key debates on the challenges faced by contemporary societies and welfare states. To simplify matters, we will start by making a rough analytical distinction between challenges the come "from above" (e.g., economic openness and Europeanization; the emergence of a human rights regime) and challenges that come "from below" (e.g., individualization and self-organization). Combined, these challenges give rise to complex and sometimes paradoxical changes in the relationships between state and citizens, especially as states and citizens appear to change at the same time.

Economic Openness and Europeanization

A more open and globalized world market, stronger competitive pressures, and increasing economic integration in Europe are all factors that have led national governments to take steps to prevent further growth in public spending, or even reduce it. It is possible that we will see a gradual shift of emphasis from redistributive welfare provision to promoting welfare objectives through "social regulation" (Majone, 1993). In contrast to redistributive policies, social regulation involves public efforts to influence the behavior of nongovernmental actors, especially actors operating in the market, in order to promote the realization of social objectives. Generally speaking, social regulation has the potential to strengthen citizens' scope for exercising active citizenship by participating in the market as workers and consumers.

These objectives and methods have been pursued by the EU, in particular, with its ambition to build a strong internal market. The European Court of Justice (ECJ) has taken on an active role in clarifying and elaborating the implications of common EU regulations for social policies (Leibfried, 2005; Pollack, 2003). Moreover, the process has extended the rights of EU citizens to have the authorities in their own country reimburse the costs of medical treatment undergone in other member states (de Burca, 2005; Ferrera, 2005). Based on the Amsterdam Treaty, the European Commission has introduced several directives that have built on complemented previous EU legislation against gender discrimination. One of these concerns the principle of equal treatment of persons, irrespective of racial and ethnic origin (Council Directive, 2000/43/EC). Another establishes a general framework for equal treatment in employment and occupation, covering discrimination on the grounds of religion or belief, disability, age, or sexual orientation (Council Directive, 2000/78/EC). Member states have been obliged to introduce new or amended laws or administrative provisions to comply with these directives.

Obviously, some sections of the population are prevented or excluded from exercising such legally based "market citizenship." People with disabilities are one of the most obvious examples, but women (especially as mothers) and people belonging to ethnic minorities are also at risk of experiencing such exclusion. Recent EU social regulation initiatives, such as nondiscrimination legislation and the setting of binding standards for universal design, have attempted to prevent such exclusion. Such regulatory measures may correct market imperfections or the undesirable consequences of unrestricted market competition, even if the need for correcting market failures was not necessarily the main impetus for introducing these measures (Majone, 2005). Compared with the introduction of new tax-financed redistributive provisions, social regulation is more compatible with the opening up and liberalization of international markets (Hvinden, 2004).

The EU also has a tradition of implementing action programs in the social field. The overarching ambition of recent programs has been to achieve greater uniformity or convergence regarding social protection and social inclusion, while allowing member states to adopt different means to achieve these objectives. Current programs of this kind cover employment, pensions, social inclusion, and other areas (Kvist & Saari, 2007). Because the EU's legal mandate in the social field has been questioned and remains weak, more recent programs have tended to follow so-called "soft law principles", such as the open method of coordination (Heidenreich & Zeitlin, 2009).

The EU has used similar soft law processes to foster a new way of thinking about welfare policies across Europe. The logic in recent programs has been to encourage a shift from "passive" to "active" policies. Since the introduction of the European Employment Strategy (1997), the EU has claimed that the primary goal of national social protection schemes should be to promote labor market participation among people of working age. Only for those who cannot work at all should the main objective be to provide adequate and secure income support. Key objectives have been to promote more employment-friendly social protection schemes, as well as "making work pay" by ensuring that the conditions, level, and duration of benefits do not create disincentives to work. Individuals are expected to improve their employability (skills, knowledge, etc.), while governments are expected to make the payment of benefits for people of working age conditional on their accepting offers to take part in employment training measures or training courses. These attempts at framing national welfare reforms are illustrations of how the EU is promoting more active citizenship in accordance with a Socio-Liberal understanding.

These aspects of EU economic integration, legislation, and action programs exemplify new constraints on the freedom of national governments to design and change their systems of welfare provisions as they would like (e.g., Ferrera, 2005; Leibfried, 2005). Yet we do not wish to overstate the degree to which "Europeanization" has diminished the decision-making capacity of member states (Cowles et al., 2001; Olsen, 2002). Social issues are still marginal within the EU-level policymaking and secondary to the complete establishment of a single (and now enlarged) European market. Scharpf warns us that national welfare states will be most affected by processes of negative integration (through market building) at the EU level and, to a lesser extent, measures involving positive integration (Scharpf, 1996). In fact, one could even argue that the focus of the EU's involvement in the "social dimension" has primarily been to ensure that national schemes of social protection do not impede the free movement of goods, services, capital, and labor within the single market.

The Incorporation of Human Rights in National Legislation

The development of an international regime of human rights and protection against discrimination has had important implications for the rights, opportunities, and scope of citizen participation. Important examples are the United Nations Convention on Elimination of all Discrimination Against Women (CEDAW, 1979), the UN Convention on the Rights of the Child (UN Doc A/44/49, 1989) and the Convention on the Rights of Persons with Disabilities (A/RES/61/106, 2007) (see also EU 2000, ILO 1989). These international conventions have challenged established national models of citizenship. However, the overall impact of this emerging international regime of human rights and protection against discrimination has yet to be fully acknowledged, mapped, and assessed.

On the one hand, these developments appear to provide a substantial improvement in the "opportunity structures" (Tarrow, 2003) for individuals and groups at the margins of welfare states and markets. Generally speaking, opportunity structures refer to institutional, political, and legal environments that can encourage or discourage individual and collective action by affecting actors' expectations of success or failure. In the context of this chapter, these structures may involve improved opportunities for achieving recognition from public authorities and presenting claims against either public agencies or nongovernmental actors. From this perspective, an international regime of human rights could stimulate agency among citizens and the organizations representing them. Yet as in any opportunity structure, agency requires that people are aware of and knowledgeable about their rights and have the necessary resources and skills to present claims (Hvinden & Halvorsen, 2003).

On the other hand, some scholars have argued that the emergence of transnational regimes of human rights and nondiscrimination provisions undermines the democratic dimension of the relationship between the (national) welfare state and its citizens (e.g., Østerud et al., 2003). However, the emergence of these regimes does not necessarily mean that the democratic basis for national welfare states is weakening. On the contrary, these regimes are probably strengthening the opportunities for citizens to exercise agency in relation to welfare states, and particularly for minorities and others whom the previous and existing policies of these states have marginalized or excluded. We see the potential for enriching social and political citizenship, contributing to improved conditions of full citizenship for a larger proportion of the total population, in terms of rights and responsibilities, freedom of choice, and participation. Such a contribution is significant, not only for concerns of equality of living conditions or economic efficiency but also for considerations of democracy.

Individualization

Contemporary welfare states are facing a number of challenges "from below." Widely accepted diagnoses of late-modern societies see a trend towards individualization and de-traditionalization (e.g., Beck & Beck-Gernsheim, 2002; Beck &

Willms, 2004). These are complex concepts that involve something greater than and different from individuals becoming more egoistic, self-centered, or simply concerned with their own well-being. One key argument is that traditional and more spontaneous forms of community, collectivity, and solidarity between people have lost much of their practical significance. The late-modern individual is becoming increasingly decoupled from these social relationships, while the spontaneous development of community and solidarity between people is found more rarely. Beck and Beck-Gernsheim (2002) suggest that "solidarity" can increasingly be achieved only through determined and conscious efforts by individuals, based on their knowledge, skills, and capacity for reflection, and their ability to negotiate a common understanding of the premises for the community or collective action. To the extent that individuals succeed in these efforts, the resulting community is likely to be more fleeting and issue-focused than more traditional and spontaneous forms of collectivity.

These discussions have important implications for our understanding of current concerns in many welfare states. The individualization thesis questions the social solidarity on which redistributive welfare states are based (Esping-Andersen, 1999). Individualization can contribute to pressures for reducing the overall scope of welfare schemes and replacing them with a greater reliance on individual responsibility when it comes to protection against loss of income and other risks (e.g., through different forms of individual saving, private insurance, or pension plans).

Individualization will represent a particular challenge to social benefit systems that are based on a long-term perspective and a fairly stable joint understanding between the affected parties. For instance, public pension systems that are not based on earlier payments into funds but operate mainly on "pay-as-you-go" principles presuppose an "intergenerational contract." According to the individualization perspective, such contracts will not only be hard to renew, they are largely a normative fiction. Due to changing public preferences, no one can take the legitimacy of established systems of social protection for granted, even when they have been planned for the long term. However, the individualization thesis does not necessarily preclude popular support for and acceptance of redistributive public provisions. One implication may be that governments should involve the public in discussions about the premises, objectives, ambitions, and time horizons of such systems and, vice versa, that the public needs to reassess and confirm its support for such arrangements. That an arrangement has been in operation for a long time does not constitute an argument for its continued existence.

Self-Organization

Many of the rights claimed by citizens or groups of citizens have not been simply bestowed upon them. Social movements involving women, ethnic minorities, and people with impairments have actively campaigned for changes in legislation and public provision. They have increased policymakers' awareness of the issues, participated in the legislation and policy process, and worked to inform their constituencies about the opportunities created by new legislation and public provision. In some cases, groups of citizens have even succeeded in bypassing national governments altogether by working through transnational networks to campaign and lobby supranational agencies or organizations to promote their case.

More generally, organizations and advocacy groups acting on behalf of these broader social movements are of great significance in understanding the process of changing or restructuring social protection policies. The significance of collective action, which is also increasingly being exercised by groups in marginal positions, has some affinity to active citizenship according to a Republican interpretation. The organizations represent not only an immediate arena for social participation and self-directed activities but also, indirectly, a route to building up self-confidence and capacity for participation in larger society and in negotiations with the representatives of public authorities. The self-activity of various citizens groups is not exclusively—or even primarily—directed towards obtaining particular material benefits. Rather, their efforts tend to involve *recognition* and *identity politics*, and symbolic as well as practical *representation* (Fraser, 2008).

Several groups are struggling against public policies that have subjected them to social and cultural domination, and denied them respect and dignity, or even their very existence. They claim their right to be heard and taken seriously by governmental bodies, and not to be forced to live invisibly and silently. In many cases, such groups insist that society recognize their difference from the majority population, in terms of culture, lifestyle, and their right to express this difference. According to some observers, issues surrounding recognition have, to some extent, come to replace issues of socioeconomic redistribution in late-modern and multicultural society (e.g., Young, 1990). Others, like Fraser, have argued that social justice requires policies of both redistribution and recognition. Even so, the international trend towards the politics of recognition is adding to the complexity of contemporary citizenship (see also Chapters 1 and 15 in this book).

THE LEGACY OF T. H. MARSHALL

A large section of the literature on social citizenship is a response to Marshall's essay (e.g., Listeret al., 2007; Turner, 2001). At the outset, Marshall defined citizenship "as a status bestowed upon those who are full members of a community. All those who possess that status are equal with respect to the rights and duties with which that status is endowed" (Marshall, 1965, 18). He outlined how civil, political, and social citizenship developed—first for a small section of the population, later widening out to a larger part of the population. In this sense,

Marshall's essay can be interpreted as a story of a progressive process of societal integration. He indicated that the three types of citizenship were mutually reinforcing, and that a person needs to enjoy all three in order to be able to exercise the rights and duties of full citizenship.

At the same time, Marshall asked how the emerging equal status of citizenship for all the inhabitants of a country was compatible with the continued existence of the substantial class differences in income, wealth, and living conditions of a capitalist market economy. He did not claim that social citizenship had the potential to completely change the capitalist system, but, being a socio-liberal rather than a liberalist, he believed that some degree of redistribution of resources between citizens was required. He argued that everybody was to be granted a minimum of economic and social welfare—that is, to enjoy a minimum level of social and economic rights (economic security, care, protection against various risks, etc.). In return, each individual had to meet certain legal and social obligations vis-à-vis the community.

Marshall did not go into detail about the exact nature of citizenship rights and obligations; rather, he claimed that there was no universal principle for defining the rights and duties of citizenship. As an emerging institution, citizenship implied a vision of what each inhabitant of a society could become, an image for societies and their citizens to strive for. Nevertheless, a fair balance between rights and obligations was necessary. The latter might include contributing to the common good, for instance by performing paid work, paying taxes, and doing military service. Avoiding the gender bias implied here, we would add obligations like taking responsibility for and undertaking care of children and other dependants, and participating in other socially valuable activities (Orloff, 2009). In addition, all citizens had to work hard and put their heart into their job, and live the life of a good citizen (see also Chapter 3 in this book).

Directions in Citizenship Theory

The debate on citizenship that has followed on from the work of T. H. Marshall has been extensive. Marshall's codification of social citizenship involves considerable complexity, even ambiguity. This is most likely due to the fact that his essay is a blend of analytical and historical arguments. This has led to a great variety in the subsequent interpretations of social citizenship and has provided ample opportunities for selective "reading in" of what one liked or disliked in Marshall's essay.

In the late 1980s and early 1990s, his theory was criticized for being too Anglo-Saxon and for failing to recognize the development of citizenship in different national contexts (Rees, 1996; Turner, 1990). Others argued that Marshall failed to consider the conflicts and struggles that constitute the driving forces behind citizenship in the 20th century, such as the civil rights movement and the labor movement (Giddens & Held, 1982).

Later, feminist scholars criticized Marshall for focusing almost exclusively on the situation of men and the historical development of citizenship for men.

He did not acknowledge the significance of motherhood, for example—that is to say, he overlooked giving birth to children and providing nurture and care in their upbringing as fundamental conditions for the continued existence of society. Marshall did not consider whether social citizenship rights, including an individual right to economic security and independence, applied to women who were carers and housekeepers for the greater part of their adult life (Lister, 2003; Pateman, 1988; Siim, 2000).

These criticisms have been influential in forming our current understandings of the notion of citizenship. However, when reviewing the citizenship debate that has taken place over recent decades one can detect a threefold development that appears to challenge certain aspects of Marshall's original codification of social citizenship: (i) a renewed emphasis on citizens' duties; (ii) a renewed emphasis on citizens' participation and agency; and (iii) the emergence of citizen consumerism.

A Renewed Emphasis on Citizens' Duties

One major criticism of Marshall's conception of social citizenship was that he placed excessive emphasis on individual social rights, especially formal and enforceable rights, while saying little about the duties or responsibilities of citizens (e.g., Marquand, 1991; Turner, 2001). For some critics, Marshall served as a straw man for a more general criticism of how generous redistributive welfare arrangements, especially income support, are supposed to have an adverse effect on citizens' attitudes to self-reliance and paid work, responsibility for personal welfare, and risk protection. These critics have argued that the proliferation of unconditional social rights, underpinned by welfare provisions, has in fact led to widespread passivity on the part of citizens, even causing economic and social exclusion, and a weakening of the work ethic (e.g., Mead, 1986, 1997).

Today, critics often link these arguments to the kind of external and internal pressures that are now facing contemporary welfare states, to which we referred previously. The general argument is that governments need to slim down their welfare provisions to prevent these provisions from becoming a liability in a more globalized system of market competition. Governments have to reduce their ambitions to provide redistributive welfare financed through taxation, while individuals and families must take greater responsibility for their own protection against risks. On the basis of these arguments, many participants in the recent debate have called for new conceptions of citizenship, striking a better balance between individual rights and duties. The slogan of "no rights without responsibilities" expresses the general thrust of these conceptions (Giddens, 1998. 65; see also Dwyer, 2000; Levitas 1998; Lister, 2001).

Arguably, much current reasoning on social citizenship exaggerates the contrast between *active* and *passive* social citizenship, where active social citizenship means that people should not only enjoy the rights associated with citizenship but also meet certain obligations. It is also possible that key writers in social policy have contributed to the understanding of social citizenship as being concerned only with the expansion of social rights. For instance, Esping-Andersen (1990, 21) makes a direct link between "decommodification" and Marshall's concept of social citizenship. Here, decommodification implies that "citizens can freely, and without potential loss of job, income or general welfare, opt out of work when they themselves consider necessary." Similarly, Dean and Melrose (1999, 82–85) focus exclusively on the rights side in their presentation of Marshall's theory of social citizenship (see also Chapter 1 and 3 in this book).

Significant changes in social security legislation, and, more specifically, attempts by governments to switch from passive to active measures in social protection, have been motivated by such concerns. We have already touched upon some of these reforms that aim to shift the balance towards the duties and responsibilities of citizens, most clearly seen in the activation of income maintenance schemes for people of working age and in pension reform. The focus is on promoting participation in paid work and prolonging working careers, providing stronger financial incentives, and in the case of activation reform, also combining "sticks" and "carrots." For instance, public authorities may offer more systematic guidance and follow-up, introduce co-determination into the planning of personalized measures, and provide the opportunities to acquire new vocational skills (the "carrots") but also enforce their requirements more vigorously, making the granting of cash benefits conditional on participation in active measures and punishing failure to comply (the "sticks"). However, different European governments have not given the same relative emphasis to these sticks and carrots (Johansson & Hvinden, 2007).

The Active/Passive Divide in Perspective

Before turning to the second main theme in current citizenship debate—the renewed emphasis on citizens' participation and agency—we need to make a few comments on the duties aspect of social citizenship. Current reasoning on social citizenship relies excessively on the arbitrary and rigid separation between active and passive dimensions. To move towards a framework that can transcend this separation, we make three points:

- Marshall's original understanding of rights/duties is richer and more complex than many critics suggest.
- Many countries' income security systems were never completely "passive" but rather hybrids, combining "active" and "passive" aspects of social citizenship (see also Chapter 15 in this book).
- Participation in gainful employment need not be the only recognized or socially valuable activity that qualifies for the status and recognition as an "active" citizen.

Firstly, Marshall was a sociologist who fully accepted the main premises and assumptions of the dominant sociological paradigm of his time. The chief concerns of this paradigm were the conditions for societal integration and social inclusion. According to this paradigm, generally shared norms for action, based on a fundamental consensus over values and norms, served as integrating mechanisms. People's acceptance of and compliance with the basic norms were ensured through socialization (the internalization of values and norms) and social control (positive and negative sanctioning of behavior). Marshall's preoccupation with integration and inclusion involved a stronger collectivist orientation than typically found in liberal thinking. Moreover, this collectivism and belief in a reciprocal or "organic" relationship between individual and society implied "duties" (the action prescribed by shared norms), as well as "rights" (the action that can be expected from others on the basis of the same norms).

In Marshall's essay, the relationship between the modern state and the individual emerges as a special case in the general relationship between the societal community and its members, as this was analyzed within the sociological paradigm. When he emphasized that citizenship involved both rights and duties on the part of the individual, these corresponded to rights and duties on the part of the state. Some of these rights and duties were of a formal and legally enforceable nature (e.g., the right and duty to schooling, the duty to pay taxes or do military service, the right to be provided income maintenance under certain circumstances). Other rights and duties were more concerned with what might legitimately be expected (e.g., from individuals to do what they can to be self-sufficient, not only to work but also to take an interest in political affairs, and exercise their right to vote). It was no accident that Talcott Parsons and other leading representatives of the sociological paradigm of the mid-20th century integrated Marshall's work into their own with ease (e.g., Bendix, 1964/1977; Bendix & Rokkan, 1971; Parsons, 1967, 1971; cf. also Ferrera, 2005).

While Marshall argued that there ought to be a balance between rights and duties, he noted with some regret that rights had proliferated more rapidly than duties under the modern welfare state. It had become more difficult to promote a sense of duty when people had to relate to a more distant and abstract construction as the nation-state. Similarly to Durkheim (1893/1947), one of modern sociology's forefathers, Marshall suggested that one should aim to develop people's sense of rights and duties in the context of intermediate institutions, for instance within their local community or the organization where they are employed. When participants in the contemporary debate on the relationship between employment and income security argue for an appropriate balance between rights and duties, Marshall would probably have agreed.

Secondly, some calls for a more active side to social citizenship are based on a selective understanding of national welfare systems. Despite much talk of universal, generous, and unconditional benefits in some countries (e.g., the Nordic countries), citizens' eligibility for many benefits has presupposed their prior participation in the labor market and/or their willingness to participate in measures to improve their employability. In other countries, means-tested, short-term, and low benefits have diminished the need for governments to enforce the work ethic; poverty and meager public provision have forced people to work.

Admittedly, the original ambition of some welfare states to achieve a balance of rights and obligations has faded away in practice. One example is Denmark, in which the level and duration of unemployment insurance or assistance almost made it into a *de facto* "citizen wage" in the 1970s and 1980s (Goul Andersen, 2002). The Danish labor market reforms of the 1990s altered this situation dramatically. Social citizenship in Denmark now relies on a strong public enforcement of the work ethic, a tightly controlled but relatively generous system of income security provision, combined with limited job protection ("flexicurity").

Thirdly, a sharp distinction between active and passive social citizenship resonates with recent claims about "the end of the work society," or "the end of the full employment society" (Beck & Beck-Gernsheim, 2002). Turner (2001) provides a more nuanced picture on the relationship between labor market participation and entitlement to social provision, arguing that wage labor, reproduction, and military service were conditions for the enjoyment of the social rights described by Marshall. Turner claims that wage labor is now undergoing considerable change; work is no longer the stable social institution and a gateway to worker-citizenship that it was during the "golden age" of the post-war welfare state. Higher levels of unemployment, new ways of organizing work, and less predictable career paths are making labor market participation a less secure route by which to gain social rights and effective entitlements. As a general claim, Turner's argument obviously has some validity but seems exaggerated, given the expansion of overall labor market participation in many European countries, even if it is largely related to the increase in employment among women. In many European countries, demographic ageing is expected to lead to labor shortages within a few years.

This prospect leads us to a fairly narrow perception of what currently counts as economically and socially valuable citizen activities. In their current welfare reforms, few governments recognize participation in activities that are *not* oriented towards paid employment or do not serve as stepping stones to the fulfillment of citizen duties, although there are some cross-national nuances in this respect. Governments tend not to fully acknowledge the value of unpaid care in the family, although in their current pension reforms they are paying lip service to it through "care credits" (Lister et al., 2007; Orloff, 2009; Siim, 2005). Governments appear to have been somewhat more willing to recognize participation in voluntary social and cultural work, self-help activities, organizational, cooperative, or "social economy" work as alternatives for people who are deemed to be distant from the mainstream labor market.

A Renewed Emphasis on Citizens' Participation and Agency

The second shift within the current debate on citizenship concerns Marshall's "failure" to recognize citizenship as *practice*—that is to say, something exercised by citizens, and not simply a set of rights and duties. By contrast, many scholars construct the citizen as an agent, with the capacity to make individual choices and take part in decision making (e.g., Deacon, 2004; Hoggett, 2001; Le Grand, 2003; Jensen & Pfau-Effinger, 2005). A more dynamic relationship between welfare states and citizens is evolving since citizens themselves expect (or are expected) to play a more active role in handling a diverse set of risks and promoting their own welfare. We need to complement Marshall's notion of social citizenship with new models of citizenship, involving *the participatory dimension of social citizenship* (e.g., citizens in the role of users, partners in dialogue with the authorities and service providers, self-organizers, etc.).

Throughout Europe, we see the emergence of new discourses on the involvement of citizens and a search for new forms of civic participation beyond representative democracy, often under the headings of "civil dialogue," "collaborative governance," or "participatory governance" (Fung & Wright, 2003; Grote & Gbikpi, 2002). The EU has made "participatory democracy" a key objective, aiming at an open, transparent, and regular dialogue with citizens, representative associations, and civil society (Kohler-Koch & Rittberger, 2007). The Lisbon Treaty introduces provisions for "Citizen's initiatives" to overcome the barriers that exist between European citizens and Brussels decision-makers. The European Parliament has installed a model of the Citizen's Agora, bringing together citizens, representatives of civil society, and elected politicians to debate the key challenges faced by the EU. Similarly, national governments are establishing new forums and channels for participation and the articulation of interests, including not only long-term actors (e.g., social partner organizations) but also self-help groups, user organizations, community-based organizations, and other civil society actors speaking on behalf of marginalized groups (Barnes et al., 2007). Across Europe, welfare states are focusing more on the role that citizens could play as co-producers of welfare, by volunteering in voluntary organizations and hence demonstrating their commitment and solidarity with society and fellow citizens (Evers & Laville, 2004).

Marshall could not have foreseen these developments, and in any case was mainly interested in (social) citizenship as a *status*, rather than the participatory side of citizenship (Turner, 1990, 1993, 2001). Nevertheless, recent calls for a more participatory and active form of citizenship can be seen as a reaction to a Marshall-inspired understanding of social citizenship. For political theorists, however, this is hardly a new aspect of citizenship. Janoski and Gran (2002, 39–40), for instance, define the active citizen as someone who participates in many political activities, is concerned about people who belong to the same group, identifies with altruistic goals, opposes established elites, and pursues some form of social change. Others list active citizenship as one of several aspects of "thick citizenship," together with elements like mutually supportive rights and duties, participation in a political community, the interdependence of public and private, and civic virtues (Faulks, 2000, 11, 108). Similarly, Habermas (1994, 24–28) conceives of active citizenship as analogous to achieving membership of a self-determining ethical community.

As argued by Siim (2000, 2005) and Lister et al. (2007), much of the current debates around the participatory vein of citizenship rest on a rigid active/passive divide. This rigid divide glosses over the historical exclusion of women and marginalized social groups from the public sphere. We need an understanding of the active/passive axis that is sensitive to a wider range of activities by various social groups, formal and informal associations in civil society, and the mechanisms by which groups may be included within or excluded from the public sphere.

Williams (1998) and Lister (1998) raise similar concerns and highlight notions of active citizenship that involve mutual aid and collective self-help, and efforts by citizens to create themselves as subjects rather than objects for others—for instance, as expressed in movements of poor or disadvantaged people. These authors point to the increasing influence of user organizations, citizen groups, and new social movements, as a challenge to much current reasoning on state/citizen models in existing welfare state research. Criticizing established models of social citizenship, Williams (1998) argues that we need a new thinking that involves a shift away from seeing people as passive beneficiaries. As a way of conceptualizing a new relationship between states and citizens, she proposes a notion of "welfare agency" to address the strategies and activities of "welfare subjects."

The core element of this new conception of citizenship is the identification of citizens (claiming benefits or services) as creative and reflexive agents, who do not respond to benefits and services in uniform ways. Fitzpatrick (2002) has made similar suggestions in relation to notions such as the "welfare democracy." He claims that even though people in marginalized positions in society are subordinated to existing power structures and possibly denied full citizenship by public institutions, they are still active agents, capable of exercising power and affecting their own welfare and well-being (see also Lister, 1998, 2003; Lister et al., 2007).

These authors create an analytical space in which we can reconsider the participatory dimensions of social citizenship. When welfare claimants challenge their ascribed identity as silent or passive objects and as occupants of fixed social categories, give voice to their opinions, and demonstrate the capability to develop strategies independently, they contest established public and professional boundaries and practices. This new dynamic might imply that citizens develop new and alternative strategies to make their voice heard in relation to public services, which they feel are violating their integrity and personal rights.

The Emergence of Consumer-Citizenship

Citizenship studies have focused increasingly on notions such as "consumer citizens" (Clarke et al., 2007), "welfare consumerism," or the "marketization of welfare" (Crouch, Eder & Tambini, 2001). These notions add yet another dimension to previous models of citizenship, by asserting that consumers are active, orient themselves in markets, and choose to maximize their welfare. Consumer-oriented conceptions of citizenship have an affinity to the Libertarian understanding of the state–citizen relationship. This defines the relationship between state and citizen as of a limited and explicitly contractual nature (Miller, 2000; Nozick, 1974). People should take responsibility for their own well-being and risk protection, and as part of this responsibility seek the best services available. Apart from its role in protecting and enforcing basic personal and property rights, it is not obvious what goods and services the state should provide. However, to the extent that the state does provide welfare services, it should operate as an enterprise with the citizen as a rational consumer of public goods (see also Chapter 1 and 3 in this book).

Crouch argues that the consumer-citizen communicates with the public through market signals (Crouch, 2001, 111–113). According to the premises of this citizenship model, individuals are to enjoy consumer sovereignty, and this is to be accomplished through choice and contract. People's role as consumer-citizens may be limited to exercising a choice between a given set of providers or "suppliers" of services, whether private or public, expressing any dissatisfaction through complaints or by demanding a change of provider. The instrument of contract means that consumers who feel they have not been given the service they are entitled to may take legal action against the provider. In this kind of mixed or semi-private welfare market, people's demands for a service may be regulated through user fees or charges covering at least part of the cost of providing it.

Jones (2005) maintains that citizens have become more assertive and critical, both as taxpayers and as consumers of social policy. But the practical impact of consumer-citizenship has so far been more limited than the widely adopted rhetoric might suggest. Nevertheless, a key analytical issue is to what extent the consumer-citizen model interacts, contradicts, or reinforces Marshall's original interpretation of social citizenship, or the participatory models of citizenship outlined in the previous section. Aberbach and Christiansen (2005, 233) express concern that the notion of consumer-citizenship will undermine the collective and participatory dimensions of citizenship. They ask whether people are beginning to be oriented more exclusively towards the consumer role, meaning that they try to influence service provision directly while neglecting other (collective) channels of participation. Others have asked what impact consumer-citizenship will have on the solidarity-based and redistributive Socio-Liberal approach to citizenship.

Whether attempts to adopt ideas of consumer-citizenship and new governance practices will actually undermine citizen practices and individuals' social rights is an issue that future research needs to explore in greater detail. Arguably, the aim of consumer-citizenship is to hand more choice and self-responsibility to the individual. This goal calls for a thorough investigation into citizens' capability to exercise this choice and self-responsibility, including the extent to which citizens feel able to take advantage of the opportunity to act as transnational citizen-consumers in the emerging European welfare market on which multinational corporations are competing to offer insurance, health, and care services.

A POST-MARSHALLIAN FRAMEWORK FOR THE ANALYSIS OF SOCIAL CITIZENSHIP

At the beginning of this chapter, we argued that we need to take a more relational approach to social citizenship and analyze the webs of interdependence between different models of citizenship—in other words, to "open up" the analysis for the relations between Libertarian, Republican, or Socio-Liberal, to use Miller's phrasings. However, in this chapter we have presented an analytical attempt to adopt a more relational approach that avoids a rigid divide between passive and active dimensions of social citizenship (regardless of how "passive" and "active" are construed), and instead seeks to view these two aspects as interdependent and mutually influencing one another. We have also suggested that researchers tend to limit their attention to just one of several possible perspectives or approaches to social citizenship, rather than asking how the elements of reality each of the researchers is focusing on may coexist and interact with each other ("opening up between").

To return to Miller's (2000) distinction between three main interpretations of citizenship, we can make the following tentative conclusions on what a post-Marshallian analytical framework needs to consider. Firstly, citizenship in a *Socio-Liberal* sense is a relationship between the individual and the state, involving encompassing sets of mutual rights and obligations. Here, a move towards active citizenship could imply that the state demands citizens to meet specific obligations more actively, such as taking part in different forms of welfare-to-work (activation) programs in return for social benefits of different kinds. Similarly, immigrants who want to become permanent residents and eventually be granted state citizenship are increasingly required to undergo specific introduction programs, courses in the language and culture of the host country, and so on.

Secondly, in a *Libertarian* sense, the relationship between state and individual is conceived more narrowly, with the emphasis on the self-responsibility and autonomy of the individual. The responsibilities and legitimate tasks of the state are therefore limited to guaranteeing and protecting the limited but fundamental rights of the individual. Individuals should be able to exercise choice and enter freely into contracts to promote their own well-being and protection against risks of various kinds. According to this understanding, a move towards active citizenship could mean that citizens have greater scope for exercising individual choice and foresight, as knowledgeable consumers in a mixed welfare market (see also Chapter 3).

Thirdly, citizenship in a (Civic) *Republican* sense generally focuses on the citizen's participation in the affairs of his or her community, and the expectation that the individual will be committed to acknowledging and promoting the well-being of the community as a whole. A shift towards active citizenship defined in this way could be a means of achieving broader and more intensive citizen participation, both in deliberation and dialogue with relevant agencies and in self-directed activity, with regard to issues of welfare and well-being. Increased participation may take both individual and collective forms. On the one hand, individual "users" may engage in a dialogue to clarify appropriate measures or courses of action; on the other hand, they might be involved in consultation and negotiation over the design and planning of new policies.

Adapting Miller's triad, we can link more clearly the passive and active dimensions of each of these understandings ("opening up within") and point to the possible coexistence of elements from each understanding of citizenship ("opening up between"), as summarized in Table 2.1.

While the "opening up within" of social citizenship concerns the horizontal relationships in Table 2.1, the "opening up between" of social citizenship refers to the vertical relationships—that is, the ways in which we may combine normative ideas and notions conventionally associated with different approaches to social citizenship.

As we have demonstrated in this chapter, the active dimension of each approach and how these dimensions are combined are of particular interest within current debates on welfare reform in Europe and most EU member-states. In several reform packages, most clearly in relation to activation and pension reforms, we can observe several attempts to *combine* notions such as fulfilling duties (obligations), exercising choice and self-responsibility, and/or participating in deliberation and decision making. Hence, one important task

Table 2.1 An Analytical Framework: Opening Up Within and Between Models of Social Citizenship

| | | Opening Up Within | |
		Passive Dimension	**Active Dimension**
Opening Up Between	Socio-liberal element	Focus on receiving and claiming of rights to benefits and services	Focus on fulfillment of duties, especially in return for entitlement to benefits and services—conditional rights
	Libertarian element	Focus on welfare consumerism on the basis of managed and circumscribed user choice or quasi-markets	Focus on the fulfilment of individual self-responsibility and exercise of choice in the private market
	Republican element	Focus on managed participation in terms of user involvement, informed consent, or agency-directed self-help	Focus on self-governed activity, combined with co-responsibility for and commitment to participate in deliberation and decision making on common affairs

for further research into social citizenship is to describe and analyze the ways in which new and "hybrid" forms of social citizenship give rise to tensions, conflicts, and ambiguities. A related task is to gain more systematic knowledge about how the Europeanization and denationalization of social policy may promote such hybridization and a relative shift in the overall configuration of social citizenship—in other words, a more prominent role for Libertarian or Republic components at the expense of Socio-Liberal components. This framework thus provides us with a vocabulary for describing and analyzing the possible strengthening of Libertarian notions of citizenship (e.g., as market citizenship or citizen-consumership) at the expense of solidaristic, inclusive, and redistributive notions of social citizenship.

ACKNOWLEDGMENTS

The chapter builds on the project "Active Citizenship and Marginality in a European Context" (p. no. 149819/599), funded by the Welfare State Research Programme, the Nordic Council of Ministers (2002–05). We give a more detailed presentation of the project's approach and results in the book *Citizenship in the Nordic Countries: Dynamics of Choice, Duties and Participation in a Changing Europe* (published by Routledge, 2007).

REFERENCES

Aberbach, J. D., & Christiansen, T. (2005). Citizens and consumers: An NPM dilemma. *Public Management Review, 7*(2), 225–245.

A/RES/61/1 06 (2007). *Convention on the rights of persons with disabilities, Resolution adopted by the General Assembly*, January 24, 2007.

Barnes, M., Newman, J., & Sullivan, H. (2007). *Power, participation and political renewal: Case studies in public participation.* Bristol: Policy Press.

Beck, U., & Beck-Gernsheim, E. (2002). *Individualization: Institutionalised individualism and its social and political consequences.* London: Sage.

Beck, U., & Willms, J. (2004). *Conversations with Ulrich Beck.* Cambridge: Polity.

Bendix, R. (1964/1977). *Nation-building and citizenship.* Berkeley: University of California Press.

Bendix, R., & Rokkan, S. (1971). The extension of citizenship to the lower classes (originally published 1962). In M. Dogan & R. Rose (Eds.), *European politics: A reader.* Boston: Little, Brown and Company.

CEDAW (1979). *Convention on Elimination of all Discrimination Against Women* (December 18, 1979).

Clarke, J., Newman, J., Smith, N., Vidler, E., & Westmarland, L. (2007) *Creating citizen-consumers: Changing publics and changing public services.* London: Sage.

Council Directive 2000/43/EC. Implementing the principle of equal treatment between persons irrespective of racial or ethnic origin. *Official Journal L 180*, 19/7/2000, pp. 22–26.

Council Directive, 2000/78/EC. (November 27, 2000). Establishing a general framework for equal treatment in employment and occupation. *Official Journal L 303*, February 12, 2000, p. 16.

Cowles Green M., Caporaso, J., & Risse, T. (2001). *Transforming Europe. Europeanization and domestic change.* Ithaca, NY: Cornell University Press.

Crouch, C. (2001). Citizenship and markets in recent British education policy. In C. Crouch, K. Eder & D. Tambini (Eds.), *Citizenship, markets and the state.* Oxford: Oxford University Press.

Crouch, C., Eder, K., & Tambini, D. (Eds.) (2001). *Citizenship, markets and the state.* Oxford: Oxford University Press.

de Burca, G. (Ed.) (2005). *EU law and the welfare state: In search of solidarity.* Oxford: Oxford University Press.

Deacon, A. (2004). Review article: Different interpretations of agency within welfare debates. *Social Policy & Society, 3*(4), 447–455.

Dean, H., & Melrose, M. (1999). *Poverty, riches and social citizenship.* Basingstoke: Palgrave Macmillan.

Durkheim, E. (1893/1947). *The division of labor in society* (first published in French 1893). New York: The Free Press.

Dwyer, P. (2000). *Welfare rights and responsibilities.* Bristol: Policy Press.

Esping-Andersen, G. (1990). *Three worlds of welfare capitalism.* Cambridge: Polity.

Esping-Andersen, G. (1999). *The social foundations of postindustrial economics.* Oxford: Oxford University Press.

EU (1997). Consolidated version of the treaty establishing the European Community. In *Consolidated treaties.* Luxembourg: Office for Official Publications of the European Communities.

EU (2000). Charter of Fundamental Rights of the European Union (2000/C 364/01). *Official Journal*, December 18, 2000.

Evers, A., & J-L. Laville (2004). *Third Sector in Europe.* Cheltenham: Edward Elgar Press.

Faulks, K. (2000). *Citizenship,* London: Routledge.

Ferrera, M. (2005). *The boundaries of welfare.* Oxford: Oxford University Press.

Fitzpatrick, T. (2002). In search of welfare democracy. *Social Policy & Society, 1*(1), 11–20.

Fraser, N. (2008). *Scales of justice. Reimagining political space in a globalizing world.* New York: Columbia University Press.

Fung, A., & E. O. Wright (2003). *Deepening democracy. Institutional innovations in empowered participatory governance.* London: Verso.

Giddens, A. (1998). *The third way: The renewal of social democracy.* Cambridge: Polity Press.

Giddens, A., & Held, D. (1982). *Classes, power and conflict: Classical and contemporary debates.* Basingstoke: Palgrave Macmillan.

Goul Andersen, J. (2002). Work and citizenship: Unemployment and unemployment politics in Denmark 1980–2000. In J. Goul Andersen, & P. H. Jensen (Eds.), *Changing labour markets, welfare policies and citizenship.* Bristol: Policy Press.

Grote, J. R., & B. Gbikpi (Eds.) (2002). *Participatory governance: Political and societal implications.* Opladen: Leske + Budrich.

Habermas, J. (1994). Citizenship and national identity. In Stenbergen, B. van (Ed.), *The condition of citizenship.* London: Sage.

Heidenreich, M., & J. Zeitlin (Eds.) (2009). *Changing European employment and welfare regimes: The influence of the open method of coordination on national labour market and social welfare reforms.* London: Routledge.

Hoggett, P. (2001). Agency, rationality and social policy. *Journal of Social Policy, 30*(1), 37–56.

Hvinden, B. (2004). How to get employers to take on greater responsibility for the inclusion of disabled people in working life. In B. Marin, C. Prinz & M. Quiesser (Eds.), *Transforming disability welfare policies: Towards work and equal opportunities.* Aldershot: Ashgate.

Hvinden, B., & Halvorsen, R. (2003). Which way for European disability policy? *Scandinavian Journal of Disability Research, 5*(3), 296–312.

Hvinden, B., & Johansson, H. (Eds.) (2007). *Citizenship in the Nordic countries: Dynamics of choice, duties and participation in a changing Europe.* Oxford: Routledge.

ILO (1989). *Convention 169: Indigenous and Tribal Peoples Convention.*

Isin, E. F., & Turner, B. S. (2007). Investigating citizenship: An agenda for citizenship studies. *Citizenship Studies, 11*(1), 5–17.

Janoski, T., & Gran, B. (2002). Political citizenship: Foundations of fights. In E. F. Isin & B. S. Turner (Eds.), *Handbook of citizenship studies.* London: Sage.

Jensen, P. H., & Pfau-Effinger, B. (2005). "Active" citizenship: The new face of welfare. In J. Goul Andersen, A-M. Guillemard, P. H. Jensen, & B. Pfau-Effinger (Eds.), *The changing face of welfare.* Bristol: Policy Press.

Johansson, H., & Hvinden, B. (2005). Welfare governance and the remaking of citizenship. In J. Newman (Ed.), *Rethinking governance: Policy, politics and the public in Europe.* Bristol: Policy Press.

Johansson, H., & Hvinden, B. (2007). What do we mean by active citizenship? In B. Hvinden & H. Johansson (Eds.), *Citizenship in Nordic welfare states: Dynamics of choice, duties and participation in a changing Europe.* London: Routledge.

Jones, P. (2005). "Consumers" of social policy: policy design, policy response, policy approval. *Social Policy & Society, 4*(3), 237–249.

Kohler-Koch, B., & B. Rittberger (2007). *Debating the democratic legitimacy of the European Union.* Lanham: Rowman & Littlefield Publishers, Inc.

Kvist, J., & J. Saari (2007). *The Europeanization of social protection*. Bristol: Policy Press.

Le Grand, J. (2003). *Motivation, agency, and public policy*. Oxford: Oxford University Press.

Leibfried, S. (2005). Social policy: Left to the judges and the markets? In H. Wallace, W. Wallace, & M. A. Pollack (Eds.), *Policy-making in the European Union* (5th ed.). Oxford: Oxford University Press.

Levitas, R. (1998). *The inclusive society? Social exclusion and New Labour*. London: Macmillan Press.

Lister, R. (1998). In from the margins: Citizenship, inclusion and exclusion. In M. Barry & C. Hallett (Eds.), *Social exclusion and social work*. Lyme Regis, UK: Russell House.

Lister, R. (2001). Towards a citizen's welfare state: the 3 + 2 'R's of welfare reform. *Theory, Culture & Society, 18*(2–3), 91–111.

Lister, R. (2003). *Citizenship: Feminist perspectives* (2nd ed.). Basingstoke: Palgrave Macmillan.

Lister, R., Williams, F., Anttonen, A., Bussemaker, J., Gerhard, U., Heinen, J., Johansson, S., Leira, A., Siim, B., & Tobio, C., with Gavenas, A. (2007). *Gendering citizenship in Western Europe: New challenges for citizenship research in a cross-national context*. Bristol: Policy Press.

Majone, G. (1993). The European Community: Between social policy and social regulation. *Journal of Common Market Studies, 31*(2), 153–169.

Majone, G. (2005). *Dilemmas of European integration*. Oxford: Oxford University Press.

Marquand, D. (1991). Civic republicans and liberal individualists: The case of Britain. *European Journal of Sociology, 32*(2), 329–344.

Marshall, T. H. (1950/1965). Citizenship and social class. In *Class, citizenship, and social development*. New York: Anchor Books.

Mead, L. (1986). *Beyond entitlement—the social obligations of citizenship*. New York: Anchor Press.

Mead, L. (1997). Citizenship and social policy: T. H. Marshall and poverty. In E. F. Paul, F. D. Miller, & J. Paul (Eds.), *The welfare state*. Cambridge: Cambridge University Press.

Miller, D. (2000). *Citizenship and national identity*. Cambridge: Polity Press.

Nozick, R. (1974). *Anarchy, state, and utopia*. Oxford: Blackwell.

Olsen, J. P. (2002). The many faces of Europeanization. *Journal of Common Market Studies, 40*(5), 921–952.

Orloff, A. S. (2009). Gendering the comparative analysis of welfare states: An unfinished agenda. *Sociological Theory, 27*(3), 317–343.

Østerud, Ø., Engelstad, F., & Selle, P. (2003). *Makten og demokratiet. En sluttbok fra Makt- og demokratiutredningen*. Oslo: Gyldendal Akademisk.

Parsons, T. (1967). Full citizenship for the Negro American? (originally published 1965). In *Sociological theory and modern society*. New York: The Free Press.

Parsons, T. (1971). *The system of modern societies.* Englewood Cliffs, NJ: Prentice-Hall.

Pateman, C. (1988). The patriarchal welfare state. In A. Gutman (Ed.), *Democracy and the welfare state.* Princeton: Princeton University Press.

Pollack, M. A. (2003). The Court of Justice as an agent: delegation of judicial power in the European Union. In *The engines of European integration.* Oxford: Oxford University Press

Rees, A. M. (1996). T. H. Marshall and the progress of citizenship. In M. Bulmer & A. M. Rees (Eds.), *Citizenship today.* London: UCL press.

Rieger, E., & S. Leibfried (2003). *Limits to globalization.* Cambridge: Cambridge University Press.

Scharpf, F. W. (1996). Negative and positive integration in the political economy of European welfare states. In G. Marks, F. P. Scharpf, P. C. Schmitter, & W. Streeck (Eds.), *Governance in the European Union.* London: Sage.

Siim, B. (2000). *Gender and citizenship: politics and agency in France, Britain and Denmark.* Cambridge: Cambridge University Press.

Siim, B. (2005). Gender equality, citizenship and welfare state structuring. In Goul Andersen, J., Guillemard, A.-M., Jensen, P. H., & Pfau-Effinger, B. (Eds.), *The changing face of welfare* Bristol: Policy Press.

Somers, M. R. (2008). *Genealogies of citizenship. Markets, statelessness, and the right to have rights.* Cambridge: Cambirdge University Press.

Stasiulis, D. (2004). Hybrid citizenship and what's left. *Citizenship Studies, 8*(3), 295–303.

Tarrow, S. (2003). *Power in movement* (2nd ed.). Cambridge: Cambridge University Press.

Taylor-Gooby, P. (2008). *Reframing social citizenship.* Oxford: Oxford University Press.

Turner, B. S. (1990). Outline of a theory of citizenship. *Sociology, 24*(2), 189–217.

Turner, B. S. (1993). Contemporary problems in the theory of citizenship. In Turner, B. S. *Citizenship and social theory.* London: Sage.

Turner, B. S. (2001). The erosion of citizenship. *British Journal of Sociology, 52*(2), 189–209.

UN Doc A/44/49 (1989). *Convention on the Rights of the Child,* G. A. res. 44/25, annex, 44 U.N. GAOR Supp. (No. 49) at 167.

Williams, F. (1998). Agency and structure revisited: Rethinking poverty and social exclusion. In M. Barry & C. Hallett (Eds.), *Social exclusion and social work.* Lyme Regis, UK: Russell House.

Young, I. M. (1990). *Justice and the politics of difference.* Princeton: Princeton University Press.

3

CHANGING PERSPECTIVES ON SOCIAL CITIZENSHIP: A CROSS-TIME COMPARISON

Jane Jenson

In recent years the composition of social citizenship rights has undergone significant redesign. In the three decades after 1945 social rights were institutionalized in response to a set of social risks—unemployment, old age, ill health, poverty, childrearing, and so on. Systems of social protection were grounded in the shared objective of providing a measure of social security via pensions, unemployment insurance, health insurance, family allowances, and other programs to the worker and his family in a primarily industrial economy. In almost all citizenship regimes the goal was to provide greater security to citizens after worldwide depression in the 1930s and then war in the 1940s. This goal was reflected in the discourse of the time. Article 22 of the 1948 United Nations Universal Declaration of Human Rights states that everyone, "as a member of society, has the right to social security."[1] Summarizing this spirit of the times, T. H. Marshall said in 1949 that the "social element" of the triptych of citizenship rights gave "the right to a modicum of economic welfare and security" (Marshall, 1965, 78).

In the past two decades policymakers have been forced to recognize, however, the need for another analysis of the risks that merit collective engagement to ensure social protection. Work and family have been transformed, as has the life course, with the result that the assumptions about industrial employment, family composition, birth rates, and life expectancy that informed social policy in the three decades after 1945 no longer hold. Coupled with a political attack from neoliberalism in the 1980s, these changes in the economy and society have prompted an analysis of new social risks and given rise to another policy perspective: the social investment perspective (Jenson, 2010a; Jenson & Saint-Martin, 2003, 2006).

Now citizenship regimes that rely on the social investment perspective rest in part on institutions created decades ago to provide social citizenship rights, such as public education and income transfers to families (Morel, Palier, & Palme, 2011). These are now being redesigned in order to be more future-oriented and refocused on children and childhood (Jenson & Saint-Martin, 2003; Lister, 2006, 461ff.). New institutions are also being created. Their objectives are to break the intergenerational transfer of poverty and to foster social inclusion by the labor market as well as civil society, all in the name of allowing individuals and families to achieve and maintain a measure of autonomy and well-being.

To map the contours of the social investment perspective, this chapter examines the design and redesign of social citizenship over the post-1945 decades. Citizenship necessarily involves two relationships: the status of members of the community with respect to a political authority, and the relationships of mutual support and solidarity that exist among such members (Bosniak, 2000). If the second reminds us of social citizenship rights, it is crucial to note that without reference to the first relationship there is no "right." Solidarity alone does not create a social right; it can be expressed via relations of mutual support, a social wage acquired by collective bargaining, or even charity.[2] Thus, both relationships must be present in order to say that social citizenship exists (Magnette, 2005, 164).

The move towards a social investment perspective involves major choices about the design of social citizenship, choices that are altering citizenship regimes. Such regimes are composed of overlapping dimensions (Jenson, 2009a; Jenson & Phillips, 1996). These incorporate a definition of rights and duties as well governance arrangements for accessing services and for delivering them. They also include an identity dimension, a definition not only of who belongs but also what belonging means. And fourthly, a citizenship regime reflects a "responsibility mix," the ideas and practices that define the boundaries of state responsibilities and differentiate them from those of markets, of families, and of communities in a "welfare diamond."[3] The result is a definition of how much of individuals' and families' security and well-being a society chooses to provide as a citizenship right. Other ways to create well-being and solidarity are, of course, by purchases in the market, via the reciprocity of kin, or via collective support in communities.

Citizenship regimes differ both across time and across space, creating varied content to these dimensions and therefore to the particular regime mix.[4] Some have been quite stingy in their definition of citizenship rights, while others have been generous. Some have relied almost exclusively on public provision, with citizens' access provided by democratic politics, while others have encouraged private, third-sector actors with their own rules of responsibility and participation to play a key role in the delivery of social rights (Evers, 2009). These differences follow from the varied historical traditions of social citizenship.

This chapter first examines historical traditions that gave rise to the shared ideas about social citizenship and security that shaped many post-1945 citizenship regimes. These regimes all faced challenges from the 1980s on. The chapter then presents the responses to the challenges, and the emerging practices of social citizenship that can be labeled the social investment perspective. Doing all this in a single chapter means that the presentation might remain at only a general level; to avoid this danger it uses two iconic examples—the UK and Sweden—to illustrate change over time in social citizenship. No Bismarckian (continental-corporatist) regime is treated in detail because these regimes lag behind the others in their adoption of the social investment perspective (Palier, 2010, 386–387).

CONJUGATING EQUALITY AND DISTINCTIONS—SOCIAL CITIZENSHIP ACCORDING TO MARSHALL AND ESPING-ANDERSEN

There is general agreement that the concept of social citizenship was given its current persona by the sociologist T. H. Marshall in his reflections on the British situation just after World War II.[5] For Marshall, there was never any question that the market economy and the capitalist system would continue to structure social relations; he anticipated no socialist economy or classless society. But he argued that social rights could alter the effects of inequalities generated by markets, especially those inequalities that were transferred from one generation to another as "original endowments" determining access to institutions such as education and labor markets as well as income.[6] For Marshall (1965, 121), "citizenship operates as an instrument of social stratification" by limiting market effects, but also by promoting new sources of inequality such as those of the stratification effects of education (1965, 117 ff.; see also Chapter 2).

Reflecting on the deep distress of the British working population in the 1930s and the visions of change embodied in programs such as those proposed by William Lord Beveridge, Marshall defined social citizenship in two general ways at the start of his essay: "the right to a modicum of economic welfare and security" and "the right to live the life of a civilized being" (1965, 78). By the mid-20th century, the British government had initiated a series of policies to increase equality of opportunity as well as to protect against life risks. For example, during World War II the British government finally made a commitment to universal and free secondary education. This reform, plus the creation of the National Health Service in 1946, significantly altered social rights to be sure—but they also altered the very identity of the nation, transforming the poor, whether workers or not, into full citizens. The 19th-century Poor Law stripped an individual of his citizen rights (Magnette, 2005, 161).[7] When the stigmatizing and exclusionary Poor Law was finally abolished in 1948, at long last, finding oneself in receipt of public support would no longer make one less a citizen in the eyes of the state or the community.

For Marshall, social citizenship's primary effect was, then, to create citizens by altering initial endowments (via education) as well as providing for old age and protecting against the "bad luck" of illness or unemployment. In the terms of the concept of citizenship regime, he described a responsibility mix in which the effects of market relations and family circumstances were tempered by a solid state sector. Moreover, the community sector of the welfare diamond was also assigned less responsibility than in earlier decades, because supports and services that had previously been provided as charity to the poor and disadvantaged— whether housing, income, or schooling—would now be provided publicly.

Marshall located his analysis in the tradition of social liberalism. Thus, just as people's survival depended on instituting a measure of "smoke abatement" in polluted industrial cities, the goal of social rights was "class abatement"—that is, smoothing over the inherent tensions within a market economy due to the inequalities generated by markets (Marshall, 1965, 95; see Chapter 1). Social liberalism was an ideology that profoundly shaped the actions of the first British Labour governments in the 1940s and 1950s as they designed the responsibility mix of the citizenship regime, its social rights and duties, and its governance arrangements. As L. T. Hobhouse's *Liberalism*, which served as a sort of manifesto for the New Liberals (social liberals) in the interwar years, said (quoted in White, 2000, 511):

> The function of the State is to secure conditions upon which its citizens are able to win by their own efforts all that is necessary to a full civic efficiency. It is not for the State to feed, house or clothe them. It is for the State to take care that the economic conditions are such that the normal man who is not defective in mind or body or will can by useful labour feed, house, and clothe himself and his family ... [In this sense the] 'right to work' and the 'right to a living wage' are just as valid as the rights of person or property.

The role of the state was to provide a balance to the market, because the market was incapable of guaranteeing to all citizens access to security and well-being. For Marshall, then, the governance dimension of this citizenship regime was in the hands first of a democratic government ("the State," as he put it, employing the European convention of using a capital letter).[8] But also important for him were trade unions, who shared with political parties the responsibility for ensuring the well-being of the "working man" by claiming his rights.

Marshall focused on the way that the existence of social rights and duties in the citizenship regime was reallocating power as well as status within the class structure. The primary institutional locales were the educational system and the occupational structure, where recognition of political rights as well as social provision permitted groups and individuals to contest the legitimacy of market relations by "an invasion of contract by status, the subordination of market price to social justice, the replacement of the free bargain by the declaration of rights" (Marshall, 1965, 121–122, also 127).

This Marshallian insight about the capacity of social citizenship to redraw the stratification system was elaborated by Gøsta Esping-Andersen as he created his typology of welfare regimes (Esping-Andersen, 1990, 23, 21). He claimed that the liberal welfare regime that inspired Marshall was one that did the least to contest the legitimacy of market relations, precisely because "only rarely have such schemes been able to offer benefits of such a standard that they provide recipients with a genuine option to working" (Esping-Andersen, 1990, 23). Thus the stratification system was dualistic, with the poor differentiated—and stigmatized—from the better-off. They could count on some income security to be sure, and benefits were equal for all recipients, but their level was miserly.

In social democratic welfare regimes, market earnings remained important and the duty of all citizens, including women, was to work. This notion of duty was a foundational principle of social democratic regimes, although in liberal regimes the idea of "duty" was much less emphasized (therefore its arrival in the past two decades struck some observers as a break with the past) (see Chapters 2 and 6). In his work, Esping-Andersen also described the effects on social stratification of a universalistic regime that promotes equality of status. In social democratic regimes, dualism was avoided by offering high-quality (rather than bargain-basement) services and benefits, such that there would be an "equality of the highest standards" (Esping-Andersen, 1990, 27). Class distinctions would be mitigated, although not eliminated: "all strata are incorporated under one universal insurance system, yet benefits are graduated according to accustomed earnings" (Esping-Andersen, 1990, 28).

Both liberal regimes and social democratic ones, to use the standard labels, were built on principles whose intent was to redraw the lines of social stratification, altering access to services and income in the name of greater security and national solidarity. The social citizenship rights, as Goodin et al. (1999, 39) claim, are not fundamentally different in design. Indeed, "'Beveridge'-style welfare regimes—by virtue of their emphasis upon universal flat-rate entitlements—clearly represent the social-democratic pole." As Esping-Andersen pointed out, however, the essential difference is in the generosity of the benefits and the willingness to override market effects more in the social democratic type than the liberal, where the greatest fear is discouraging labor force participation.

Thus the social citizenship offered by both social democratic and liberal regimes differed significantly from continental-corporatist or Bismarckian ones, whose principal goal was, and still is, to adequately recognize acquired status. "As far as social justice is concerned, these schemes are less concerned about poverty or inequalities than about ensuring the proportionality of benefits with regard to former wages" (Palier & Martin, 2007, 536).

When the challenges to initial design and instruments began to be recognized, the liberal and social democratic regimes were thus the first to initiate the social investment perspective. As we will describe, to develop their social investment perspectives, they reached back to retrieve first principles about equality, about ensuring life chances and therefore patterning social stratification, and about the meaning of security and solidarity. Continental-corporatist (Bismarckian) welfare regimes had much greater difficulty in moving towards social investment, because their foundational principles were not the same (for example, Häusermann, in Palier, 2010, 207, 223–224).

FROM ENSURING SECURITY TO PROMOTING SOCIAL INVESTMENT

By the 1970s welfare regimes, conjugating capitalist economies and democratic politics, had been solidly institutionalized across Europe. While recognizing that there were many key differences among them, we can still summarize them as corresponding, in a variable mix, to the six moral values identified by Goodin et al. (1999, 22–23): promoting economic efficiency, reducing poverty, promoting social equality, promoting social integration and avoiding social exclusion, promoting social stability, and promoting autonomy. These values, of course, generated policy objectives, with programs and their instruments attached to each (for a further discussion of instrument change see Chapter 15).

The differences across liberal and social democratic citizenship regimes can be attributed to the different understanding of the responsibility mix embedded in each. The social citizenship rights offered by a classic liberal welfare regime after 1945 were always granted with an eye to protecting markets from too much interference. Thus, as John Myles summarizes, liberal welfare regimes have always displayed "a preference for market solutions to welfare problems" (Myles, 1998, 342). Another key motivation has been avoiding the supposed moral hazard of discouraging work among those able to work, by failing to distinguish between "deserving" and "undeserving" poor and those who are employable from those who are not. Thus targeting has been strict and cutoffs have been low so as not to discourage people from taking low-paid work if that is all that is available. By the 1970s these ideas had helped generate social rights that were not very generous, that were conditional on having demonstrated the legitimacy of a claim, and that tended to be "passive" rather than actively helping with labor force participation (Goodin et al., 1999, 40–45).

There was, however, a large and very significant exception: liberal welfare regimes were almost as concerned about maintaining traditional gender roles and relations as were the familialist corporatist regimes. They sometimes allowed, indeed encouraged, women to refrain from seeking paid employment. In some cases, such as Britain, trade unions had fought hard for the right to earn a family wage, one that would be sufficient to support a stay-at-home wife, and wives obtained significantly different benefits from men and single women. Such differentials and disincentives began to be eliminated in the 1970s, with one notable exception: through the post-1945 decades, women heading lone-parent families were also permitted to follow the social norms of the traditional gender division of labor and devote themselves full time to parental care.[9] Social assistance was designed in such a way that they would lose much of their benefit if they began to earn income, because these programs were means-tested.

Not surprisingly, then, liberal welfare regimes in the EU had low rates of mothers' employment. In 1990, British women aged 22 to 60 reported very high rates of work interruption for family reasons (at 80% it was the highest country average in the EU 12) and fully 10 percentage points lower than the average for having worked during the preschool years of their first child. Ireland was little different, with 75% having interrupted work for family reasons and only 26%, the lowest rate in the EU, having been employed when their first child was pre-school age (Lelièvre & Gauthier, 1995, 474). Similarly, among lone parents, rates of nonparticipation in the labor force soared above the average of the EU. In the mid-1990s, 55% of Irish lone-parent families were simply outside the labor force, while another 7% were unemployed. The corresponding UK figures were 46% and 9%. The EU average was only 31% and 10% (Chambaz, 2001, 662).

In social democratic welfare regimes, the approach to the gender division of labor was different. All citizens had a general duty to work, and lone parents no more or less than mothers in general were not expected to provide full-time care for their children. Rather, they could access programs such as parental leaves and childcare services to support their labor force participation as well as family responsibilities. Social citizenship rights were designed to encourage employment. Generous universal family allowances were available, as were parental leaves at high replacement levels. Thus, in 1996 lone parents in the two Nordic welfare states in the EU had rates of nonparticipation in the labor force well below the European average (20% for Denmark and 22% for Finland, the EU average being 31%), while in 1990 76% of Danish women aged 22 to 60 reported having been employed while their first child was preschool age. This was the highest rate in the EU 12 (Chambaz, 2001, 662; Lelièvre & Gauthier, 1995, 474).[10]

For its part, social assistance was a very minor part of the welfare economy, with other programs carrying the weight of income support. This is the case because, as the wide consensus describes it, the key principle of social demo-cratic welfare regimes is promoting social equality (Esping-Andersen, 1990, 27; Korpi, 1980). Two main tools, both based on social policy interventions, are available to achieve these goals. One is redistribution of income so as to flatten, although not eliminate, income differentials, so as to foster a sense of "equal worth," to encourage full participation in the life of the community, and to avoid social exclusion. Such tools built a social architecture of rights and duties (full participation in the community included seeking employment and paying taxes) and promoted the identity of citizen. The second tool is to expand the state sector of the welfare diamond by restricting the borders of the market sector. In practice this has meant de-commodification. "What social democratic welfare states do is simply to try to take certain goods and services out of that [market] realm.... No longer bought and sold, their distribution is no longer dictated by the underlying distribution of income and wealth within the community" (Goodin et al., 1999, 49).

The principles and practices of both liberal and social democratic welfare regimes were solidly institutionalized by the 1970s. By the end of that decade, however, neoliberals were gaining political visibility (Margaret Thatcher's neoliberal Conservative party was elected in 1979), and they mounted their assault on post-1945 social citizenship. The goal of this ideology and the politics following from it was to shrink to almost zero the state sector of the welfare diamond by denying it any legitimate responsibility for ensuring security. According to the standard and strident claims of neoliberals, faulty state action was actually undermining security. For neoliberals, "too much state" had not only usurped the rightful space for the market but had undermined the family. They wished to assign the family a significantly larger responsibility for managing the interface with the market at the same time that the role of the state would contract. An example from quintessential Margaret Thatcher illustrates this narrative:[11]

> I want to talk to you tonight about building "the healthy society." By "the healthy society" I mean a society in which three complementary ideals are combined. First, it is a society in which the vast majority of men and women are encouraged, and helped, to accept responsibility for themselves and their families, and to live their lives with the maximum of independence and self-reliance. Second, it is a society where everyone feels himself a responsible member of the community in which he lives and works; where he is inspired to play his part in ensuring the well-being of that community; and, in particular, where he shows a practical concern for those members who—for reasons of age, handicap or other disability—cannot fend for themselves without help. And, third, the healthy society is one founded on the family. Family life is the bed-rock on which the healthy society must be built. … The citizens of the healthy society are people who care for others and look first to themselves to care for themselves. I hope that we can together see that society grow and flourish.

For the "purest" neoliberals, as this quote illustrates, the community or voluntary sector was responsible for picking up the pieces of social dislocation. However, civil society was also to help organize the distribution of well-being, relying on social capital ties as well as self-help to ensure that families could realize their projects. This is a vision without social citizenship, a call to redesign the welfare diamond so that it could become a triangle without a corner for the state.

Neoliberals had, of course, their day. Nonetheless, prescriptions such as these were soon found wanting, and this from a variety of political positions and institutions. In reaction, the social investment perspective began to take shape and to be institutionalized, with a rehabilitation of the state (Evers, 2009, 253ff; Jenson & Saint-Martin, 2006). In an initial step, concerns arose that acceptance of certain neoliberal prescriptions and departures from the principles of post-1945 social policy were creating new threats. For example, this was the case in the mid-1990s for the Organisation of Economic Cooperation and Development (OECD), which had been an early enthusiast of a standard neoliberal position. The OECD had been the leader of the "welfare as a burden" position; in a 1980 conference on the "welfare state in crisis," the organization had begun diffusing the idea among its members and within policy communities that "social policy in many countries creates obstacles to growth" (quoted in Deacon, 1997, 71). By the middle of the next decade, however, concerns about stability and the negative effects of "structural adjustment," in the OECD and elsewhere, were circulating. Social cohesion and social exclusion became key words in policy discussion, and warnings appeared of the need to balance attention to economic restructuring with caution about societal cohesion in order to sustain that very restructuring (Jenson, 1998, 3, 5). The 1996 high-level conference, "Beyond 2000: The New Social Policy Agenda," concluded with a call for a "new framework for social policy reform," labeled a social investment approach, in which "the challenge is to ensure that return to social expenditures are maximised, in the form of social cohesion and active participation in society and the labour market" (OECD, 1997, 5–6).

Political struggle was also the driver of the new perspective. In post-Thatcher Great Britain, as the Labour Party moved toward electoral victory, it significantly rejigged its program, following on the work of its Commission on Social Justice (explicitly intended to update the Beveridge Report on its 50th anniversary), which reported in 1994 (Lister, 2006, 457–459). It provided a vision of social citizenship that was one of the first summaries of the social investment perspective. The Commission wrote, "The first and most important task for government is to set in place the opportunities for children and adults to learn their personal best. By investing in skills, we raise people's capacity to add value to the economy, to take charge of their own lives, and to contribute to their families and communities" (Commission on Social Justice, 1994, 119–120), while its Chair made the point that social justice—that is, a modernized welfare state—is "an economic not merely a social necessity" (Borrie, 1996). If the Commission's report was rarely explicitly referenced by New Labour led by Tony Blair or by his Chancellor, Gordon Brown, its themes were developed over the next decade as "social investment" was promoted (Dobrowolsky & Jenson, 2005).[12]

A similar political project was mounted in and around the institutions of the EU, where a grouping of policy entrepreneurs, experts, politicians, NGOs, and unions all were working to legitimate the idea that it was necessary to "correct" the pro-business bias and neoliberalism of monetary union by "revalorizing" social policy and identifying how it contributed to rather than hindered economic growth. Building on the key notion that social spending is not a burden but an investment in economic growth, such efforts bore fruit when under the Dutch Presidency of 1997 the EU described social policy as a productive factor (Hemerijck, 2007, 2). This analysis of how to achieve the value of economic efficiency informed the 2000 Lisbon Agenda, which promised to make Europe "the most competitive and dynamic knowledge-based economy in the world capable of sustainable economic growth with more and better jobs and greater social cohesion." It took a while for the EU to take up the notion of social investment *per se*, but by 2005 and the midterm review of the Lisbon Strategy the EU had fallen in behind the social investment perspective (Jenson, 2009b, 4 and passim).[13]

Finally, policy intellectuals and epistemic communities within these institutions but also autonomously began in the mid-1990s to promote the social investment perspective. For example, Anthony Giddens (1998) called in the mid-1990s for a "social investment state" that would invest in human and social capital. As the idea of social investment spread through European policy communities, by the time of the British Presidency of the EU in 2005 (for which Giddens and the Policy Network organized the social policy analysis) and in a key document prepared for it, Maurizio Ferrera's first policy proposal to European leaders was for "a specific *focus on children*" (in Diamond et al., 2006, 30).[14] In the same document, Joachim Palme vaunted the Nordic model because of its "family policy for children" (in Diamond et al., 2006, 40).

Of course, the best-known intellectual promoting social investment in the European context, and in terms very similar to those already developed by the OECD in the mid-1990s, was Esping-Andersen (Esping-Andersen et al., 2002; Esping-Andersen with Palier, 2008). His intello-political project called for a "child-centred perspective," with a "child-centred social investment strategy" (Esping-Andersen et al., 2002, 51). This strategy is essentially one to ensure "social inclusion and a competitive knowledge economy" via activation, making work pay, and reducing workless households (see Chapter 2 on child-centered social investment in Esping-Andersen et al., 2002).

These examples document the multiple entry points of the calls for more attention to social investment as a way of coping with the negative consequences of the neoliberal years and in order to modernize social citizenship for the future, without abandoning its underlying principles. What is this social investment perspective on social citizenship?

THE SOCIAL INVESTMENT PERSPECTIVE—NEW ROUTES TO ACHIEVING WELFARE GOALS

In an earlier section the initial goals of welfare regimes, and therefore social citizenship, were summarized as promoting economic efficiency, reducing poverty, promoting social equality, promoting social integration and avoiding social exclusion, promoting social stability, and promoting autonomy. Examining the social investment perspective at this level of generality, there is little evidence that it has contributed to the abandonment any of these values. Again at this high level of generality, there is little evidence that new values have been identified.

Where there is change, however, is at the level of policy objectives and the creation or reinforcement of certain policy instruments. The result is that policy interventions in the name of social citizenship are sometimes quite different from those of the post-1945 decades.

What are the policy objectives and instruments of this policy perspective? A general description would include the notion that there should be less emphasis on social protection and more on being preventive and proactive. Its announced goals are to increase social inclusion and minimize the intergenerational transfer of poverty as well as to ensure that the population is well prepared for the likely employment conditions (less job security; more precarious forms of employment) of contemporary economies. Policymakers claim that moving towards this perspective will allow individuals and families to maintain responsibility for their well-being via market incomes and intra-family exchanges, much as male wages and full employment promoted the goals of autonomy and integration in the earlier design of welfare regimes. Labor market participation of most adults is a goal. Exemptions, for example for lone mothers, have been cut back, and leaves for caring or other family activities are usually designed so as to be short and minimize the long-term negative effects on employment. An additional goal is to lessen the threats to social protection regimes themselves coming from aging societies and high dependency ratios, such that pension systems can stabilize. The state's role is to define its interventions and social citizenship practices so that these conditions will be met. In policy terms this implies increased attention to and investment in children, human capital, and making work pay.

Just as with Keynesianism after 1945,[15] the perspective takes on different coloration depending on the political circumstances and intellectual influences that shape it in each case. Yet there are a number of shared premises that underpin it. It is possible, therefore, to construct an ideal type, in the Weberian sense. Three key building blocks can be identified.[16]

First is the notion of constant learning. The claim is that individuals' security no longer means protection from the market. Security has come to mean the capacity to confront challenges and adapt, via lifelong learning to acquire new or update old skills as well as via early childhood learning. The metaphor is of a trampoline rather than a shield or a net. Acquisition of human capital is proposed as a response to the changes associated with de-industrialization, the growth of services, and, particularly, the emergence of a knowledge-based economy. It is promoted as the way to ensure continued connection to a rapidly changing labor market.

Second is an orientation to the future. The metaphor of "investment" is most obviously linked to this dimension. Investing implies adopting a particular notion of time. Investments generate dividends in the future, whereas spending is something that occurs in the present. These notions reframe state spending from "passive expenditures" towards proactive and preventive "investments," and re-legitimate the role of the state intervening, among other things, to overcome new social risks, as we saw above with respect to the OECD's *virage* in 1996 as well as that of New

Labour. They also legitimate a policy stance that pays less attention to poverty in the here-and-now as long as it is "only" short term and does not undermine future child well-being. With this orientation to time, fighting intergenerational transmission of disadvantage as well as a life-course perspective takes on all their meaning.

And finally, as in any social policy framework, there is a link between individuals' circumstances and the collective well-being. The social investment perspective promotes the notion that investments in individuals enrich our common future and that ensuring success in the present is beneficial for the community as a whole, both now and into the future. Rather than stressing promotion of equality as a basis for social justice, claims for the social investment perspective are framed such that policy instruments providing some measure of income security now (via state spending on active labor market measures and supplementing earnings with work-tested transfers or tax credits) will break the intergenerational cycle of poverty, thereby leading to school success, less crime, and positive school–work transitions. These benefit everyone less by limiting expenditures now than by promising to limit those of the future.

Each of these building blocks—or dimensions—of the ideal type can usually be found in each citizenship regime, but some jurisdictions usually emphasize one dimension more than the others. For example, social democratic Nordic welfare regimes have concentrated more on human capital, adjusting the training components of their activation policies as well as their approach to early childhood education and care.

Sweden provides a good example of how a single policy domain can be altered to bring it into conformity with the social investment perspective. Although Sweden has been a leader in providing childcare services since the 1970s, the goals and instruments have not been the same over the four decades. It is not correct, in other words, to argue, as enthusiasts sometimes do, that the Nordic welfare states have been "doing social investment" for decades (for example, Esping-Andersen et al., 2002, 51).

In the early 1970s, childcare had "the aim ... to bring about a powerful democratisation of activities for children, and introduce a progressive pedagogy for creating equivalent conditions for growing up" (Korpi, 2007, 24). In other words, the goals focused on the individual child's development and on Swedish society's equality goals, including to ensure "the opportunity of [children] developing their social competence in democratic processes" (Korpi, 2007, 24). Then, in the mid-1990s, as the social investment perspective began to emerge, Sweden worked a major realignment both in the organization of childcare and its philosophical grounding. Prime Minister and leader of the Social Democrats, Göran Persson, announced "a major change" and did so using the classic language of the social investment perspective (quoted in Korpi, 2007, 61):

> Lifelong learning should be a foundation stone in Government policy for
> combating unemployment. Sweden should be able to compete with high

competence, and the prerequisites for this are to be provided through high quality in all school forms, from pre-school to higher education. The pre-school should contribute to improving the important early years of the compulsory school.

Then, responsibility for childcare was transferred from the National Board of Health and Welfare to the Ministry of Education, to ensure that the transition to a human-capital approach was fully institutionalized. By 1998 a national pre-school curriculum had been developed, focused on the skills the child should have in order to enter and succeed in school rather than on equality and demo-cratic citizenship, as earlier (Korpi, 2007, 63).

Liberal welfare regimes have tended to emphasize more the second dimension of the social investment perspective, stressing investments for the future. British policy toward children provides an example here. Addressing child poverty was one of the big policy ideas of the New Labour government after 1997; Tony Blair in his 1999 Beveridge Lecture pledged to end it in 20 years.[17] The Prime Minister contextualized this promise by offering to implement "good spending" on pro-grams such as the Child Benefit and to cut back "bad spending on the bills of eco-nomic failure," by which he meant social assistance and other forms of income support (full quote in Dobrowolsky & Jenson, 2005, 208). This policy stance was also promoted by Blair's Chancellor of the Exchequer, Gordon Brown, whose pre-budget documents for that financial strategy in 2005 made standard claims drawn from a social investment perspective (quoted in Dobrowolsky & Jenson, 2005, 207):[18]

> Tackling child poverty will both improve individuals' life chances and con-tribute to the development of an educated and highly-skilled workforce. The Government has an ambitious, long-term goal to eradicate child pov-erty by 2020. The Government's strategy is to provide financial support for families, with work for those who can and support for those who cannot; and to deliver high-quality public services, which are key to improving poor children's life chances and breaking cycles of deprivation.

Stressing one dimension over another has consequences for the policy instruments via which investments are made. Therefore, in Nordic citizenship regimes as well as liberal ones, early childhood education and care (ECEC) is a key instrument for implementing the social investment perspective because it addresses both human capital goals and anti-poverty goals (by allowing parents to seek employment). It also promises, according to the literature on child development, to help break the intergenerational transfers of disadvantage.[19] For example, the Irish National Economic and Social Council, in its massive analysis calling for a "developmental welfare state," put greater investment in childcare front and center, relying exten-sively on the OECD's analysis of the advantages of ECEC (NESC, 2005). We have already seen Sweden's emphasis on ECEC, and the public services that Gordon Brown promised in the quotation above are, among others, childcare.

But agreement on where to invest does not always bring consensus on how to invest. Indeed, the trajectories of social citizenship regimes remain influential, including longstanding visions of the proper welfare diamond. Thus, Sweden's childcare services remain primarily public. When private services expand, as they have been doing in recent decades, it is often the community sector that expands; these private services are provided by parental cooperatives and other forms of third-sector provision. In addition, they have been and remain a controversial political choice (Korpi, 2007, 55). In the UK, in contrast, most public effort went to supporting developmental programs for poor children, such as Sure Start, and part-time preschool. In the second case, parents are left to fill in the rest of the day by hiring babysitters or paying for other services. In addition, there are substantial childcare benefits in the programs supporting labor force activation. These allow parents to purchase the form and amount of childcare they want in the market. In this model we see that the "preference for market solutions to welfare problems" remains front and center in the policy instruments chosen.

Labor market programs of the social investment perspective, both those promoting activation and those aimed at "making work pay," have been grafted onto existing trajectories of social citizenship. The deep recession of the 1990s massively struck the Nordic countries, and the future of their social citizenship practices seemed in jeopardy. Sweden was hard hit, with the negative consequences being most pronounced for Swedes younger than 30 (OECD, 2008, 21). The labor market challenges associated with the crisis as well as policy changes mean that since 1990 there has been a widening of the income distribution. Labor market nonparticipation and even exclusion have increased.[20] There was a consequent increase in the proportion of the working-age population receiving some form of income support. Not surprisingly, child poverty began to rise.

In a social democratic welfare regime like Sweden's, "perhaps the most salient characteristic ... is its fusion of welfare and work" (Esping-Andersen, 1990, 28). When the crisis hit in the first years of the 1990s, programs were retrenched, and as conditions improved many of these cutbacks were reinstated, but employment never returned to its pre-1990 level (Palme et al., 2002, 334). The response has been to push forward the approaches we associate with social investment, in particular efforts to increase labor force participation and supplement earnings in order to make work pay.

This has meant a stiffening of the rules that allow individuals to remain out of the labor force. In September 2007 the center-right government announced that the 2008 budget would emphasize "further reforms aimed at creating clearer incentives to work and more and better ways back for people who are now outside the labour market."[21] It promised "new start jobs" in the private sector by reducing employers' contributions to social security when they hired someone from one of the target groups.[22] A second measure in place since 2007 introduced a requirement of labor market participation for the long-term unemployed and recipients of social assistance. Presented as a guarantee of employment, after a year and a half in the program and still without a job, participants can be assigned work.[23]

There is also a new emphasis on measures to "make work pay." By far the largest tax expenditure (and expenditure in general) of the government in 2008, 2009, and 2010 would go to the in-work tax credit (*jobbskatteavdrag*), one of the standard programs associated with the social investment perspective. Its objectives are to reduce poverty by reducing dependence on benefits and limit government expenditures. The new tax credit was instituted the same year the replacement levels for unemployment insurance were reduced (Aaberge & Flood, 2008, 7–8).

In all this, social citizenship practices continue to exhibit some continuity with past practices. For example, the Swedish design of its instrument for supplementing earnings is somewhat particular in comparison to those developed elsewhere, which tend to target low-income earners and to cut off benefits before reaching the middle class. In Sweden there is no minimum (termed a "phase-in region") and no low-income target group. The tax credit can be claimed universally (Aaberge & Flood, 2008, 7–8).

The UK's design of its in-work benefits is different. They continue to be targeted and focused on the "deserving"—that is, individuals in employment. There is a significant difference with the previous instruments, however. Social assistance has declined in importance, as money is transferred into benefits for "jobseekers," the employed, and especially the working poor. The first in-work benefit introduced after 1997 by New Labour (replacing a less generous Family Credit) was the Working Families Tax Credit (WFTC). Creation of this benefit marked a major move towards using the tax system (and its agencies, such as the Treasury and Inland Revenue) to deliver social policy and social benefits. In addition to providing a tax credit, scaled to earned income, the WFTC included a childcare credit for all claimants and more generous credits for families with children. The childcare credit could cover up to 70% of childcare costs, up to a maximum (Rake, 2001, 218). The design was clearly meant to "reward" earned income, and particularly to support families with children, as the name suggested.

In 2003 the WFTC was ended. The Working Tax Credit that replaced it was no longer both child-tested and income-tested; access depended only on levels of earned income. For families with young children, the second earner need have only 16 hours of employment instead of 30. The same adjustment applies to lone-parent families, where the only earner also has responsibility for young children.

It is here that we can also see an important break with the past, and a redesign of the welfare diamond and social rights in ways that broke with the familialism and gender exceptionalism described earlier. The New Deal for Lone Parents of 1997 set a target for 2010 of 70% in the active labor force, but at first there was no break with the tradition of "conservative" practices that permitted lone parents to substitute childcare for paid employment even after their children reached school age. It was only in 2008 that lone parents with a child aged 12 or more would no longer be entitled to social assistance benefits and would receive only the Jobseeker's Allowance, which imposed work requirements. A further reduction to age 7 was announced for 2010 (Knijn, Martin, & Millar, 2007, 647).

CONCLUDING REMARKS

T. H. Marshall was a social liberal of his times. His discussions of social citizenship demonstrated the complexities involved in conjugating the spatial mix within the welfare diamond assigned to markets, families, communities, and the state. In the past six decades the social and economic world has changed immensely, while political currents such as neoliberalism and feminism have de-legitimated some of the practices of social citizenship that he considered normal. Feminists have claimed since the 1960s that "full employment" can no longer mean for only half the population, while the very goal of the "family wage" has been discredited. They called instead for social services and adequate income transfers so that women as well as men could achieve full citizenship. Neoliberals took another tack, of course, striving to discredit the earlier design of the welfare diamond and its social rights. They claimed that the state corner of the welfare diamond needed to be shrunk, leaving markets, communities, and families to take up most of the responsibility for well-being.

Neoliberalism's promises of more well-being for all never materialized, of course. In the UK, for example, from 1975 to 1995, when Margaret Thatcher's Conservatives were in power (1979–1997), the child poverty rate *tripled*. By 1995 the country had the fourth highest rate of relative poverty (only slightly behind the United States) and the sixth highest by the measure of absolute poverty (UNICEF, 2000, 21, 5, 7). But even without the virulent neoliberal politics experienced in Britain, the effects of the worldwide turn to neoliberal thinking as well as economic crisis affected many European countries. Sweden provides one such example (Blomqvist, 2004).

Then, as all sort of indicators turned in a negative direction, governments, civil society actors, international organizations, and policy communities began to rethink their ideas about and practices of social citizenship. Out of this rethinking came the social investment perspective for "modernizing" social citizenship. As documented in this chapter, it has involved in part an exercise in retrieval. New ways of delivering on longstanding values of social citizenship have been developed, with the corresponding redesign or invention of policy instruments. As a liberal welfare regime, the UK's social citizenship practices still emphasize market solutions to welfare problems, via a preference for tax credits and targeting. Its childcare programs illustrate this continuity. Nonetheless, with this rethinking there has also been change. The UK's targeting reached farther into the middle class and policy finally reflected a lessened commitment to the traditional family division of labor and policies that discourage women from taking up work. When the Conservatives came to power in 2010 they did not abandon these positions, although they did seek to reshape the welfare diamond with the concept of the "Big Society." In Sweden's social democratic welfare regime, whose active labor market policies have for decades been meant to ensure that all citizens gain employment, the policy instruments have been rejigged by introducing a somewhat larger dose of compulsory work requirements and substantially more space in program delivery for both the market and the community sector.

In both of these cases, as well as elsewhere where the social investment perspective has made headway, we see that social citizenship continues to have effects, just as Marshall saw it did. The emphasis on improving the circumstances of the elderly and retired, which drove so much of post-1945 thinking and policy, is less present; public pension schemes often are seen as burdens, when the future belongs to children. These future workers and their parents, the workers of the present, win most attention. Here there are differences, of course. In social democratic regimes, the deeply implanted belief that citizens have a duty to work as well as the right to be "de-commodified" at key moments of the life course has brought redesign of policy instruments and redeployment of others (childcare, for example) to new purposes. The social investment perspective marks less of a break with previous large principles and ideas, however, than in liberal regimes where the notion of "citizen duty" (especially to seek employment) had been little emphasized and miserly social rights had sometimes been termed "entitlements." Nonetheless, in both cases the social investment perspective marks a break with neoliberalism, which granted very little legitimacy to the state. In both cases there had been a rebalancing of the welfare diamond that re-legitimated the very concept of social citizenship.

With the "great depression" of 2008, the predominance of the social investment perspective was challenged in several countries by a return to "infrastructural Keynesianism" that diverted spending to large projects that would generate primarily male employment. Then the crisis of the Euro and the fragility of several European economies plagued by high deficits and huge debt also threatened commitments to social spending for social citizenship. Whether these events signal the end of the social investment "moment" or only a difficult time in its history, however, is still a story to be written.

NOTES

1 This Declaration summarizes well the progressive thinking about social citizenship of the time, at least in Europe and North America. See: http://www.un.org/en/documents/udhr.

2 Particularly but not exclusively in liberal welfare regimes, the portion of an employee's compensation paid in the form of a private benefits—supplementary health insurance or private pensions, for example—is significant. This "private welfare state" merits attention to understand the welfare mix, but it does not provide citizenship rights.

3 The metaphor of the welfare diamond underpins the responsibility mix. It disaggregates the three "welfare pillars" described by those employing the concept of welfare regime (for example, Esping-Andersen, 1990, 21). Where the three pillars of welfare regimes are state, market, and family, we suggest that it is important also to consider *four* sources of well-being. Distinguishing the community sector from both the family and the market provides a better handle on processes of shifting responsibilities and governance. For a similar diamond see Evers et al. (1994).

4 There is also a European, and increasingly an international, approach to social citizenship (Auvachez, 2009; Jenson, 2007). Barbier (see Chapter 5) does not, however, share this view of the situation.

5 This chapter uses the 1965 edition of *Class, citizenship and social development*, introduced by S. M. Lipset with an essay in retrieval of historical sociology. Marshall's original "Citizenship and Social Class" was presented as the Alfred Marshall Lecture at Cambridge in 1949. One of the ironies of intellectual history is, of course and as Lipset points out, that the essay now treated as an iconic classic was seen at the time as "old-fashioned sociology" (Marshall, 1965, vi).

6 For additional elaborations of Marshall's analysis see Chapters 1 and 2 of this volume.

7 Marshall understood clearly that earlier notions of "protection" deprived whole groups, such as women and children, as well as dependent males, of the status of citizenship. In the United States as well as Britain, legislation reducing working hours and monitoring conditions of work "meticulously refrained from giving this protection directly to the adult male—the citizen *par excellence*. And they did so out of respect for his status as a citizen, on the grounds that enforced protective measures curtailed the civil right to conclude a free contract of employment" (Marshall, 1965, 89). Feminists' suspicion of "protective legislation" arises from the same recognition that "protection" in the form of mothers' allowances or limitations on hours were often less a "right" than a way of infantilizing women and therefore denying them citizenship (Jenson, 1989).

8 See for example, Marshall on the role of parliament and local councils in protecting rights (1965, 115).

9 For example, in the liberal welfare regime of the Canadian province of Ontario, the Ontario Mothers' Allowance Commission in the interwar years said: "the mother is regarded as an applicant for employment as guardian of future citizens of the state" (quoted in Boychuk, 1998, 35) and the state was employing her, in the absence of any male breadwinner.

10 Finland was not in the EU 12.

11 Speech to Social Services Conference Dinner, Dec. 2, 1976. http://www. margaretthatcher.org/speeches/displaydocument.asp?docid=103161. In this same speech she describes "industry, the basic social service" and the roles of the voluntary sector and self-help.

12 British analyses tend to hew to the concept of the "social investment state," although it is now little used elsewhere. See for example Lister (2006) and Newman and McKee (2005).

13 Esping-Andersen participated in the analytical work organized by the Portuguese Presidency in 2000 (Rodriques, 2002) and the Belgian Presidency in 2001. In both, he called for attention to social investment, but his ideas made little headway at the time; indeed, the Belgian Presidency was very resistant (Jenson, 2010b, 25–26).

14 In 2000, Maurizio Ferrera's report to the Portuguese Presidency in preparation for the Lisbon Council provided a classic analysis of whether globalization threatened European welfare regimes. Neither care nor children as objects worthy of policy analysis were mentioned (Ferrera et al., 2000).

15 As Peter Hall wrote of the adoption of Keynesianism: "To be Keynesian bespoke a general posture rather than a specific creed. Indeed the very ambiguity of Keynesian ideas enhanced their power in the political sphere. By reading slightly different emphases into these ideas, an otherwise disparate set of groups could unite under the same banner" (Hall in Hall, 1989, 367).

16 The three building blocks were identified by Jenson and Saint-Martin (2006), who provide examples of their various expressions in policy discourse and design.

17 Blair announced: "Our historic aim will be for ours to be the first generation to end child poverty, and it will take a generation. It is a 20-year mission, but I believe it can be done."

18 For a similar analysis, drawing on 2002 documents, see Lister (2006, 457–461).

19 The research by economist James Heckman as well as experts in early childhood development is cited frequently in order to justify increased spending on ECEC (see for example the sources cited in Saint-Martin & Dobrowolsky, 2005, and Jenson, 2009b, 5).

20 Over the decade 1991–2001, Sweden experienced one of the largest declines in labor market activity registered in the OECD, putting it in the company of the central and eastern European countries and Turkey (OECD, 2003, 26–27).

21 See Press Release, "Budget Bill for 2008: Putting Sweden to work—increasing opportunities" on http://www.sweden.gov.se/sb/d/8186/a/88569. Accessed May 15, 2010. The category of greatest concern was recipients of sickness benefits, and therefore many of the work incentives targeted them.

22 The target groups are individuals who are aged 25 years or older and have been unemployed, participated in employment policy programs, received sickness benefit, sickness or activity compensation, or obtained social benefits for more than a year; young people between the age of 20 and 25 years, who have been unemployed, participated in employment policy programs, received sickness benefit, sickness or activity compensation, or obtained social benefit for up to six months; refugees or related immigrants. See *eironline*, SE0703019I http://www.eurofound.europa.eu/eiro/2007/03/articles/se0703019i.htm.

23 This program aims to develop individually designed measures to get participants into employment as soon as possible, moving through three phases: intensified job-seeking activities including personal coaching; access to unemployment policy programs, such as job training, a work experience placement, or a subsidy for employment and skills development; after 450 days, if participants have not been able to obtain work, they are assigned an "appropriate" job corresponding to their personal skills. See: *eironline*, SE0705019I, http://www.eurofound.europa.eu/eiro/2007/05/articles/se0705019i.htm

REFERENCES

Aaberge, R., & L. Flood (2008). Evaluation of an in-work tax credit reform in Sweden: effects on labor supply and welfare participation of single mothers. *Working Papers in Economics*, No. 319. School of Businesses, Economics and Law, University of Gothenburg. Available at http://gupea.ub.gu.se/dspace/bitstream/2077/18215/1/gupea_2077_18215_1.pdf.

Auvachez, É. (2009). Supranational citizenship and the United Nations: Is the UN engaged in a citizenization process? *Global Governance, 15*(1), 43–66.

Blomqvist, P. (2004). The choice revolution. Privatization of Swedish welfare services in the 1990s. *Social Policy & Administration, 38*(2), 139–155.

Borrie, Lord. (1996). *Is Social Justice affordable?* Speech to the Centre for the Understanding of Society and Politics, Kingston University, 20 March. Available at: www.kingston.ac.uk/cusp/Lectures/Borrie.htm. Consulted March 2005.

Bosniak, L. (2000). Citizenship denationalized. *Indiana Journal of Global Law Studies, 7*, 447–509.

Boychuk, G. W. (1998). *Patchworks of purpose. The development of social assistance regimes in Canada*. Montreal: McGill-Queen's University Press.

Chambaz, C. (2001). Lone-parent families in Europe: A variety of economic and social circumstances. *Social Policy & Administration, 35*(6), 658–671.

Commission on Social Justice. (1994). *Social Justice: Strategies for National Renewal. Report of the Commission on Social Justice*. London: Vintage.

Deacon, B., with M. Hulse & P. Stubbs (1997). *Global social policy. International organizations and the future of welfare*. London: Sage.

Diamond, P., et al. (2006). *The Hampton Court Agenda. A social model for Europe*. London: Policy Network.

Dobrowolsky, A., & J. Jenson (2005). Social investment perspectives and practices: a decade in British politics. In M. Powell, L. Bauld, & K. Clarke (Eds.), *Social Policy Review, 17. Analysis and Debate in Social Policy, 2005* (pp. 203–230). Bristol: The Policy Press.

Esping-Andersen, G. (1990). *The three worlds of welfare capitalism*. Princeton, NJ: Princeton University Press.

Esping-Andersen, G., with B. Palier (2008). *Trois leçons sur l'État-providence*. Paris: Seuil.

Esping-Andersen, G., D. Gallie, A. Hemerijck, & J. Myles (2002). *Why we need a new welfare state*. Oxford: Oxford University Press.

Evers, A. 2009. "Civicness and Civility: Their Meanings for Social Services." *Voluntas, 20*, 239–259.

Evers, A., M. Pilj, & C. Ungerson (Eds.) (1994). *Payments for care. A comparative overview*. Aldershot: Avebury.

Ferrera, M., A. Hemerijck, & M. Rhodes. (2000). "Recasting European Welfare States." *European Review 8*, 427–446.

Giddens, A. (1998). *The third way. The renewal of social democracy*. Cambridge, UK: Polity Press.

Goodin, R. E., B. Headey, R. Muffels, & H-J. Driven (1999). *The real worlds of welfare capitalism*. Cambridge: Cambridge University Press.

Hall, P. A. (Ed.). (1989). *The political power of economic ideas. Keynesianism across nations*. Princeton, NJ: Princeton University Press.

Hemerijck, A. (2007). *Joining forces for social Europe. Reasserting the Lisbon Imperative of 'double engagement' and more*. Lecture to the Conference Joining Forces for a Social Europe, organised under the German Presidency of the European Union, Nuremburg, Feb. 8–9.

Jenson, J. (1989). Paradigms and political discourse: Protective legislation in France and the United States before 1914. *Canadian Journal of Political Science, 22*(2), 235–258.

Jenson, J. (1998). *Mapping social cohesion. The state of Canadian research*. Ottawa: CPRN. Available at www.cprn.org.

Jenson, J. (2007). The European Union's citizenship regime. Creating norms and building practices. *Comparative European Politics, 5*(1), 53–69.

Jenson, J. (2009a). Making sense of contagion: Citizenship regimes and public health in Victorian England. In P. Hall & M. Lamont (Eds.), *Successful societies. How institutions and culture affect health* (pp. 201–225). New York: Cambridge University Press.

Jenson, J. (2009b). Lost in translation. The social investment perspective and gender equality. *Social Politics, 16*(4), 446–483.

Jenson, J. (2010a). Diffusing ideas after neo-liberalism: The social investment perspective in Europe and Latin America. *Global Social Policy, 10*(1), 59–84.

Jenson, J. (2010b). *Ideas and policy: The European Union considers social policy futures*. American Consortium on European Union Studies, ACES Cases, # 2010.2. Available at: http://transatlantic.sais-jhu.edu/ACES/ACES_Cases/cases.

Jenson, J., & D. Saint-Martin (2003). New routes to social cohesion? Citizenship and the social investment state. *Canadian Journal of Sociology, 28*(1), 77–99.

Jenson, J., & D. Saint-Martin (2006). Building blocks for a new social architecture: the LEGO™ paradigm of an active society. *Policy & Politics, 34*(3), 429–451.

Jenson, J., & S. D. Phillips (1996). Regime shift: New citizenship practices in Canada. *International Journal of Canadian Studies, 14*, 111–136.

Korpi, B. M. (2007). *The politics of pre-school—intentions and decisions underlying the emergence and growth of the Swedish pre-school* (3rd ed.). Stockholm: Ministry of Education.

Korpi, W. (1980). Social policy and distributional conflict in the capitalist democracies: A preliminary framework. *West European Politics, 3*(3), 296–316.

Knijn, T., C. Martin, & J. Millar (2007). Activation as a common framework for social policies towards lone parents. *Social Policy & Administration, 41*(6), 638–652.

Lelièvre, E., & A. H. Gauthier (1995). Women's employment patterns in Europe: inequalities, discontinuities, and policies. In A-M. Guillemard, J. Lewis, S. Ringen, & R. Salais (Eds.), *Comparing welfare states in Europe* (vol. 1, pp. 461–486). Oxford Conference in the collection *Rencontres et Recherches de la MIRE*. Paris: MIRE.

Lister, R. (2006). Investing in the citizen-workers of the future: Transformations in citizenship and the state under New Labour. In C. Pierson & F. G. Castles (Eds.), *The welfare state reader* (2nd ed., pp. 455–472). London: Polity.

Magnette, P. (2005). *Citizenship: The history of an idea*. Colchester, UK: ECPR Monographs.

Marshall, T. H. (1965). *Class, citizenship and social development*. Garden City, NY: Anchor.

Morel, N., B. Palier, & J. Palme (Eds.) (2011). *Towards a social investment welfare state? Ideas, policies and challenges*. Bristol, UK: Policy Press.

Myles, J. (1998). How to design a 'liberal' welfare state: A comparison of Canada and the United States. *Social Policy & Administration, 32*(4), 341–364.

National Economic and Social Council, Ireland (NESC). (2005). *The developmental welfare state*. Dublin: NESC.

Newman, J., & B. McKee (2005). Beyond the new public management? Public services and the social investment state. *Policy & Politics, 33*(4), 657–673.

OECD (1997). Beyond 2000: The new social policy agenda. *OECD Working Papers*, vol. V: #43. Paris: OECD.

OECD (2003). *Employment outlook 2003: Towards more and better jobs*. Paris: OECD. Available at http://www.oecd.org/dataoecd/62/59/31775213.pdf.

OECD (2008). *OECD economic surveys: Sweden, 2008*. Paris: OECD. Available at http://www.oecd.org/document/26/0,3746,en_2649_33733_41733540_1_1_1_1,00.html.

Palier, B. (Ed.). (2010). *A long goodbye to Bismarck? The politics of welfare reform in continental Europe*. Amsterdam: Amsterdam University Press.

Palier, B., & C. Martin (2007). Comparing welfare reforms in continental Europe? *Social Policy & Administration, 41*(6), 535–554.

Palme, J., Å. Bergmark, O. Bäckman, F. Estrada, J. Fritzell, O. Lundberg, O. Sjöberg, & M. Szebehely. 2002. "WelfareTrends in Sweden: Balancing the Books for the 1990s". *Journal of European Social Policy* 12:4, 329–346.

Rake, K. (2001). Gender and New Labour's social policies. *Journal of Social Policy, 30*(2), 209–231.

Rodriques, M. J. (Ed.). (2002). *The new knowledge economy in Europe. A strategy for international competitiveness and social cohesion*. Cheltenham, UK: Edward Elgar.

Saint-Martin, D., & A. Dobrowolsky (2005). Social learning, Third Way politics and welfare state redesign. In A. Lecours (Ed.), *Historical institutionalism in political science* (pp. 132–156). Toronto: University of Toronto Press.

UNICEF (2000). *A league table of child poverty in rich nations*. Innocenti Report Card #1. Florence, Italy: Innocenti Research Centre. Available on: http://www.unicef-icdc.org

White, S. (2000). Review article: Social rights and the social contract—political theory and the new welfare politics. *British Journal of Political Science, 30*, 507–532.

4

CITIZENSHIP IN THE ENABLING STATE: THE CHANGING BALANCE OF RIGHTS AND OBLIGATIONS

Neil Gilbert

Over the past several decades arrangements for social protection in most, if not all, of the advanced industrialized nations have undergone a series of changes. Some see these changes as amounting to no more than a marginal adjustment in the borders of the welfare state, a "fine tuning" of existing policies (Pierson, 1996, 2; S. O. Hort [2001] characterizes recent policy changes in the Swedish welfare state, including the unprecedented move toward the privatization of old-age pensions, as "fine tuning"). Summarizing a study of the adaptations of welfare states in the mid-1990s, for example, Gøsta Esping-Andersen (1996, 265) concludes that almost everywhere, political forces have conspired to maintain the existing principles of the welfare state. This means that cutting occurs at the margin and that trimming is largely limited to the "fat." Curiously, the claim that only "fat" was being cut is followed on the very next page with a description of successful welfare state cutback policies, including "the succession of increasingly severe cutbacks in the Swedish welfare state, including the most cherished programmes such as pensions, sickness absence and parental leave" (Esping-Andersen, 1996, 266). Others, including myself, see these changes as major revisions not so much in government spending as in the policy, principles, and philosophy that guide social spending, which are transforming the essential character of modern welfare states—amounting to an emergent shift in the conventional welfare state paradigm (e.g., Ferge, 1996). For a wide-ranging analysis of the current debate about how to legitimize care work and provide caregivers with income security, see Daly (2001). As Evers and Guillemard point out in the concluding chapter of this book, contemporary social welfare reforms in response to demographic,

80

social, and economic challenges of the post-industrial era have fundamentally altered the prevailing paradigm. This is not to say that the modern welfare state's programs of social security, health, welfare, social services, unemployment, and disability insurance are being demolished—they are being reshaped. To transform is not to dismantle or obliterate institutional arrangements for social protection—what is being altered involves the basic framework for social policy on which the most progressive welfare states were modeled.[1]

In this chapter I will present a theoretical perspective on the reasons for this transformation and analyze how it has changed the substantive character of social protection and the rights of citizenship associated with the welfare state in the United States and many European countries. This analysis will summarize some broad trends, which I have more thoroughly documented elsewhere. Much of the discussion in this section draws upon Gilbert (2002) (also see Gilbert, 2001; Gilbert & Parent, 2004; Gilbert & Van Voorhis, 2002).

THEORETICAL PERSPECTIVES ON CHANGE: STRUCTURAL AND SOCIOPOLITICAL ORIENTATIONS

The transformation of the welfare state is a story most clearly articulated by starting from a vantage point that places the currents of change in their theoretical context. Among the various accounts of the rise of the modern welfare state, much of the theory and research is concentrated along two apparently competing lines of analysis, which emphasize the influence of either impersonal structural forces or sociopolitical pressures (for a comprehensive study of these lines of analysis see Van Voorhis [1998]). These orientations (which reflect the longstanding tension between structure and agency in theories of social change) frame the major theoretical debates on the development of the welfare state.

Analyses of structural forces, such as economic growth, industrialization, and demographic shifts, are associated with convergence theory. Simply put, convergence theory posits that in response to disruptions caused by structural changes, countries tend to increase public expenditure on a similar set of institutional arrangements—programs such as public assistance for the poor and social security for the elderly—that perform the functions of social protection previously rendered by the extended family, church, and feudal traditions.[2] Coming from a different angle, studies on the impact of sociopolitical pressures are associated with the theory of distinct welfare state regimes, which holds that different institutional arrangements for social protection evolve depending on the actions of people and groups—which are influenced by cultural norms, values, knowledge, and the strength of contending interest groups. Initially three distinct welfare state regimes were identified by Esping-Andersen (1990). Castles and Mitchell (1990), Ferrera (1996, 17–37), and others argued that the "southern model,"

Table 4.1. Structural and Sociopolitical Pressures for Change

Structural Forces
Demographic Shifts
Aging
Divorce rates
Extramarital births
Female labor force participation
Globalization of the Economy
Mobility of capital to where production costs are low
Mobility of labor to where benefits are high
Sociopolitical Forces
Knowledge of Unanticipated Effects
Disincentives to work
Dependency traps
Rising Faith in Market Economy
Privitization
Consumer choice
Women's liberation and equality

which includes Italy, Spain, Greece, and Portugal, constitutes a fourth regime; as an alternative to Esping-Andersen's three worlds, Leibfried distinguishes among Germanic, Scandinavian, Anglo-Saxon, and Levantine regimes, the latter including the "Latin Rim countries" (see Leibfried, 1992). In contrast to the case for a distinct "southern model," Katrougalos' reading of the data suggests that arrangements for social protection in Greece, Portugal, and Spain are "merely underdeveloped species of the Continental model" (Katrougalos, 1996, 43).

Over the past several decades, one can perceive the transformation of the welfare state as being driven by both structural and sociopolitical pressures generated from four sources (Table 4.1). Among the structural changes, the most dramatic demographic shift—the aging of the population—has yet to make its full impact. The steep rise in aging has just begun and will take off at the end of this decade. As illustrated in Figure 4.1, the ratio of the working population to the inactive elderly accelerates after 2010. In 2010 the OECD countries will have on average three workers for every inactive elderly person. By 2050 this 0.33 ratio will climb to about 0.66—an average of 1.5 workers contributing to the support of one inactive elderly person. At that time, the dependency ratio in the United States, at 0.50, will be somewhat lower than the projected OECD average.

The growing social costs associated with the aging of the population are compounded by other demographic trends. Extramarital births and divorce rates, for example, are at almost record heights. Between the 1980s and 1990s the number

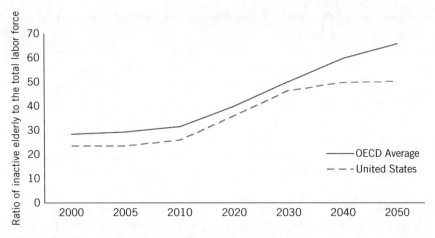

Figure 4.1 Dependency Projections for U.S. and OECD Average

of lone-parent families increased by 83% in France, 43% in Germany, and 32% in both the United States and the Netherlands. The proliferation of two-income households, as well as lone-parent families, has reduced the modern family's capacity to provide in-person care for children, elderly, and other infirm relatives, which creates additional demands for the state to supply care, financial assistance, and other supportive services. Although many of the OECD countries are lifting the standard age of retirement in an effort to mitigate the crushing costs of aging, since 1970 the labor force participation rates for men over 65 have declined (20%) and declined substantially for men aged 60 to 64.[3]

The demographic transition reflects that fact that on the one hand life expectancy has increased—people are living and collecting retirement pensions for much longer than in the past. (When Otto von Bismarck introduced the first state-sponsored social security scheme in 1889, average life expectancy was only 45 years—retirement was at age 65.) And on the other hand the average fertility rate for the OECD countries has fallen well below the 2.1 replacement level (although the U.S. rate is relatively high, at just about the replacement level). Overall, the near-future forecasts illuminate a period of sociodemographic change that will generate new demands for welfare state benefits and eliminate practically no existing needs (Cantillon, 1990).

While demand for social spending continues to push upward, the constraints on additional spending are tightening in response to the pressures of the global economy, which have magnified interdependencies, heightened competitive markets, and shrunk time and space. There are differences of opinion about what exactly the process of globalization represents and its implications for the future of state-sponsored social protection. (It might have contradictory tendencies.) However, many analysts I think would agree with Guy Standing's assessment that globalization has intensified pressures to scale back labor rights and welfare benefits (which is supported by Fritz Scharpf's analysis) (Scharpf, 2000; Standing, 1999).

In addition to the pressures emanating from large-scale structural changes such as demography and the globalization of the economy, there are also sociopolitical pressures for change stemming from increased knowledge about the impact of social policies and a growing appreciation for the values of the economic market. Regarding the impact of social policy, the weight of accumulated experience gained over the decades of welfare state growth has told us much about the unanticipated consequences of social benefits, particularly their disincentive effects. The idea that generous welfare benefits might inhibit one's inclination to work was once viewed as heresy by welfare state advocates—in the United States they charged it was a case of "blaming the victim." Yet after decades of rising welfare and disability rolls, by the late 1990s the same idea, that welfare benefits produce "poverty traps" or "enforced dependency"—prudently worded not to blame victims—was widely accepted in OECD countries (for discussion of concerns about the "poverty trap" in relation to various groups see Bradshaw & Miller, 1990; Euzeby, 1988; and OECD, 1988). One report goes so far as to say that "dependency traps are an unintended outcome of most social security systems" (OECD, 1991b).[4] Indeed, one might well conclude that Charles Murray's rendition of the disincentive to work bred by public welfare, which was viewed as heresy by welfare state advocates in the mid-1980s, had became the received wisdom of the late 1990s (Murray, 1989).

Finally, the collapse of the command economy of the USSR has raised the stock of capitalism's public approval to record levels in the marketplace of ideas—this development has been accompanied by a rising faith in the virtues and abilities of the private sector, and growing appreciation for the value of consumer choice. Not only was the private market seen as an effective mechanism to satisfy consumer wants and needs, it also came to be viewed as the main arena through which women could achieve economic equality and social liberation. Although this enthusiasm for the private market dampened somewhat after the worldwide recession that began in 2007, privatization and consumer choice remain well received.

Thus, complex and multiple forces have lent impetus to the transformation of the welfare state. It is not demographic factors or globalization alone, or new perceptions shaped by knowledge and experience with social policies, or the rising faith in the market economy that by themselves account for the fundamental change in the character of social protection—it is the combination of these forces. And what give these pressures for change particular weight is that they all push in the same direction—that is, away from the progressive welfare state model based on government delivery of an expanding range of social benefits that provide social protection against loss of income under a system of broad-based entitlements.

FROM WELFARE TO THE ENABLING STATE

To suggest that the welfare state as we knew it is being left behind somewhere along the path of institutional evolution does not signify the end of social welfare programs. No one imagines that social security, health insurance, disability benefits, public assistance, unemployment insurance, daycare, and the rest will be jettisoned. But the social policy environment in which they are reshaped will be constrained by a set of demographic and economic conditions and informed by knowledge and values that are different than those underlying the development of social welfare programs through the early 1980s.

If a new institutional framework for social protection is in the offering, it needs a name—a conceptual representation that differentiates it from the conventional welfare state model. In the final chapter of this volume Evers and Guillemard identify the new framework as one that redefines the role of the state from providing benefits that compensate for risks to one that enables beneficiaries to actively exercise responsibility in coping with risks. In a flourish of neologisms—the Schumpeterian Workfare State, the Hollow State, the Contract State, the Hidden Welfare State, the Social Investment State, the Mixed Economy of Welfare, the Third Way, the Post-Modern Welfare State, and the "active" welfare state (discussed in this volume by Ruth Lister in Chapter 6)—welfare theorists around the world have made efforts to capture the essential features of change (Eardley, 1997; Evers & Svetlik, 1993; Milward & Provan, 1993; Weatherley, 1994).[5] Finally, there is the "Enabling State," a term that has been used to illustrate the essential character of change in the United States (and by some in England), which is captured by the tenet of public support for private responsibility, where "private" responsibility includes individuals, the market, and voluntary organizations. For a sample of this usage see Evandrou et al. (1990), Gilbert (1995), Gilbert & Gilbert (1989), Marshall & Schram (1993), and Wattenberg (1993, A12). I use the term the "Enabling State" to represent the emerging paradigm for social protection. The directions of change and substantive character of the Enabling State are illustrated in Table 4.2, which captures four critical dimensions in the transformation of the welfare state.

First, since the mid-1980s there has been an increasing move toward the privatization of social welfare activity through purchase of service contracting and the provision of benefits in cash and vouchers and through tax credits, which allow individuals to make private arrangements for health, education, care services, and retirement. Over the past decade 30 countries have incorporated private individual accounts into their mandatory pension systems (Kritzer, 2005, 32–36). Pension schemes are not the only beneficiaries of privatization. For example, the Netherlands privatized sick leave care for workers in 1996, and Germany has experienced an extraordinary increase in for-profit providers in the realm of long-term care services.

Table 4.2. Shift in Central Tendencies from Welfare to Enabling State

Welfare State	Enabling State
PUBLIC PROVISION	PRIVATIZATION
Delivery by public agencies	Delivery by private agencies
Transfers in the form of service	Transfers in cash or vouchers
Focus on direct expenditure	Increasing indirect expenditures
PROTECTING LABOR	PROMOTING WORK
Social support	Social inclusion
De-commodification of labor	Re-commodification of labor
Unconditional benefits	Use of incentives and sanctions
UNIVERSAL ENTITLEMENT	SELECTIVE TARGETING
Avoiding stigma	Restoring social equity
RIGHTS OF CITIZENSHIP	SOCIAL OBLIGATIONS OF CITIZENSHIP
Benefits as social entitlement	Benefits contingent on responsibility

With the private share of the mixed economy of social welfare on the rise, it has become increasingly difficult to distinguish substantive differences between the political left and the right. The political compass has lost its conventional bearings. Where is the left? In the 2000 Republicans running for president in the United States wanted to expand private activity through the use of educational vouchers and a shift in social security financing that (the commission co-chaired by Moynihan proposed) would allow individuals to invest 22% of their total contributions in private equity accounts. Democrats opposed these measures, which never passed. At the same time, the privatization of 2% (or 14% of total) of social security contributions and the use of educational vouchers (75% of public education costs, which today cover independent schools that include more than one quarter of a million people) have been approved in Sweden, which has been traditionally politically to the left of both parties in the United States.[6]

Second, it has become almost universally accepted that social policies heretofore providing "passive" income supports to unemployed people should be replaced by measures designed to promote employment. Since the mid-1990s, a wave of work-oriented reforms swept through the OECD countries (Gilbert & Van Voorhis, 2001). Stretching across the political spectrum from Sweden to the United States, active labor market policies created new incentives and firm pressures for moving social welfare beneficiaries, particularly those receiving unemployment, disability, and public assistance payments, into the paid labor force. As Streeck (2007, 545) explains, these reforms represented "an almost universal restructuring of national welfare states in the direction of investment rather than consumption, re-commodification instead of de-commodification, strengthening 'employability' instead of raising workers' reservation wage, 'activation' for the market instead of protection from it." In a similar vein, Alber views the new emphasis on activation as a profound transformation of European social democracy which is of historic proportions (Alber, 2010). He suggests that around the turn of the 21st century, the European labor movement abandoned support of welfare policies designed to de-commodify labor by providing benefits that endowed a means of livelihood outside the market in favor of work-oriented measures to enable people to participate in the market.

The 1996 U.S. welfare reforms were arguably the most stringent work-oriented policies, introducing lifetime limits on eligibility, firmly administered incentives and sanctions, and a "work-first" approach to activating the unemployed that favored job placement over increasing human capital via skills training and education. If social safety nets for the unemployed are perceived as mechanisms that can be adjusted to be made more or less taut, then the "work-first" approach represents a tightly strung net, which acts as a trampoline that quickly springs workers back into the paid labor force. The slack safety net absorbs the shocks of workers falling off the ladder of employment, providing a soft landing that includes longer benefits and training opportunities aimed at increasing human capital.

Although social safety nets for the unemployed in Europe tend to have greater slack than those in United States, the 1990 policy reforms moved in the same direction on both sides of the Atlantic—tightening eligibility criteria, trimming benefits, and contracting to activate people receiving public assistance, unemployment, and disability benefits. The 1992 White Paper on Rehabilitation, for example, introduced what Norwegians termed the "Work Approach" to social welfare policy, a basic premise of which was "that individual rights are not exclusively tied to cash benefits; each individual has, as far as possible, a right and a duty to work, to participate in rehabilitation programs or enter education." The reconfiguration of social protection in the OECD countries was aptly summarized by the motto of the Dutch "purple coalition" (red Social Democrats and blue Liberals), which formed a new government in the mid-1990s: "Work, work and work again!" (Gilbert, 2002).

Indeed, since the 1990s public assistance, disability, and unemployment policy reforms have followed a general pattern of change that involves restricting access and accelerating exit, introducing contractual obligations, and applying diverse incentives. For example, Germany significantly reformed unemployment insurance, shifting what were long-term (over one year) benefits into the system of social assistance (at a much lower benefit rate); countries such as Denmark, the United Kingdom, Finland, Spain, and the Netherlands have extended the period of paid employment required to access benefits; Sweden, Finland, Belgium, and France have introduced or extended waiting periods for benefits. Of the many countries that implemented more rigorous examination to qualify for disability benefits, the 1991 Dutch reforms are among the most extensive and widely cited (OECD, 1991a); Norway intensified the requirement to demonstrate a causal link between the claimant's medical condition and the reduced capacity to earn a living.

Almost everywhere, work contracts (activation or action plans) have been introduced along with conditions attached to benefits that were heretofore distributed without requirements. Conditionality has shaped contemporary reforms even among the Nordic welfare states, which Esping-Andersen strongly identified with policies that de-commodified labor. The Social Services Act of 1991 gave local administrations in Norway authority to institute work requirements as a condition of eligibility for welfare benefits. After Swedish welfare expenditures nearly doubled in the first half of the 1990s, similar reforms were initiated that qualified the longstanding social right to public assistance. Although it was not adopted everywhere, the Uppsala model (named after Sweden's fifth largest municipality) required public assistance applicants to develop individual career plans in consultation with welfare officers and employment counselors and to search actively for work. The Danish Social Assistance Reform of 1997 required that all persons receiving social assistance must participate in formulating individual action plans, which are designed to improve their working skills and to facilitate gainful employment. Activation entails job placements, training, and educational opportunities, and all recipients under the age of 30 are expected to be activated within their first 13 weeks on welfare. Those who reject a fair offer of activation can have their welfare benefits reduced by up to 20%.

The third dimension of change involves the increased targeting of benefits. This is reflected not only in the upswing of means-testing but in other reforms, which include the narrowing of diagnostic criteria for disability and the lifting of the age of retirement in many countries. The tax system has been employed to make public benefits universal at the point of distribution but selective at the point of consumption—an approach dubbed by Theda Skocpol (1990, 59–67) as "selectivity within universalism." (However one describes it, what we have is a sleight of hand through which the state distributes more in the way of social expenditures than citizens are eventually allowed to consume.) In France, what began as a universal policy of family allowances has become increasingly means-tested over the past several decades. According to one estimate, means-tested allocations rose from 13.5% of all family benefits in 1970 to 45% at the end of the 1980s and climbed to 60% in the 1990s, if the *revenue minimum d'insertion* program is included (Martin, 1998). Bruno Palier (1997, 104) notes that the new orientation towards means-tested benefits identifies the "transformation of social protection in France as a 'liberal' rather than 'universal' dynamic."

Finally, there has been a normative swing from an emphasis on welfare provisions being given as the social rights of citizenship to the social responsibilities of recipients to behave well, contribute to society (and their individual defined-contribution pension plans), and become independent as quickly as possible. This shift is embodied in the contractual agreements/activation/action plans that beneficiaries of public benefits are being required to develop, sign, and implement. It is also evident in the increasing use of defined-contribution pension plans and indeterminate retirement dates, under which social insurance benefits no longer ensure recipients a degree of adequacy. The signal here is that the elderly will get what they put into the retirement scheme, and if that is not enough they have the responsibility to work additional years to build up the account.

The emerging emphasis on individual responsibility (to work and be self-sufficient) and the tightening of eligibility criteria for social benefits have recalibrated the social rights of citizenship—rights that T. H. Marshall saw as a defining element of citizenship, which fostered a common sense of belonging and social cohesion. According to Marshall the status of citizenship endows residents of a nation with social rights "to a modicum of economic welfare and security," which reinforce a sense of affiliation to the larger polity. However, as Evers and Guillemard noted in the introductory chapter, Marshall recognized that beyond access to health and education services, the right to social benefits was not necessarily unconditional. He was fully cognizant that social rights of citizenship had to be balanced by obligations requiring citizens to behave with "a lively sense of responsibility toward the welfare of the community." And among these responsibilities, the duty to work was of paramount importance. Less widely acknowledged is Marshall's observation that the right to social benefits does not necessarily imply the right to receive them free of charge. The costs of benefits might be recovered, he suggests, "by levying ad hoc charges in proportion to the ability to pay, ranging from the full cost of the service received down to nothing" (Marshall, 1964, 123).

In sum, the new policy orientation represents a change from (1) the guiding principles of progressive policies that were framed by a universal orientation to publicly delivered benefits designed to protect labor against the vicissitudes of the market and firmly held as social rights, to (2) policies framed by a selective approach to private delivery of provisions designed to promote labor force participation. In the process, the balance between the rights and responsibilities of citizenship has shifted toward the responsibility to be self-sufficient. The transformation, as I see it, is from a welfare state to an Enabling State, which functions under the guiding principle of "public support for private responsibility." Within the new framework, social welfare policies are increasingly designed to enable more people to work and to enable the private sector to expand its sphere of activity.

I think there is a fair amount of agreement among social policy scholars that over the past few decades reforms have been framed with an increasing emphasis on privatization, work-oriented measures, targeting, and social responsibility. Reasonable people, however, may disagree about the magnitude of this change. Has it moved social policies only a few degrees one way or the other, or has it veered so far as to signify a major change, on the order, perhaps, of paradigm shift, toward the Enabling State (or whatever label one might give it)? This is difficult to pin down. At some point a change in degree becomes palpably a change in kind—when, for example, a pot of cool water is brought to a boil. Whether the policy reforms described above have only raised the temperature a few degrees or have created enough heat to brew some new tea is a matter I must leave for the reader to decide.

To suggest that there is a convergence toward the Enabling State is not to say that all the systems for social protection will be exactly the same. Of course, there will be assorted renditions of the Enabling State. Freud's axiom concerning the "narcissism of minor differences" suggests that the closer nations come to resemble each other, the more they magnify minute dissimilarities as a means to reinforce social cohesion. If this proposition is correct, with English rapidly becoming the *lingua franca* of the European Union and the Enabling State identified most closely as an Anglo-American construct, policymakers from other countries are likely to go to great lengths to differentiate their social welfare initiatives from those of the United States and the United Kingdom. The Nordic countries will have their version of the Enabling State, as will France, Germany, and the eastern European countries.

But when one peels back the outer layers of rhetoric and sorts through the different measures to advance privatization, targeting, employment, and individual responsibility, we arrive at a common core of market-oriented social policies that in essence represent the triumph of capitalism. This might be seen as a paradigm shift recasting some of the basic purposes of the welfare state—from social protection to social activation and from income maintenance to social inclusion. This shift is advanced by an inspirational political discourse of reform, which emphasizes *activation, social inclusion, empowerment, and social responsibility*— terms that represent several ways of conveying to citizens how important it is that social policies be designed to get them back to work as soon as possible.

RECALIBRATING RIGHTS AND RESPONSIBILITIES: A NEW SOCIAL CONTRACT?

In the United States and many other OECD countries the longstanding acceptance of welfare as a social right has been replaced by a new emphasis on the recipients' social responsibilities. From the 1960s to the mid-1980s the political discourse on welfare was animated by efforts to extend the range of benefits available to the poor. The new benefits included medical care, food stamps, daycare, legal aid, and work training. With memories of the Great Depression still in mind, the poor were perceived by many people as innocent victims of capitalism and as such entitled to be compensated for the system's failures—welfare was seen as among the "social rights of citizenship." In a popular book, William Ryan's admonitions against "blaming the victim" struck a prominent chord in the zeitgeist of the 1960s and early 1970s. Ryan saw even the use of financial incentives to encourage voluntary participation in work training and employment as "coercive and repressive" (Ryan, 1971).

By the late 1980s, concerns about the nature of welfare entitlement shifted away from elaborating social rights to delineating the social obligations of citizenship. Although Marshall (1950, 129) recognized the need to balance social rights with the duty to work, he did not explain how the right to tangible benefits might be modified if citizens did not discharge their duties. Following Marshall's concern about balancing rights and responsibilities, Lawrence Mead's influential work *Beyond Entitlement; The Social Obligations of Citizenship* takes this line of analysis a step further by stipulating tangible responsibilities of citizens. He identified several duties that constituted the core of expected behavior for U.S. citizens. At the very least, according to Mead, able-bodied adults are expected to work in available jobs, to contribute to the support of their families, to acquire fluency in English, to learn enough in school to be employable, and to respect the law as well as the rights of others (Mead, 1986).

As public support for "passive" benefits—unconditional social rights to economic assistance through cash grants—has waned in many OECD countries, another manifestation of social rights is gaining widespread endorsement. That is, the right to welfare has morphed into the right to work and earn a living wage. As the obligation to work has been intensified, advocates for social rights are moving to reframe the orientation to policy reforms to focus on the social rights to earn a living wage for low-income workers, whose ranks have expanded as welfare recipients move off the rolls and into the labor force. The right to a living wage attracts a broader spectrum of political support than a guarantee of cash assistance for people who do not work. It is easier to mobilize public opinion in support of government intervention that helps people who work hard and play by the rules to provide their families a decent standard of living, than programs that pay poor people to stay home and care for their children.

There are several approaches to providing income supplements for working families. (See Chapter 3 for Jenson's comparison of efforts to make work pay in Sweden and the UK.) For those receiving welfare benefits, policymakers can increase the level of income by raising the amount of pay for their jobs that recipients are allowed to retain without having their welfare allotment reduced. In the United States over a dozen states currently permit recipients to make up to $1,000 in earnings before losing welfare payments under the Temporary Assistance for Needy Families program (TANF) (Gilbert & Terrell, 2005). Another approach involves boosting the minimum wage. Advocates for the right to a living wage in the United States, for example, propose lifting the federal minimum wage to 50% of the average wage (which was its level relative to the average wage in the 1950s).

In addition, various measures have been designed to supplement low-income wages through tax expenditures. These involve expanding the earned income tax credit to minimum-wage workers. Thus, for example, the earned income tax credit that subsidizes low-wage employment in the United States has been expanded (Greenberg et al., 2007). In 2009, it paid a maximum of $5,657 to low-income working families with three children. Similar subsidies have been implemented through the family tax credit in New Zealand and the working families tax credit in the United Kingdom. The French version of public supplements for low-paid workers is called a "job bonus." Introduced in 2001, this subsidy is paid by local tax authorities to those earning less than 140% of the minimum wage, with adjustments for dependents.

In addition to subsidizing low-income work, progressive efforts to bolster the right to work and earn a living wage also seek to reframe the issue of what counts as work, particularly in relation to care work and the extent to which it meets the demands of conditionality for welfare benefits. Under the 2005 TANF welfare reforms in the United States, the core activities that count as work include providing childcare, which enables another recipient to participate in a community service program—but not providing childcare for welfare recipients' own children. A movement is afoot to recognize care work as equivalent to other work, advanced by a new strand of feminist thought in the United States—sometimes referred to as "care feminism" or relational feminism. For a wide-ranging analysis of the current debate about how to legitimize care work and provide caregivers with income security, see Daly (2001). This strand of feminist discourse emphasizes the value of care work and the need for women to have meaningful opportunities to choose how much of their lives to invest in paid work and childrearing (Gilbert, 2008). Supporting this position, Alstott (2004) proposes the development of caretaker resource accounts that would pay an annual grant of $5,000 to assist individuals who provide continuity of care for a child, and who sacrifice their own opportunities in doing so.

The debate about care work goes well beyond the United States. In Germany, Leipert and Opielka (1999), for example, have argued for a new social contract based on the understanding that parental childcare work is functionally equivalent to gainful employment. Calculating the monetary value of childcare, they propose a monthly salary of approximately $1,360 for the first child and $680 for additional children up to age 7. Although this proposal stirred public debate in the late 1990s, it did not carry the day. Many countries provide a cash allowance for home care for the elderly, which can be used to pay relatives. And cash payments for home care of children are already offered in several European countries, including Norway and Finland (for a detailed discussion of home-care allowances, see Gilbert, 2008).

In sum, a new social contract is being forged about the right to welfare benefits, which seeks to change the balance between entitlements and conditionality. Politically, this contract is driven by two agendas. The responsibility agenda emphasizes the obligation to work and socially acceptable personal behavior; the rights agenda seeks to broaden the definition of work and emphasizes the assurance of work training, employment opportunities, and a living wage. All of the clauses of this contract are not yet entirely worked out, but the indications to date suggest that social benefits as a right of citizenship in the welfare arena have fundamentally changed from providing income maintenance to the poor to creating public supports to promote private responsibility—following the tenet of the Enabling State.

NOTES

1 Observing a worldwide consensus "that social security is at a critical juncture in its development," Dalmer Hoskins, Secretary General of the International Social Security Association, expresses the need to resolve basic issues of social welfare such as what risks should be covered and where state responsibility for protection should end and individual responsibility begin. And he sees the process of redefining a new social contract with respect to income security also under way (Hoskins, 1998).

2 Analyzing patterns of social welfare policy development in Sweden, Norway, Germany, and the UK from 1960 to 1993, for example, Olli Kangas finds that countries that often have been described as representing different welfare state models at specific points in time show distinct signs of convergence when analyzed from a longitudinal perspective. He concludes that "much of what is happening is structural," although politics will eventually influence how countries respond to structural problems (Kangas, 1994, 79–94). At the same time, a number of empirical studies generated findings that challenged the soundness and utility of convergence theory. Some of these studies found no relationship between levels of industrial development and timing of the adoption of social insurance programs (see, for example, Collie & Messick, 1975; Flora & Alber, 1981).

3 Although there is much variation among countries. In 1998, for example, 70% or more of those aged 55 to 64 did not participate in the labor force in Hungary, Belgium, Luxembourg, Italy, and Austria. In the past few years there has been a slight uptick in the age of retirement, but it still remains well below that of 1970.

4 And even in Sweden, the paragon of the modern welfare state, in the early 1990s, Prime Minister Carl Bildt declared that benefit levels had become so high as to reduce the incentives to work (Stevenson, 1993).

5 The distinction between the "Keynesian Welfare State" and the "Schumpeterian Workfare State" is the intellectually toniest conceptualization, contrasting John Maynard Keynes's ideas about the merits of state intervention in the market with Joseph Schumpeter's views on the fiscal limits of taxation beyond which the state would sabotage innovative activity and entrepreneurial drive.

6 A member of the Swedish parliament observes that the introduction of private pension accounts "has turned the Swedish people into one of the most capitalist societies in the world, creating an atypical popular interest in the stock market's ups and downs" (Rojas, 2005).

REFERENCES

Alber, J. (2010). What the European and American welfare states have in common and where they differ: facts and fiction in comparisons of the European Social Model and the United States. *Journal of European Social Policy, 20*(2), 102–125.

Alstott, A. (2004). *No exit: What parents owe their children and what society owes parents.* New York: Oxford University Press.

Bradshaw, J., & J. Miller (1990). Lone-parent families in the U.K.: Challenges to social policy. *International Social Security Review, 43,* 4.

Cantillon, B. (1990). Socio-demographic changes and social security. *International Social Security Review, 43(4),* 399–425.

Castles, F. G., & D. Mitchell (1990). *Three worlds of welfare capitalism or four.* The Australian National University Discussion Paper, No. 21, Canberra.

Collie, C., & R. Messick (1975). Prerequisites versus diffusion: Testing alternative explanations of social security adoption. *American Political Science Review, 69,* 1299–1315.

Daly, M. (Ed.) (2001). *Care work: The quest for security.* Geneva: International Labour Office.

Eardley, T. (1997). *New relations of welfare in the contracting state: The marketisation of services for the unemployed in Australia.* Social Policy Research Center Discussion Paper 79. SPRC, University of New South Wales.

Esping-Andersen, G. (1990). *The three worlds of welfare capitalism.* Princeton: Princeton University Press.

Esping-Andersen, G. (Ed.) (1996). *Welfare states in transition: National adaptations in global economies.* London: Sage Publications.

Euzeby, A. (1988). Unemployment compensation and unemployment in industrialized market economy countries. *International Social Security Review, 41,* 1.

Evandrou, M., J. Falkingham, & H. Glennerster (1990). The personal social services: Everyone's poor relation but nobody's baby. In J. Mills (Ed.), *The state of welfare: The welfare state in Britain since 1974.* Oxford: Clarendon Press.

Evers, A. & I. Svetlik (Eds.) (1993). *Balancing pluralism: New welfare mixes for the elderly.* Aldershot: Avebury.

Ferge, Z. (1996). *The change of the welfare paradigm—The individualisation of the social.* Paper presented at the Annual Conference of the British Social Policy Association, Sheffield, July 16–18, 1996.

Ferrera, M. (1996). The "southern model" of welfare in social Europe. *Journal of European Social Policy, 6*(1), 17–37.

Flora, P., & J. Alber (1981). Modernization, democratization, and the development of the welfare state in western Europe. In P. Flora & A. J. Heidenheimer (Eds.), *The development of welfare states in Europe and America.* New Brunswick: Transaction.

Gilbert, N. (1995). *Welfare justice: Restoring social equity.* New Haven: Yale University Press.

Gilbert, N. (Ed.) (2001). *Targeting social benefits: International perspectives on issues and trends.* Rutgers, N.J.: Transaction Publishers.

Gilbert, N. (2002). *Transformation of the welfare state: The silent surrender of public responsibility.* New York: Oxford University Press.

Gilbert, N. (2008). *A mother's work: How feminism, the market and policy shape family life.* New Haven: Yale University Press.

Gilbert, N., & B. Gilbert (1989). *The Enabling State: Modern welfare capitalism in America.* New York: Oxford University Press.

Gilbert, N., & A. Parent (Eds.) (2004). *Welfare reform: A comparative assessment of French and U.S. experiences.* New Brunswick, N.J. : Transaction Publications.

Gilbert, N., & P. Terrell (2005). *Dimensions of social welfare policy.* Boston: Pearson.

Gilbert, N., & R. Van Voorhis (Eds.) (2001). *Activating the unemployed: A comparative analysis of work-oriented policies.* New Brunswick, N.J.: Transaction Publishers.

Gilbert, N., & R. Van Voorhis (Eds.) (2002). *Changing patterns of social protection.* New Brunswick, N.J.: Transaction Publications.

Greenberg, M., I. Dutta-Gupta, & E. Minoff (2007). *From poverty to prosperity: A national strategy to cut poverty in half.* Washington, D.C.: Center for American Progress.

Hort, S. O. (2001). From a generous to a stingy welfare state? Sweden's approach to targeting. In N. Gilbert (Ed.), *Targeting social benefits: International perspectives on issues and trends,* New Brunswick, N.J.: Transaction Publishers.

Hoskins, D. (1998). *The redesign of social security. Developments and trends in social security 1996–1998.* Geneva: International Social Security Association.

Kangas, O. (1994). The merging of welfare state models: Past and present trends in Finnish and Swedish social policy. *Journal of European Social Policy, 4*(2), 79–94.

Katrougalos, G. (1996). The south European welfare model: The Greek welfare state, in search of an identity. *Journal of European Social Policy, 6*(1), 39–60.

Kritzer, B. (2005). Individual accounts in other countries. *Social Security Bulletin, 66*(1), 32–36.

Leibfried, S. (1992). Towards a European welfare state? On integrating poverty regimes into the European Community. In Z. Ferge & J. Kolberg (Eds.), *Social policy in a changing Europe.* Boulder, CO: Westview Press.

Leipert, C., & M. Opielka (1999). *Child-care salary 2000: A way to upgrade child care work.* Bonn: Institute for Social Ecology.

Marshall, T. H. (1950). *Citizenship and social class.* Cambridge: Cambridge University Press.

Marshall, T. H. (1964). *Class, citizenship and social development.* New York: Anchor Books.

Marshall, W., & Schram, M. (Eds.) (1993). *Mandate for change.* New York: Berkley Books.

Martin, C. (1998). *Reframing social policies in France towards selectivity and commodification: The case of family and frail elderly policies.* Presented at the European Forum, Centre for Advanced Studies Conference on Reforming Social Assistance and Social Services: International Experiences and Perspectives, December 11–12, 1998, Florence, Italy.

Mead, L. (1986). *Beyond entitlement: The social obligations of citizenship.* New York: Free Press.

Milward, B., & K. Provan (1993). The Hollow State: Private provision of public service. In H. Ingram & S. Rathgeb Smith (Eds.), *Public policy for democracy.* Washington, D.C.: The Brookings Institution.

Murray, C. (1989). *Losing ground: American social policy: 1950–1980.* New York: Basic Books.

OECD (1988). *The future of social protection.* Paris: OECD.

OECD (1991a). *Economic surveys: The Netherlands.* Paris: OECD.

OECD (1991b). *Shaping structural change: The role of women.* Paris: OECD.

Palier, B. (1997). Liberal dynamic in the transformation of the French social welfare system. In J. Clasen (Ed.), *Social insurance in Europe.* Bristol: The Policy Press.

Pierson, P. (1996). The new politics of the welfare state. *World Politics, 48,* 2.

Rojas, M. (2005). *Sweden after the Swedish model: From tutorial state to enabling state.* Stockholm: Timbro Publishers.

Ryan, W. (1971). *Blaming the victim.* New York: Random House.

Scharpf, F. (2000). *Globalization and the welfare state: Constraints, challenges and vulnerabilities.* In "Social Security in the Global Village: The Year 2000 International Research Conference on Social Security." Geneva: ISSA.

Skocpol, T. (1990). Sustainable social policy: Fighting poverty without poverty programs. *The American Prospect, 2,* 59–67.

Standing, G. (1999). *Global labour flexibility: Seeking distributive justice.* London: Macmillan.

Stevenson, R. (March 14, 1993). Swedes facing rigors of welfare cuts. *New York Times.*

Streeck, W. (2007). "Globalization": nothing new under the sun? *Socio-Economic Review, 5,* 3.

Van Voorhis, R. (1998). Three generations of comparative welfare theory: From convergence to convergence. *European Journal of Social Work, 1*(2), 189–202.

Wattenberg, B. (Jan. 20, 1993). Let Clinton be Clinton. *Wall Street Journal,* A12.

Weatherley, R. (1994). From entitlement to contract: Reshaping the welfare state in Australia. *Journal of Sociology and Social Welfare, 3*(13), 153–173.

5

TO WHAT EXTENT CAN THE EUROPEAN UNION DELIVER "SOCIAL CITIZENSHIP" TO ITS CITIZENS?

Jean-Claude Barbier

INTRODUCTION

T. H. Marshall's view of citizenship had little to do with what, in 1992, the Maastricht Treaty was to call "EU citizenship." Indeed, the relationship between the latter and what is meant by the Marshallian concept is not easy to grasp. Researching this point will be a useful exercise, however, because in analyzing the substance of EU citizenship we will at the same time shed light on the appropriateness of Marshall's concept for understanding contemporary developments in social protection across the member states of the EU. These developments should certainly include the consequences of what is happening at the EU level.

For the purposes of this chapter, we will refer to the definition of citizenship presented in the introduction by the editors and to the one we use in our chapter about France. For each of its dimensions (social rights and duties, social conditions, political and social participation), it is possible to ask whether an EU dimension exists alongside the national ones and to assess its importance. Here, again, the notion of "wage-earner citizenship" is essential to bear in mind: wage-earner societies (*sociétés salariales*) have largely retained their national characters, a fact that is illustrated by the diversity and separateness of social protection systems and industrial relations systems. For all the normative enthusiasm for presumed "postnational" or cosmopolitan Europe (Beck, 2003) and despite far-reaching Europeanization, access to social protection has, since the Treaty of Rome in 1957, remained firmly national. Moreover, very often European influence exerts its effect only negatively in this respect, as a result of increasing clashes between social rights (national) and economic freedoms. The same applies for labor law. Our first task will thus be to explain how competences set down in the initial treaty evolved in the initial years. The year 1991 was a turning point, because citizenship was specifically inserted into the Maastricht Treaty (ex-Article 8, now Articles 20 to 24 in the Treaty on Functioning of the European Union [TFEU]). We will address the changes brought by *European citizenship* in the second section and try and assess their substance, a reality that is far more prosaic and modest than one might expect after reading literature that systematically and unilaterally characterizes Europeanization as progress from the dark ages of *national citizenship*. Finally, the actual substance of *social citizenship* in the EU will be analyzed: we shall explain why social citizenship has remained at the national level for numerous and good reasons, and, on the other hand, why this national setting is threatened by legal integration at the EU level, because, as Scharpf (2009) has aptly noted, alternative forms of social protection and social citizenship have not been put in place, even though economic and legal integration are jeopardizing the national arrangements. As will be seen in the following sections, the previous assessment should certainly be qualified with regard to the different situations existing in so-called "new" member states, if compared with EU-15 countries. However, empirical findings as to how the incorporation of the *acquis communautaire* has been transposed in central and eastern Europe are just starting to be documented (Falkner & Treib, 2008; Schimmelfennig & Trauer, 2009). Although new research insights have started to emerge, it is thus still difficult, in 2010, to really appreciate the overall importance that provisions related to "EU citizenship" have acquired.

JURISDICTIONS AND SOCIAL CITIZENSHIP

European integration still bears the imprint of its origins in the initial treaty establishing the European Coal and Steel Community in 1951, and this is essential to explaining the limits of "European citizenship." The building of the EU has, since the start, involved economic integration, and little else. While it was always a political process, the rationale of which originally was linked to establishing peace in Europe, economic transformation was the means chosen by its initiators. The original division of jurisdictions (*competences*) has remained basically the same: the "social" (including education) is a matter for the national (or subnational) level, notwithstanding the limited introduction of qualified majority voting in the Council of the EU for certain social matters. At the same time, the hierarchy of legal norms has been radically altered through a series of particularly inventive decisions by the Court of Justice of the European Union (ex-ECJ[1]), imposing the Community legislation's supremacy over domestic (national) legal systems of all member states, in spite of their initial resistance.

A Firm and Overarching Legal Basis

The initial, *economic*, logic of the founding act has continuously informed subsequent developments. The goal of promoting or increasing social rights was absent from the original treaty. Even admitting that the social dimension has since been addressed more extensively,[2] as the Court of Justice's evolving jurisprudence demonstrates (de Schutter, 2004), EU law still does not treat economic and social rights in an equivalent way, despite the formal adoption of texts establishing social rights.[3] A basic asymmetry (imbalance) prevails. While freedom of movement and freedom of establishment constitute a hierarchically superior legal base for the Union, because they are supposed to allow better competition and an improved functioning of the single market, social rights are taken into consideration only to the extent that they might be affected by the functioning of this market (or, conversely, affect the market's functioning). Their application "for their own sake" does not, strictly speaking, constitute an explicit political task for the EU. Moreover, when conflicts arise—a more and more common situation—CJEU's case law retains the upper hand by making use of the "proportionality" principle: social and labor rights should be implemented, according to this very elastic principle, in a proportionate manner; that is to say, in such a way that economic freedoms are not jeopardized. Applied to social protection as a whole, a second principle concerns the supremacy (if not the exclusivity) of national jurisdictions. In the core areas of social protection, member states have until now succeeded in their resistance (Ferrera, 2005), even if important rules constrain national decisions, and notably rules established by the Court of Justice.

In the area of social protection, as in other matters, three principles prevail: the *direct effect* of Community law, the *supremacy* of EU law over domestic law, and the dominant position of economic *freedoms* (freedom of establishment and free movement of persons, goods, services, and capital—often referred to as the "fundamental freedoms"), associated with the principle of fair competition. Gradually consolidated, these principles now "command" member states' law, directly or indirectly, in all areas. When a matter is submitted to the Court of Justice, it provides the basis for the latter's interpretations. Admittedly, these interpretations may be overturned, but this requires a decision of the Council of Ministers, which is not easy to achieve, as demonstrated by the lengthy battle, probably only just getting under way, over the free circulation of services, which should be seen as essential for the future of citizenship in the EU.

At the end of the day, however, despite the existence of the two powerful constraints constituted by EU law and by the Stability and Growth Pact, the Europeanization of social rights has remained limited in practice. Similarly, the essential legal basis for labor market regulation and social protection remains predominantly at the national level. It is also true that, despite the apparently strict constraints imposed by the euro, the majority of economic policies are still also devised, chosen, and implemented at the national level. In this respect, Europeanization is often superficial. Many scholars fail to spot this superficiality because they use tools that are unable to grasp diversity, and some of them conclude that all countries are converging towards a uniform and homogenous single type of social protection (see Gilbert, 2002, as a typical proponent of the convergence thesis, and Chapter 4 in the present book). Some also assumed that, once it was introduced by the Maastricht Treaty, European citizenship transformed the situation significantly in European social protection, notably through the Open methods of coordination (Jenson, 2007, 59–62). However, seen with hindsight the actual, empirical situation is certainly more prosaic. Much more attention is often given to common trends, the dissemination of common norms, the framing of policies through similar perspectives, and the sharing of similar policy instruments and even language (provided it is English). As a result, mainstream research gives unbalanced precedence to general trends while brushing diversity under the carpet of its universalistic interpretation (Barbier, 2008, 2012). At the same time, according to the official political EU discourse too, it would be easy to believe that EU member states not only already participate in a common "social model" that differs from others in the world, but are converging ever more closely by learning from each other and exchanging best practices (Barbier, 2007). Nevertheless, an immense gap exists between the claims of the European political parlance about the existence of a common model, and the more prosaic reality. In view of this gap, the fact that the process of coordinating employment and other social policies in the EU stalled after 2005 should come as no surprise: coordination, common goals, and open methods of coordination never penetrated beyond the *surface* of things: this also applies to the new members joining the EU after 2004 (Keune, 2008). In the meantime, as the Court of Justice case-law decisions demonstrated in the late 2000s (e.g., Laval, Viking, among the most important), one could see that member states were fighting as individuals to fend off attacks on their "national model." All in all, when one tries to take stock of the state of "EU citizenship" in 2010, the outcome of the interaction and intermingling of EU law and national laws appears ambivalent: on the one hand, ever greater influence upon the social rights of European citizens can be *indirectly* observed, because of the growing power of *EU economic law* (the freedoms of movement); at the same time, apart from the specific area of equality and nondiscrimination, few traces exist of any new, *positive and substantive rights* that have originated from European law. Limited positive integration has been the rule, against a background of a powerful negative integration (i.e., the discarding of legal and other obstacles brought about by the systematic introduction of mechanisms aimed at promoting the common market and "free" or "fair" competition) (Scharpf, 1999).

STAGES OF A MODEST POSITIVE INTEGRATION
OF SOCIAL RIGHTS

With such powerful legal justification for the persistent role of the national level of social protection, industrial relations, and labor law systems, it is not surprising that only modest progress has been made so far in the domain that politicians and voters sometimes refer to as "Social Europe" (admittedly more easily in some countries than others[4]). This is not to say that the EU level is unimportant in the current systems of governance for social protection and their links with labor markets, industrial relations, and employment: quite the contrary, it is certainly important. However, one must ascribe the "federal" level its appropriate significance within the multilevel system of governance that now prevails in the EU. Here again the role played by the EU level of governance will be different when articulated with the diverse institutions and political compacts across the 27 member states (Falkner et al., 2005; Falkner & Treib, 2008, see also Chapter 11 in the present volume).

When one looks at the diversity of administrative and political activities that have been organized by the Commission in the "social domain" since the beginnings of the European Communities and the Treaty of Rome, they appear wide-ranging. In fact, they can be summed up and presented in three simple stages: (1) A first, long period stretches from 1957 to the early 1990s; (2) a period of true innovation then started, lasting until 2005; (3) the present situation will probably remain as the third stage for a very long time. Leaving aside the essential facts of "negative integration" and its damaging influence on social protection and social rights (Scharpf, 1999, 2009), a considerable gap has existed throughout all these stages between the demands for social policy and social protection and the limited interventions that European institutions have been permitted *and able* to make: when they are met, demands have inevitably been met at the national level. This gap has become more and more visible recently, precisely at a time when the issues dealt with at the EU level appear increasingly politicized.

The first stage has been documented largely by Ferrera (2005) and Leibfried and Pierson (1995). The main elements of this period are the following. Firstly, the Court of Justice gradually established the legal basis of its influence upon national social protection systems; this influence has grown as a consequence of the consistent implementation of the principles of free movement. Additionally, member states—sometimes with great reluctance—have gradually accepted that the EU's legal order prevails over the national legal orders. Over the whole period, this form of homogenization ("Europeanization") via the EU legal order was practically unnoticed in national public debates; the obligations and constraints that resulted from it for national systems pertain to "negative integration." Secondly, the main domain in which European influence was exerted was the coordination of social security systems for migrant workers and employees—a very small group indeed. The main legal instrument used was Regulation 1408/71: in a nutshell, its goal was to open up national systems in such a way that workers (and their families) would be eligible for benefits if they went to work in another member state: for instance, family benefits were paid to the family of a Portuguese worker employed in France by way of a mechanism coordinating family funds in France and Portugal.[5] Subsequently, the influence of this EU legislation was to extend beyond the marginal situation of migrants (about 2% of European citizens currently work in another member state) (see below). Thirdly, the "hard-law" influence of the EU level over national legislation was at its highest in the domain of health and safety at work on one hand, and equal opportunities for men and women (equality and anti-discrimination in general) on the other. In these domains, directives were adopted that significantly transformed social rights (Davies et al., 1996). Nevertheless, apart from this varying influence upon national systems, it can be argued that the essential substance of social citizenship, its national jurisdiction, as well as the social justice and solidarity principles upon which it have rested, were left consistently as matters of national competence during this first period.

The second period—which could in a way be seen as the "golden age" of Social Europe—started in the late 1980s. With hindsight, the period starting with the Agreement on Social Policy of February 1992 can be seen as when previous modest efforts to harmonize were dropped and the influence of "soft law" continued to increase. True, when the UK had not yet accepted the Social Protocol of the Treaty of Amsterdam (1992–97), the notion of "upward harmonization" was still used as a principle (Davies et al., 1996, 7–12).[6] However, important as they may be, especially in countries with lower levels of social provision,[7] social directives had essentially been limited to introducing minimum requirements into social and labor rights. Yet the mere transposition of directives into domestic law does not entail that they are effectively enforced (Falkner et al., 2005). Moreover, from the beginning, and more so recently, EU law has always been primarily concerned with social matters inasmuch as it has involved economic principles (the economic freedoms, competition, and market functioning). It is nevertheless undeniable that, after a period in which harmonization was discussed, there followed another period in which only restricted scope was given to "social matters" (in spite of Jacques Delors's particularly active presidency). The Delors presidency was evidently instrumental in upholding and extending the role of the social partners within the EU governance system (Ross, 1994).

Yet, beyond the minimal provision directives, this golden age never came to mean anything more than coordinating ideas, cognitive frameworks, and processes more closely, as well as including social partners very explicitly in the mechanisms of governance. One of its main distinctive characteristics lay in the creation of the open methods of coordination (OMC) in social policy. The intellectual and political origins of these methods are not always sufficiently stressed: there was a convergence of efforts and initiatives between the Delors group (the publication of the White Paper on Growth, Competitiveness and Employment in 1993) and some Scandinavian politicians and experts (Barbier, 2004, 45–46; Johansson, 1999) that supplied the Intergovernmental Conference in 1995–96 with innovative ideas and proposals, with the help of Luxembourg's Prime Minister Juncker and the Party of European Socialists (PES). The Scandinavian Joint Committee of the Nordic Social Democratic Labour Movement (SAMAK) was very active, with Allan Larsson, the former Swedish Finance Minister and later Director of the Commission's DG Employment, as a key player. With other EU policies, OMCs share a characteristic that is stressed by many researchers (Muller, 2000, 204–205): they contribute to the *decoupling*[8] of the sphere of policies from the sphere of compromise in which social systems are based. In this respect, Open methods of coordination can easily be seen—although of course falsely—as "technical" or "apolitical." Yet they do to a certain extent become *depoliticized*. Radaelli (2003) has astutely noted that there was a tension at the very core of the European Employment Strategy (EES) (and one may add in Open methods of coordination in general) because as "there [was] no attempt to forge a European vision of capitalism" (ibid., 20), it was all the more important to "avoid politicization" (ibid., 21). However, when translated to national politics, this depoliticized discourse was swiftly *repoliticized*, a process that revealed how important the national level of "Social Europe" has been and will remain. Indeed, the EES, for example, did not consist *mainly* of a complex web of political and administrative activities, and a discourse resulting from a controversial process between governments pushing forward their conflicting views, but it ultimately relied upon the existence of *national policies,* which were legitimated at the domestic level through a great variety of institutions and political cultures. OMCs have now existed for 10 years in various social policy domains, and the situation has not changed significantly: convincing empirical literature (Büchs, 2007; Kröger, 2008, to quote only a few references) has now established rather firmly that changes brought about by the methods of coordination amount to three essential ones: (1) the existence of the Open methods of coordination modifies previous relationships between actors by providing some with new resources at certain points in time; (2) what happens beyond the reach of the implementation of the methods is often more important than what happens in their limited domain (pensions are a case in point there [Hartlapp, 2007], but healthcare is another [Martinsen, 2005]); (3) OMCs certainly contribute to the dissemination of ideas, ideologies, conceptions, and decontextualized values and norms. The latter process is certainly not neutral, but it is incapable by itself of altering the substance of national political compromises significantly (the actual identification of learning and even more of "transfers of practices" or "recipes" from one to another country has remained marginal). It means that the substance of social citizenship in Europe has so far been affected only very marginally by the presence of a great variety of coordinations in pensions, healthcare, social inclusion, and so forth.

This is because, not only in legal terms (the competencies conferred to the EU by the EC Treaty), but also in political terms (the process of the political legitimization of policies within national polities), national programs and policies, however cognitively and normatively coordinated, have remained and will remain a determining variable. Here lies the core substance of social citizenship, a national "wage-earner citizenship," where bonding and bounding (Ferrera, 2005) prevail. In spite of coordination at the EU level, specific national features and institutions prevail, in a context of domestic politicization and partisanship. Reforms will remain legitimized and contested within national polities, even if the OMCs provide national governments—and sometimes other actors (Barbier, 2004)—with power and cognitive resources. This explains why, despite the reluctance of many member states to accept an increased role for the Commission, the EES continued to function rather successfully, in terms of the states' expectations, during its first period of existence until 2002. However, the fundamental limitations of the EES and other OMCs were to be reached rather rapidly, and they could hardly be seen as vehicles to building a future substantive and genuine "Social Europe," beyond a cognitive/discursive mechanism of coordination between states. Conflicts between values and politicization were bound to occur, somehow or another, and the accession of eastern and central European members were to increase their likeliness. Neither can one say that the creation and adoption of the Charter of Fundamental Rights in 2000 (see next section) fundamentally transformed European citizenship, at least not so far. As was again demonstrated in 2007, at the European Council in June that adopted a new "reform treaty," the exact legal status of this document is still very fragile.[9]

2004–05 opened a third period, in which the EU was still engaged in 2010. The beginning of this period was marked by three events, all of which threw up obstacles to furthering the practice of Open methods of coordination as innovative (and alternative) ways of reinforcing the influence of the EU level in social policy. The first change was a clear shift in the balance between the "economic" and the "social" actors within the Commission, and within the policy arenas deciding over this balance. This was exemplified by the change of tune and substance that characterized both the "Kok reports." The first one, "Jobs, Jobs, Jobs," published in 2003, was positioned in continuity with the 2003 reform of the EES. However, the second one, "Facing the Challenge," published in autumn 2004, marked a shift towards the clear affirmation of the necessity of structural reforms in the context of orthodox economic supply-side policies. The second important change introduced in 2004 was the effective accession of 10 (later 12) new member states as part of the enlargement process. Unlike previous enlargements, these countries were significantly poorer and had very different social protection and legal institutions, and their membership immediately made the existing coordination processes of the various OMCs more complicated and tricky. The deep divide between the two groups of member states with regard to the "social dimension" was illustrated by the publication in February 2007 of a manifesto in favor of new social measures by a group of countries (Belgium, France, Luxembourg, Hungary, Italy, Greece, Spain, Bulgaria, and Cyprus), while this declaration was sharply opposed by countries like Poland and the Czech Republic. Last not but not least, of course, the third event that almost prompted the collapse of "Social Europe" was the havoc triggered by the failure of referendums in the Netherlands and France for the adoption of the project for a Constitutional Treaty in 2005. This latter event had to do, particularly in France, but also less directly in the Netherlands, with the national boundaries of *social citizenships* (in the plural) and the fear of the negative influence that the supranational level would exert upon them. During the referendum in Ireland in 2008 and in 2009, the politicization of European social questions was demonstrated again (farmers' income, the provision of public services, workers' rights, etc.[10]).

All in all, the painstaking process of building of the first two stages of the "social dimension" in the EU has now ended in a state of "near collapse." It is certainly not incidental that, for the first time in 2005, on a large and explicit scale, measures pertaining to this "social dimension" were directly present and debated within the mainstream processes of politics and elections in the Netherlands and France. For instance, in France, the "Bolkestein" service directive was used widely by opponents of the project for a Constitutional Treaty to support their contention that European integration was gradually destroying public services and social protection. In a way, although distorted and difficult, a new kind of national democratic debate was indeed launched at that time—one that focused specifically on social issues, and the emergence of this debate could well count as progress towards a certain kind of European citizenship because it meant greater political participation of citizens in many member states. Amid the prevailing indifference towards European issues in the European elections of 2009, the politicization of European debates was nevertheless again shown among certain groups of voters or on certain issues specific to certain areas of social policy (for instance, the fate of services of general economic interest in the social domain, or the consequences of EU law on labor law in member states). Similar issues played an important role in the rejection of the "Lisbon Treaty" in the June 2008 Irish referendum. Summarizing the past stages of "Social Europe" demonstrates its structural inability, so far, to alter the basic substance of social rights in a positive manner—that is to say, by introducing new positive rights—apart from the decisive influence of EU legislation in the domain of equality between men and women, a domain that stands out as an exception. However, some maintain that the introduction of "European citizenship" in the Maastricht Treaty has had far-reaching consequences. Is that really the case?

THE SUBSTANCE OF EU CITIZENSHIP AND SOCIAL CITIZENSHIP/ ECONOMIC FREEDOMS: THE AMBIGUITY OF "JANUS-FACED" RIGHTS

At the EU level, unlike at the national level, citizenship—particularly social citizenship—is "framed" or effectively "embedded" in the freedom of movement of persons, a right that could variously be said to be economic or "fundamental" (a civil right if we use Marshall's classification). This is why, since its inclusion in the Maastricht Treaty, European citizenship has unfortunately remained, *de facto,* the preserve of only a limited number of citizens in Europe: those *who are able to move.* This is very clearly illustrated in the formulation of the treaty: the only social rights presented are those of migrants (Article 21.3, TFEU). In fact, one dimension that is perhaps difficult to understand for nonspecialists, and citizens themselves, is that EU law in the area of citizenship targets situations of movement between member states (Rodière, 2008, 195, 265). A paradoxical situation may arise when, for instance, a citizen does not exercise his or her freedom of movement. Then, for instance, he or she will not be able to claim the application of EU law in the area of family reunification (ibid.) nor could he or she, if the movement took place within the territory of the member state of which he or she enjoys citizenship. In both cases, citizens are not deemed really to have "moved," and they will be subject to national legislation in the domain of family reunification.

The only dimension of EU citizenship that is not directly or indirectly linked to movement is that citizens have the right to vote for the European parliament. To this, protection against discrimination established in the same part of the treaty (in Part 2, Articles 18 and 19 of TFEU deal with discrimination, just before Article 20 deals with EU citizenship) may also be added, although this is not a citizenship right in the strict sense. One aspect of this discrimination is linked directly to movement—that is, the prohibition of discrimination on "grounds of nationality." However, the other aspect is much broader, because it concerns (Article 19) all the most common grounds for discrimination ("sex, gender, racial or ethnic origin, religion or belief, disability, age or sexual orientation"). Here again, the ambiguous and "Janus-faced" nature of EU citizenship is apparent: on one hand, it belongs to fundamental rights (also present in the list of the Charter of Fundamental rights of the EU), and, on the other hand, it is a consequence of the freedom of movement. Freedom of movement is also a "Janus-faced" right. All the major components of EU citizenship concern citizens who want to move: they enjoy diplomatic protection in other member states, and they enjoy the right—under certain very limited conditions—to reside in any member state of their choice. The right to vote in another member state, in either municipal or European parliament elections, is also strictly linked to free movement. All in all, the major dimensions of EU citizenship, except the right to vote for the European parliament, in reality concern the tiny number of people who work or reside in another member state. As already mentioned, the main exception in terms of significant European influence on social and labor rights has been equality between men and women, because of the unexpected spillover effects of the initial provisions in the Treaty of Rome (namely, ex-Article 119, see Davies et al., 1996).

The great majority of legal experts we have been interviewing since the 2009 implementation of the Lisbon Treaty share the view that the reference to the Charter of Fundamental Rights (Article 6, TEU) will not modify this situation in the future. As was already the case before the adoption and the reference to the Charter, in matters of human rights the Court of Justice's case law refers to legal sources originating in member states' legislation and constitutions, as well as to the European Convention of Human Rights (Council of Europe). The recent row about the situation of the Roma people exemplifies this problem, and the issue remains uncertain as to how the conflict between the European Commissioner Viviane Reding and France will be solved eventually.

Hence, European citizenship—which incidentally is explicitly presented in the treaty as auxiliary (the formal term is "additional," cf. Article 20.1, TFEU), cannot compare with the classic model of national citizenship (nationality/*nationalité*). It is, by definition, partial. Moreover, even after the important adoption of Directive 2000/43 of April 29, 2000 (on the right to move and reside freely—a text that has regrouped various piecemeal legislation), European citizenship has remained fragmented according to the status of the person concerned—whether he or she is a worker or inactive, a student, a family member of a European citizen, whether he or she has sufficient financial means or not. Additionally, in a transitory phase that may continue until 2014 at the latest, certain restrictions are in place for citizens from the EU's newest member states (notably Bulgaria and Rumania). Finally, as far as explicitly social rights are concerned—social protection and social security rights—EU law deals with them, but only from the essential perspective of citizens (mainly workers) who move from one member state to another. An essential piece of EU social legislation in this regard, as noted above, was Regulation 1408/71, now updated and applicable (Regulation 883/2004, April 19, 2004). These are the essential limitations that affect European citizenship in general, and social citizenship in particular. It is thus clear that substantive and positive social rights are provided for at the national level, by the way of existing national systems of social protection. This is not to say, apart from the potential but marginal role that the OMCs may have in the medium-term future, that one should not stress the importance of the Charter of Fundamental Rights for the future development of social policy in Europe (Ferrera, 2005, 240–244). However, even if the EU will become a member of the European Convention for Human Rights,[11] the fundamental rights applicable to citizens will in the *first instance* be those that the nation states are responsible for implementing once they themselves are members of the Convention. All these elements amount to severe limitations on the extent of European citizenship in general. One should thus take a sober view of the opportunities presented by the existence of European citizenship, rather than overstating them for normative reasons (Kostakopolou, 2008, 286). Such overestimation is often encountered on the part of North American scholars, who tend to stress the symbolic importance of Europeanization and the latest developments of federalism. Not only is national citizenship not outmoded, it still provides the essential core of the rights, social or nonsocial, enjoyed by European citizens. For all the enthusiasm that some European citizens may express—though they remain a small minority in all member states—this is a hard, empirical fact. Some might think that this amounts to a gloomy perspective (Ferrera, 2005) or even a hopeless situation, but it remains a fact. And there are strong reasons for thinking that it will be perpetuated, as we will see in the next section.

WHY SOCIAL CITIZENSHIP HAS REMAINED AND WILL REMAIN AT THE NATIONAL[12] OR INFRANATIONAL LEVEL

Contrary to common assumptions, the actual role of national institutions, national political cultures, and compacts is still essential, and its empirical documentation certainly does not fall into the category that some tend to see as obsolete "methodological nationalism" (Beck, 2003). As Giraud (2005, 113) remarked, nation states have remained central with regard to authority, solidarity, and democracy. The empirical fact is that, despite the pervasive internationalization of markets and despite all the obvious signs of globalization, working conditions and wage-labor nexuses—to borrow from the vocabulary of the *Régulation* school of economists—are still nationally embedded (Boyer, 2004). A purely cross-national view of elites (Fligstein, 2008) fails to understand that even when these elites are in a very different position vis-à-vis European integration compared to other social groups, they are nevertheless part of *distinct* national compacts (Streeck, 2009).

The "closure" of social protection systems along national lines (Ferrera, 2005) has seldom been studied extensively and it is most often taken for granted as an *implicit fact*. Yet the *relative* closure[13] of social protection has remained a clear characteristic in building solidarity since the beginnings of modern systems between the late 19th century and the 1930s. This "bounding" dimension is associated with the "bonding together" of citizens (and possibly, denizens, *immigrants*, and *Mitbürger*), and the possibility of "sharing" something between them. Many characteristics that relate to the nation as a closed community are relevant in social protection: territory, nationality (or nationhood)—in the sense of *nationalité*, or *Bürgerschaft*—residence, language, citizenship, identity—as the shared sentiment of belonging to a community, and identification—that is, the process of identifying with such a "collectivity" (*collectivité historique*, to use Schnapper's vocabulary). The propensity for sharing between the members of this collectivity is constructed both individually and collectively (Rothstein, 1998). This obviously applies to the rights of workers and the way their employment conditions are, to varying degrees, protected and regulated. When studying the Swedish welfare state, Rothstein (1998, 222) rightly remarked that "the future of welfare policy lies in how it functions internally, rather than in surrounding factors. If it is true that the shape of welfare policy is decided by the social norms established among citizens, and if these norms in turn are determined by the type of political institutions we have analyzed, then the future of the welfare state of whatever type is something that lies in the hands of its political leaders and citizens, since they decide whether they want to change our political institutions or not."

To understand the implications of this situation fully, it is necessary to identify more precisely the relevant sociologic characteristics of nations that have a direct bearing on the social construction of the question of work, labor markets, and social protection. For my discussion, I only need to stress that both (1) subjective (affective, normative, imaginary, and cognitive, both individual and collective) and (2) objective, practical and institutional phenomena, are grouped together under the term "nation." Firstly, because social protection links politics, economics, and family in a structural way (Barbier & Théret, 2009), it is based on social conditions of legitimacy; secondly, citizenship and the identification processes linked with it are essential; and thirdly, material, territorial, and linguistic constraints have a crucial bearing on the very possibility of implementing social protection programs.

Three Main Roles for Nations in the Construction of Social Justice

Firstly, nations provide *practical frameworks for the daily legitimization of choices* and collective actions that are aimed at the collectivity (whether by tax or social contributions), the allocation and redistribution of public money, linked to a complex process of identification by individuals. Despite the Europeanization of politics in many guises, as is empirically obvious, these choices are only distantly affected by what happens at the EU level. As has been shown in many studies, support for redistribution ultimately relies on the opportunity for individuals to appraise the "moral" justification of their contribution, including the sentiment of reciprocity (Rothstein, 1998). Individual assessments would be impossible without the existence of a (national) political community with *actual* institutions for a debate usually conducted *in one language*. Moreover, the building processes of solidarity in societies involve *identification* with the national political systems that provide an indispensable and pragmatic support—that is, the sentiment of belonging to a particular community, notwithstanding the multiple identifications that individuals may have. For social protection decisions to be taken and legitimized, individual and collective (from political parties, associations, trade unions, or business associations) support is needed, whether it is implicit or explicit. A public sphere—to use Habermas's *Öffentlichkeit* concept—along with specific policy community forums and decisional arenas are necessary to debate these decisions (Kraus, 2008). As Goul Andersen showed in detail in the Danish case, support for welfare schemes is never straightforward, uniform, and constant: "macro-level factors" are also at stake ("perceived fairness," "reciprocity or trust in the fairness of the system") (Goul Andersen, 2008). Such mechanisms— which are so routinely basic at the national level—have no counterpart at the EU level, in the absence of significant redistribution and of a proper political community. Perhaps contrary to rational economic choice expectations, the importance of groups who try not to share in some national solidarity by resorting to market de-territorialized social provision has remained small (Ferrera, 2005).

Secondly, *citizenship matters immensely for social justice and solidarity*. Access to social protection is (at least in theory) extended to permanent and regular residents (or denizens), among whom some are close to acquiring fully fledged rights (and obligations) if they gain full citizenship. Van Oorschot (2006) has shown that in all countries, migrants are viewed unfavorably in terms of "deservingness perceptions," especially in the "new member states." At the same time, a survey conducted in May 2007 showed that in the five bigger member states, interviewees agreed with the assertion that there were too many legal immigrants in their countries, except in France.[14] Eurobarometer does not publish regularly updated data on this question. However, in September 2007, only four respondents out of ten in Europe approved the statement according to which immigrants were "contributing much" to their country. Some politicians and researchers do not attach the due importance they should to a legal fact that is often ignored: "solidarity," in *legal terms*, is a domain where EU law (i.e., the prevailing economic freedoms) stop being enforceable. When a social protection program, a solidarity scheme of any sort, exists, free competition and the economic freedoms cannot apply. Indeed, as the first pillar of pensions demonstrates—an excellent illustration of what solidarity entails—redistribution among members of a social insurance fund is not concerned by EU law, which would be applicable only for the provision of pension services on the market. The same situation prevails across what is usually in Europe considered as "social protection," including social assistance. Last but not least, as is well known that solidarity always means significant redistribution of money from the better-off to the less well-off: the EU level—fortunately or not—has failed in this respect to feature among the institutions that redistribute money (Majone, 1993) and that constitute the practical basis for solidarity to exist at all. The marginal EU budget (1% of aggregated GDPs) provides obvious evidence in this respect, when social expenditure, in each EU member, is in the range of 20% to 30% of each GDP.

Thirdly, the *very possibility of solidarity and sharing* remains at the level of the nation state in an even more trivial sense, and from a triple perspective: the sharing of a national language (or, in some cases of federalism, like Belgium or Spain, multiple languages); a firm anchoring within a national territory with formal institutions and organizations; a legal system, which—despite its subordination to a higher European legal order—remains nation-specific and links citizenship, nationality, rights, and obligations. One trivial aspect of social protection *in practice* is generally overlooked: there is no such thing as social protection without an administration, and every administration speaks one national language—or, exceptionally, a handful of official languages. Similarly trivial for social protection is the necessity of its territorial, physical, circumscription. Social protection needs buildings, IT systems, official documents, application forms, leaflets, websites, social security identification documents, records of contributions, and so on. This means that people claim their rights and enjoy their share of social protection in places situated in their neighborhood, where they may phone or visit the local agency at the counter. As citizens of the country they work in, migrants from other member states do that as well, and since the beginning of the EU, its various systems have been coordinated to cater for migrants. Obviously, the legal basis of social protection is directly linked to national definitions of citizenship. But law is not only a way of ascribing an identity to individuals; it also provides the ultimate statement and confirmation of the legitimacy of the particular arrangements that determine whether a particular category is eligible to particular protection or support. In many countries, this supposes an extensive discussion by the social partners (the Scandinavian countries, Germany). Even in countries where industrial relations systems are more recent or fragile (Spain, Italy) or where union density is low (France), the participation of unions in decisions on benefits, the rules for unemployment insurance, early retirement schemes, or assistance in the local communities remains essential. Despite "direct effect" or European law, national law is the ultimate mechanism of legitimization. No equivalent procedures can be imagined at the EU level today, and this explains, at least partly, why voters rejected the documents they were asked to approve in successive referendums, in Denmark in 1992, in the Netherlands and France in 2005, and in Ireland in 2008. Without national legal rules, it is not possible to define a beneficiary, a participant in a scheme, or an insurance claimant, or to enforce a claim on taxpayers. In this respect, the fundamental asymmetry that exists between the legal order of the EU and the national legal orders has in no way been reduced since the beginnings of the European Community. As recent rulings by the Court of Justice in the area of labor law have shown (the Viking, Laval, and Rüffert cases), this asymmetry is structural, and the influence of EU law has rightly been described in terms of "negative integration" (Scharpf, 1999). In the near future, this situation will remain unchanged, presenting a formidable obstacle to any possible development of a new "layer of social protection" at the EU level. Even if the Court of Justice continues to expand its powers, legal rules governing social protection systems will in practice remain dependent on specific national choices and normative compromises over the role of nationality, residence, family ties, gender, occupational status, contributions, and employment record. Indeed, none of this should come as a surprise when one considers how long the closure of national systems of social protection and of industrial relations has been in place—since the end of the 19th century (Ferrera, 2005, 37–52). There exists a basic rationale for systems to remain national, both *in terms of legitimacy* and *in terms of practical feasibility*.

CONCLUSIONS: "SOCIAL EUROPE" IN THE MIDST OF THE ECONOMIC CRISIS, ANOTHER TEST

There are certainly few opportunities to test the capacity of the EU level of governance in shaping the substance of social policies. The present economic and political crisis is one of them. The strict constraints that the EU, and its executive, the EU Commission, are confronted with was amply illustrated during the French Presidency in 2008 and again shown during the Czech Presidency in 2009. The amount of funding the EU was able to add to national recovery plans was marginal because of its budgetary rules and the very limited size of the EU budget. Perhaps the case of the "European adjustment globalization fund" (EGF) is the best illustration of the EU's powerlessness in this regard. This fund was created by the Council in December 2006 with the aim of enabling "the EU to show solidarity with and provide support to workers made redundant as a result of major structural changes in world trade patterns" (EGF Regulation, SEC [2008, 16.12.2008], p. 2). When the economic crisis started, it became clear that in 2007 and 2008, the number of such workers who were supported by the EU was less than 15,000 people. This figure grew to less than 76,000 in 2011. The number of people concerned and the tiny budget earmarked for supporting them (€500 million) clearly illustrate the true balance between the national European levels of governance when it comes to social policy in times of economic crisis. In other domains, the difficulty of the EU to make significant advances on important social questions was also illustrated in 2009 by the dismal failure of the Commission to put a consistent compromise proposal to the European Parliament for the rewording of the 1993 Working Time directive. After 16 years waiting for the necessary update to this key legal instrument, the failure to do so sent out a terrible signal to employees across Europe. At the beginning of 2010, the struggle about whether it was acceptable to support Greece was an additional and excellent example of the absence of genuine solidarity between the nation states that make up the EU—which, in a way, presented us with an apt counterpoint to the kind of de-territorialized and universal citizenship being promoted by the Court of Justice in Luxembourg.

These hard facts should be taken into consideration when one wants to forecast whether any more substantial "EU social citizenship" might emerge in the future. The most probable will be the continuation of some sort of *status quo*

(Barbier, 2008): the room left to social questions in the fresh so-called "EU 2020 strategy" is but another evidence of the credibility of this scenario. However, as the "Greek crisis" had shown, a *status quo* scenario is bound to meet many contradictions, not only because in case of crisis member states are forced to cooperate more closely and to put up some form of solidarity (between states, not among citizens). A considerable new interest for more "federalism" has been visible since the first "bailout" plan for Greece in May 2010, and putting in place the new European Stability Mechanism by the end of 2013 is a further illustration of the fact that economic constraints and increased interdependence push the member states for increased integration of certain decisions and for more *de facto solidarity*. But political elites are walking this path with extreme reluctance and with the difficult task of keeping in touch with electorates that are not prone to easily accept cross-European solidarity (Barbier, 2012). This is a reason for keeping another scenario where states would walk again the "Long March to Social Europe," as they did during the "golden age," albeit with dogged reluctance.

NOTES

1 The European Court of Justice was renamed the Court of Justice of the European Union (CJEU) when the Treaty of Lisbon entered into force in January 2009. For the sake of simplicity we will use the term "the Court of Justice" throughout the present text instead of the common acronym "ECJ" standing for the European Court of Justice.

2 For instance, in the important domain of discrimination and equality.

3 For example, the Community Charter of Fundamental Social Rights for Workers, adopted in 1989, and the European Charter of Fundamental Rights, which deals with social rights in Chapter IV (Solidarity), adopted at the Nice Summit in December 2000. Reference to the Charter is now made at Article 6 of the Treaty on European Union (TEU).

4 Surveys in many countries, analyzing the meanings of words and expressions apparently common in Eurospeak, show that these expressions don't have the same connotations. For instance, as "social Europe" will dominantly echo positive meanings in France, it will be seen as a potential threat to the Danish welfare state in Denmark, while in other countries, for instance Bulgaria, things labeled "social" tend to evoke the memory of past communism (Barbier, 2008, 210–211).

5 I refer here to the matter discussed in the Judgement of the Court "Pinna vs Caisse d'allocations familiales de la Savoie" in 1989 (March, 2, 1989), a judgement that started a controversy and led to an updating of Regulation 1408.

6 Article 151 of the Treaty (TFEU) still talks about *égalisation dans le progrès* (Rodière, 2008, 26–50). In English, member states "shall have as their

objectives the promotion of employment, improved living and working conditions, so as to make possible their harmonization while the improvement is being maintained."

7 The situation is different for the new member states, however, to the extent that the introduction of EU legislation has modified the way they have implemented social legislation since the demise of communist regimes (see further).

8 "Decoupling" is a general feature of the entire EU-level system, as Mény (2004) notes: "*Dans la pratique, le découplage entre débats, programmes électoraux et politique européenne est presque total, à la fois en raison de la faiblesse—de l'inexistence diraient certains—d'une opinion publique européenne, de la faiblesse du Parlement et de sa médiocre influence sur une partie de l'exécutif européen, de l'absence de lien entre l'organe conseil des ministres et l'électorat.*"

9 The UK government successfully negotiated to exempt Britain from the application of the Charter, because it said it was incompatible with the common-law tradition. Poland and ultimately the Czech Republic joined in the opt-out.

10 In this regard, nothing is perhaps more telling than the list of reassurances the Council felt obliged to address to the Irish voters (see for instance the "solemn declaration" of the European Council in Brussels in June 2009, which made promises to the people of Ireland not only on moral questions but also on items such as "social progress and the workers' rights," "services of general economic interest," and even "public services," a quite unusual move. See Presidency Conclusions, June 18–19, 2009, p. 20).

11 The Council of Europe and the European Commission have issued a project for an agreement on the accession of the EU to the European Convention on the Protection of the Human Rights and Fundamental Freedoms, on October 14, 2011.

12 The very category of "nation" has remained tricky, difficult to handle, and controversial. Schnapper (1991, 26) once rightly wrote that *le national* (what is national) has a bad reputation because it is intrinsically associated with empirical nationalisms and the wars they helped to foster. Social scientists often experience "surprise" when confronted with the reality of nationalism (Taguieff, 1991, 47), a surprise that partly accounts for the discredit of the concept, often seen as a mere artificial construction by political interests for manipulative purposes. Some, as Brubaker (1996), seem to deny the possibility of a distinct analytical substance to the term. This author systematically added brackets when he wrote "nation," a "putative" category, which for him can describe neither a substantive community nor an empirical entity. He suggested distinguishing between "nationness," "nationhood," and "nation," three words that do not translate easily into French, or in German for that matter.

13 Evidently, this closure has always been historically relative (Werner & Zimmermann, 2004).
14 Harris Poll, 46, May 29, 2007.

REFERENCES

Barbier, J.-C. (2004). La stratégie européenne pour l'emploi: genèse, coordination communautaire et diversité nationale, avec la contribution de Ndongo S. Sylla. *Document de Travail CEE*, No. 16: Noisy le Grand.

Barbier, J.-C. (2007). The French activation strategy in a European comparative perspective. In A. Serrano Pascual & E. Magnusson (Eds.), *Reshaping welfare states and activation regimes in Europe* (pp. 145–172). Brussels: PIE-Peter Lang.

Barbier, J.-C. (2008). *La longue marche vers l'Europe sociale.* Paris: PUF.

Barbier, J.-C. (2012). *The Road to Social Europe. A Contemporary Approach to Political Cultures and Diversity in Europe.* Abingdon: Routledge [translation and adaptation of *La longue marche vers l'Europe sociale*].

Barbier, J.-C., & B. Théret (2009). *Le système français de protection sociale.* Paris: La Découverte, Repères.

Beck, U. (2003). *Pouvoir et contre-pouvoir à l'ère de la mondialisation.* Paris: Aubier.

Boyer, R. (2004). *Une théorie du capitalisme est-elle possible.* Paris: Odile Jacob.

Brubaker, R. (1996). *Nationalism reframed, nationhood and the national question in the new Europe.* Cambridge: Cambridge University Press.

Büchs, M., (2007). *New Governance in European Social Policy, The Open Method of Coordination.* Basingstoke: Palgrave.

Davies, P., A. Lyon-Caen, S. Sciarra, & S. Simitis (1996; 2nd ed. 2005). *European Community law, principles and perspectives, Liber Amicorum Lord Wedderburn.* Oxford: Clarendon Press.

de Schutter, O. (2004). *The implementation of the EU Charter of Fundamental Rights through the Open Method of Coordination.* Jean Monnet Working Paper 07/04, New York School of Law.

Falkner, G., & O. Treib (2008). Three worlds of compliance or four? The EU-15 compared to new member states. *Journal of Common Market Studies, 46*(2), 293–313.

Falkner, G., O. Treib., M. Hartlapp, & S. Leiber (2005). *Complying with Europe: EU harmonization and soft law in the member states.* Cambridge: Cambridge University Press.

Ferrera, M. (2005). *The Boundaries of Welfare, European Integration and the New Spatial Politics of Social Protection.* Oxford: Oxford University Press.

Fligstein, N. (2008). *Euroclash, the European Union, European identity and the future of Europe.* Oxford: Oxford University Press.

Gilbert, N. (2002). *Transformation of the welfare state, The silent surrender of public responsibility.* Oxford: Oxford University Press.

Giraud, O. (2005). Nation et globalisation, mécanismes de constitution des espaces politiques pertinents des comparaisons internationales. In J.-C. Barbier & M.-T. Letablier, *Politiques sociales/Social Policies: Enjeux méthodologiques et épistémologiques des comparaisons internationales [Epistemological and methodological issues in Cross National Comparison]* (pp. 97–118). Brussels: PIE Pieter Lang.

Goul Andersen, J. (2008). Public support for the Danish welfare state. Interests and values, institutions and performance. In E. Albæk, L. Eliason, A. Sonne Nørgaard, & H. Schwartz (Eds.), *Crisis, miracles and beyond: Negotiated adaptation of the Danish welfare state.* Aarhus: Aarhus University Press.

Hartlapp, M. (2007). Intra-Kommissionsdynamik im Policy-Making: EU-Politiken angesichts des demographischen Wandels. *Politische Vierteljahresschrift* 40(PVS-Sonderheft 2007/2), 139–160.

Jenson, J. (2007). The European Union's citizenship regime. Creating norms and building practices. *Comparative European Politics, 7,* 53–69.

Johansson, K. M. (1999). Tracing the employment title in the Amsterdam treaty. *Journal of European Public Policy, 6*(1), 85–101.

Keune, M. (2008). *EU enlargement and social standards: exporting the European Social Model?* ETUI Working Paper 2008.01.

Kostakopolou, D. (2008). The evolution of European Union citizenship. *European Political Science, 7,* 285–295.

Kraus, P. (2008). *A union of diversity, Language, identity and polity building in the EU.* Cambridge: Cambridge University Press.

Kröger, S. (2008). *Soft governance in hard politics. European coordination of antipoverty policies in France and Germany.* Wiesbaden: VS Verlag.

Leibfried, S., & P. Pierson (Eds.) (1995). *European social policy between fragmentation and integration.* Washington, DC: Brookings Institution.

Majone, G. (1993). The European Community between social policy and social regulation. *Journal of Common Market Studies, 31*(2), 153–170.

Martinsen, D. S. (2005). The Europeanisation of welfare—the domestic impact of intra-European social security. *Journal of Common Market Studies, 43*(5), 1027–1054.

Mény, Y. (June 12, 2004). Europe, la grande hésitation. *Le Monde,* p. 18.

Muller, P. (2000). L'analyse cognitive des politiques publiques, vers une sociologie de l'action publique. *Revue française de science politique, 50*(2), 189–208.

Radaelli, C. (2003). *The open method of coordination, a new governance architecture for the European Union?* SIEPS 2003–1, Stockholm.

Rodière, P. (2008). *Droit social de l'Union européenne.* Paris: LGDJ.

Ross, G. (1994). *Jacques Delors and European integration.* Oxford and New York: Polity Press and Oxford University Press.

Rothstein, B. (1998). *Just institutions matter, the moral and political logic of the universal welfare state.* Cambridge: Cambridge University Press.

Scharpf, F. (1999). *Governing Europe, effective and democratic.* Oxford: Oxford University Press.

Scharpf, F. (2009). Legitimacy in the multilevel European polity. *MPIfG Working Paper 09/1.*

Schimmelfennig, F., & F. Trauer (2009). Introduction: Post-accession compliance in the EU's new member states. *EIoP Papers,* special issue 2, vol. 13, pp. 1–8.

Schnapper, D. (1991). *La France de l'intégration, sociologie de la nation.* Paris, Gallimard.

Streeck, W. (2009). Review symposium, N. Fligstein, Euroclash: the EU, European Identity and the Future of Europe. *Socio-Economic Review, 7,* 545–552.

Taguieff, P.-A. (1991). Le nationalisme des 'nationalistes', un problème pour l'histoire des idées en France. In G. Delanoi & P.-A. Taguieff, *Théories du nationalisme.* Paris, Kimé.

van Oorschot, W. (2006). Making the difference in social Europe: deservingness perceptions among citizens of European welfare states. *Journal of European Social Policy, 16*(1), 23–42.

Werner, M., & B. Zimmermann (2004). *De la comparaison à l'histoire croisée.* Paris: Seuil.

PART II

COUNTRY CASES: WESTERN EUROPE

6

SOCIAL CITIZENSHIP IN NEW LABOUR'S NEW "ACTIVE" WELFARE STATE: THE CASE OF THE UNITED KINGDOM

Ruth Lister

The late 20th century saw the renegotiation of the postwar welfare settlement in the UK, starting with the direct challenge of Thatcherism and continuing with New Labour's third way. Social citizenship rights have been at the heart of this renegotiation. The New Right challenged their very validity and, although government actions did not always match the rhetoric, there was an erosion of social citizenship rights during its period in office. This chapter focuses on the subsequent rearticulation of social citizenship over the past decade since New Labour came to power in 1997.

It is divided into six main parts. The first elaborates on social citizenship as a theoretical concept. The second explains how the concept has been understood in the particular context of the UK, which leads into the third part: a discussion of New Labour's broad philosophical approach to social citizenship. As the central area in which this philosophy has been reflected in policy has been the social security system, this will be the main focus of the chapter. The fourth and fifth parts explore how New Labour's philosophy of social citizenship translated into policy in relation to (a) rights and responsibilities and (b) in less detail, social investment. The sixth part discusses briefly the more traditional theme of the balance between universalist and targeted, means-tested, social security, which was more implicit than explicit in the Labour government's welfare reform policy statements. The conclusion pulls the paper together and speculates briefly on the implications of the change of government.

THE CONCEPT OF SOCIAL CITIZENSHIP

Citizenship in general and social citizenship in particular can be conceptualized in either broad or narrow terms. A broad understanding is articulated by Pnina Werbner and Nira Yuval-Davis, who define citizenship as "a more total relationship, inflected by identity, social positioning, cultural assumptions, institutional practices and a sense of belonging" (1999, 4). This sense of belonging involves "a set of social and political relationships, practices and identities" and participation, as well as a legal status with its attendant rights and obligations (Lister et al., 2007, 9). Here, the *social* dimension of citizenship focuses on social *relations* (Isin, 2008). It is as much about the relations between individual citizens as it is about the relationship between individuals and the state. As a relational concept it embraces the politics of recognition—both of difference and of the need for respect of the dignity of human beings—as well as redistribution. Its terrain stretches from the intimate and the domestic through to the global (Lister, 2007a).

More traditional conceptualizations of social citizenship focus more narrowly on the relationship between individuals and the state (which would now include the European Union as well as the nation state). The notion of social citizenship derives from T. H. Marshall's tripartite classification of civil, political, and social rights. Marshall explained that "by the social element" of citizenship he meant "the whole range from the right to a modicum of economic welfare and security to the right to share to the full in the social heritage and to live the life of a civilised being according to the standards prevailing in the society" (1950, 11). This represents a potentially expansive notion of social citizenship that offers much more than a minimalist "modicum of economic welfare."

Although it has received less attention in subsequent work on citizenship, Marshall also acknowledged that social citizenship involves duties as well as rights (see also Chapter 1). However, he did not invoke a contractual relationship between the two. For instance, he wrote that "if citizenship is invoked in the defence of rights, the corresponding duties of citizenship cannot be ignored; these duties require that the citizen's acts 'should be inspired by a lively sense of responsibility towards the welfare of the community" (1950, 43, 70). Subsequent, more recent, theorization of social citizenship has placed greater emphasis on specific duties and responsibilities, and much of the literature has been concerned with what those duties and responsibilities should be and with the nature of the relationship between them and social rights. Broadly, this relationship is articulated in either reciprocal or conditional terms (Dwyer, 2004; White, 2003).

Eschewing the kind of broader conceptualization of citizenship developed elsewhere (Lister, 2007a), a narrower approach is more appropriate for this analysis, which is centered on the increasing contractualization of the relationship between the individual and the state and between social rights and obligations—a "socio-liberal" understanding following Johansson and Hvinden (see Chapter 2).

UNDERSTANDINGS OF CITIZENSHIP IN THE UK CONTEXT

Three main waves of political preoccupation with citizenship have been identified in the UK since the start of the 20th century: the three decades prior to the First World War; the period between the Second World War and the 1960s; and the last two decades of the 20th century (and the first of the 21st). What marks these periods out is a political concern with the appropriate welfare settlement between the state and individual citizens (Rees, 1996). The re-emergence of the language of citizenship in the late 20th century reflected factors that were not, by and large, unique to the UK but that took on a particular resonance in what has been described as the "chief European testing ground for new right theory" (Marquand, 1991, 329). In some ways, the UK provided a conduit for new right ideas as they were carried from the United States to Europe on the wave of broader global economic trends (Lister, 1998). For many on the center-left, the notion of citizenship offered a key intellectual tool in their defense of the values of the welfare state (King, 1987; Plant, 1988).

In terms of popular discourse, however, the notion of citizenship does not have deep roots. Despite Marshall's pivotal contribution to the theorization of citizenship, a report by a Commission on Citizenship in 1990 observed that "an immediate difficulty" in defining citizenship "is that in our society the term 'citizenship' is an unfamiliar notion" (Speaker's Commission, 1990, 3). More recently, David Miller has made a similar point: "citizenship—except in the formal passport-holding sense—is not a widely understood idea in Britain. People do not have a clear idea of what it means to be a citizen" (2000, 26). Empirical research bears this out. Dean with Melrose found that "citizenship is not a term that is current in everyday popular discourse" (1999, 105), and a qualitative longitudinal study of how young people negotiate the transitions to citizenship notes that "citizenship was not part of the everyday language of the young people" (Lister et al., 2003, 237). This may be changing, however, with the advent of compulsory citizenship education (although this is now under threat) and a more prominent political (and academic) discourse of citizenship.

The lack of popular resonance of the term (compared with, for example, in France) reflects constitutional, political, and legal traditions. At the heart of these is the notion of "subjecthood." For a long time, this stood in place of citizenship to describe the relationship between the individual citizen and the government and the citizen's membership of the national community, in the absence of a written constitution and a Bill of Rights. However, the European Convention on Human Rights was incorporated by New Labour into a Human Rights Act (although the Coalition Government is considering replacing this with a specifically British Bill of Rights).

The Commission on Citizenship set out what it called "a traditional British analysis of citizenship which, so far as we can judge, seems to match British people's perceptions of it" (Speaker's Commission, 1990, 6). This reflected the Marshallian approach, with a particular emphasis on social and civil rights and a generalized duty to respect the law. In addition, the Commission drew attention to a more participatory (republican) understanding of citizenship, in terms of both voluntary contribution and politics, which has become more vocalized in the past couple of decades.

One of the few empirical studies of how citizens themselves perceive the meaning of citizenship found that it tended to be seen as a formal legal status, involving legal entitlement and obligations (Conover et al., 1991). In contrast, Lister et al. (2003) found that young people were more likely to understand citizenship in terms of belonging, constructive social participation, and economic independence. What was striking was that the young people found it markedly more difficult to identify their rights than their responsibilities; they were also less likely to identify social than civil rights. A larger-scale government Citizenship Survey, which presented respondents with a list of rights, identified strong support for rights to free education and healthcare and "to be looked after by the state if you cannot look after yourself" (Green et al., 2004; see also Pattie et al., 2004). Successive polls for the Joseph Rowntree Reform Trust have found that "large majorities ... say economic and social rights should take their place alongside civil and political rights; they ranked some socio-economic rights as higher than civil and political rights" (Weir, 2007, 10).[1]

NEW LABOUR'S PHILOSOPHY OF SOCIAL CITIZENSHIP

Introducing new pensions legislation, the then Work and Pensions Secretary, Peter Hain, told the House of Commons that "it is the duty of every Government to keep the contract between the state and the individual under constant review to ensure that the balance between rights and responsibilities is properly maintained (*House of Commons Hansard*, January 7, 2008, col. 54). His successor, James Purnell, explained, in his first speech in the post, that:

> We need to rewrite the terms of the welfare contract. On one side: a decency floor to wage rates, making work pay through in-work benefits, tax credits, a credible ladder of opportunity from low paid jobs to higher skills and better pay ... In return those who can work will be obliged to look for work or train for work and if they do not then they will face sanctions. There should be no free riding on the welfare state. (Purnell, 2008)

These quotations are just recent examples of how, from the outset, New Labour articulated social citizenship in explicitly contractual terms. Its first welfare reform policy document was titled *New Ambitions for our Country: A New Contract for Welfare*. This heralded two important themes in its thinking; these concern the nature of the state and of the contract between the state and citizens.

The two are combined in twin processes of contractualization: the contracting out of some of the state's welfare functions, especially with regard to activation, and the explicit exposition of the state's contract with its citizens. Paradoxically perhaps, what has been described as a more light-touch "enabling" state, in place of the providing state, is more intrusive in the ways it enforces the welfare contract, with potential implications for civil rights of citizenship.

With regard to the first theme, the enabling state operates increasingly in partnership with the third (voluntary) and private sectors. As under the Conservatives, the ethos is that of managerialism, individual rational action, and a consumerist model of citizenship (Needham, 2003; Taylor-Gooby, 2009). As part of this model, "the demanding, sceptical, citizen-consumer" expects improved standards from public services in line with those in the private sector (DSS, 1998, 16).[2] This element is more in line with Johansson and Hvinden's "libertarian" understanding, although "market consumerist" perhaps captures it better.

Turning to the second (and for our purposes more central) theme, the "new contract for welfare" places greater emphasis on obligations than on rights. The need to match rights with obligations and responsibilities has been underlined by the key architects of New Labour's thinking on citizenship, such as Anthony Giddens, and has been a recurrent theme in the speeches of both New Labour prime ministers. For instance, in his first speech as leader to the Labour Party's annual conference, Gordon Brown stated:

> We have not done enough in the last ten years to emphasise that in return for the rights we all have, there are responsibilities we all owe. New rights to better health care but you have to show up and not miss your appointment. New rights to education maintenance allowances but you have to show that you are working hard. New rights to higher maternity allowances but you have to meet with a health visitor. The right for company boards to make their own decisions, but obligations to the rest of society too. And an understanding that if you come to our country you not only learn our language and culture: you must play by the rules. (Brown, 2007a)

Another key move in New Labour thinking, with implications for social citizenship, was a shift from the earlier democratic socialist ideal of equality to that of equality of lifelong opportunity and social inclusion. This meant that the redistribution of opportunities through education and other forms of investment in human capital in order to achieve greater *future* prosperity is now seen as more important than traditional forms of redistribution through the tax-benefit system, designed to achieve greater *current* equality of outcome. This futurist orientation stands at the heart of the "social investment state" (see further below and Chapter 3).

RIGHTS AND RESPONSIBILITIES

As explained above, the main arena for the translation of New Labour's philosophy of social citizenship into policy has been the social security system. It is worth noting that the responsible government department has been renamed the Department for Work and Pensions and some of its traditional functions have been transferred to the tax system. One Work and Pensions Secretary underlined the significance of the new name in his inaugural speech when he noted that his title:

> embodies an ideological break with the past. It is not all that long ago that my predecessors were called the Secretary of State for Social Security. What a telling name: security as something handed down; welfare as bureaucratic transfer; people as recipients of funds ... The new title, Secretary of State for Work and Pensions, tells a wholly different story. It tells you that work is the best route to personal welfare and well-being: it tells you that if you work hard and contribute then you deserve your retirement to be free from anxiety about money. (Purnell, 2008; see also Millar, 2003, 6–7)

This section therefore focuses mainly on this area of policy, looking first at the emphasis on responsibilities over rights and second at the implications for social rights of more personalized delivery methods. The overall approach was summed up by a former Work and Pensions Secretary (subsequently Chancellor of the Exchequer): "There is no unconditional right to benefit ... It is right that we should ask ourselves if there is a role for the benefit system as part of the wider system in asserting the values we hold and asserting the kind of behaviour that we want to see" (Darling, 2002).

The rest of this section explores three main ways in which obligations of social citizenship are being asserted in what has been dubbed "the conditional welfare state" (Dwyer, 2008): activation policies to enforce and extend paid work obligations; policies to encourage desirable behavior; and policies to prevent or punish undesirable behavior. The first is the central focus of policy and therefore will be discussed in greater detail than the other two. Together, they reflect a wider interest in government in using policy to achieve behavioral change (Halpern & Bates, 2004) and what has been described as a "new politics of conduct [that] reflect notions of self-regulation and responsible citizenship" (Nixon & Prior, 2009, 71).

Activating into Paid Work

Activities associated with paid work represent the principal form of behavior asserted through the rules governing social security. As well as being available for work, these activities involve the active seeking of work and/or work preparation, skills acquisition, and attendance at work-related interviews. Income replacement benefits for people classified as unemployed have always been conditional on the willingness to take suitable paid employment. What has changed over the past couple of decades has been a steady intensification of the rules governing this conditionality and, more recently, the gradual extension of activation measures to groups classified as "workless" rather than unemployed, notably lone parents and disabled or otherwise incapacitated benefit recipients.

Under New Labour, these changes were made initially in the name of the principles of "reforming work around the work ethic" and "work for those who can, security for those who cannot," reflecting the confluence of a number of rivers of thought (Lister, 2002).Subsequently the principle of conditionality was evoked more explicitly and linked to the welfare contract:

> Conditionality embodies the principle that aspects of state support ... are dependent on citizens meeting certain conditions which are invariably behavioural. This aims to encourage people to engage in actions and activities that help themselves. It also draws on the notion that the welfare system rests on a fair bargain of mutual obligations between citizen and state, in simple terms: 'something for something' ... Conditionality is one way in which the Government tries to encourage active citizenship. (DWP, 2008b, paras. 1, 39)

To develop further the application of the principle of conditionality, the government commissioned an independent review. The ensuing report put forward "a vision for a single personalised conditionality regime where virtually everyone claiming benefits and not in work should be required to engage in activity that will help them to move towards, and then into employment" (Gregg, 2008b, 7). The government accepted "the key components of this vision" and took forward most of the report's recommendations in a welfare reform White Paper published shortly afterwards (DWP, 2008c, 73).

The responsibility of benefit claimants to take up opportunities for paid work and training as the route to social inclusion and antidote to "welfare dependency" was constantly reiterated in government statements, as it introduced "a stronger framework of rights and responsibilities to move benefit claimants from being passive recipients to active jobseekers" (DWP, 2007b, 9). Reflecting the individual rational actor model (Taylor-Gooby, 2009), this is typical of how the new "active" welfare state is contrasted with the "passive," "dependency"-inducing, support previously provided. This false active/passive dichotomy has been criticized by commentators such as Adrian Sinfield, who observes that even the OECD has acknowledged that "a generous benefits system can itself be active—effective in promoting employment and preventing poverty" (Sinfield, 2007; see also Lister, 2001).

Intensification
Under the Conservatives, contributory unemployment benefit (paid for 12 months) was replaced by jobseeker's allowance (JSA), paid on a contributory basis for only 6 months (and income-based or means-tested thereafter); qualification

for it requires entering into a jobseeker's agreement. This agreement formalizes the welfare contract at the level of the individual (although its contents are not legally binding on either party). New Labour retained the JSA and further tightened the sanctions regime in association with the introduction and development of its New Deal welfare-to-work programs. It then proposed "a new contract for job seekers, promising help with skills and help with employability," as well as tougher conditionality (DWP, 2008c, 111).

The New Deal programs, which provide various forms of assistance with job searches and overcoming barriers to employment, follow a primarily "work-first" approach. However, there is growing acknowledgement of the need for greater emphasis on skills acquisition and on support once in work in order to sustain employment and help people move into better jobs (Harker, 2006). There was to be "a new emphasis on skills as the key to sustainable employment, so that there is a focus on **retention and progression** not just job entry" (DWP/DIUS, 2007, 8, emphasis in original). Skills were now seen as "the key driver to achieving economic success and social justice" in the face of the challenges of the global economy (*op. cit.,* 30). The unemployed citizen who lacks the necessary skills will be expected to undertake the necessary training as part of "the contract between the citizen and the state" (*op. cit.,* 6). In the words of the Prime Minister, "We will combine tough sanctions for those who refuse to work or train with better and more targeted support for those most in need to give them the skills and advice they need to get back onto the jobs ladder" (Brown, 2007b, 2). It is proposed "to test the approach of requiring people to deal with their skills needs or risk losing benefit" (DWP, 2008a, p13). "Piloting skills conditionality for benefits customers will enable us to understand better how this supports individuals back into employment" (DWP, 2008c, 122). In an earlier speech, Brown explained that the government is proposing a transfer of "resources from welfare to education" and a transformation of "claimants from passive recipients of welfare benefits to active job and skill seekers." Such changes are, he declared, necessary to "fit the aspirational society the Britain of the future needs to be" (Brown, 2007a).

Further steps in the steady process of intensification are spelled out in the White Paper *Raising Expectations and Increasing Support: Reforming Welfare for the Future* (DWP, 2008c). They include further toughening of the sanctions regime; a "Work for Your Benefit scheme [, which] will require people who have been on Jobseeker's Allowance for two years to participate in full-time activity, to develop their work habits and employability skills in return for their benefit," which represents a form of "workfare"; and benefit sanctions for "problem drug users" who fail to engage in "an agreed rehabilitation plan" without "good cause" (DWP, 2008c, 16, 118). These were robustly criticized by the Government's own Social Security Advisory Committee (SSAC) when published in an earlier Green Paper (SSAC, 2008). Although the proposals were modified in the face of widespread opposition, including from drugs agencies and medical experts, the Welfare Reform Act 2009 includes the power to introduce pilot schemes. These:

will offer additional support to those problem drug users already in treatment. In return, and in order to receive benefit payments, they will also test
an approach in which claimants with a drug dependency that is a barrier
to employment, and who are not already receiving drug treatment, will be
required to sign up to a rehabilitation plan that will outline how they will
engage with the help that is available to them to overcome their addiction.
That is to say that doing nothing will no longer be an option for this group.
While these provisions will also allow for people on benefits to be required
to take drug tests in certain limited and prescribed circumstances, there
will be no loss of entitlement as a result of any positive test. (*House of
Commons Hansard*, Written Answers, col. 177W, December 7, 2009)

Again, such measures have potential implications for civil citizenship rights.

Extension

An increasingly stringent regime of compulsory work-focused interviews has
been introduced for those classified as "workless": lone parents, partners, and
disabled people. This is now being extended to embrace measures that effectively recategorize an increasing proportion of these groups as unemployed
jobseekers. Following the review of conditionality, there will be an "expectation that nearly everyone on benefits is preparing or looking for work" (DWP,
2008c, 17). Working-age benefit recipients will be divided into three groups: the
"work-ready"; a "progression to work group" for whom work is a future possibility and who will be required to produce a personalized "back-to-work plan"
with a personal adviser; and a smaller "no conditionality" group comprising
carers, lone parents of very young children, and severely disabled people (*op.
cit.,* 13). The Government pressed on with these measures despite the warning
from many organizations, including SSAC, of the likely harmful effects in the
face of recession.

   Although the UK remained unusual among OECD countries in not having required lone parents to be available for paid work while their children are
aged under 16, lone parents have been under increasing pressure to consider
work-related activities and think of themselves as prospective workers. This
has paved the way for a radical shift in policy, the announcement of which was
framed by the active/passive discourse (referred to above). The press release was
headed "Moving benefit claimants from passive dependants to active job seekers" (DWP, December 13, 2007). The policy document itself set out "our strategy
to move people from being spectators on the margins—as recipients of passive
benefits—to becoming participants, actively seeking and preparing for work"
(DWP, 2007b, 10).

   For lone parents, this will mean "a presumption" that they "will have to be
actively seeking work in order to claim benefits, once their youngest child is
12 and over from October 2008, 10 and over from October 2009, and 7 and

over from October 2010" (DWP, 2007b, 14). In other words, with limited exceptions, they will be treated as unemployed. It is intended that these "increased obligations will be supported by good quality, affordable childcare, flexible jobs and tailored pre-employment and skills provision" (*ibid.*). Lone parents should not, it is claimed, be sanctioned for not taking a job, if appropriate, affordable childcare is not available. In addition to this new work obligation, lone parents with younger children aged 3 or over will be placed in the "progression to work group." Legislation has been introduced "that will enable advisers to require lone parents with a youngest child aged three or over to undertake work-related activity, a skills health check and training where a lack of skills is identified as a barrier to employment" (DWP, 2008c, 124). Lone parents of younger children, aged 1 or 2, will continue to be required to attend work-focused interviews.

Organizations working with lone parents are very critical of this extension of conditionality. They point, on the one hand, to an 11-percentage-point increase, since 1996, in the proportion of lone parents employed despite no requirement to seek work (Lane, 2008). On the other hand, they note the failure of the existing obligation to engage in work-focused interviews, "with high numbers of New Deal for Lone Parents participants being sanctioned for not attending repeat interviews, which parents say are humiliating and a waste of time" (CPAG press release, December 13, 2007). This gradual increase in the pressure on lone parents, leading to the new work obligation, has also prompted concerns in some quarters (including SSAC) about the devaluing of caring work as an expression of citizenship responsibility. Moreover, some commentators have warned of a possible tension between expectations that lone mothers will enter the labor market on the one hand and new legislative duties to prevent truancy and anti-social behavior, as well as general exhortations to take an active interest in their children's education, on the other.

The introduction of joint claims to income-based JSA (paid after the 6 months contribution-based benefit) for most childless couples has "resulted in increased conditionality for dependent partners (overwhelmingly women), who now also have to be available for work and actively seeking work, in the same way as their partners. It also gives them the same access to employment services as their partners have had in the past" but not access to an independent benefit entitlement (Bennett, 2005, 52–53). This conditionality is now being extended to couples with children, on the same basis as lone parents, and to some couples claiming other benefits.

The most intensive extension of activation measures has been in relation to incapacity benefit recipients, who, it was generally agreed, had previously "been left behind in the welfare to work programmes" (Bennett, 2004, 55–56). A series of measures since 1999 has aimed at both reducing the inflow to and increasing the outflow from incapacity benefit (Kemp, 2005). The mechanism for achieving the latter has been a set of Pathways to Work pilots, designed to encourage and help claimants into work, which have gradually been extended on a compulsory basis. It is reported that over 64,000 people have been helped into work through the scheme (DWP, 2008a).[3]

The final stage under New Labour was the replacement of incapacity benefit by an employment and support allowance (ESA) for new claimants from October 2008, with a phased extension to existing recipients. A new "work capability assessment," which "focuses far more on what an individual can do rather than what they cannot," will determine what help will be received and the conditions attached to that help (DWP, 2008a, 69). ESA is regarded as a temporary benefit for the great majority: "only the most severely disabled people or those people with health conditions ... should see ESA as a long-term benefit" (*op. cit.*, 70). While there is broad support for the aims of helping disabled people into employment, particularly among disability organizations, some are concerned about the further extension of conditionality to this group.

Making Work Pay

Conditionality and sanctions represent the "stick" to activate benefit recipients. The "carrot" has been various measures to "make work pay." The most important have been the introduction of a national minimum wage; the replacement of a means-tested family credit for low-income working families (and children's additions to social assistance) with a more generous means-tested child tax credit; a new working tax credit, which both replaces the adult element of previous support for families with children and extends the subsidy to low wages to childless adults for the first time (it also includes a childcare element); and various payments designed to facilitate work-focused activities and the transition from benefit to paid work and to cushion a return to benefit for disability benefit recipients who are unable to sustain a job (Dornan, 2006).

A Brief Assessment

The government's assessment of its welfare-to-work programs over the first 10 years was upbeat: "the New Deals have been the most successful innovation in the history of the UK labour market. In the last decade, the New Deals have helped more than 1.85 million people into work. Overall, prior to the onset of recession, employment was at record levels and the total number of people on key out-of-work benefits had fallen by a million since 1997" by 2007 (DWP, 2007a, 6). The government cites independent research and international organizations such as the IMF in support of these claims. More skeptical observers point to the high level of repeat claims: for example, in 2006 47% of leavers from the New Deal for Young People and 36% of those leaving the New Deal for 25-plus claimed benefit again within 12 months of leaving the program (*House of Commons Hansard*, December 17, 2007, col. 939W). It would appear that attendance at work-focused interviews has contributed to an increase in employment rates among workless groups (Gregg, 2008a). The government claimed success in reducing the numbers receiving incapacity benefit by 200,000 from its peak

(DWP, 2008c, 24). However, the evidence also suggests that existing forms of conditionality and sanctions have had only very limited effects on labor market behavior and may have reduced levels of benefit take-up without raising employment levels (Bunt & Maidment, 2008; Goodwin, 2008; Griggs & Bennett, 2009; SSAC, 2006, 2008).

Moreover, from the perspective of welfare-to-work's contribution to tackling child poverty, despite the attempts to "make work pay," a number of reports have drawn attention to the fact that around half of children living in poverty are in a household containing a wage-earner (Cooke & Lawton, 2008; Lawton, 2008). There is also evidence that sanctions hit the most disadvantaged hardest and can cause significant hardship (CPAG, 2008; Griggs & Bennett, 2009). They may therefore "conflict with other important government goals, such as the reduction of poverty" (Griggs & Bennett, 2009, 35).

Encouraging Desirable Behavior

A number of measures were adopted to promote forms of behavior, other than job-seeking, that the government regarded as desirable. Saving is a prime example. "Saving is being elevated from a private aspiration of the prudent individual to a core duty of the good citizen supported by government" (Hewitt, 2002, cited in Kemp, 2005, 26). A key aim of pensions policy has been to encourage greater personal responsibility through investment in private pensions during working life: "individuals must take personal responsibility by saving for later life as part of a renewed social contract designed to avoid the nightmare of a pensions crisis in years to come" (DWP, press release, January 7, 2008). Moreover, "working beyond pension age will be encouraged and incentivised" (Kemp, 2005, 27).

Saving was also actively stimulated by novel "asset-based welfare" policies. Most important of these is a new Child Trust Fund (CTF). This provides a fixed endowment for every child at birth, topped up at age 7, with higher payments for children in low-income families.. According to proponents of assets-based welfare, "the CTF establishes an important principle: the right of the individual, as a citizen, to capital" (Paxton & White, 2006, 6). The other main mechanism was a new Savings Gateway, to be introduced in 2010. This aimed to encourage low-income adults to build up shorter-term savings by providing matching savings (up to a fixed limit). (Both of these have been abandoned by the Coalition Government.)

An early example of the use of social security policy by New Labour to encourage desirable behavior was the attachment of conditionality to entitlement to the maternity grant (which was simultaneously increased significantly in value). The grant is now conditional on attendance at child health checks. Over 8,000 claims were disallowed as a result in 2001–02 (Dwyer, 2008). In the education field, previously discretionary educational maintenance allowances were converted into a national statutory scheme in order to encourage young people from low-income families to stay on at and attend school beyond school-leaving age. Payment was conditional on attendance, with the possibility of bonus payments for effort. From September 2008, the criteria for payment of bonuses and weekly payments were amended "to include punctuality, completing coursework on time and achievement of agreed learning goals" in order to "emphasise the 'something for something' approach" (*House of Commons Hansard*, Written Answers, January 13, 2009, col. 651–2W). Evaluation of the pilot found its impact was greatest on families with incomes below £20,000 (*ibid.*) Again the scheme has since been abolished.

Future 16- and 17-year-olds (who reached the age of 11 in 2009 or later) will be required to stay in some form of education or training. The legislation was described by the Secretary of State as "a bill of responsibilities as well as a bill of rights. Because if young people fail to take up these opportunities there will be a system of enforcement—very much a last resort—but necessary to strike the right balance between new rights and new responsibilities" (Balls, 2007b).

Housing benefit (means-tested assistance with housing costs for people on low incomes) was also reformed. The "overarching purpose is to transform passive housing support into an enabling provision that places responsibility and choice firmly in the hands of tenants and that strongly encourages financial inclusion and the development of skills that can help smooth the transition into work" (DWP, 2006, 86). Tenants are thus "expected to become active and responsible consumers in the marketplace armed with their LHA [local housing allowance], rather than being passive recipients of Housing Benefit that is paid directly on their behalf directly to the landlord" (Kemp, 2005, 29).

Discouraging Undesirable Behavior

The main deployment of social security policy to discourage undesirable behavior was as part of the government's antisocial behavior strategy. Legislation made provision "for a reduction in housing benefit where someone has been evicted from their home on grounds of antisocial behaviour and refuses to co-operate with the support that is offered by the local authority to improve behaviour" (*House of Commons Hansard*, 2006, col. 627). The sanction was piloted. In the words of the then Work and Pensions Secretary: "an active welfare state, with rights and responsibilities at its heart, must send a clear signal to those evicted for antisocial behaviour that they are at the end of the line and cannot simply expect to move to another property and continue their bad behaviour at the expense of decent hard-working families" (*ibid.*). This new sanction is in addition to the power already introduced to evict families from social housing in cases of persistent antisocial behavior. Research has revealed its gendered impact, as women-headed households have been at greatest risk of eviction, often because of the women's inability to control boyfriends' and/or teenage sons' behavior (Hunter & Nixon, 2001).

In the education field, (non-social security) penalties were introduced as part of a "package of support and sanctions to reinforce parental responsibility for school attendance and behaviour" (Halpern et al., 2004, 57). Parenting contracts were introduced and the numbers issued in cases of irregular attendance increased steadily (*House of Commons Hansard*, January 16, 2008, col. 1279W). In extreme cases parents can be sent to jail. Thus, the social citizenship right of education for children, which has only recently been enshrined explicitly as a right in law, is matched by tough sanctions for parents unwilling or unable to ensure their children avail themselves of the right.

Legislative power was also taken to deny the right to social security to convicted criminals who breach a community order. The aim was to send out "a clear message … to individuals that their rights to benefits have to be matched by their responsibility to comply with their community sentence" (DWP press release, October 15, 2001). This was piloted for 8 years and the sanctions were found to be ineffective (SSAC, 2008). The scheme was finally discontinued (*The Guardian*, February 18, 2009).

Policy towards asylum-seekers has been cited as a further example of use of social security "to control and to influence" behavior (Dornan, 2006, 92). To discourage asylum, a parallel income maintenance system pays benefit at a rate lower than that received by the resident population and can withdraw it "from those whose asylum claims are rejected" or deny it to "those not registering as required" (Dornan, 2006, 92). This and other measures, in particular the denial of legal access to the labor market, have resulted in evidence of destitution among some failed asylum-seekers and in "the marginalisation of asylum seekers from mainstream services and society" (Burchardt, 2005, 224; Hobson et al., 2008; Lewis, 2007). This raises questions too about human rights (see Chapter 1).

The treatment of asylum-seekers is an example of a parallel development: the increased exclusivity of social citizenship rights (Lister, 2009). The contractual construction of social citizenship is to be extended to immigrants in the form of "earned citizenship." To "earn" citizenship, newcomers must demonstrate their commitment to the UK by, for instance, learning the language and contributing to the community. Access to most benefits and services will be confined to British citizens and permanent residents after a probationary period of a minimum of 6 years.[4] Access to full political citizenship will also be postponed. John Flint comments that "the concept of 'earned' citizenship thereby reconfigures the idea of a 'right' to citizenship, which is based on proactive endeavour rather than passive qualification and provides an additional mechanism of conditionality for classifying potential citizens" (2009, 89).

Personalizing Delivery

On the delivery side, a customer-focused, post-Fordist "business model" is increasingly dominant (Carmel & Papadopoulos, 2003, 47). A "*passive one-size-fits-all model*" is contrasted with "an *active, enabling* system, where *tailored support* to help people back into work is matched by personal responsibility for people to help themselves" (DWP, 2006, 2, emphasis added). The New Deal was developed in ways that decentralize provisions within a national framework. The aim was to "give more freedom and flexibility to front-line staff [personal advisers] so that they can develop tailored help and implement innovative solutions" (DWP, 2004, 1), using a proportion of their employment budgets and a "menu of modular provision."

One of the core principles set out in the welfare reform document, *Ready for Work*, is "a personalised and responsive approach" so that the support available "better responds to individual need" (DWP, 2007b, 10). The document promises to "**empower advisers and give increased discretion both to Jobcentre Plus staff** and to public, private and third sector providers" (*ibid.* emphasis in original). The reference to "private and third sector providers" leads in to another core principle: "partnership—the public, private and third sectors working together" (*ibid.*). In the name of customer choice, individual responsibility, and "what works," the government has been "systematically testing the impact of opening up the design and delivery of labour market support to private- and voluntary-sector competition" (DWP, 2006, 74). Personalization is a central theme running through a 2008 welfare reform White Paper, which explains that the reforms it proposes "mark a decisive step towards a personalised welfare state" (DWP, 2008c, 17).

While personalization is generally regarded as a positive development, there is also growing concern in some quarters about the implications for claimants' social citizenship rights of this increased emphasis on personalized delivery through voluntary- and private-sector providers. Greater reliance on discretion erodes rights, "increases the likelihood that claimants will receive differential treatment ... and can leave the way open for prejudice" (Griggs & Bennett, 2009, 43). The contracting out of delivery weakens accountability. The then Chief Executive of the Child Poverty Action Group (a leading anti-poverty organization) warns that:

> while the Government has invested substantially in the welfare state in recent years, it has also quite casually dismantled and undermined the notion of citizenship and citizenship rights that should lie at its heart. Policies have proved, in practice, to be discriminatory, discretionary and judgemental. A fragmented system of financial support and lack of appeal rights and accountability lead to poor understanding of what support is available, and can lower take-up as a result. Complexity and poor administration in the tax credit system, the increasing application of discretion, greater conditionality to participate in work-related activity or face benefit sanctions, and the 'outsourcing' of more and more of the functions of Jobcentre Plus to an army of voluntary and private sector providers, all give cause for concern. (Green, 2006, v)

Similar concerns have been expressed by SSAC, who have asked whether "'flexibility' for individual customers can be achieved without sacrificing the transparency and equity of outcome that are the foundations of a regulated benefits system" (SSAC, 2007, 3).

Together with personalization, "empowerment" is presented as "at the heart of our welfare reforms" (DWP, 2008c, 57). One example is "developing a right to choose between providers for people on employment programmes" (*ibid.*). The principles of personalization and empowerment do not, however, extend to user involvement. Although a government document on modern policymaking includes consultation with and feedback from "those affected by policy" as a feature, user involvement has not been built into the social security system (Carmel & Papadopoulos, 2003; Finn et al., 2008). This contrasts with other areas of the welfare state and neighborhood regeneration programs, where emphasis is placed on user involvement and active resident participation. The DWP has nevertheless been involved in a participatory initiative designed to enable people with experience of poverty to feed their views into the 2006–08 National Action Plan on Social Inclusion, as required by the European Commission (Get Heard, 2006; Lister, 2007b). Although such initiatives tend to be circumscribed and limited, they could be interpreted as a more republican approach to social citizenship in Johansson and Hvinden's schema (Chapter 2).

SOCIAL INVESTMENT

The erosion and circumscribing of rights detailed above notwithstanding, the emergence of the "social investment state" in some ways represents a strengthening of social citizenship. New Labour's philosophy of social investment (see also Chapter 3) was translated most concretely into its policies for children, particularly children living in poverty (Dobrowolsky & Lister, 2008).

The government was committed to the eradication of child poverty by 2020, with milestone targets for reductions by a half and a quarter.[5] These targets were missed; nevertheless, 900,000 children were lifted out of poverty under New Labour (Jin et al, 2011). In a document updating its child poverty strategy, it proposed a "contract out of poverty." Under this contract "all parts of society will do their bit to tackle the blight on children, communities and future prosperity"; "the Government will provide all families with a clear route out of poverty"; and "on the other side of this contract, the Government looks to families to make a commitment to improve their situations where they can and to take advantage of the opportunities on offer" (HM Treasury, 2008, 55, 3, 55). Brown spelled this out: "matching new opportunities to support their children with new responsibilities to take up work, to acquire new skills, to make the most of their lives" (2008). The case made by some anti-poverty NGOs and commentators on the center-left that eradicating poverty requires an assault on economic inequality, which is extremely wide from both an historical and cross-national perspective, was not accepted by the government despite concerns expressed by some individual ministers and some taxation measures in the wake of the credit crunch.[6]

The establishment of a childcare and early years strategy was a particularly significant element of social investment. While there are many criticisms of the details of the strategy, it represents a breakthrough in British social policy in its recognition that childcare is a public as well as private responsibility. Childcare was presented by ministers as a new frontier for the welfare state. Although childcare was not represented as a social citizenship right as such (unlike in, for instance, the Nordics [Lister et al., 2007]), a limited entitlement to free nursery education for 3- and 4-year-olds was introduced. A new statutory duty has also been placed on local authorities to "improve child outcomes and secure a sufficient supply of childcare and a new system of regulation and inspection for childcare and early education" (HM Treasury, 2006, 107). The main new institutional mechanisms for the delivery of early years provision was the creation of a network of Sure Start Children's Centres, which, as well as childcare, "bring together early education, health, family support and employment support for young families" (HM Treasury, 2006, 108). In addition, extended schools are providing out-of-school facilities including childcare between 8 a.m. and 6 p.m. throughout the year. UNICEF has ranked the UK in the middle of 25 OECD countries, using 10 benchmark standards for early childhood services (Adamson, 2008).

Parental social citizenship rights have also been strengthened, within limits, through improved leave arrangements in the name of "flexibility in balancing work and family life" (HM Treasury, 2006, 107). The main vehicle has been paid maternity leave (and limited paternity leave). Parental leave, in contrast, has been introduced on an unpaid basis, and the government has resisted calls to implement the Nordic "daddy month" model, which would encourage greater paternal involvement and challenge the traditional gendered division of labor (Lister, 2006a). (The Coalition government is now considering this.)

As well as investment in the early years, a "guiding principle" of the government's social exclusion policy, revised in 2006 in *An Action Plan on Social Exclusion*, was "early intervention." This was seen as "vital to breaking the cycle of disadvantage and deprivation." According to the responsible cabinet minister, "this is not only beneficial to the children and families concerned, but it also saves the taxpayer from the high costs of treatment and communities from the side-effects of exclusion" (*House of Commons Hansard*, December 13, 2006, col. 1156W). Early intervention was seen as particularly important in preventing criminal and antisocial behavior. Again, personalization of services was the watchword in place of "a one-size-fits-all approach [which] lets down our most needy and hard to reach" (Armstrong, 2006, 6). The reference to "our most needy and hard to reach" signalled a renewed emphasis in the social exclusion strategy on "small groups of people whose needs are unique and complex" and who experience "entrenched exclusion" (Cabinet Office, 2006, 9).

Both early intervention and investment are marked by their future orientation (Jenson, 2004, 2006, and Chapter 3). One consequence is that although some aspects of social citizenship have been strengthened as a result, the child herself is positioned not as a citizen in the here and now but as a citizen-worker of the future (Lister, 2003, 2006b). The child as cipher for future economic prosperity overshadows the child as child-citizen and the quality of childhood and children's well-being as experienced through, for instance, education and play (Lister, 2006b, 2008). This has led to some criticism of the instrumentalist nature of the social investment approach, even among those who welcome the increased investment in children. The government's record on children also came under public scrutiny following the considerable media coverage of the UK's dismal showing in the UNICEF child well-being international league table.

The creation by Gordon Brown of a new Department for Children, Schools and Families, together with the subsequent publication of a Children's Plan (2007) and a Play Strategy (2008), signaled something of a shift in orientation. Although the plan is subtitled "Building brighter futures," one of its principles is that "children and young people need to enjoy their childhood as well as grow up prepared for adult life" (DCSF, 2007, 4). Moreover, in one of his first speeches as Secretary of State in the new department, Ed Balls (2007a) spoke of the importance of a "happy childhood" and acknowledged the role of play in achieving this.

Another source of criticism has been that not all children have equal strategic significance as future citizen-workers. Since this criticism was directed towards the treatment of disabled children by Fawcett et al. (2004), the government has published a strategy to improve support for disabled children (Strategy Unit, 2005; see also HM Treasury/DfES, 2007). The Children's Plan commits resources to the achievement of the government's "ambition ... for a transformation in services for families with disabled children by 2011" (DCSF, 2007, 26).

Two other groups of children whose rights are fragile at best are gypsy and traveler children and asylum-seeking children.[7] An essay on the former group argues that the high risk of poverty they face "tends to reflect the group's wider relationship with the dominant settled society and the discrimination and denial of human rights they endure across a range of aspects of day-to-day living" (Cemlyn & Clark, 2005, 150). Research reveals that "gypsies and travellers remain among those most overlooked by service providers and policy makers. Indicators include low health status and a lower likelihood of accessing services and a higher likelihood of homelessness" (Warrington, 2006, 38).

The position of asylum-seeking children is even more insecure. The reduction in asylum-seekers' welfare rights was detailed earlier. In a foreword to a study by the charity Barnardo's, its chief executive reveals "the shocking truth ... that, despite all our assertions that every child matters, children in asylum-seeking families do not seem to matter to our society as much as others" (Narey, 2008, 2). An earlier study "highlights the fact that despite their obvious vulnerability, children seeking asylum face constant discrimination, and it illustrates (in children's own words) how their rights are violated and routinely infringed by a state that seems to have forgotten that they are children" (Hewett et al., 2005, 1; see also Lister,

2006a, 325–326). The authors' recommendation that "asylum-seeking families and separated (unaccompanied) children should be treated on the basis of equality with the general population in terms of welfare benefits" (Hewett et al., 2005, 7) is echoed by a number of children's and anti-poverty organizations as well as those working with refugees and asylum-seekers.

"PROGRESSIVE UNIVERSALISM"

"Progressive universalism" was the term adopted by the government to describe an approach that aimed to provide "support for all and more help for those who need it most when they need it most" (HM Treasury, 2004, para. 5.2). It framed income maintenance policy towards children and pensioners in particular. Thus, for children, the Child Trust Fund (described earlier) combined a universal basic child endowment with higher payments for children in low-income families. Similarly, the government maintained the value of the universal child benefit, with some real increases for first children. However, it targeted most of its new investment into means-tested tax credits for children, which themselves provide, through a tapering mechanism, some support for the majority of families but maximum support for those on low incomes. Responsibility for both child benefit and tax credits now lies with HM Revenue and Customs, an example of the "fiscalisation" of social rights (Bashevkin, 2000, 2). It is also sometimes represented as a step towards fuller integration of the tax-benefit system.

For pensioners there have been some limited improvements in universal support, in particular the basic pension and winter fuel payments. The main additional assistance, though, has been targeted on the poorest pensioners through a pension credit, which is made up of a minimum guarantee and a savings credit, designed to encourage small savings for retirement.

The priority given to means-tested support for children and pensioners reflects the emergence of "a clear strategy … in social security policy … to increase the role of means tests" (Brewer et al., 2002, 513). One consequence has been a shift in the fulcrum of the income maintenance system as between means-tested and contributory national insurance benefits, continuing the direction of policy under the previous Conservative administrations. Contributory benefits, which represented the hallmark of social citizenship in the postwar Beveridge model, have become increasingly marginal, despite some reforms that have made the national insurance system more inclusive (Bennett, 2005).[8] For unemployed and disabled people the distinction between contributory and means-tested benefits has been blurred in the jobseeker's allowance and new employment and support allowance, which combine contributory and means-tested elements (Bennett, 2008). The government's view was that "the contributory principle, means-tested benefits or universal benefits are not an end in themselves but merely a means of delivering the Government's policy objectives—it is the outcomes which are important"

(DSS, 2000, para. 2). Nevertheless, in response to a House of Commons Work and Pensions Select Committee report on simplification, the Department for Work and Pensions has conceded that "the extent to which the system relies on means-testing as a targeting mechanism is an important question for future reform." But it also warned that the scope for increasing the scope of universal provision "is likely to be very limited," despite acknowledging the contribution of means-testing to the system's complexity (Work and Pensions Committee, 2007, 2). The perennial issue of complexity is increasingly driving the welfare reform agenda. The increased reliance on means-testing has emerged as an issue in public debate. John Hills has warned that there "may be limits to how much further" a strategy of redistribution through means-testing can be pushed because of the effects on effective marginal tax rates and incentives and because of its unpopularity (2004, 255; see also Dornan, 2006). The backlash on means-testing has been most vocal in relation to pensions, where a broad consensus has emerged that the cornerstone of pensions policy must be an adequate (contributory or universal) state pension. As a consequence, both the main parties went into the 2010 general election committed to restoring the statutory up-rating link between earnings and pensions, which had been abolished by the Conservatives when they first came to power. Although less prominent, there is also concern about the extensiveness of means-testing in financial support for children. This has been fueled by the complexities of the tax credits system and administrative problems associated, in particular, with the calculation of tax credits on the basis of annual rather than weekly income, leading to the widespread clawing back of overpayments. Thus instead of contributing to security of income, these social rights have, in many cases, created considerable *in*security. A wide range of bodies is now calling for a rebalancing between universal and means-tested support and in particular an increase in the child benefit paid for second and subsequent children, which is considerably lower than that paid for the first child.

Reports from the former Equal Opportunities Commission (Bennett, 2005) and the Fawcett Society (Bellamy et al., 2006) have drawn attention to the negative implications for women of the increased reliance on means-testing. This has been less of an issue in public debate. However, the unfavorable treatment for pension purposes of time spent out of the labor market (mainly by women) to provide care has been acknowledged and is being addressed through legislation. The government estimated that, as a result, around three quarters of women will qualify for a full pension by 2010 and around 90% by 2020, compared to around half were the system not reformed (DWP press release, January 16, 2007).

CONCLUSION

This chapter has outlined a number of developments in the nature of social citizenship rights in the UK under New Labour. The watchwords have been responsibility and a more "active" welfare state, as social rights have become increasingly conditional. While labor market activation has been the most visible goal of this increased conditionality, there were also attempts to use social rights to change behavior more generally. The "active" welfare state was contrasted not only with a "passive" welfare state but also, through the notion of personalization, with a one-size-fits-all welfare state. More personalized forms of delivery, often in partnership with the third and private sectors, spell greater discretion and reduced accountability.

Means-testing has played an increasingly prominent role: contributory national insurance benefits have been marginalized (albeit with some exceptions) and spending on means-tested tax credits for children has outstripped that on the universal child benefit as a key plank in the strategy to eradicate child poverty. Such spending, and also spending on child care and early years support, was portrayed as investment in the nation's future in what has been dubbed a "social investment state" in which children represent citizen-workers of the future.

These shifts reflect a number of interacting factors—some associated with the particularities of British social democracy, some more general. After four electoral defeats New Labour repositioned itself by adopting the "third way" of "neither old Left nor New Right," which represented both a reaction against and accommodation with neoliberal Thatcherism. The rearticulation of its understanding of social citizenship was a key tenet of the third way. However, as Rebecca Surender observes, "to understand the emergence of either Third Way policies or rhetoric, an analysis of the interaction between macro-socio-economic factors and political dynamics is required" (2004, 7). Thus, at another level, the shifts also represent a post-Fordist reading of how to respond to global economic change, interpreted through a totalizing discourse of modernization.

As such, New Labour's stance represented elements of both continuity (with Thatcherism and with its own social democratic past) and change. Its emphasis on responsibility and personal agency drew heavily on communitarianism, which resonated with the Christian socialist strand in Labour's own history to create an "Anglicanized communitarianism" (Deacon, 2000, 2002). New Labour similarly absorbed other American influences, notably in its welfare-to-work policies, but combined with learning also from Australian and Nordic experience (Deacon, 2002). The changing nature of social citizenship in the UK therefore needs to be understood both in the particular context of New Labour's political heritage and in the wider context of Western welfare states' responses to demographic, social, and global economic change (Lewis & Surender, 2004). One welfare reform document makes explicit reference to drawing "on the best of international welfare systems, such as the Dutch and Scandinavian models" (DWP, 2008b, 14). At the same time, the government liked to present itself as a beacon of welfare reform. In an early media interview, Work and Pensions Secretary Purnell asked, "Why do people round the world look to Britain? Because of our ability to reform" (*The Observer*, January 17, 2008).

John Clarke has analyzed New Labour's policy on social citizenship as "a *political and governmental project* ... of remaking the relationships between state and citizens" (2005, 456–457, emphasis in original). It is an explicitly contractual relationship between state and citizens, which governs social citizenship in line with the socioliberal model (see Chapter 2).

Following the change of government at the 2010 general election,, it is clear that the Conservative-Liberal Democrat coalition will travel further down the same path on welfare reform. The weight placed on responsibilities and obligations is even greater than under New Labour and the emphasis on social rights even weaker. When he took office as prime minister, David Cameron declared, "I want to try to help and build a more responsible society here in Britain. One where we don't just ask what are my entitlements but what are my responsibilities" (2010). Responsibility subsequently became one of the trinity of values guiding the coalition.

It is given expression in the Welfare Reform Act 2012 through the further extension and intensification of work obligations and provision for conditionality to be extended to some in-work recipients of the new universal credit. Following the August 2011 riots, it was suggested that benefits might in future be denied to criminals given noncustodial sentences. This is part of a reframing of the right to social security as at best an entitlement and at worst a privilege. Both ministerial pronouncements and early policy developments point to a further shift in the mix of socioliberal, libertarian (or market consumerist), and republican models of citizenship, bound together by the paramount virtue of responsibility.

NOTES

1 The Human Rights Act 1998, which incorporates the European Convention on Human Rights, does not include social and economic human rights, and the government resisted UN pressure to incorporate the International Covenant on Economic, Social and Cultural Rights. A parliamentary committee has recommended that a planned Bill of Rights should include certain social and economic rights.

2 For a discussion of "this peculiar hybridised and hyphenated combination of citizen and consumer," see Clarke et al. (2007, 1).

3 A qualitative study, reported by the DWP, suggests that despite a significant impact on attendance at work-focused interviews, subsequent positive engagement with the Pathways to Work program was rare. The sanctions applied to participants in the pilots who failed to attend a work-focused interview had a damaging impact on mental health in a number of cases and hit "the more socially deprived or isolated, or longer-term benefit recipients" hardest (Bunt & Maidment, 2008, 1).

4 In an exclusive interview, the Immigration Minister suggested that some immigrants will face a waiting period of ten years (*The Sun*, December 8, 2008).

5 This commitment is now to be enshrined in law.

6 Most notably, a new 50% top rate of tax for those earning over £150,000 a year from April 2010 marks the reversal of New Labour's refusal to raise the taxes of the highest paid. However, it has been presented as a revenue-raising measure rather than as part of a strategy to reduce inequality.

7 Neither of these two groups is identified in a discussion of "vulnerable groups" in a discussion paper published as part of the government's policy review of children and young people (HM Treasury/DfES, 2007). They are mentioned briefly in the Children's Plan, which does acknowledge that unaccompanied asylum-seeking children "are first and foremost children" (DCSF, 2007, 26).

8 For example, changes in the entitlement threshold have brought more low earners, mainly women, into the system. Also, a new civil right for gays and lesbians in the form of the right to enter into civil partnerships has meant the extension of certain social rights also, notably the right to bereavement benefits and survivors' pension rights. These rights have not, however, been extended to heterosexual cohabiting couples, even though they too are treated as couples for the purposes of entitlement to means-tested benefits (Bennett, 2005; Kemp, 2005). The treatment of civil partnerships as equivalent to marriage has also meant that homosexual couples are now subject to the cohabitation rule applied to heterosexual couples (McKay, 2007).

REFERENCES

Adamson, P. (2008). *The child care transition*. Florence: UNICEF Innocenti Research Centre.

Armstrong, H. (2006). Foreword. *Reaching Out: An Action Plan on Social Exclusion*. London: Cabinet Office.

Balls E. (2007a). *Every child matters*. Speech to the National Children's Bureau, London, July 18.

Balls, E. (2007b). *Raising the participation age: Opportunity for all young people*. Fabian Society Lecture, London, November 5.

Bashevkin, S. (2000). *Road-testing the Third Way: Welfare reform in Canada, Britain and the United States*. Jerusalem: The Hebrew University of Jerusalem.

Bellamy, K., F. Bennett, & J. Millar (2006). *Who benefits? A gender analysis of the UK benefits and tax credits system*. London: Fawcett Society.

Bennett, F. (2004). Developments in social security. In N. Ellison, L. Bauld, & M. Powell (Eds.), *Social Policy Review 16*. Bristol: The Policy Press.

Bennett, F. (2005). *Gender and benefits*. Manchester: Equal Opportunities Commission.

Bennett, F. (2008). Celebrating sixty years of the welfare state? *Poverty, 131*, 12–17.

Bochel, H., & A. Defty (2007). *Welfare policy under New Labour. View from inside Westminster.* Bristol: The Policy Press.

Brewer, M., T. Clark, & M. Wakefield (2002). Social security in the UK under New Labour. *Fiscal Studies, 23*(4), 505–537.

Brown, G. (2007a). Speech to Labour Party Conference, Bournemouth, September 24.

Brown, G. (2007b). Foreword to DWP, *Transforming Britain's labour market.* London: Department for Work and Pensions.

Brown, G. (2008). Speech to Welsh Labour Party Conference, February 15, 2008.

Bunt, K., & A. Maidment (2008). *Qualitative research exploring the Pathways to Work sanctions regime.* London: Department for Work and Pensions.

Burchardt, T. (2005). Selective inclusion: asylum seekers and other marginalised groups. In J. Hills & K Stewart (Eds.), *A more equal society? New Labour, poverty, inequality and exclusion.* Bristol: Policy Press.

Cabinet Office (2006). *Reaching out: An action plan on social exclusion.* London: Cabinet Office.

Cameron, D. (2010). Speech outside 10 Downing Street, May 11.

Carmel, E., & T. Papadopoulos (2003). The new governance of social security in Britain. In J. Millar (Ed.), *Understanding social security.* Bristol: The Policy Press.

Cemlyn, S., & C. Clarke (2005). The social exclusion of Gypsy and Traveller children. In G. Preston (Ed.), *At greatest risk.* London: Child Poverty Action Group.

Clarke, J. (2005). New Labour's citizens: activated, empowered, responsibilized, abandoned? *Critical Social Policy, 25*(4), 447–463.

Clarke, J., J. Newman, N. Smith, E. Vidler, & L Westmarland (2007). *Creating citizen-consumers.* London: Sage.

Conover, P. J., I. M. Crewe, & D. D. Searing (1991). The nature of citizenship in the United States and Great Britain: empirical comments on theoretical themes. *Journal of Politics, 53*(3): 800–832.

Cooke, G., & K. Lawton (2008). *Working out of poverty.* London: Institute for Public Policy Research.

CPAG (2008). *No one written off." Response to the July 2008 welfare reform Green Paper.* London: Child Poverty Action Group.

Darling, A. (2002). Address to the Parliamentary Press Gallery, reported in *The Independent*, May 16.

DCSF (2007). *The Children's Plan. Building brighter futures.* London: Department for Children, Schools and Families.

Deacon, A. (2000). Learning from the USA? The influence of American ideas on New Labour thinking on welfare reform. *Policy & Politics, 28*(1), 5–18.

Deacon, A. (2002). *Perspectives on Welfare*. Buckingham: Open University Press.

Dean, H., with M. Melrose (1999). *Poverty, riches and social citizenship*. Basingstoke: Macmillan.

Dobrowolsky, A., & R. Lister (2008). Social investment: the discourse and the dimensions of change. In P. Dwyer (Ed.), *Modernising the welfare state. The Blair legacy*. Bristol: The Policy Press.

Dornan, P. (2006). Social security policies in 2005. In L. Bauld, K. Clarke, & T. Maltby (Eds.), *Social Policy Review 18*. Bristol: The Policy Press.

DSS (1998). *New ambitions for our country: A new contract for welfare*. London: Department for Social Security/The Stationery Office.

DSS (2000). *Report on the contributory principle. Reply by the Government to the 5th Report of the Select Committee on Social Security*. London: The Stationery Office.

DWP (2004). *Building on New Deal: Local solutions to meeting individual needs*. London: Department for Work and Pensions.

DWP (2006). *A New Deal for welfare: Empowering people to work*. London: Department for Work and Pensions.

DWP (2007a). *Transforming Britain's labour market*. London: Department for Work and Pensions.

DWP (2007b). *Ready for Work*. London: Department for Work and Pensions.

DWP (2008a). *No one written off: Reforming welfare to reward responsibility*. London: Department for Work and Pensions.

DWP (2008b). *More support, higher expectations: The role of conditionality in improving employment outcomes*. London: Department for Work and Pensions.

DWP (2008c). *Raising expectations and increasing support: Reforming welfare for the future*. London: Department for Work and Pensions.

DWP/DIUS (2007). *Opportunity, employment and progression: Making skills work*. London: Department for Work and Pensions/Department for Innovation, Universities and Skills.

Dwyer, P. (2004). *Understanding social citizenship*. Bristol: The Policy Press.

Dwyer, P. (2008). The conditional welfare state. In M. Powell (Ed.), *Modernising the welfare state. The Blair legacy*. Bristol: The Policy Press.

Fawcett, B., B. Featherstone, & J. Goddard (2004). *Contemporary child care policy and practice*. Basingstoke: Palgrave.

Finn, D., D. Mason, N. Rahim, & J. Casebourne (2008) *Problems in the delivery of benefits, tax credits and employment services: Findings*. York: Joseph Rowntree Foundation.

Flint, J. (2009). Subversive subjects and conditional, earned and denied citizenship. In M. Barnes & D. Prior (Eds.), *Subversive citizens*. Bristol: The Policy Press.

Get Heard (2006). *People experiencing poverty speak out on social exclusion*. London: UK Coalition against Poverty.

Goodwin, V. (2008). *The effects of benefit sanctions on lone parents' employment decisions and moves into employment.* London: Department for Work and Pensions.

Green, H., H. Connolly, & C. Farmer (2004). *2003 Home Office Citizenship Survey.* London: Home Office.

Green, K. (2006). Foreword. In S. Osborne (Ed.), *Welfare benefits and tax credits handbook* (8th ed.).London: Child Poverty Action Group.

Gregg, P. (2008a). *UK welfare reform 1996 to 2008 and beyond.* CMPO Working Paper No. 08/196. Bristol: University of Bristol.

Gregg, P. (2008b). *Realising potential: A vision for personalised conditionality and support.* London: Department for Work and Pensions.

Griggs, J., & F. Bennett (2009). *Rights and responsibilities in the social security system.* London: Social Security Advisory Committee.

Halpern, D., & C. Bates (2004). *Personal responsibility and changing behaviour.* London: Cabinet Office.

Harker, L. (2006). *Delivering on child poverty: What would it take?* London: Department for Work and Pensions.

Hewett, T., N. Smalley, D. Dunkerley, & J. Scourfield (2005). *Uncertain futures. Children seeking asylum in Wales.* Cardiff: Save the Children Wales.

Hewitt, M. (2002). New Labour and the redefinition of social security. In M. Powell (Ed.), *Evaluating New Labour's welfare reforms.* Bristol: The Policy Press.

Hills, J. (2004). *Inequality and the state.* Oxford: Oxford University Press.

HM Treasury (2004). *Budget report 2004.* London: HM Treasury,

HM Treasury (2006). *Investing in Britain's potential: Building our long-term future.* London: The Stationery Office.

HM Treasury (2008). *Ending child poverty: Everybody's business.* London: HM Treasury.

HM Treasury/DfES (2007). *Aiming high for disabled children.* London: HM Treasury.

Hobson, C., J. Cox, & N. Sagovsky (2008). *Safe return. The Independent Asylum Commission's second report.* London: Independent Asylum Commission.

Hunter, C., & J. Nixon (2001). Taking the blame and losing the home: women and anti-social behaviour. *Journal of Social Welfare and Family Law, 23*(4), 395–410.

Isin, E. (Ed.) (2008). *Recasting the social in citizenship.* University of Toronto Press.

Jenson, J. (2004). Changing the paradigm. Family responsibility or investing in children *Canadian Journal of Sociology, 29*(2), 169–194.

Jenson, J. (2006). The LEGO TM paradigm and new social risks: consequences for children. In J. Lewis (Ed.), *Children, changing families and welfare states.* Cheltenham/Northampton, Mass.: Edward Elgar.

Jin, W., R. Joyce, D. Phillips, & L. Sibieta (2011) *Poverty and Inequality in the UK: 2011,* London: Institute for Fiscal Studies.

Kemp, P. (2005). Social security and welfare reform under New Labour. In M. Powell, L. Bauld, & K. Clarke (Eds.), *Social Policy Review 17*. Bristol: The Policy Press.

King, D. (1987). *The New Right: Politics, markets and citizenship*. Basingstoke: Macmillan.

Lane, K. (2008). *Lone parents and the challenges of working*. London: Citizens Advice.

Lawton, K. (2008). *Nice work if you can get it*. London: Institute for Public Policy Research.

Lewis, H. (2007). *Destitution in Leeds: The experiences of people seeking asylum and supporting agencies*. York: Joseph Rowntree Charitable Trust.

Lewis, J., & R. Surender (Eds.) (2004). *Welfare state change. Towards a Third Way?* Oxford: Oxford University Press.

Lister, R. (1998). Vocabularies of citizenship and gender: the UK. *Critical Social Policy, 18*(3), 309–331.

Lister, R. (2001). Towards a citizens' welfare state. *Theory, Culture and Society, 18*(2–3), 91–111.

Lister, R. (2002). The dilemmas of pendulum politics: balancing paid work, care and citizenship. *Economy and Society, 31*(4), 520–532.

Lister, R. (2003). Investing in the citizen-workers of the future: Transformations in citizenship and the state under New Labour. *Social Policy & Administration, 37*(5), 427–443.

Lister, R. (2006a). Children (but not women) first: New Labour, child welfare and gender. *Critical Social Policy, 26*(2), 315–335.

Lister, R. (2006b). An agenda for children: investing in the future or promoting well-being in the present? In J. Lewis (Ed.), *Children, changing families and welfare states*. Cheltenham/Northampton Mass.: Edward Elgar.

Lister, R. (2007a). Inclusive citizenship: realizing the potential. *Citizenship Studies, 11*(1), 49–61.

Lister, R. (2007b). From object to subject: including marginalised citizens in policy-making. *Policy & Politics, 35*(3), 437–455.

Lister, R. (2008). Investing in children and childhood: a new welfare paradigm and its implications. *Comparative Social Research, 25*, 383–408.

Lister, R. (2009). Poor citizenship: social rights, poverty and democracy in the late 20th and early 21st centuries. In A. Kessler-Harris & M. Vaudagna (Eds.), *The Two Wests: Social rights and democracy in twentieth century Europe and United States*. Torino: Otto Editore.

Lister, R., N. Smith, S. Middleton & L. Cox (2003) "Young people talk about citizenship: empirical perspectives on theoretical and political debates." *Citizenship Studies, 7*(2),235–253.

Lister, R., F. Williams, A. Anttonenon, et al. (2007). *Gendering citizenship in western Europe*. Bristol: The Policy Press.

Marquand, D. (1991). Civic republicans and liberal individualists: The case of Britain. *Archive Européenne de Sociologie, 32*, 329–344.

Marshall, T. H. (1950). *Citizenship and social class.* Cambridge: Cambridge University Press

McKay, S. (2007). Laying new foundations? Social security reform in 2006. *Social Policy Review 19.* Bristol: The Policy Press.

Millar, J. (2003). Social security: means and ends. In J. Millar (Ed.), *Understanding social security.* Bristol: The Policy Press.

Miller, D. (2000). Citizenship: what does it mean and why is it important? In N. Pearce & J. Hallgarten (Eds.), *Tomorrow's citizens.* London: Institute for Public Policy Research.

Narey, M. (2008). Foreword to J. Reacroft, *Like Any Other Child?* London: Barnardo's.

Needham, C. (2003). *Citizen-consumers: New Labour's marketplace democracy.* London: The Catalyst Forum.

Nixon, J., & D. Prior (2009). Disciplining difference—introduction. *Social Policy and Society, 9*(1), 71–75.

Pattie, C., P. Seyd, & P. Whiteley (2004). *Citizenship in Britain.* Cambridge: Cambridge University Press.

Paxton, W., & S. White (2006). Introduction: The new politics of ownership. In W. Paxton & S. White (Eds.), *The citizen's stake.* Bristol: The Policy Press.

Plant, R. (1988). *Citizenship, rights and socialism.* London: Fabian Society.

Purnell, J. (2008). Speech to "Ready to Work, Skilled for Work" conference, London, January 18.

Rees, A. (1996). T. H. Marshall and the progress of citizenship. In M. Bulmer & A. Rees (Eds.), *Citizenship today.* London: UCL Press.

Sinfield, A. (2007). Response to the DWP Green Paper *"In work, better off,"* unpublished.

Speaker's Commission (1990). *Encouraging citizenship: Report of the Commission on Citizenship.* London: HMSO.

SSAC (2006). *Sanctions in the benefits system.* London: Social Security Advisory Committee.

SSAC (2007). *Reducing dependency, increasing opportunity: Options for the future of welfare to work. Response by the Social Security Advisory Committee.* London: SSAC.

SSAC (2008). *No one written off: Reforming welfare to reward responsibility—the response of the Social Security Advisory Committee.* London: SSAC.

Strategy Unit (2005). *Improving the life chances of disabled children.* London: Cabinet Office.

Surender, R. (2004). Modern challenges to the welfare state and the antecedents of the third way. In J. Lewis & R. Surender (Eds.), *Welfare state change. Towards a Third Way?* Oxford: Oxford University Press.

Taylor-Gooby, P. (2009). *Reframing social citizenship.* Oxford: Oxford University Press.

Warrington, C. (2006). Gypsy and traveller children ought to be engaged more by mainstream services. *Community Care,* 14 September, 38–39.

Weir, S. (2007). Unequal Britain. *Newsletter of the British Institute of Human Rights,* Summer, 10.

Werbner, P., & N. Yuval-Davis (1999). Introduction: Women and the new discourse of citizenship. In N. Yuval-Davis & P. Werbner (Eds.), *Women, citizenship and difference.* London & New York: Zed Press.

White, S. (2003). *The civic minimum.* Oxford: Oxford University Press.

Work and Pensions Committee (2007). *The government's response to Work and Pensions Committee report, Benefits Simplification.* HC 1054. London: Stationery Office.

7

CHANGES IN SOCIAL CITIZENSHIP IN FRANCE IN A COMPARATIVE PERSPECTIVE: "ACTIVATION STRATEGIES" AND THEIR TRACES

Jean-Claude Barbier

INTRODUCTION: SOCIAL PROTECTION SYSTEMS IN AN ERA OF "ACTIVATION"

Beyond the rhetoric of political discourse, one of the main reforms of national social protection systems in the last 20 years preceding the economic crisis has certainly been the gradual introduction of "activation" strategies across an increasing number of policy fields in Europe and the United States (pensions, unemployment insurance, social assistance, family benefits, etc.). This is the reason why one should be careful not to limit the meaning of "activation" to a common (and inevitably vague) political concept. In this chapter, we are looking for the effective transformation of citizenship linked to what we will call the "activation of social protection." To summarize, "activating" systems, individual programs or policy sectors of social protection, has meant making them more "employment-friendly" and more dependent on employment; "activating" people in all sorts of individual ways has basically meant encouraging—and sometimes compelling—them to work more. Many analyses have sought to understand what has rightly been seen as the ideological shift brought about by the reforms. Far-reaching research has also been devoted to identifying institutional change in the systems, documenting macro-trends (Barbier, 2006; Serrano Pascual, 2004; Van Berkel & Møller, 2002). More than 20 years after the introduction of the first reforms that we can call "activation" reforms, it is certainly time that empirically based judgments were made about the consequences of these trends. The reflection is especially timely because Europe has been deeply affected by its economic and political crisis since 2009. This chapter intends to contribute to this task by focusing on "micro-transformations" in citizenship, and especially "social citizenship."

It is possible to list the main areas of social policy where activation reforms have brought significant change in systems and in the lives of citizens/persons. There are four such areas. Firstly, the normative discourses that justify social policy, and benefit distribution in particular, have changed in tone: an ideological shift has been documented to the effect that a common superficial discourse now prevails everywhere, in all European languages, incorporating a rhetoric concerning "duties" and "rights." Originating in the United States, the ideology contends that benefit recipients have been too passive in the past and that it is now fair that they should be more active in return for the support they receive. Secondly, this discourse was universally accompanied by three promises for societies and individuals: (a) poverty would be significantly reduced if people accepted their duty to work; (b) more employment would be created (in some countries, quality jobs) for an increasing number of people (one of the most explicit slogans in this respect was in Denmark in the early 2000s, "*flere i arbejd*"—"more in work"); (c) "social inclusion" would reward individuals who accepted their duties and social exclusion would be reduced. Thirdly, the architecture and instruments of programs (sometimes also the relative levels of benefits) have, to varying degrees, been adapted to enhance the defining role of work (the French *activité professionnelle* is a suitable term, meaning an effective occupational commitment of individuals). This has been translated, for instance, into restrictions on the eligibility for benefits according to behavioral criteria, and sanctions, but it has also meant transforming the funding of social protection (the decrease in social contributions, the introduction of tax credits, etc.). Fourth, social citizenship has effectively been altered, in certain countries, at certain times, and for certain groups. In this chapter, we shall concentrate on this aspect, showing that it is not only the levels of benefits available that have changed, but that much broader "benefits" are involved, that individuals gain from participating in society, including for instance the right to share the advantages of full employment with others, and they also benefit from the "right" not to be pigeonholed or put in a stigmatized category and to have their autonomy as an individual respected. Our contention is that more can be learned in this respect about "activation reform" than general trends and ideological shifts.

However, one should not ignore the fact that disagreements remain in the academic community about exactly how "activation" should be interpreted. There are three main reasons for this. (1) The concept of activation can be used in both broad and narrow senses. In the broader sense, it reaches well beyond what is commonly described as "activation" in political discourse (all sorts of "welfare-to-work" programs and "making-work-pay" policies). (2) There is no such thing as a universal activation rationale (moral and political logic); a diversity of solutions persists. (3) The assessment of the meaning and impact of activation requires knowledge not only about formal rules, but also about both the broader context and the empirical praxis of activation. Last but not least, one needs an analytical and robust notion of citizenship, which is not easy to agree upon if one wants to separate normative debates from analytical research.

True, though not comprehensive, some assessments of the various effects brought by the reforms have started to be published, with the hindsight of about 20 years (Barbier, 2008b; Bothfeld, 2008; Handler & Hasenfeld, 2007; Lødemel & Trickey, 2000; Paugam & Duvoux, 2008; Serrano Pascual, 2004; Van Berkel & Møller, 2002, to quote only a few). Producing an exhaustive research is probably too exacting a task. A thorough assessment would have to begin with the comprehensive identification of all the social (and economic) programs that have been transformed since 1988. And 1988 is an interesting date: it was the year in which the United States adopted the Family Act and with it its famous "workfare" programs; it was also the year that the RMI (*Revenu minimum d'insertion*) was created, a benefit that for the first time on this scale in France included the active support for its recipients normatively based on the republican principle of solidarity. The 1988 RMI Act unambiguously quoted texts from the French Revolution to justify the attribution of a benefit to the poor without having to register as unemployed and actively seek work (Barbier, 2002). Hence "workfare" and "insertion" appear, in hindsight, as two polar examples of "activation." It is beyond the scope of this chapter to inquire about all the various models that have emerged in practically all developed countries since the late 1990s. We hope our readers will excuse us for referring them to other publications: we have shown elsewhere that, even according to cautious estimates, the main conclusion to be drawn is that activation programs and reforms have failed to deliver any of the three promises just mentioned (Barbier, 2009).

We will also leave aside the torrent of papers published by international organizations (the OECD and the European Union are at the forefront): "activation" has indeed been one of their key political recommendations since the mid-1990s and, not surprisingly, these organizations have also been eager to evaluate whether their recommendations have been followed, and to what effect. Economic evaluations have been carried out on the impact or effects of programs in certain countries, over a certain period, in terms of what programs were deemed to have brought to "beneficiaries." However, there is much more to understanding the real effect that "activation strategies" have had on our societies than simply synthesizing the increasingly standardized evaluation discourse disseminated by international organizations and the so-called best practices they promote, in an universalistic and normative manner (Martin, 1998). Contrary to what the producers of such "evidence-based" material claim, the lessons drawn from piecemeal studies can never be used as templates with which to reproduce "best practice" in other contexts. Neither will we address the question of why "activating strategies" have happened at all. We have addressed that question elsewhere (Barbier & Nadel, 2003; Barbier & Théret, 2009): economic and monetary transformations in the capitalist world can only partly explain the pressures for activation, with other explanations being political and institutional. It is in any case certain that many activation programs were designed to contain the costs of social protection (Pierson, 2001).

Section 1 will discuss the notion of citizenship. Starting from T. H. Marshall's notion, we choose to follow J. Goul Andersen's explicit attempt (2005) at bringing forward what he terms an "operational" definition of citizenship. In Section 2, we test this definition against two typical French reforms from the late 1990s and early 2000s, which are considered highly indicative of the type of strategies employed in France to "activate" the poor and the unemployed. Although this is not a comparative study, we are nevertheless able to set these French empirical developments alongside our empirical observations in other countries: Denmark (as a typical example of an "universalistic" "activation strategy") and the United Kingdom (as a typical representative of a "liberal" strategy) provide polar mirror cases. In conclusion, we sum up some of the consequences the reforms have had on the *substance* of what we define as citizenship and put them in the perspective of the current crisis.

Citizenship, Social Citizenship and the "Wage-Labor Nexus"

As Goul Andersen (2005) rightly noted, the notion of citizenship has been discussed in the literature in a huge number of publications and across a number of academic disciplines. The basic approach is normative,[1] and it is not easy to separate facts from values in this discussion. Attempts have been made to devise normative "models of citizenship" (Republican, Liberal, Communitarian, etc.). Because of the influence of the English-speaking tradition on international social policy research, much work has been devoted to a narrower concept of "social citizenship," following T. H. Marshall's influential work. In Chapter 6, Lister notes a key distinction between "popular discourse" and the use of the concept. She rightly observes that the notion of citizenship (*citoyenneté*) is popular in France, yet *citoyenneté sociale* is not used in mainstream public debates about social protection. "*La protection sociale*" is clearly preferred (Barbier & Théret, 2009). On the other hand, an explicit equivalent to "social citizenship" is seldom discussed in French social science literature.

While the reference to the Marshallian conception of citizenship has tended to function as a standard international reference, its limits have also been exposed: the idea that three historical stages order civil, political, and social rights tends to overemphasize the separation of these types of rights. The assumption that these historical steps apply universally is also empirically inadequate (Hassenteufel, 1996; Théret, 1992). The unilateral emphasis placed on rights is a further limit of the Marshallian approach. Finally, it has also been rightly remarked that Marshall's analysis did not take into account the gendering of citizenship. It is nevertheless logical that the concept of "social citizenship" has been discussed more frequently by researchers familiar with one or both of the Beveridgean welfare regimes—the British or the Scandinavian. In the 1990s, the concept was discussed explicitly in a small number of French papers (Birnbaum, 1996; Hassenteufel, 1996; Théret, 1992). The reluctance to adopt a French equivalent of social citizenship might be explained by the normative tradition of the "Republican" approach to citizenship (Schnapper, 1994), and by the rather late insertion of the French case into the international comparison of systems of social protection. However, the use of "*citoyenneté sociale*" has certainly gained greater currency in the last years (Castel, 2006). In comparative research, French social scientists today often use the term when they write in English, although they often do it in a rather loose manner: "social citizenship" generally stands for a *loose equivalent of the current set of rights to social protection* in a certain country. Such an interpretation is not so different, in fact, from mainstream practice in international research projects. To put it in extreme terms, the objectification of the effects of activation strategies on unemployed or assisted persons is too often seen simply as a reduction of social entitlements, and as a direct threat to "social citizenship." Yet we contend that the question is much more complex that an assumed simple relationship between the provision of benefits and the substance of citizenship, for two main reasons: citizenship should be seen from a holistic, societal, perspective; secondly, the concept should be broken into dimensions to be studied empirically.

The Wage-Earner Society: The Difference Full Employment Makes to "Rights and Obligations"

First, one important aspect of the discussion is whether one considers citizenship (not only "social citizenship") in the light of macro-societal processes (economic and political). Here one can draw on the approach advocated by the French "regulation school" (*école de la régulation*[2]) of economists (Boyer, 1986), which stresses the fact that, since Fordism, societies should be considered as "wage-earners societies." Historical regimes of regulation are made up of certain elements, with one essential element being the "*rapport salarial*" ("wage-labor nexus").[3] Extending this framework, Théret has proposed a comprehensive structural approach of "citizenship regimes," contending that the wage-labor nexus is not only an economic but also a *political* nexus, which sets the private status of wage-earners as equal and free in general (1992, 19). Théret's contention is empirically grounded and, in this sense, contemporary citizenship in advanced countries is a "wage-earner citizenship," in which political and social rights are closely interlinked to and overdetermined by the fact that the great majority of citizens are wage-earners. In all welfare regimes, social protection finds a fundamental basis in both economic and political *régulation* processes involving a *citoyenneté salariale* or *citoyenneté fondée sur le salariat*. In certain countries—France and Germany are prime examples—where the mainstream substance of the right to social protection has been linked to the status of wage-earner, the very changes in the prevalence of this status within the working population, as well as its actual quality, should be key indicators of the *possible* consequences of activation.

Indeed, this leads to putting the emphasis on full employment as a determining factor for "wage-earner citizenship." The impact of activation policies such as the UK's "welfare to work," the Danish *"aktivering,"* or the French *"insertion"* programs on the "rights" and "social conditions" of individuals is bound to be profoundly marked by the overall economic circumstances of the country in which the policies are implemented. When "quality jobs" are available and numerous on the market, the quality of citizenship will necessarily be affected very differently by programs designed to "activate" people, when compared to situations where there is a scarcity of jobs on the market, or where only "dead-end" or "precarious" jobs are available, and where the state does not act as a provider of employment of last resort. When, for instance, the state—or the various implementation authorities of "welfare-to-work"–type programs—forcefully demand that individuals take jobs and become (or be again) active, the substantive nature of this demand is different in both cases. All this demonstrates that the meaning of activation reforms cannot be assessed without understanding the wider economic opportunities open to "activated" individuals.[4]

An Analytical Grid

Secondly, our goal in this chapter is to expand on T. H. Marshall's concept. To do this, we will follow Goul Andersen's suggestion of using the notion of citizenship as a "perspective and a benchmark" (2005, 76)—that is to say, take his definition as an instrument with which to identify how the rationale of "activation of social protection" transforms the individual's social conditions. We will add supplementary dimensions to Marshall's original grid. Goul Andersen's approach has the great advantage of being explicitly articulated in a non-normative manner. We focus on the first elements he suggests (rights and duties; social conditions), and we bear in mind the others (participation and identities). The main aspect considered here pertains to social rights (benefits and services) and social conditions (autonomy and actual inequality), but their linkage to political and social participation should certainly not be overlooked. The assessment we shall conduct is conceived of as an attempt to detail empirical manifestations of the changes brought by "activation reform" in one country. Whereas these changes have mostly been considered in the literature in very general terms so far, we go into the details of both French programs analyzed—although we certainly do not claim that a thorough examination of all the dimensions evoked by Goul Andersen will be achieved at the end of the exercise. The six dimensions are derived directly from his definition. "Social conditions" are considered particularly from the perspective of equality and freedom of individuals. To these we add the *access to quality jobs in the context of full employment.*

Box 7.1 The Activation "Machinery" in France (1988–2007)

In a nutshell, the French activation strategy consisted of a combination of five main elements: (1) Employment and training programs, well entrenched, mostly wage-based (with some resemblance to Scandinavian programs). (2) Activation was initially introduced from the late 1980s in unemployment insurance and "assistance" (in 1988, with the introduction of *Revenu mimimum d'insertion* [RMI]), but also later with reforms targeting the remaining regulations leading to possible "inactivity traps," especially for the recipients of minimum income benefits, with the introduction of "incentives" to take jobs. (3) Large sectors of social protection (social services, family and housing benefits) were spared any particular linkage to work incentives. (4) The gradual decrease in employers' social contributions has played a leading role in the activation dynamics, and it was "embedded" into the working time reduction process (1997–2001), along with emerging tax credits—a conjunction of reforms that have thoroughly altered the traditional Bismarckian principle of the dominant funding of social protection via social contributions. (5) Finally, in this period, the introduction of a consistent activation strategy did not really materialize in the domain of "active ageing." Over the whole 20-year period, these features were introduced and implemented in the context of an extremely low job-creation rate (with the exception of two short labor market boom periods in 1986–88 and 1997–2002). Hence, universal access to quality full employment has certainly never featured among the rights of citizenship in France since the late 1980s, unlike in postwar Fordist France and the Danish or Swedish situations in the same years, for instance.

Activating the Insured and Assisted Unemployed (1988–2007)

Since it is not possible to go into the details of the French activation strategies (Barbier, 2008b), the main features are presented in Box 7.1. The period for which both programs selected are considered representative covers the years 1988 to 2007. From 2007 on, a renewed rationale of reform changed the context, and this will not be considered empirically here (for more details, see Barbier, 2009).

Our choice may be seen as broadly representative of the French programs of the decades in question in terms of (1) eligibility for one form or the other of "minimum income" benefits and (2) support for the unemployed and those assisted to enter (or re-enter) the labor market. This situation has not been significantly changed since, because of the economic crisis, despite the reforms introduced in 2008. We will review PARE (*Plan d'aide au retour à l'emploi*—the standard unemployment insurance "individual plan") and RMI (*Revenu minimum d'insertion*—the standard assistance minimum income, which, since 1988, has been accompanied by a personal plan—*contrat d'insertion*). Both of these were applied to working-age beneficiaries and were affected by the activation dynamics of the 1990s. In early 2008, a new reform strategy was implemented, but the crisis destroyed its potential.[5]

Contrary to what has happened in most countries in the European Union, the French assistance and unemployment system has never been really simplified. Before the 2008 reform, the system was made of "three tiers" for working-age individuals: those with a sufficient employment record had rights to unemployment insurance; when their rights were exhausted (and if they had worked more than 5 years) they became eligible for *Allocation spéciale de solidarité* (ASS), the mainstream unemployment assistance benefit; when they were not eligible for either of the former, and if their resources were under a certain threshold, they were eligible for RMI. Except for RMI, traditional requirements for looking for work applied. In all three cases, however, benefit recipients were eligible for various employment programs.

"ACTIVATION REFORM" 1: ACTIVATING UNEMPLOYMENT INSURANCE BENEFITS

In July 2001, ARE (*Aide à la recherche d'emploi*) became the standard provision for all newly unemployed people claiming unemployment insurance. Along with access to benefits, it involved an individualized "project" (recipients negotiated an action plan [PAP, *projet d'action personnalisé*]), including the provision of services (skills assessment, job search and counseling, vocational training courses, and so on). The introduction of this reform was triggered by explicit demands from MEDEF, the main employers' association, which had considered the previous system too "passive." This first empirical example of "activating the unemployed" will be assessed against the grid in Box 7.1.

Freedom of Choice and Autonomy, Access to Quality Services

The scope for individual choice was balanced by the obligations imposed upon (or discussed with) the unemployed. One of the main justifications for the PARE reform advanced by the employers' organizations and the trade unions, which were in favor of it, was that it would lead to enhanced, more effective choice. Basically, new entrants eligible for benefits discussed their *projet d'action personnalisé* with advisors from the PES[6] and ASSEDIC,[7] taking their skills and job experience into consideration, as well as the prevailing labor market conditions. The introduction of the personal project led to a significant increase in the workload[8] of PES employees (who resorted to "creaming" practices when the unemployed were considered able to look for themselves). The formal rights of the unemployed to influence the content of the project and choose between the services available were also inevitably curtailed by the lack of resources. However, this was not a new situation that was brought about by the introduction of "activation." The activation reform simultaneously tended to upgrade services (although not for all) and to reduce the access to training for some.[9]

At the time, France's ranking among European countries in terms of its labor market public expenditure was intermediate, spending more than Britain, Italy, and Spain, for instance, but significantly less than Scandinavia. An important comparative feature of the system was the unequal access to programs and the inadequate service coverage. While in theory specific programs for the long-term unemployed were designed as universal, the number of places was always limited. In the case of temporary employment in the public and nonprofit sectors, for instance, the ratio of offers to the number of potential participants varied from less than 10% to 27% and fell in the 1990s. This feature also explains why, during periods of low employment creation combined with limited provision of places, the PES could not enforce strict rules in place for certain categories of the unemployed. It has also been shown that before the 2001 reform, less than 20% of those insured had access to specific "activation" measures (Tuchszirer, 2002). So while it was possible to present the PARE reform as an opportunity to extend the unemployed's freedom of choice, this assumption was not ultimately vindicated.

Organizations for the unemployed and the unions were critical of the reform from its inception because it did not counter the existing dualism and inequality of services between the more employable and those "harder-to-place" or potentially even "excluded" from the labor market.

Generosity and Duration of Benefits

In 2001, benefit rates were increased and the previous rule according to which they decreased over time was abolished. So overall, generosity was enhanced. In terms of their comparison to the minimum wage, benefits were certainly less generous than in the Scandinavian countries (Barbier, 2005) but more generous than the UK's flat-rate benefits. Moreover, while the social partners had decided to shorten the duration of the benefits as of January 2004, the reform was abandoned by the government just after its defeat in the French regional elections, and after law courts ruled the reform unlawful. While the ratio of the unemployed eligible for insurance (vs. for assistance) had tended to decrease in the 1980s and 1990s (Daniel & Tuchszirer, 1999), this trend was reversed during the course of the PARE reform and remained fairly stable (before the economic crisis). While mean figures certainly conceal wide discrepancies between part-timers and full-timers, the amount paid to beneficiaries did not decline over the period in question.

All in all, in the first period, the duration of benefits remained practically unchanged by the reform, while the conditions for eligibility were eased for recipients with limited work experience and benefits were upgraded. In this respect, activation went hand in hand with the enhancement of social rights, firstly in the context of the unions negotiating the initial reform with employers' associations and, secondly, the government canceling the second reform after court rulings in April 2004. However, from 2005 to 2006, the shorter eligibility period was again introduced. Although this cannot be compared unfavorably with other continental countries, it was much less generous than in Denmark or Sweden, for example.[10]

Sanctions and Conditionality

There is a lack of data as to the precise effects of the enhanced activation dynamics on the unemployment insurance system. In France, there is no automatic link between a person's registration as unemployed (at the PES) and his or her eligibility to receive a benefit. Before the economic crisis began in 2008, the numbers of those leaving the PES (ANPE) register had remained fairly constant for years (when the obvious influence of labor market fluctuations is taken out). The 2001 reform did not alter the formal provisions regarding sanctions significantly. However, while formal sanctions before 1992 had been very marginal when compared with the rate of leaving the PES register, a first shift was experienced in the early 1990s: the monthly mean number of sanctions in 1991 was about 4,000 (compared to roughly 130,000 who left the register for unknown reasons) and rose to more than 16,000 in 1993, particularly due to the implementation of a special program for the long-term unemployed. Subsequently, it fell again to a level of about 7,000. At the beginning of 2001, the rate jumped to about 16,000. Although it is impossible to attribute this rise directly to the PARE reform, this number rose again sharply from 2001: the mean number was between 30,000 and 40,000 monthly after 2004. If the proposed January 2004 reform had been implemented, in the context of increasing sanctions, the general conclusion— and again with the caveat that independently assessed data are scarce—would have to be that activation would in this case have involved a downgrading of rights. Following a new reform introduced in 2005, the sanction regime was formally tightened.

Participation in Policy Formulation and Implementation

As a mainstream program, PARE was managed by the unemployment insurance fund, which was jointly administered by social partners in ever closer cooperation with ANPE, the other branch of the PES. There was intense and heated public debate about the reform, unlike with previous reforms of the unemployment insurance, which had been passed "by stealth." The actions and arguments of political parties and trade unions eventually succeeded in heading off any stricter regulations on active job-seeking or new definitions of what a "decent job"[11] was.

This led to increased political participation compared to previous reforms. The main aspects that were widely debated were (and they have remained so since, even into the crisis): (i) What demands can be legitimately imposed on the insured unemployed? (ii) Precisely what is the nature of the services to be provided to the unemployed in the new system, as opposed to rhetorical promises and formal rules? (iii) Would the new system reduce or reinforce the existing dualism of service provision to the *insured* unemployed and the *assisted* unemployed? (iv) What new balance was to be established between the role of the unemployment insurance system managed by the social partners on one hand and the role of the state, as the actor responsible for the employment service and for guaranteeing the principle of equal treatment, on the other hand? At the end of the day, the generosity of benefits was broadly maintained,[12] and the debate also resulted in the cancellation of the most controversial aspects of the initial blueprint for the reforms—namely, the imposition of stricter behavioral requirements on the insured unemployed until 2005. The legal definition of the obligations of the unemployed remained unchanged, despite proposals to the contrary from the employers' side (Tuchszirer, 2002). The duration of the benefits was reduced in 2004–05, in the context of the regular negotiations between the social partners who regularly negotiate about this parameter, depending on the cycle of the economy.

Age and Gender: Equality of Opportunity

In the past, the quality offered by "activation measures" and the quality and level of unemployment compensation have been highly unequal (in terms of the younger compared to the older, women compared to men, for example) (Daniel & Tuchszirer, 1999). These inequalities persisted (Tuchszirer, 2002). Moreover, critics of the new reform argue forcefully that, because of insufficient funding of the new services and because of new orientations in the provision of training courses, the existing dualism was reinforced between those eligible for insurance benefit and those eligible for assistance benefit, and between the hard-to-place and the more employable. This latter inequality, however, has been a permanent feature of the French system, and even one experienced—although with a lower relative prevalence—in universalistic systems such as in Denmark (Abrahamson, 2001). Recent surveys about the comparative access of women and men to various types of employment programs (and especially younger women compared to younger men) have shown that gender inequality is still prevalent: labor market programs closer to the mainstream labor market are gender-biased in favor of men, whereas vocational training programs and *insertion* programs, which are less effective, are gender-biased towards women. We conclude, then, that the implementation of this reform has not significantly altered the previous bias against the young and women in France.

"ACTIVATION REFORM" 2: INTRODUCING THE RMI, THE MAINSTREAM MINIMUM INCOME BENEFIT AND ITS INDIVIDUAL CONTRACT

From its inception in 1988, the RMI was designed as a universal benefit, the right to which was explicitly linked to citizen participation in the community. In this respect, the RMI would pertain to a (Republican) universalistic model. At the same time, it was also designed as a safety-net benefit. In this second respect, the RMI would appear to be more at home in the liberal welfare model. This mixed character can also be seen in the local variations of its implementation.

Freedom of Choice and Autonomy, Offer of Services

When compared to other programs in other countries, one distinctive feature of the RMI was—even after its reform in 2004—the absence of any obligation to work.[13] Local implementation introduced different interpretations of this rule (Mahé, 2002), but nationally, a "punitive" orientation never prevailed during this period. Plans were discussed with beneficiaries and an individualized contract was drawn up. The degree to which there was effective consideration of the latter varied according to local circumstances and according to the social worker's discretion and local labor market conditions. It was overwhelmingly assumed that all recipients should engage in a series of activities, which, in the medium or long term, should result in their integration into the labor market (*insertion professionnelle*). However, particularly in the case of the long-term unemployed (Demazière, 1992), the imposition of a strict "obligation to work" upon the recipient was always limited. Only about half the recipients registered with the public employment service.

Until 2007, and in a comparative perspective, the activation rationale behind the RMI was certainly not punitive and, in relative terms, was positively affected by the explicit link it established with the citizenship of the beneficiaries (in the political sense). However, the services offered were of low quality—due to the lack of resources and the lack of employment opportunities available. In 2004, after a failed partial reform, the RMI was further decentralized, which meant that the scope for local variations was extended. Yet variation had already existed (Bouchoux et al., 2004). Beneficiaries of the RMI (as well as their families) had been among the priority target groups for employment programs since the early 1990s. Yet because of the limited number of places available in such programs (as with those for insured unemployed people), the proportion of RMI recipients who were eligible in practice was always lower than the proportion of the insured unemployed, although when labor market conditions became more favorable, the proportion of RMI recipients grew. Clearly, the range of choices open to RMI recipients was narrower and of lower quality. However, quality should also be assessed with regard to the variety of social services. Many RMI recipients—whatever their limited autonomy and choice—had access to social services other than directly work-related activities (traditional social services, counseling, medical or housing support, etc.). Only some[14] of the "*contrats d'insertion*" were concerned with "*insertion économique*" or "*insertion professionnelle*" (i.e., a work or training content). Moreover, depending on their own choices and strategies, RMI recipients could be engaged in employment of some sort without having signed any *contrat d'insertion*. Indeed, this was increasingly encouraged.[15] All in all, the quality of services for assisted persons seems to have been lower than in the case of the insured, and universality was clearly lacking.

Generosity and Duration

The RMI rates for one person were fixed at roughly half the minimum wage in order to ensure that engaging in employment would always generate additional income for a workless household. To counter supposed "unemployment traps," new regulations enhanced these incentives. RMI rates were obviously less generous than comparable benefits in Scandinavian countries, but compared favorably with those in the UK. A high proportion of beneficiaries were long-term recipients. Statistics showed, for instance, that 9% had been eligible since the start of the program in 1989.[16] Long-term recipients compared unfavorably in terms of employability and social conditions. Long-term RMI recipients, especially those living alone, thus undoubtedly belonged to the socially excluded in France, were entitled to a relatively low-value benefit, and had a lower quality of citizenship.

Sanctions and Conditionality

This explains why social provision in the case of the RMI always compared unfavorably with analogous programs in Scandinavian countries. Conditionality, on the other hand, was very limited, in contrast to the situation in the UK and Denmark. When the RMI Act was passed in 1988, one of the main debates in Parliament was directly related to the theme of "welfare to work" or "workfare": a controversy arose over the "compensation" that beneficiaries were supposed to give society in return for their benefit. Yet the RMI was eventually introduced as an explicit entitlement, national rather than local, differential and nonconditional (Belorgey, 1996). While a minority of members of Parliament favored the total absence of any link between entitlement and the recipient's behavior, this was not the case for the majority. The compromise resulted in what Belorgey has termed an "ambiguous situation," in which the benefit that emerged was somewhere in between a totally nonconditional benefit and a benefit that was conditional on compliance in the form of taking up the *insertion* opportunities he or she was offered. However, in fact only a very small proportion (5% to 6%) of the claimants were ever sanctioned for noncompliance. Again, local implementation led to significant discrepancies in this respect.

Although not representative of the overall situation, one interesting study of two contrasting cases shows that at least two types of implementation occurred at the local level, with sanctions differing considerably (Mahé, 2002). In a first type, the stigma attached to the benefit was minimized; it was effectively implemented in a universal manner, as if the entire population may need to make use of the RMI at some time in their lives. This form of implementation was accompanied by the strict monitoring of beneficiaries, and a strict sanctions regime. A key factor was the fact that the local market yielded interesting opportunities both in terms of quality and quantity. Hence, a contract between the employment (or social) services appeared credible in terms of outcomes for the recipients if they complied with the obligations on their side of the contract. In such cases, sanctions were considered more legitimate. Under a second type of local implementation, the target population tended to be more homogeneous and less employable, and local labor market opportunities were scarce. In such situations, only the more employable would leave the program early, while social workers tended to classify the others as traditional targets for medium- or long-term income support. In such cases, sanctions were rarer and were certainly not considered legitimate, either by social workers or by recipients. Mahé commented in her study of both local sites that recipients in the first case "express the perception that they are fully-fledged citizens more often" (2002, 74). This analysis is consistent with a wider and more representative analysis (Bouchoux et al., 2004).

Participation in Policy Formulation and Implementation

As a universal citizenship right, the RMI was voted through unanimously across the political spectrum. Access to and the exercise of the rights of political citizenship figured explicitly among the objectives of the legislation (Articles 1 and 2 of the 1988 Act). Despite recurring controversy about the evaluation of the program over the years, and particularly over its effectiveness in terms of actual integration of unemployed persons into employment, no government sought to reform it before 2004, and even then the reform failed and the basic tenets of the program were not altered for the overwhelming majority of recipients. Real reform was only implemented from 2007 to 2008, after a period of consultation of social actors, especially nonprofit organizations. Actual implementation, which started from 2009, was then directly confronted with the aggravation of the employment crisis.

Age and Gender: Equality of Opportunity

Now replaced by the RSA (*Revenu de solidarité active*), the RMI was a typically biased program in terms of the age groups it targeted. Because it was part of the "third tier," so to speak, of the unemployment compensation system (as opposed to the mainstream insurance system and unemployment assistance benefit), the fact that older people were eligible was always an indication of persistent inequalities in the labor market. This was especially true for long-term recipients, who were more likely to be in the age bracket of 50 to 54. As for gender bias in the program, this was associated with the other characteristics of the recipients: qualifications and the gender bias in the access to employment programs. For instance, female recipients of RMI were more likely to sign insertion contracts, but these were predominantly oriented towards training courses and temporary employment in the nonprofit and public sectors.

CONCLUSION

From the empirical analysis of two emblematic activation reforms in France (which are contrasted with the British and Danish cases), five essential conclusions may be drawn, which illustrate the complexity of the influence of activation reforms upon citizenship. This influence has certainly not remained stable over the years and across all the benefits available in any given system of social protection. Institutional constraints, economic developments, territorial inequalities, and political activity all play a role in eventual outcomes. This is especially the case in the midst of the present crisis: as new austerity measures are expected by the financial markets and announced by the French government, it is of course extremely difficult to predict the actual consequences for citizens.

The first conclusion is that, even having undergone "activation" reforms, France has nevertheless remained in a sort of "intermediary" position between the generous Scandinavian system and the liberal-market UK approach. After the reforms, the common tendency towards activation across the three countries left them in the same relative position to one another. However "activated" it has become, the French system remained hybrid: it has clearly manifested its "incompatibility with universalism" in practice, although it has maintained this commitment in rhetorical terms. On the other hand, it has also been unable (and unwilling) to go down the UK route of strict punitive, self-help programs. This has produced results with regard to social citizenship.

The French system's incompatibility with universalism was illustrated by the case of the RMI, the entitlements and rights of which, although theoretically universal, were *de facto* targeted. This can be explained by many factors (overloaded services, scarcity of resources, targeting and means-testing mechanisms), but it led to polarization (the opposition between quality mainstream insurance-linked provisions and lower quality assistance-linked provisions, and also to the increasing emergence of a working poor stratum in French society). Here, employment and training programs are a case in point. In times of very bad labor market conditions, the French state only achieved the function of employer of last resort to a limited extent (and at times very reluctantly). Accordingly, the services delivered by the public employment service were of lower quality than those provided in, for instance, the Scandinavian countries. Moreover, benefits were much less generous than in these latter countries, when compared with mean minimum market wages. Given such circumstances, the comparatively limited enforcement of the obligation to work would appear logical. This activation pattern also appears consistent with the wider mix of policies, which, since the late 1980s, has gradually shifted towards an emphasis on the overall reduction of employers' social contributions, rather than emphasizing the incentive for individuals to take jobs. Thus, the limited pressure that was put on the unemployed/the assisted was linked to both (i) a *de facto* acknowledgement of scarce labor market opportunities and (ii) the acceptance of a certain degree of freedom of choice and balance between legitimate individual needs and the legitimate demands of society. As a result, the French transforming system has simultaneously displayed elements of an upgrading of social citizenship and moves in the opposite direction, depending on schemes, programs, locations, modes of implementation, and target populations and groups.

The second feature was related precisely to the differential treatment of groups: the French system showed a persistent gender bias. Caught in their legal "universalistic" tradition, French policymakers have only recently begun to address the gender question in social policy seriously (in the second half of the 1990s). This situation is obviously linked to the gender division of labor, but also to the issue of de-familialization. The third important characteristic pertaining to a transformed, "activated," French "social citizenship" is linked to the treatment of the young in social policy. Despite significant exceptions,[17] over the past 20 years the young have tended to be eligible for lower-quality social benefits and provision of programs overall. This is also linked to the French "familialistic" tradition (the way the young are treated in French social policy is certainly determined by this historical dependency). Many rights, entitlements, and benefits for those under the age of 20 to 25 still depended on the family policy system and were not individualized. Moreover, the young faced worse conditions than adults and older employees in terms of labor market participation and the precariousness of their employment (Barbier, 2004), especially the less qualified and young women. Extreme examples of the unfavorable situation of the young also include territorial and ethnic discrimination against certain groups (Castel, 2006). Activation reforms in this respect certainly did not deliver positive outcomes in terms of social citizenship for these groups, nor for the young in general. Although certainly not as marked as the Italian one (see Chapter 8), this fragmentation of rights and opportunities has remained a feature of recent French reforms.

The fourth conclusion concerns the particular form taken by "political" participation as part of a wider wage-earner citizenship (mostly in the sense of policy formulation and program implementation). Each in its own specific way, the activation reforms studied above have a common element. In the RMI program, *insertion professionnelle* retained the positive function of political integration. The last-resort safety net was characterized explicitly by the fact that political citizenship was seen as a higher objective than mere participation in the labor market for reasons of self-help; accordingly, value was also placed on participation in "social" or "intermediate" activities. Although questioned to an increasing extent, the latter activities did not disappear into some labor market participation panacea, as seems to have been the case in the UK for instance. While this characteristic was obviously explained in terms of longer-term history, this did not prevent a subsequent sharp diversion in the course of policy after 2007. The PARE reform illustrates another aspect of the complex interaction between political and social rights. When France is compared to Scandinavian countries, for instance, "collective" participation in the definition of rights is characterized by the dominant role of government and the relatively subordinated role ascribed to social partners. Yet, unlike under British reforms, the PARE reform and the subsequent cancellation of reforms in 2004 demonstrate that there had developed a significant margin for dissent, negotiation, and action by unions, union members, and civil society. Just before the crisis, this was again demonstrated when the government organized a process of significant consultation with social actors ahead of the passing in Parliament of the RSA Act in 2007.

Finally, reforms introduced to foster job creation and the demand for new employees through the fundamental overhaul of the social contributions system were never able to deliver full employment: for all the talk of "activation," the "wage-earner citizenship" that existed in the 1970s was replaced by growing segmentation in the labor market and, as a consequence, growing inequality in access to wage-earner citizenship. Empirical evidence drawn from the design and implementation of the programs reviewed here tends to discourage any analysis in terms of a generalized downgrading of social citizenship's "rights," and an accumulation of "duties" in the direction of an overwhelming liberal and residual welfare system dominated the requirements of the labor market. True, as we have seen, effects varied across the policy fields. Yet, for all their "solidaristic" promises, French activation reforms in the 1980s and the 1990s obviously did not deliver their promise of integrating everyone into the labor market. While to a certain extent (employment programs) activation strategies contributed to keeping a significant proportion of the working-age population in tune with the needs of the labor market, the growing polarization of statuses was not countered by the trend towards activation. Behind the comprehensive "solidarity" logic, the inequality of access to social and wage-earner citizenship came to be an increasingly blatant failure in 2005–06. Such realities were bound to be emphasized even more with the economic downturn from 2009.

More General Lessons

Could more general lessons be drawn from this analysis of two typical French programs? Comparative indications relative to the well-documented cases of the UK and Denmark are provided in the text, which suggest that the impact of "activation" on social citizenship strategies has also been very uneven across countries (see Chapter 8, and for an eastern European case Chapter 11). Country variations, documented elsewhere (Barbier, 2006, 2009), are thus made up of sectoral, temporal, and territorial variations within one single country. The main lesson, perhaps, is that once general trends are left aside and the many dimensions of substantive citizenship are considered in empirical terms, the assessment of the far-reaching group of reforms that one can categorize as "activation" ultimately appears ambiguous and mixed. There is, moreover, one aspect that was not dealt with in detail in this chapter: national "normative frameworks" influence the judgment of the impact of activation reforms on the lives of citizens. Countries differ in their political culture or the "moral and political logic" according to which they operate (Rothstein, 1998). Reforms introducing stricter demands may be seen as "acceptable" in a particular national context and "unacceptable" in another. To use the interesting German notion, some reforms will not be "*zumutbar*"[18] (Barbier, 2008a). This does not mean, however, that citizens and groups of citizens will not experience a relative degradation of their situation (Goul Andersen, 2005). However, in this domain, studies and surveys that are truly comparable between countries are very rare: national exploratory studies exist (Paugam & Duvoux, 2008, for France; Bothfeld, 2008, for Germany; and Bothfeld & Betzelt, 2011). Yet two problems arise when seeking to conduct a really comparative appraisal of the question for two reasons. The first is the difficult question of how to objectify the legitimacy of reforms: such support and legitimization only takes place at the national level, in a particular polity and it is always difficult to assess this legitimacy and support, which varies according to population groups as well as over time and with adaptation to the reforms implemented in a given national setting. Secondly, considerable national variation has persisted in this respect (Barbier, 2008b). In certain countries, the strategy for activating social protection, including its reinforced behavioral demands, has over the years been accompanied by a broad and open public debate. In the Scandinavian countries, where just such a debate took place, the construction of a broad legitimizing consensus, albeit of a conflictual nature, has been based on the perception of extensive reciprocity (Rothstein, 1998). The situation has been very different when activation reforms were introduced in other countries, such as Germany, France, or the UK. However, appraising this question in comparative terms is a difficult task because legitimization processes occur within national boundaries (or, sometimes, within infra-national spaces). The national solidarity and reciprocity formed by these legitimization processes does not leave the nation state level—at least so far—to the EU level (Barbier, 2008b). On all these questions, however, no really comparative cross-national research exists to date. The major difficulty lies in rendering the different national normative settings compatible with each other, while at the same time distancing themselves from their own inevitable national bias[19]; in this respect, the widest contrast existing among countries in Europe is perhaps to be seen between central Europe (see Chapter 11) and the continental countries like France and Germany (Barbier & Knuth, 2011).

NOTES

1 Schnapper (1994) identifies two main normative traditions, which she terms "pluralist" (relating to Burke's thought) on one side and "unitary" (relating to Rousseau's theory of general interest).

[2] Distinct from the English meaning, "*régulation*" is not "regulation"; it is the process through which the economic system (and society in general) is able to adjust and reproduce itself in articulation with other processes of social integration (self-adaptation).

3 There are no easy equivalents for the French notion of *salariat*, with its multiple meanings: (i) the social group (class) composed of all the wage-earners, as opposed to the social group of employers (*patronat*); (ii) an individual's social status/condition as a wage-earner, a status that has also a political dimension.

4 Interestingly, Sen (1999, 94–96) has pointed out the very different situation in this respect of the United States and Europe, although he does not explicitly address the wide divergences existing across Europe.

[5] With respect to the policy areas we are reviewing, two main reforms were introduced in 2008: one was the merger of the unemployment insurance funds (ASSEDIC) and the Employment Service (see next footnote); the second one was a complete overhaul of the RMI benefit, replaced by *Revenu de solidarité active* (RSA).

[6] In the French system, the benefit was delivered by ASSEDIC and registration was made at the PES (ANPE [*Agence Nationale Pour l'Emploi*]), but services were delivered by both. From Jan. 1, 2008, regional funds and ANPE were merged into a new public service, "Pôle Emploi."

7 The regional unemployment insurance fund.

8 Basically, the French PES was, in comparative terms, underfunded and understaffed; the adjustment to these bad conditions was often made through the quality and quantity of service delivery. Recent adjustments to more "individualized" action plans echo the difficulties experienced in Denmark when individual action plans were introduced. With the merger, and the concomitant economic slump, the PES entered into a phase of acute crisis from 2009.

9 Although this access was also very unequal before the reform (Tuchszirer, 2002), mainstream vocational courses tended to be shorter, less concerned with the long-term employability of the unemployed.

10 Before the crisis, the lowest assistance benefit served by ASSEDIC was (January 2007) €430 monthly (to compare with an amount of €1254 for the national monthly minimum wage—this amount was before social contributions, so that the net minimum monthly wage [full-time job] was a little over € 1,000). After the reform, the mainstream insurance benefit was served for 23 months, once recipients could demonstrate that they contributed their social contributions for 16 out of the previous 26 months. This period was reduced to 12 months for those who contributed only 12 out of the previous 20 months. For the less employed (6 months out of the 22 previous ones), the period was reduced to 7 months.

11 At the time, French law did not define what a decent job was; rather, reasons were defined in broad principles, which allowed the unemployed to refuse a job (or training) offer (articles L 311–315 and 351–317 of the Labour Code). The law was altered in 2008 but could not really be implemented because of the twin consequences of the economic slump and the merger alluded to above.

12 In the first phase of the economic crisis (2008–10), benefits were globally maintained. In certain cases, benefits were even extended to new recipients, such as the young who had patchy employment careers. However, this situation started to alter from 2010.

13 At the end of 2005, around 15% of RMI recipients nevertheless had access to a special employment program.

14 This part is not easily calculated, because of the limits of the monitoring system. Statistics showed, in 1993, that two thirds of activities mention either job search or various forms of work. Data indicate that about 40% of recipients only had signed a "*contrat d'insertion.*"

15 At the end of 2006, the ministry of social affairs reported that 190,000 RMI recipients combined some form of employment with their eligibility. This meant that the overwhelming majority of RMI recipients who were employed did not have access to special programs.

16 As a universal benefit, RMI catered for a very heterogeneous population. A very common assessment among practitioners was that the RMI target group comprised one third of recipients who left the program rapidly (Afsa & Guillemot [1999] showed that one third left in less than 6 months). At the other end of the spectrum, one third experienced important problems preventing them from a rapid return to the labor market. National statistics in the early 2000s estimated the proportion of recipients present in the program for more than 4 years at around 25%.

17 One was the Socialist government flagship program of the *Nouveaux services-emplois jeunes* (NSEJ), providing 5-year "temporary" jobs in the public and nonprofit sectors (1997–2002).

18 The verb *zumuten* points to the demand made from someone, and there is a moment when, if demands are too high, it is not possible to *zumuten* (to accept them). Hence *zumutbar* and *Zumutbarkeit*.

19 I especially discuss this point with regard to central European ideological and cultural political frames of reference (Barbier, 2008b, 208–212).

REFERENCES

Abrahamson, P. (2001). L'activation des politiques sociales scandinaves, le cas du Danemark. In C. Daniel & B. Palier, *La protection sociale en Europe, le temps des réformes* (pp. 123–140). Paris: DREES, Documentation française.

Afsa, C., & D. Guillemot (1999). Plus de la moitié des sorties du RMI se font grâce à l'emploi, *INSEE Première, 632*, février.

Andersen, J. Goul (2005). Citizenship, unemployment and welfare policy. In J. Goul Andersen, A. M. Guillemard, P. H. Jensen, & B. Pfau-Effinger (Eds.), *The new face of welfare. Social policy, marginalization and citizenship* (pp. 75–92). COST A13 Book Series. Bristol: The Policy Press.

Barbier, J.-C. (2002). Peut-on parler d' "activation" de la protection sociale en Europe ? *Revue française de sociologie, 43–2*, avril-juin, 307–332.

Barbier, J.-C. (2004). A comparative analysis of "employment precariousness" in Europe. In M. T. Letablier (Ed.), *Learning from employment and welfare policies in Europe* (pp. 7–18). Available at http://www.xnat.org.uk/

Barbier, J.-C. (2005). Citizenship and the activation of social protection: A comparative approach. . In J. Goul Andersen, A. M. Guillemard, P. H. Jensen, & B. Pfau-Effinger (Eds.), *The new face of welfare. Social policy, marginalization and citizenship* (pp. 113–134). COST A13 Book Series. Bristol: Policy Press.

Barbier, J.-C. (2006) (with N. S. Sylla & A. Eydoux). *Analyse comparative de l'activation de la protection sociale en France, Grande-Bretagne, Allemagne et Danemark, dans le cadre des lignes directrices de la stratégie européenne pour l'emploi.* Rapport pour la DARES (ministère du travail), CEE, janvier. http://eucenter.wisc.edu/OMC/Papers/EES/barbier.pdf

Barbier, J.-C. (2008a). *La longue marche vers l'Europe sociale.* Paris: PUF, Le Lien Social.

Barbier, J.-C. (2008b). L' "activation" de la protection sociale, existe-t-il un modèle français. In A. M. Guillemard (Ed.), *Où va la protection sociale.* (pp. 165–182). Paris: PUF, Le Lien Social.

Barbier, J.-C. (2009).. Le *workfare* et l'activation de la protection sociale, vingt ans après: beaucoup de bruit pour rien? Contribution à un bilan qui reste à faire. *Lien social et politiques, 61*, Printemps, 21–34.

Barbier, J.-C., & M. Knuth (2011). Activating social protection against unemployment, France and Germany compared. *Sozialer Fortschritt, 60*(1–2), 15–24.

Barbier, J.-C., & H. Nadel (2003). *La flessibilità del lavoro et dell'occupazione*, introduzione di L. Castelluci e E. Pugliese. Roma: Donzelli.

Barbier, J.-C., & B. Théret (2009). *Le système français de protection sociale*. Repères, Paris: La Découverte, 2è ed.

Belorgey, J. M. (1996). Pour renouer avec l'esprit initial du RMI. In "Vers un revenu minimum inconditionnel," *Revue du MAUSS semestrielle*, n°7, premier semestre. Paris: La Découverte, pp. 297–299.

Birnbaum, P. (1996). Sur la citoyenneté. *L'Année sociologique, 46 (1)* 57–85.

Bothfeld, S. (2008). *Individual autonomy, a normative and analytical core of welfare statehood*. Paper for the RC 19 conference, Stockholm, September 6.

Bothfeld, S., & S. Betzelt (2011). How do activation policies affect social citizenship? The issue of autonomy. In S. Betzelt & S. Bothfeld (Eds.), *Activation and labour market reforms: Challenges to social citizenship* (pp. 15–34). Basingstoke: Palgrave McMillan.

Bouchoux, J., Y. Houzel, & J. L. Outin (2004). Revenu minimum d'insertion et transitions : une analyse des inégalités territoriales. *Revue Française des affaires sociales, 4*, octobre-décembre, 107–132.

Boyer, R. (1986). *La flexibilité du travail en Europe*. Paris: La Découverte.

Castel, R. (2006). La discrimination négative, le déficit de citoyenneté des jeunes de banlieue. *Annales, Histoire, Sciences sociales, 4*, juillet-août, 777–808.

Daniel, C., & C. Tuchszirer (1999). *L'État face aux chômeurs*. Paris: Flammarion.

Demazière, D. (1992). *Le chômage en crise ? La négociation des identités des chômeurs de longue durée*. Lille: Presses Universitaires de Lille.

Handler, J. F., & Y. Hasenfeld (2007). *Blame welfare, ignore poverty and inequality*. Cambridge: Cambridge University Press.

Hassenteufel, P. (1996). L'État providence et les métamorphoses de la citoyenneté. *L'Année sociologique*, 46(1),127–149.

Lødemel, I., & H. Trickey (2000). *An offer you can't refuse: Workfare in international perspective*. Bristol: Policy Press.

Mahé, T. (2002). Le RMI à Rennes et à St Etienne: des dynamiques locales différentes. *Recherches et Prévisions*, CNAF, n° 67, Paris, pp 67–75.

Martin, J. P. (1998). What works among active labour market policies: evidence from OECD countries' experiences. *Labour Market and Social Policy Occasional Papers, 35*, Paris.

Paugam, S., & N. Duvoux (2008). *La régulation des pauvres*. Paris: PUF.

Pierson, P. (Ed.) (2001). *The new politics of the welfare state*. Oxford: Oxford University Press.

Rothstein, B. (1998). *Just institutions matter: The moral and political logic of the universal welfare state*. Cambridge: Cambridge University Press.

Schnapper, D. (1994). *La communauté des citoyens, sur l'idée moderne de nation*. Paris: Gallimard.

Sen, A. (1999). *Development as freedom*. New York: Anchor Books.

Serrano Pascual, A. (2004). Conclusion: Towards convergence of European activation policies? In A. Serrano Pascual (Ed.), *Are activation policies converging in Europe? The European employment strategy for young people* (pp. 497–518). Brussels: ETUI.

Théret, B. (1992). Esquisse d'une conception topologique et régulationniste de l'interdépendance entre le rapport salarial et l'Etat-providence. *Cahiers du GRETSE, 11*, décembre.

Tuchszirer, C. (2002). *Réforme de l'assurance chômage, du PAP au PAP-ND, le programme d'action personnalisée pour un nouveau départ*, Document de travail, n° 02.02, février, Noisy le Grand: IRES.

Van Berkel, R., & I. H. Møller (2002). *Active social policies in the EU: Inclusion through participation?* Bristol: The Policy Press.

8

ITALY: A TERRITORIAL AND GENERATIONAL DIVIDE IN SOCIAL CITIZENSHIP

Valeria Fargion

THE ITALIAN "ORIGINAL MODEL OF CITIZENSHIP"

Within the overall framework of this book, this chapter will focus on the case of Italy and show whether and to what extent recent social policy reforms reflect a post-Marshallian conception of citizenship that—as Johansson and Hvinden suggest in Chapter 2—seems to be emerging across Europe. However, if Italy never followed the path that Marshall identified for the development of citizenship in the first place, the question appears rather more complicated. As I shall seek to illustrate, in the case of Italy the "original model of citizenship" is profoundly different from the British one, and these origins can hardly be ignored if we are to fully grasp all the subsequent steps in the development and combination of civil, political, and social rights.

To make my point quite clear, I want to recall first of all that throughout his famous lecture on "Citizenship and Social Class," Marshall built his theoretical arguments by referring constantly and exclusively to the historical experience of England. Among the many examples that one could choose, the following passage appears particularly indicative: "If I am right in my contention that citizenship has been a developing institution in England at least since the latter part of the seventeenth century, then it is clear its growth coincides with the rise of capitalism, which is a system not of equality but of inequality. Here is something that needs explaining. How is it that these two opposing principles could grow and flourish side by side on the same soil?" (Marshall, 1965, 92). Yet, during the decades that followed, Marshall's considerations on the virtuous cumulative process of civil, political, and social rights were often decoupled from the specific case of Britain, meaning that sweeping and misleading generalizations developed. Luckily, this was not always the case. In the introduction to a collection of Marshall's essays published in 1965, Seymour Lipset acknowledged that Marshall's theorization was nation-bound in the following terms:

> Many of T.H. Marshall's writings have been concerned with the emergence of a modern class structure based on the divisions inherent in industrial society in his native Britain. This was the first country to experience the industrial revolution, and, more significantly from the sociological point of view, it is one of the few nations that have successfully admitted the new classes of industrial society—first the bourgeoisie and later the workers—into the polity, while preserving the monarchy's and the aristocracy's traditional status and aura of legitimacy. In most of the European nations, the aristocracy resisted granting rights to the new strata, a reaction that often had the effect of inhibiting economic growth or precipitating revolution. In Britain alone, of the major European countries, economic development was paralleled by peaceful changes in the social and political structure that made a stable democracy possible. (Marshall, 1965, ix)

But if Lipset is moving in the right direction when he points out that Britain represents more of an exception than the rule, and I believe this to be the case, then it becomes crucial to shed light on the path individual countries have followed in addressing similar problems, on the specific constellation of internal and external factors that have influenced the way in which societies admitted new strata to participation in the polity and hence defined the actual profile of citizenship and its evolution over time. By taking this approach, the contrast between the British and the Italian experience could hardly be greater. Nothing of the following description by Marshall fits the Italian case:

> Citizenship requires a bond of a different kind, a direct sense of community membership based on loyalty to a civilization which is a common possession. It is a loyalty of free men endowed with free rights and protected by a common law. Its growth is stimulated both by the struggle to win those rights and by their enjoyment when won. We see this clearly in the eighteen century, which saw the birth, not only of modern civil rights but also of modern national consciousness. The familiar instruments of modern democracy were fashioned by the upper classes and then handed down, step by step to the lower: political journalism for the intelligentsia was followed by newspapers for all who could read, public meetings, propaganda campaigns and associations for the furtherance of public causes. Repressive measures and taxes were quite unable to stop the flood. And with it came a patriotic nationalism, expressing the unity underlying these

controversial outbursts. How deep or widespread this was is difficult to say, but there can be no doubt about the vigour of its outward manifestation. (Marshall, 1965, 101)

What happened in Italy instead? Although this work does not aim to provide a historical account of the development of citizenship in Italy, for the purposes of my argument I need to pay special attention to the very origins of the Italian state. Notably, among the European nation-states, Italy was a latecomer. The unification of the country only occurred in 1861 under the House of Savoy, which had previously reigned over Piedmont and Sardinia. Most importantly, involvement in the national liberation movement—the *Risorgimento*—was largely confined to the country's cultural and socioeconomic elite in the north. The myth of Italy, namely the idea of restoring the country to the splendors of ancient Rome after centuries of foreign domination, excited intellectuals and other social groups in urban areas. But it was alien to the peasantry and, thus, to the bulk of the population, which was overwhelmingly illiterate, spoke only local dialects, and very often lived under feudal conditions, especially in the south. D'Azeglio, a prominent statesman in the early days of the new kingdom, made this very clear by suggesting: "We have made Italy. Now we must make Italians." But the ruling class in power during the second part of the 19th century made very little headway with this task and in fact chose a quite different strategy—as Giovanna Zincone (1992) suggests in an insightful comparative study on the different configuration of citizenship development in Europe.

Zincone starts by pointing out that in the mid-19th century "on the overall Italy was still a periphery of Europe and the south was, therefore, a *periphery in the periphery*" (1992, 145, italics added). According to the author, the north of the country was itself too far behind in the race for economic development and industrialization to be able to invest in a cultural and economic policy aimed at integrating the south. Neither was northern civil society sufficiently strong. Furthermore, the head-on clash with the church—stemming from the fact that the new kingdom had also been built at the expense of the Vatican's own territory—undermined any potential political aggregation along class lines. Zincone argues that rather than pursuing a strategy aimed at acquiring mass legitimacy, and fully aware of its own fragility, the governing coalition of the new kingdom chose to focus on its most powerful opponents. This resulted in a repressive strategy with respect to the church (including the confiscation of its properties across Italy), and in buying out the disloyal landed aristocracy in the south at the cost of leaving the traditional social order untouched in that part of the country. Historians have often described this arrangement as a sort of non-interference compromise between the northern and the southern elites; from the perspective of this study, this would appear to be a bifurcation of the country into a southern land of subjects and a central and northern land in which the seeds of citizenship were able to start growing, despite adverse conditions, not least the huge debt accumulated during the wars of independence.

The consequences of this initial settlement are still with us, 150 years later. As just mentioned, in return for maintaining their privileges, which were often of a feudal nature, large landowners from the south pledged allegiance to the new monarchy; but this also implied that while northern Italy was starting to industrialize, especially in the triangle between Turin, Genoa, and Milan, economic modernization was blocked entirely in the south. Further, the Italian government opted for a highly centralized political and administrative system, by extending Piedmont's rules and institutions to the rest of the country. In principle, this was meant to avoid the resurgence of pre-unitary states and force national standards upwards, but in practice, it was perceived, especially in the south, as an imposition, which soon came to be known as *Piedmontization*. In the backward, impoverished areas of the *Mezzogiorno*, the Italian state essentially meant new taxes, the repression of revolts by peasant asking for land by the armed forces, and compulsory military service—the exact opposite of what might have helped to integrate the southern lower strata into the new polity.

In the light of Marshall's discussion on the incompatibility between modern civil and political rights and traditional rules and norms, one can appreciate the distinctiveness of the Italian case: under the same flag and despite the same national anthem, two quite separate social, cultural, and economic formations developed, with very little evidence of any convergence between them. As I have argued elsewhere, Italy is in fact two countries in one (Fargion, 2009), and this is especially true when it comes to the profile of citizenship and the particular intertwining of political and social rights. In over a century and a half, there were only two moments when the two separate paths could have merged into a single path, but in both cases, albeit for different reasons, that "window of opportunity" quickly closed, leaving things largely unchanged. I am referring to the years immediately following World War I and World War II. In 1919, against the backdrop of considerable social turmoil and instability, Italy witnessed a huge leap forward in the area of both political and social rights: universal male suffrage was introduced and the newly elected Parliament—which for the first time had a majority of representatives from the industrial working class and peasants—passed a far-reaching insurance program providing coverage for old age and unemployment, a risk that most European countries started taking into consideration only much later. Agricultural workers were among the beneficiaries. In short, Italy turned from a laggard to a frontrunner, but this experience was short-lived. In reaction to the unprecedented mobilization of the working classes in the northern "industrial triangle" and in fear of the revolutionary winds blowing from Russia, large industrialists and the landed aristocracy supported the rise of the Fascist movement, which catalyzed protests by right-wing groups and nationalists dissatisfied with the war settlement.

As is well known, in October 1922 the democratic regime collapsed and the Fascist Party seized power: this was clearly the end of the inclusive strategy that moderate and reformist parliamentary representatives had stubbornly been pursuing in a deliberate attempt to avoid either a left-wing or a right-wing revolution. Not surprisingly, free elections were discontinued and trade unions and opposition parties were soon outlawed, elected local government was abolished, as was the free media, and the judiciary lost its independence. But one of the first measures introduced by Mussolini was to repeal the extension of social insurance benefits to the agricultural sector. While this move was clearly done to secure support from large landowners and helped to block the potential emancipation of the peasantry, the strategy pursued with respect to the northern industrial working classes envisaged a skillful use of social protection for control purposes and consensus building: Mussolini attempted a regimentation of the workers by imposing a corporatist structure that parceled out benefits on a categorical basis. In short, for over 20 years the development of citizenship was frozen, and it was only with the end of World War II that the thread was again picked up.

The two years immediately following the end of the war represent the second historical juncture in which north and south could at last have begun to tread a common path. The coalition government formed by the Socialist, the Communist, and the Christian Democratic Party initially endorsed the idea of recasting social protection along the lines of the Beveridge report. As a result, the new Republican Constitution reflected a broad conception of social rights, but the shift in 1947 from a cooperative climate to Cold War confrontation once more put an end to what could have developed into a fully fledged strategy of inclusion.

A DUAL WELFARE STATE FOR A DUAL POLITY

The elections of 1948 opened a new phase: Christian Democracy gained the absolute majority of the vote in an outright clash against the Socialist and Communist parties, acquiring a pivotal position that remained unchallenged for almost 45 years. Indeed, despite changes in coalition partners, the Christian Democratic Party remained in office until the early 1990s, when the old party system collapsed entirely. Throughout this period, the major opposition party was the Communist Party—the largest in western Europe—but nevertheless with no hope of ever gaining office because of the international settlement of the Cold War. Thriving on its permanent incumbency, the Christian Democratic Party had the opportunity to expand the public sector and penetrate state administration to a degree unparalleled elsewhere. However, it never used social policy measures to help bridge the gap between north and south, in contrast to what happened, for instance, in Canada—a country that had a similar and perhaps even more complicated territorial cleavage because of an overlapping ethnic and linguistic divide. The literature amply documents the integrative role played by the Canadian welfare state, but nothing similar occurred in Italy. In fact, in many ways the various governments running the country over the past 60 years deepened the north–south divide even further. To illustrate the point, I shall try to assess the extent to which the distribution of social policy benefits mirrors a territorial pattern. Considering that during the postwar period the lion's share of social spending in Italy consistently went towards pensions, the pension system appears the most obvious starting point for my argument.

Pension Benefits

As Figure 8.1 shows, at the beginning of the 1950s, pension expenditure represented 45% of total expenditure on income maintenance programs, equal to spending on family allowances. But over the subsequent three decades, pension benefits increased to the point that, by 1980, they accounted for 80% of total social insurance expenditure, while spending on family allowances decreased to about only 10%, with sickness, work injuries, and unemployment insurance making up the remaining 10% (Ferrera, 1984).

Given the occupational basis of the social insurance system, and the radically divergent profile of the economy in the north and south of the country, one would expect an unequal distribution of pension benefits, favoring the more industrialized areas of the north. Historical data on contributory private sector pensions fully confirm this expectation. In the mid-1980s, in northern regions, on average one in two retired persons received a relatively generous benefit from a private-sector pension scheme; in central Italy the corresponding figure was

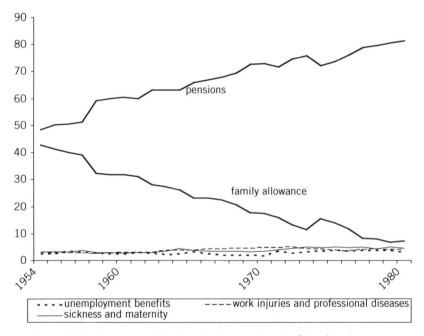

Figure 8.1 Expenditure on income maintenance programs by type of benefit, Italy, 1954–1980 (percentage distribution). Source: Ferrera, M. (1984). *Il welfare state in Italia. Sviluppo e crisi in prospettiva comparata* (p. 53). Bologna: Il Mulino.

only one in three, dropping to one in five in southern regions—with the exception of Apulia (Fargion, 1992). In the following years, as the pension system increasingly reached maturity, the gap widened even further.[1] If this is clearly the result of the interplay between a dual economy and an insurance program designed primarily for the core sectors of the workforce with regular jobs and standard long-term contracts, to get the full picture one needs to focus on the kind of benefits the Italian social protection system funneled to the poorer southern areas. By taking this approach, the conclusions are unequivocal: the structural disadvantage of the south was perversely counterbalanced by granting discretionary second-class benefits that appear well tuned to the logic of southern politics and apt to reinforce it. I am referring particularly to disability pension benefits and their abuse. In his well-known article on the "southern model" of welfare, Ferrera provided international readers with an accurate analysis of the highly sophisticated mechanisms that underpin the "clientelistic welfare market" of invalidity pensions (1996, 26–27), which largely served as a functional equivalent for missing unemployment benefits. This peculiar market—namely the exchange of invalidity pension benefits for preference votes—was able to thrive primarily in the south at least until the mid-1980s, with devastating political and institutional consequences.

To fully appreciate the role played by invalidity pensions in the south, we need to recall the peculiar political dynamics of the south of Italy. As most studies point out, throughout the second part of the 20th century the political process in southern Italy displayed remarkably different features to the center-north of the country: prepolitical particularism; an instrumental approach to politics; the absence of collective action; vertical channels of articulation; and aggregation of demand (Graziano, 1980). From a historical perspective, none of this is actually surprising. As the previous section highlights, the long-term features of public intervention in this part of the country were certainly not conducive to building trust in state institutions in the south. Against this backdrop, the type of answers the welfare state provided to meet the economic needs of large sectors of the population that suffered from unemployment and/or underemployment reinforced this negative trend. The lack of a broad-based social insurance scheme granting adequate unemployment compensation as a right,[2] and the availability instead of largely discretionary disability benefits—which could only be captured through particularistic relations—severely undermined the standard functioning of democratic institutions.

Family Allowances

Although social policy studies usually concentrate on invalidity pensions when referring to the clientelistic profile of the Italian welfare model, southern regions witnessed a similar misuse of family allowances, especially during the Italian economic boom at the end of the 1950s and early 1960s. The literature usually overlooks this program, or simply mentions its rapid decline in the postwar period and the marginal role of family policies in the Italian social protection system.

In fact, the specific operation of family allowances in the less-advantaged areas of the country further confirms the dual nature of the Italian welfare state. Let us try to briefly illustrate why. First of all, in contrast to most other countries, family benefits were granted to workers' parents; in addition, coverage could be extended to a long list of other relatives. All that was needed was a deed legally signed by the worker stating that he was responsible for supporting, among others, his brother, sister, or even nephews. Under these circumstances, it was legally possible for a worker to receive family allowances for as many as 15 to 20 people. This situation allowed widespread misuse of the program, especially in economically deprived areas. The large number of court cases during those years confirms that fraudulent behavior on the part of employees, and also on the part of employers, was not rare. Perhaps even more interesting is that politicians and trade union officials openly showed a benevolent attitude towards this state of affairs. By examining cash flows for family benefits in the different parts of the country, one can begin to understand why this kind of misuse was not openly condemned. Elsewhere (Fargion, 2010a), I have analyzed official data from the National Insurance Fund (INPS) on revenues and spending for family benefits in each of the three main occupational sectors of salaried workers. The relevant breakdown by region during the years of the "economic miracle" documents a remarkable redistribution from the northern to the southern part of the country for the industrial and the trade sector, while agriculture displays a negative balance between social contributions and benefits throughout the country. In the case of Sicily, for instance, benefits paid out were eight times higher than the social contributions that were collected in the region that year. The following statement published in the official journal of the social insurance fund (INPS) provides an illuminating comment:

> The current system might enhance fraud attempts, but we should not forget that in fact what is certainly a fraud also achieved the goal of alleviating poverty among the people who have not benefited from the golden rain of the economic miracle or have received only a few drops of it; in many cases it served to guarantee social peace in economically depressed areas; in other cases it granted more humane living conditions to underoccupied categories of workers—in conjunction with a benefit which is inappropriately named agricultural unemployment compensation but is in fact another wage complement. (Masini, 1962, 15)

The evidence presented thus far suggests that Italian family benefits did not work exactly in the same way as in other Bismarckian welfare states. However, what is most important for the purposes of this essay is that overall, monetary social transfers reinforced the original Italian model of citizenship, and particularly the entrenched condition of southern people as subjects rather than citizens. As illustrated, during the first decades following World War II, rather than guaranteeing basic social rights, the cash transfers available enhanced the subordination of southern Italians to the local ruling elite. The devastating consequences of this policy course are well captured in the following passage by Cartocci (1994, 59):

> Whenever particularistic criteria—rather than universalistic norms—define the functioning of a public institution or access to its services, the integrative capacity of such an institution is lost. The latter will operate according to ad hoc successive aggregations on the basis of partial and uncertain criteria, building in turn on political exchange or personal bonds. Under these circumstances, the guarantees typical of entitlements—which place all citizens on equal footing—are no longer there, benefits and services become instead provisions, that is to say the granting of favors.[…] Individuals start competing against one another in what they perceive as a zero-sum game: anyone's advantage (access to the services and benefits granted by an institution on particularistic grounds) turns out to be a disadvantage for everyone else. As a result, the connective texture of society, which is made of horizontal, egalitarian and informal relations based on trust and solidarity, gets systematically destroyed. What develops in its place is a series of vertical and asymmetrical links ending in the hands of a variety of institutional representatives controlling the relevant resources and their allocation. Within this context, individuals give up their citizenship rights to obtain favors; or, to put it in Dahrendorf's terms, they give up entitlements to obtain provisions.

Social and Healthcare Services

When we turn from monetary benefits to services, unfortunately the picture does not improve. Following the establishment of the regions in 1970, the national government entrusted the latter with legislative responsibility in the field of social care services. The results of the extensive research I carried out on regional policies and expenditure in this sector between the 1970s and 1990s (Fargion, 1997) leave very little room for hope: while central and northern regions have used their powers to address—albeit without adequate resources—emerging social care needs with respect to children and the elderly, southern regions have maintained a very limited and archaic system of social provision. Actually, the very title of the Italian volume that discusses the relevant findings (translated as "The Geography of Social Citizenship in Italy") conveys a message that any reader can understand at a glance.

With the introduction of a national health service in 1978, the regions also acquired an increasingly wide range of competences in the health sector.[3] The devolution of powers, however, only really gathered pace in the early 1990s. What is the outcome of this process with respect to the territorial disparities and imbalances that apparently run across the entire Italian welfare state? In a nutshell, over 30 years after the establishment of the Italian National Health Service, the north–south divide remains practically intact. Despite repeated commitments to redress regional disparities in healthcare with respect to both the quantity and the quality of the services being provided, the gap between the two parts of the country is not narrowing. Although the issue has been extensively discussed in academic and political circles for some considerable time, over the past couple of years it has acquired unprecedented media attention in connection with the ongoing political debate on fiscal federalism, and because of major political scandals in a number of regional health systems (Fargion, 2010b).

The President of the Senate Commission on the national health service,[4] Ignazio Marino, made the point very strongly. Senator Marino, a leading figure of the major opposition party—the Democratic Party—anticipated the results of a comprehensive review carried out on behalf of the Commission by focusing on just a few revealing indicators (Ministero della Salute, 2009): (a) hospitalization rates; (b) inpatient discharges from surgical wards with medical DRGs; (c) cesarean deliveries as a share of total births; (d) surgery within two days of a femur fracture; (e) coverage of breast cancer screening. The data show that hospitalization rates range from 169 per 1,000 inhabitants in Emilia Romagna to as many as 235 in Sicily. Turning to the second indicator—which measures inappropriate use of expensive surgical wards—while Emilia Romagna and Lombardy display figures of 17% and 22% respectively, the corresponding value for Campania is as high as 45%. The third indicator points to an even more dramatic variation in the quality of healthcare across the country. Looking at the number of cesarean deliveries as a percentage of total births, Italy generally fares much worse than all other highly industrialized countries, with an average of 37% cesareans, in contrast, for instance, to 19% in France, 25% in Spain, and 13% in the Netherlands. But if one looks at the breakdown by region, the situation is even more worrying, with Campania showing an incredible 62% of cesareans, in contrast to 26% in Tuscany. A similar picture emerges from the fourth indicator: while in the southern city of Catanzaro only 9% of patients with a fractured femur received surgical treatment within 48 hours of the event, the corresponding figure is 83% in Bolzano. The last indicator, which addresses preventive healthcare measures, also confirms the gap existing between the north and the south. The available data show that the percentage of women aged 50 to 69 who were screened using mammography varies from 72% in Emilia Romagna to only 39% in Sicily.[5]

The above data are the tip of the iceberg. Quite clearly, the problem lies with the mismanagement of the healthcare system in the south, which involves regional politicians as well as administrative and professional staff. Until recently, legislation endorsed a perverse public–private mix and geared the system to the interests of service providers rather than patients: in detail, keeping performance standards low in the public sphere helped divert patients to private facilities that the doctors themselves often owned or where they might work on a part-time basis, supplementing their regular salary considerably. Considering the overall profile of politics in the south, particularly the role of clientelistic relations and behavior, and not to mention the grip over the economy that the Mafia has in a number of regions—it is not surprising to find misuse or overt abuses of loose healthcare regulation, and the accumulation of huge deficits by regional health-care systems. To appreciate the consequences of such mismanagement from a citizenship perspective, one can look at hospital inpatients' mobility from south-ern to northern regions: this indicator is the litmus test for the unequal opportu-nities that are offered to Italians living in the *Mezzogiorno*.

Recent policy developments offer some hope, but there is still a long way to go in order to effectively redress the existing healthcare imbalances. In the light of the current legislative framework—apart from defining the total resources allo-cated to the health sector—the state monitors regional financial management and has more stringent sanctioning powers with respect to regions running a def-icit. As envisaged in the 2006–08 health pact between the national and regional governments, this can lead to both partners signing specific recovery plans with stringent obligations on the part of failing regions—a process that now involves most southern regions and only one region in the north.

So far, the discussion has concentrated on the dual nature of benefits and ser-vices available under the Italian welfare state; however, to get the full picture one also needs to refer more specifically to the profile of the Italian labor market.

Labor Market Policies

At least until the mid-1990s, the literature constantly referred to Italy as one of the most rigidly regulated labor markets in the industrialized world. Notably, since the 1960s and especially following the 1970 Workers Code, labor legisla-tion has strengthened the rights and entitlements of workers at the expense of employers, a process progressively leading to a system characterized by wage-setting rigidity, stringent hiring and firing rules, and very limited openings for atypical contracts. Yet this is only one face of the coin, and to grasp how the Italian labor market really works, it is highly misleading to exclusively concen-trate on the rigidity stemming from the regulatory framework: this is offset by a complex mix of decentralized small firms, which are subject to lesser constraints on employment relationships, and by the sizeable "gray economy" and the num-ber of self-employed. By looking at some quantitative data, one gets an even better picture of the contradictions—or perhaps the paradoxes—that character-ize the Italian labor market. According to Ichino's estimates (1996), in the mid-1990s workers effectively covered by labor market regulations—namely work-ers in firms with more than 15 employees plus the public sector—accounted for only about 40% of total employment. On the other hand, the proportion of small firms and the self-employed remains much higher than in most other European countries still today, and more importantly the gray sector of the economy finds no European equivalent, with non-regular work accounting for as much as 22% of the total work done. In short, in one of the world's most highly regulated labor markets, a large share of the workforce is in fact not covered by such regulations and therefore does not enjoy the employment and social protection associated with it. To put it differently, the development of labor legislation has resulted in high barriers around those who already had regular permanent jobs, to the disadvantage of growing numbers of outsiders. This has promoted the consolidation of a dual labor market, with highly negative implications from economic, social, political, and fiscal points of view. Not surprisingly, such a dual market has reiterated the north–south cleavage, with the bulk of non-regular work concentrated in the southern part of the country.

RECENT SOCIAL POLICY REFORMS: ADDING AN INTERGENERATIONAL DIVIDE

The end of the first Republic in 1992 and the collapse of the party system that had run the country over the previous 40 years marked a new phase in the development of the Italian welfare state. The reforms that the technocratic governments introduced in the first part of the 1990s allowed pension expenditure to be brought under control and improved efficiency in healthcare. In their well-known book *Rescued by Europe?* Ferrera and Gualmini provide a detailed account of the social policy measures adopted over the period; most tellingly, they entitle the section devoted to the period 1992–2000 "a Copernican revolution?"

At a distance, however, one can notice that the distributive distortions of the Italian social protection system have not been corrected and that in fact a further generational cleavage has been added onto the territorial cleavage discussed in the previous section. As a result of the labor market deregulation measures introduced during the late 1990s—which Parliamentary law no. 30 of 2002 expanded even further—and in the absence of any concurrent reform of the social guarantees attached to atypical work, Italy now is witnessing a generational split that is stronger than ever, which cuts across geographical and firm-size differences. On top of the disparities stemming from the entrenched contrast between the formal and the informal sectors of the economy and between large and medium to small firms, a new dividing line is increasingly emerging within the individual enterprise: the adult core sector labor force that enjoys standard permanent job contracts is being confronted every day by growing numbers of young workers on part-time, fixed-term, temporary jobs. These so-called "atypical workers" can only count on much lower social protection levels but, given their precarious position, they are also ready to accept less-favorable working conditions.

To illustrate the extent to which the Italian welfare state now reflects this intergenerational divide, I shall refer to the outcome of the policymaking process concerning three issues that have played a primary role in social policy developments over the past 15 years: (a) the 1995 pension reform; (b) the 2007 "welfare protocol"; and (c) the measures recently adopted to address the consequences of the international financial crisis, particularly unemployment.

The 1995 Pension Reform

Many authors have written on the so-called "Dini reform" of the Italian pension system, emphasizing its crucial contribution to the long-term stabilization of pensions expenditure. Moreover, the literature usually refers to the reform—which introduced notional defined contribution pensions—as a turning point with respect to the distributive approach that underpinned the micro-sector legislation passed during the 1970s and 1980s. However, the studies available tend to overlook phasing-in procedures—which in fact included quite significant drawbacks, especially from the perspective of our study. New entrants into the labor market as of January 1996 are in fact the only ones to which the less-generous new method fully applies, while all the workers who were already in the labor market when the reform was introduced are subject to favorable transitory provisions. In greater detail, workers with at least 18 years of contributions at the cutoff date remain in the earnings-related regime, while a mixed regime—combining the earnings-related with the notionally defined contribution formula—applies to workers with less than 18 years of contributions at the end of 1995. In sum, the law established an artificial barrier between younger and older workers that openly favored the latter: a political choice that can hardly be considered equitable from an intergeneration point of view.[6] Moreover, taking into consideration that increasing numbers of young people spend long spells in "atypical work"—which is characterized by lower contributory requirements compared to standard permanent jobs—the younger generations can expect to receive largely inadequate pension benefits when they retire.[7]

The 2007 "Welfare Protocol"

The second issue I want to consider refers to the new regulations introduced in 2007 concerning a particular type of pension—the so-called *pensioni di anzianità*, which the international social policy literature usually refers to as seniority benefits. To place into perspective the specific measure I intend to discuss—namely the 2007 "Welfare Protocol"—a few words are in order on this particular program, which represents an anomaly in the context of European old-age protection. Until the mid-1990s, seniority benefits were linked only to contributory requirements, with no age threshold. More precisely, private-sector workers could receive this type of pension well before the legal retirement age as long as they had paid social contributions for 35 years. In the case of public-sector employees, the requirement was even lower: only 20 years of contribution! During the 1990s, various governments—especially the center-left governments in power during the second part of the decade—tightened the rules by first introducing an age threshold and then gradually increasing that threshold to 57 years by 2001.[8] The center-right coalition that won that year's national elections picked up the issue and, albeit reluctantly due to internal controversies, ended up introducing even stricter age requirements in the context of its 2004 pension reform: the relevant provisions moved the age threshold for seniority benefits from 57 to 60 years of age, which was still 5 years lower than the normal retirement age, but to avoid excessive opposition the new requirement was postponed to January 2008 (hence beyond Berlusconi's term of office).

From 2004 until the end of 2007—just before the deadline for enforcing the 60-years-of-age threshold—this remained one of the most controversial issues, not only between the center-right and center-left blocks but also within the latter. When Prodi came to power once again, following his electoral victory in May 2006, the new government officially stated that one of its first targets was to repeal the provision on the 60-years-of-age threshold. Over the first year and a half of Prodi's second Cabinet, this problem monopolized the entire social policy debate, to the detriment of any serious discussion on new social needs related to atypical work, youth unemployment, the frail elderly, social exclusion, or child poverty. In short, the divide between old and new social risks dominated the debate, just as it had during the 1996–2001 center-left government, and the social policy responses showed a similar bias in favor of the older generation. Although according to official estimates the workers who would suffer from the restrictive rules were only just over 600,000, the three labor confederations and the refounded Communist Party adamantly supported their claims and ended up securing €10 billion to cover the cost of setting back the age threshold from 60 to 58 years. The so-called "Welfare Protocol" that was signed between the government and the major workers' trade unions in December 2007 endorsed this agreement, which once more confirmed the strong bias of Italian social politics and policies in favor of the older generations. The protocol did envisage some improvements for atypical workers, particularly concerning their pension rights. Yet all the other issues were totally marginalized compared to the question of seniority benefits. To put it differently, instead of addressing the emerging social needs of the younger generation in particular—concerning the level of social protection attached to atypical work but also housing, childcare services, and social exclusion—the government responded primarily to the organized pressure of older workers. Rather than disentangling the inequities of the southern welfare model, its action paradoxically resulted in further overprotection of the already overprotected.

Measures Addressing Unemployment in the Context of the International Crisis

The third issue I want to discuss brings us even closer to the present. In this section, I shall try to shed light on the measures the current government introduced to address growing unemployment as a result of the international economic crisis. Notably, in the case of Italy, unemployment protection is extremely low and highly inequitable compared to all other continental and northern European countries; for this reason the reform of "social shock absorbers" has been on the political agenda for over 15 years, but no reforms have ever gotten off the drawing board. For those unfamiliar with the intricacies of Italian unemployment protection, it is best to recall the main features of existing programs. There are four main types of benefits: (a) standard unemployment benefit, which today guarantees 60% of lost earnings, provided the dismissed worker has been insured for at least two years and has paid contributions for a total of one year of the previous two years; (b) reduced standard unemployment benefit, which is meant to provide a small income integration to seasonal workers or to workers who have only worked a limited number of months during the previous year[9]; (c) so-called "mobility benefit," which is more generous than the ordinary unemployment benefit (covering about 80% of lost earnings) but is available only on the basis of tripartite agreements in the case of collective dismissals by large and medium-sized firms; (d) ordinary and special temporary wage compensation for cases where working hours have been reduced due to contingent market difficulties or industrial restructuring, respectively.

As I have illustrated in detail elsewhere (Fargion, 2001), Italy witnessed extensive misuse of this latter type of benefit, first of all because it was far more generous than the ordinary unemployment benefit[10] while protecting workers in the event of redundancy. Eligibility was subject to negotiation between trade unions and employers, and until 1988 the scheme was entirely financed by the state. In short, the program was very palatable to both unions and employers because it allowed for a freezing of redundancies while permitting firms to externalize the financial and social costs of industrial restructuring. Highly unionized large firms were obviously in a better position to take advantage of the discretionary procedures involved in the operation of the program. Although over the past decade the Wage Compensation Fund (*Cassa Integrazione Guadagni*) was brought back to its original purpose, no concurrent measures were introduced to effectively increase coverage levels of the ordinary unemployment benefit—despite the growing numbers of atypical workers unable to meet the relevant contributory requirements—nor has a public assistance safety net ever been established.

Against this backdrop, it is easier to appreciate the policy measures the Italian government introduced to address the social consequences of the international economic crisis, particularly concerning unemployment protection. As the government clearly stated in a number of official documents, its first and preferred option was to extend the coverage of temporary wage compensation (*Cassa Integrazione Guadagni*) by relaxing current rules that largely confine potential beneficiaries to large industrial enterprises and the construction sector. According to the executive, this solution has a number of advantages: (a) it limits dismissals and keeps workers attached to the firm; (b) it invests employers with responsibility for their workers; (c) it requires tripartite agreements between the social partners and public institutions; (d) it provides more generous coverage compared to ordinary unemployment benefit. Yet, reading the list of dispensations in law no. 2/2009,[11] one quickly discovers that the categories temporarily admitted to enjoy the benefits of the Wage Compensation Fund exclude a considerable proportion of the workforce. What happens to all the others? The answer is not easy because one has to read through a patchwork of detailed provisions referring to specific groups of workers. The less-generous ordinary unemployment benefit is extended, for instance, to the handicraft sector, including workers on lease, and to apprentices, but in this case only for the period 2009–11. For the first time, the law also introduced some kind of unemployment protection for a particular category of atypical workers—the *collaboratori coordinati a progetto*—which includes around 550,000 people, mostly young people and women. For 2009, the benefit corresponded to only 20% of the worker's earnings for the previous year,[12] but nevertheless—according to Berton, Richiardi, and Sacchi (2009a)—only 12% of potential beneficiaries meet the qualifying conditions. The authors also contend that although the law formally extends unemployment protection, on the basis of the specific regulations, as many as 50% of workers employed by temporary work agencies will actually remain without unemployment protection, along with 40% of workers on fixed-term contract and 80% of apprentices.

Criticism has not been confined to the academic sphere. The major opposition party—the Democratic Party—supported the need to introduce an unemployment benefit for all workers losing their job, irrespective of contractual arrangements. The following statement by the parliamentary representative Enrico Letta—the Democratic Party's spokesman on welfare policy—provides a clear-cut evaluation of the government's strategy: "To address this unprecedented crisis by adding money to the existing system of unemployment benefits and merely resorting to temporary dispensations from the rules currently in force is like trying to shoot at airplanes with bows and arrows."[13]

The real world is, however, more complex than the political rhetoric might suggest. In this particular case, one should not forget that when in power, the Democratic Party was also unable to comprehensively reform the social shock absorbers and introduced only minor improvements. On the opposite side, the strategy of the center-right certainly eased the negative social consequences stemming from the recession, particularly by softening the impact of the closure of a number of small and medium-sized firms. However, the evidence suggests it has been much less effective for the weakest types of workers, who have been hit the hardest by the current crisis—namely atypical workers. Yet, if this is the case, it is also true that the crisis came on top of a situation that was already extremely critical. Considering that coverage levels of unemployment protection remain highly inadequate, it was practically impossible for the government to enforce activation measures, along the lines of most other European countries. The relevant policy measures did pay lip service to conditionality, especially concerning the need to combine cash benefits with vocational training, but in fact the latter's role remained largely marginal.

ATYPICAL WORK AND THE ITALIAN WELFARE STATE

In the light of the current scenario, it is most useful to outline in greater detail the profile of atypical work in the case of Italy. The latest data available from EU-SILC (relating to 2006) provide a good starting point. However, one needs to keep in mind that as far as atypical work is concerned, the above dataset refers exclusively to workers on fixed-term contracts. According to calculations by Raitano (2010), the following picture emerges: (a) in 2006, workers with fixed-term contracts represented 14.8% of total private and public employees; (b) they were mostly low-skilled workers and concentrated in the service sector; (c) their net hourly salary was 78.2% of the corresponding figure for permanent workers; (c) their net average yearly income was 55% of the average income earned by workers with full-time permanent jobs. As a result, Raitano calculates that as many as 56% of temporary workers were in the lowest quintile of income distribution and that 14% fell below the poverty line and could thus be classified as "working poor" (net monthly wage below €680). These disadvantages are not counterbalanced by adequate social protection measures. As the literature amply documents, because of the existing insurance and contributory requirements, once their contract expires many workers on fixed-term contracts are only entitled to the "reduced unemployment benefit" (*indennità di disoccupazione a requisiti ridotti*) mentioned above, which is paid out one year later and for a very limited period. If we now turn to other forms of atypical work—particularly to the workers labeled in the Italian debate as *parasubordinati* and *"false" partite IVA,* the situation appears even worse. These workers are formally self-employed but are in fact working for a single employer. Employers are increasingly resorting to these forms of contractual relations to reduce their costs: whereas in the case of workers with fixed-term contracts (which cannot be usually renewed for more than three years) social contributions amount to 33% of wages—two thirds of which are paid by employers, in the case of the *parasubordinati* (which include *Collaboratori Coordinati a Progetto* or *Co.Co.Pro,* and in the public administration *Collaboratori Coordinati Continuativi* or *Co.Co.Co*), the burden for the employer is definitely lighter because contributions amount to 25.7% of wages—of which employers again cover two thirds. Resorting to a formally independent "professional" is even cheaper, since then the social contributions entirely fall on the worker's shoulders.

To make an adequate assessment of the implications of this situation, it is important to remember that 60% of new jobs fall into one of the many categories of atypical work and that at present atypical workers represent 20% of Italy's labor force. Not only are workers in these new forms of employment relationship inadequately protected against unemployment, they also suffer from an insufficient protection with respect to maternity leave, sickness leave, and family allowances. Berton, Richiardi and Sacchi (2009b) devote an entire chapter of their latest volume to this subject. Tellingly, the book is entitled *Flex-insecurity*. To illustrate the point—among the many examples in the book—one can refer to sickness allowances in the event of hospitalization, which were introduced in 2000 for all workers registered with the special INPS fund for atypical work (*Gestione Separata INPS*). If hospitalized, the worker is then entitled to a daily allowance (which is proportionate to the contributions actually paid with a daily maximum of €39), provided he has contributed for at least three of the twelve months preceding the event. However, if the contribution is below a certain amount, it will not be registered when actually paid but only from the following January. As a result, a registered contribution might fall outside the twelve months preceding hospitalization, thereby excluding the worker from access to the benefit. In fact, according to the authors' estimates, one out of three *parasubordinati* cannot actually receive the benefit. The overall outcome appears paradoxical but the authors provide an insightful analysis, which is worth reiterating. On the one hand, they coin the concept of "cognitive illusion" to highlight the gap between the legislation, which formally extends social protection coverage to particular categories of atypical work, and how it is implemented. On the other hand, they point to the intrinsic conflict between atypical work and the insurance rationale that underpins the relevant social protection measures. In summary, contributory requirements are designed using full-time, permanent jobs as their reference point, but the conditions of atypical work reflect an entirely different world.

As mentioned above, rather than using the current economic and financial crisis as an opportunity to overhaul the existing social protection system for atypical workers (which is extremely fragmented and highly inequitable), and providing instead a universal floor of basic social rights, starting with an effectively accessible unemployment benefit, Berlusconi's government opted for a patchwork strategy that leaves the dualistic nature of the Italian labor market untouched, and actually further consolidates the long-term divide between insiders and outsiders.[14] Women and young people have suffered particularly from recent developments. These two groups were largely engaged in a variety of atypical forms of work before the crisis and unsurprisingly have been the first to lose their jobs as a result of the crisis, in many cases moving—as a last resort—to what the authoritative CENSIS Report (2009) has labeled as "molecular work" in the context of an emerging "fourth sector" (*Quaternario*) that is developing within the hidden economy. There is no hard quantitative evidence relating to this new phenomenon, but it would be short-sighted to ignore it. Increasing numbers of young workers are disappearing from social insurance registries and official statistics because there is little benefit in paying sky-high payroll taxes. As noted above, due to obnoxious contributory requirements, in many cases the worker would not even receive social protection benefits in any case. Moving to the "gray economy" might appear the best course of action for these workers in the short run, but in the long run this could mean that an entire generation are excluded from social protection.

CONCLUDING REMARKS

The first two sections provide ample evidence that Italy never developed a fully fledged social citizenship that one could label as Marshallian. But then, how can we interpret the more recent trends in the country's social protection system? The answer to this question is less straightforward. If we look at the measures introduced with respect to unemployment protection, the evidence puts Italy in a quite distinct position compared to other European countries. For instance, while most other countries have increasingly made unemployment benefits more conditional, this has not been the case in Italy. However, this is not because Italian policymakers rejected the neoliberal paradigm that is internationally predominant and the associated redefinition of citizens' rights and duties *vis-à-vis* the state, in the name of maintaining a conception of unemployment protection as a right. Given that unemployment protection still covers a small minority of the unemployed and cannot therefore be considered a fully fledged citizens' entitlement, one can hardly use moral hazard arguments to promote a restrictive strategy. As the above section illustrates, the real problem is in fact quite the opposite, namely the extension of coverage to all workers.

Yet there are also signs that Italy might move directly to a post-Marshallian phase without ever having developed or endorsed a model of social citizenship along Marshall's lines. For the moment, these "signs" are primarily confined to public discourse and official government documents, but Berlusconi's center-right coalition did start to implement its ideas on a comprehensive reduction of the public sphere (Fargion, 2010b). The main components of this vision—which is a mix of neoliberal and neocorporatist elements—can be found in the green and white papers that the Labor and Social Policy Minister, Maurizio Sacconi, issued in 2008 and 2009 respectively.

The green paper—which was published within a few months of Berlusconi's electoral victory with the intent of outlining the new government's strategy—claims that "the crisis of the Italian social model is primarily a cultural crisis which stems from the fact that the importance of the person has been overlooked and the role of the family has been repeatedly denied."[15] The practical implications of this statement appear especially worrying for social and long-term care policies: in the name of prioritizing the family, there is a risk that public services might be scaled back even further; in fact, it is precisely the families' readiness to shoulder the caring needs of their dependent members that has so far counterbalanced the inadequacy of public services. Notably, the family is described in the international literature as "the clearing house of the southern welfare model," and in fact what the family needs most is to offload some of these caring burdens, in other words to receive more concrete support. But the executive's budgetary decisions seem to be a move in exactly the opposite direction. The first move of Berlusconi's government was to cut personnel in primary, secondary, and higher education—a decision that is now being fully implemented with a heavy reduction of school hours, especially in nursery and primary school.[16] Secondly, it postponed any allocation of funds for long-term care, and only at the end of 2009 did it reluctantly and insufficiently refinance the National Dependency Fund originally established by the previous center-left cabinet. Lastly, in reaction to the Greek crisis, the budgetary law for 2011 focused particularly on drastically reducing the resources allocated to regional and local governments. This is sure to have a negative impact on families, by reducing the quantity and quality of educational and social care services, and making it even more difficult for mothers to combine work and family life, not to speak of the negative implications on female occupational levels.

Building on the premises set out in the green paper, the subsequent white paper on welfare openly suggests that the current balance between state, market, and family should be shifted more in favor of the market and the family, and away from the state (Ministero del Lavoro e delle Politiche Sociali, 2009). In the context of shrinking resources, the white paper calls for a new model of welfare based primarily on "opportunities and responsibility." The document also suggests enhancing the role of the social partners in extending private insurance schemes to complement public provision in the pension system and in the healthcare sector, a prospect that could widen the gap between over- and under-protected citizens even further—as the data on coverage by supplementary pension funds clearly indicate. In the case of healthcare, it is also interesting to note that supplementary schemes are required to devote at least 20% of their resources to address long-term care needs, rehabilitation, and dental care—three sectors that are currently underdeveloped within the public system. The emphasis on bilateral agencies, which—as mentioned above—are supposed to play an important role also in the field of unemployment protection, indicates yet another problem: neocorporatist arrangements appear the least apt to address the social needs in an economy that is increasingly characterized by rapid change and flexibility.

According to Laura Pennacchi (2009), a well-known Italian scholar who is also a leading figure of the major opposition party, the most critical aspects of the white paper can be summarized as follows: (1) the document endorses an alteration of the constitutional framework of citizenship; (2) it envisages a substantial reduction of public and collective responsibility; (3) it aims to privatize key components of the Italian social model, concerning in particular the health and pension sector. While I agree on the latter two points, I have some reservations about the first, as the far-reaching social commitments enshrined in the 1948 republican constitution were never fully realized during the postwar period. In my view, the white paper reinforces long-term trends by undermining even further the bonds of social solidarity that the Italian welfare state developed to only a very limited extent. The policy measures adopted to address migration issues—which represent a relatively recent phenomenon compared to continental and northern Europe—move in the same direction. While the national government is pursuing a restrictive and repressive strategy, local authorities—which are primarily responsible for addressing the social needs of immigrant workers and for promoting integration policies—are providing very different sets of answers, depending on geographical location and political profile.[17] As Laura Dragosei (2010) suggests in her comments on the government's white paper, Italy is becoming more than ever a welfare state in which citizenship entails "varying social entitlements for each and every one."

Postscript

At the very moment the book was being sent to the publisher, Berlusconi lost his majority in a crucial Parliamentary vote and had to resign. This event represents the end of an era and can hardly be ignored. In the midst of a dramatic international financial crisis, which is progressively involving the entire European Union (and not only its weaker member states), once again Italy placed its fate in the hands of a technocratic cabinet. What can we expect from the new prime minister, Mario Monti, and his government?

There are good reasons to expect a reversal of recent trends. The current situation offers policymakers an unexpected policy window to try and redress both the territorial and the generational divide. The literature amply documents that the major reforms introduced in the 1990s were primarily the result of exogenous pressures (Ferrera & Gualmini, 2004). Now history gives the country a second chance, and even in this case external constraints will be turned into an opportunity. At the risk of being overly optimistic one can say that this Cabinet will engage in a serious attempt to combine economic sustainability of the welfare state with adequate and accessible social protection. The problem is whether the political parties—which are in standby—will give the new government enough time and room for maneuver to introduce at least the basic elements of its reform package. Italian parties have often pursued self-destructive strategies, and what appears as a rational strategy cannot be taken for granted. However, if the Monti government manages to stay in power until the next electoral turn, which is due in the spring of 2013—and a lot depends on how the European scenario evolves—it will be very difficult to revert to the old course of action. The welfare reforms the Executive is bound to introduce over the next months—first of all because of binding requirements by EU institutions—will represent an institutional wedge with far-reaching implications for whoever wins the next elections. In short, there are all the prerequisites for Italy to distance itself at last from the distortions and anomalies of its largely unfair model of social citizenship. But will the country make it?

NOTES

1 As an example, one can consider the current breakdown by geographical area of seniority benefits. Apart from being an anomaly of the Italian pension system, the latter are notably more generous compared to regular old-age pension benefits. The evidence presented by the 2009 CENSIS report shows first of all that in 2007 the total number of seniority benefits for the Private Employees Pension Fund (which is the largest of the entire system) was 1,886,697 as

compared to 3,715,947 old-age pensions. But the territorial distribution of recipients appears even more remarkable: 44.9% of beneficiaries were from the northwest and 22.4% from the northeast, while the remaining 15.1% and 17.7% were from central and southern regions respectively. Quite the contrary holds true for noncontributory pensions. In this case southern regions are disproportionately overrepresented. In detail, whereas beneficiaries of public assistance pensions represented only 14.7% and 20.9% of pensioners in northern and central regions, in the south the corresponding figure was 28.4%.

2 Available comparative data on unemployment protection constantly place Italy at the bottom of EU rankings, along with the other Mediterranean countries and new member states.

3 In line with constitutional provisions, the regions had already acquired responsibility for hospital care in 1974, but it was only after 1978 that they were entrusted with responsibility for the planning and organization of local health districts.

4 In October 2008, the Senate set up this special Commission to investigate inappropriate functioning of regional health systems.

5 The region of Tuscany pioneered the monitoring of healthcare services by entrusting a group of researchers from the prominent Scuola Superiore Sant'Anna at the University of Pisa with the task of working out a monitoring system to be tested in a limited number of local health agencies and then applied to the entire region. The monitoring system—which became fully operational in 2008—is based on 130 indicators. The national ministry apparently evaluated the experiment positively to the point that it entrusted the same group of researchers to work out a simplified monitoring system to be applied throughout the country. Instead of the original 130 indicators, only 36 indicators were selected, covering the following main areas: (a) hospital care; (b) community care services; (c) pharmaceutical expenditure; (d) public health prevention. In April 2010, the health minister announced that the relevant monitoring had been completed for both 2007 and 2008. Currently, anyone can have free access to all the relevant information by simply clicking on the dedicated website: http://www.salute.gov.it/imgs/C_17_pubblicazionI_1239_allegato.pdf

6 As a result of the very long transition period envisaged by the 1995 reform, up until 2013–15 people will continue to retire on the basis of the more generous earnings-related regime; from 2013–15 to 2033–35 a mixed regime will apply, with the defined-contribution method progressively acquiring greater importance, while defined-contribution pensions will be fully phased in only from 2033–35 onwards.

7 In the case of Italy, the current profile of supplementary pension schemes does not appear to be able to offset the reduction in statutory pensions. First, occupational pensions are mostly spread among private employees, while they are still considerably underdeveloped for the self-employed and absolutely marginal in the public sector. Available statistical information

concerning age, gender, and territorial distribution of pension fund members provides an even more accurate picture. According to the 2009 annual report by COVIP (the authority in charge of monitoring and controlling private pension funds), members are mostly concentrated in the age group 35 to 54. The younger cohorts are strongly underrepresented: workers up to 35 years of age represent only 23% of total membership, while their share of total employment corresponds to 34%. The gender distribution is also very unbalanced, with male workers representing as much as 67% of total membership. Thirdly, take-up rates reflect the entrenched socioeconomic gap between the north and the south of the country, with an overrepresentation of northern and an underrepresentation of southern regions. For an overview of more recent developments in the pension sector see also Fargion (2010b).

8 In 1996–97, to be entitled to a seniority pension a private-sector employee with a contribution record of 35 years had to be at least 52 years old; in 1998 the age requirement was increased to 54, and in the following three years it was moved further upward, first to 55, then to 56, and lastly to 57.

9 There are separate programs for the industrial, the agricultural, and the building sector in the case of both the ordinary and the reduced unemployment benefit.

10 Until 1998, the replacement rate for ordinary unemployment benefits was only 30% compared to 80% for short-term wage compensation.

11 The law is complemented by the agreement signed by the national government and the regions in February 2009. The agreement is characterized by following major points: (a) €8 billion will be allocated over the period 2009–10 to provide unemployment protection in the context of an active inclusion strategy; and (b) funding is mainly provided by regional and national resources related to the European Social Fund: within this context, the regions will funnel their allocations (€2.65 billion) into measures to enhance employability through vocational training and skills upgrading, which should accompany income-support measures. However, in September 2009, Minister Sacconi stated that until then only €1.5 billion had been effectively spent and that by the end of the year he expected to spend only €500 million more.

12 The percentage was increased to 30% in 2010.

13 Parliamentary discussion of law-decree 185 (turned into law 2/2009) on January 16, 2009.

14 Even a quick look at the unemployment benefits specifically aimed at atypical workers—which the government introduced in the context of the measures addressing the economic crisis—confirms the validity of the above consideration. For the first time, the above-mentioned *parasubordinati*—a category of atypical work that comprises about 550,000 people, mostly young people and women—were granted some form of unemployment protection. The lump sum will correspond to 30% of the worker's earnings for 2009, but not all the workers meet the qualifying conditions.

15 *Libro verde sul futuro del modello sociale: La vita buona nella società attiva*, p. 10.

16 Until now, parents could choose whether to send their children to primary school for eight hours a day, including lunch, or only in the mornings, with the possibility of two long days. The eight-hour schedule has now been severely limited.

17 Among others, Francesca Campomori (2008) provides a very interesting and comprehensive analysis of local intervention in this field in *Immigrazione e cittadinanza locale.*

REFERENCES

Berton, F., M. Richiardi, & S. Sacchi (2009a). *Il sussidio lascia e raddoppia*. http://www.lavoce.info

Berton, F., M. Richiardi, & S. Sacchi (2009b). *Flex-insecurity. Perché in Italia la flessibilità diventa precarietà*. Bologna: Il Mulino.

Campomori, F. (2008). *Immigrazione e cittadinanza locale. La governance dell'integrazione in Italia*. Rome: Carocci.

Cartocci, R. (1994). *Il deficit di integrazione in Italia: una lettura culturale della crisi di oggi*. In M. Caciagli, F. Cazzola, L. Morlino, & S. Passigli (Eds.), *L'Italia tra crisi e transizione* (pp. 45–67). Bari: Laterza.

CENSIS (2009), *43° Rapporto sulla situazione sociale del Paese 2009*, Milan, Franco Angeli. http://www.censis.it

Dragosei, L. (2010*). Il Welfare del Libro Bianco. Diritti variabili per ciascuno.* www.nelmerito.it

Fargion, V. (1992). *Aspetti politici ed istituzionali della esperienza italiana in materia di distribuzione territoriale della spesa pubblica*, FORMEZ *La distribuzione regionale della spesa pubblica. Esperienze internazionali*, pp. 119–134.

Fargion, V. (1997). *Geografia della cittadinanza sociale in Italia*. Bologna: Il Mulino.

Fargion, V. (2001). Creeping workfare policies: The case of Italy. In N. Gilbert (Ed.), *Activating the unemployed: A comparative appraisal of work-oriented policies* (pp. 29–68). Rutgers, N.J.: Transaction Publishers.

Fargion, V. (2009). Italy: Still a pension state? In P. Alcock & C. Graig (eds.), *International social policy* (pp. 171–189). Houndmills: Palgrave.

Fargion, V. (2010a). Children, gender and families in the Italian welfare state. In J. Gal & M. Ajzenstadt (eds.), *Children, gender and families in Mediterranean welfare states* (pp. 105–128). London/New York: Springer.

Fargion, V. (2010b). *Annual National Report 2010: Pensions, health and long-term care— Italy*. http://www.socialprotection.eu/files_db/898/asisp_ANR10_Italy.pdf

Ferrera, M. (1984). *Il welfare state in Italia*. Bologna: Il Mulino.

Ferrera, M. (1996). The "Southern Model" of welfare in social Europe. *Journal of European Social Policy, 6*(1), 17–37.

Ferrera, M., & E. Gualmini (2004). *Rescued by Europe? Social and labour market reforms in Italy from Maastricht to Berlusconi.* Amsterdam: Amsterdam University Press.

Graziano, L. (1980). *Clientelismo e sistema politico. Il caso dell'Italia.* Milan: Franco Angeli.

Ichino, P. (1996). *Il lavoro e il mercato.* Milan: Mondadori.

Marshall, T. H. (1965). *Class, citizenship and social development.* New York: Doubleday.

Masini, C. A. (1962). Il sistema degli assegni familiari in Italia. *Previdenza Sociale, 17*(1), 5–15.

Ministero del Lavoro e delle politiche sociali (2009). *Libro Bianco sul Futuro del Modello Sociale. La vita buona nella società attiva.* http://www.lavoro.gov.it/NR/rdonlyres/376B2AF8–45BF-40C7-BBF0-F9032F1459D0/0/librobianco.pdf

Ministero della Salute (2009). *Il sistema di valutazione della performance dei Sistemi Sanitari Regionali. Primi indicatori ministeriali 2008.* http://www.salute.gov.it/imgs/C_17_pubblicazionI_1239_allegato.pdf

Pennacchi, L. (2009). La rimozione della cittadinanza. Il futuro del modello sociale secondo il Libro Bianco. *Notiziario INCA, 10,* 113.

Raitano, M. (2010). La segmentazione del lavoro in tempo di crisi: il caso italiano in prospettiva comparata. *La Rivista delle Politiche sociali, 1,* 47–77.

Zincone, G. (1992). *Da Sudditi a Cittadini.* Bologna: Il Mulino.

9

A FUZZY PICTURE: SOCIAL CITIZENSHIP IN POSTCORPORATIST GERMANY

Ingo Bode

Social scientists exploring the reality and future of modern welfare states are confronted with two different agendas: the empirical analysis of institutional and social developments, on the one hand, and the design of welfare reform following a set of (allegedly) widely shared, or personally held, convictions, on the other. Clearly, however, there are aspects that can be referred to in both senses simultaneously, one of which is the concept of social citizenship. Many view social citizenship as a valuable concept to be promoted by "real" welfare policies; accordingly, current states of welfare are judged against this ideal. This contrasts with an empirical approach, which explores whether, or to what extent, typical (Western) societies have seen the emergence of a welfare regime influenced by this concept, and how this regime is evolving. This empirical perspective includes a debate on the wider, for instance sociostructural, underpinnings of those regulatory norms endorsing social citizenship, such as the structure of labor markets, patterns of collective interests, or the evolution of the life course in modern society.

The following analysis subscribes to the second of the two aforementioned perspectives. Referring to one particular European country, namely Germany, it explores the fate of social citizenship in a corporatist welfare regime against the background of recent welfare reforms. It begins with some remarks on the analytical utility of the concept when analyzing corporatist welfare states. It proceeds by giving a picture of the major pillars of the German welfare state and examines to what extent the concept of social citizenship—which is a far from familiar concept for both speakers in the public sphere and the scientific community of Germany—can be applied to the analysis of a corporatist welfare regime. It will be

198

shown that elements of quasi-social citizenship have indeed settled in the German welfare system, albeit under other names. The chapter then examines what has happened to these elements since the end of the "golden age" (Esping-Andersen, 1996) of the corporatist era (the 1980s), and how they have been influenced by developments since then. In essence, it will be argued that these developments are indicative of a fuzzy configuration in which the work-related social rights that had *de facto* instilled elements of social citizenship in the German welfare regime during the 20th century have been exposed to a shift towards "marketization" (or re-commodification) even though, paradoxically, new universalistic elements have also occurred that loosely connect with a citizenship-related concept of social welfare provision but are ultimately insignificant to those who are the most dependent on welfare state entitlements.

The final section of the chapter embarks on a speculative discussion about the reasons behind such changes. In particular, it takes issue with approaches that contend that pressures on the institutional setup of Western welfare systems correspond to the emergence of "new risks." Referring to the case of Germany, it will be argued that the new risk account, while it concords with some contemporary societal phenomena, cannot explain the background to current welfare reforms. Other factors will have to be brought into the equation if we are to understand why "old" ideas relating to social citizenship have fallen out of fashion, and not only in Germany.

SOCIAL CITIZENSHIP AND ITS FATE: AN ANALYTICAL PERSPECTIVE CENTERING ON CORPORATIST WELFARE REGIMES

Throughout the Anglo-Saxon world, the groundbreaking work of Thomas H. Marshall (1965) has popularized the idea by which social citizenship has become a reference to public policies in Western nation states taking shape particularly in the aftermath of World War II (Dwyer, 2004, 51–76). Although the concept was not awarded much paradigmatic value outside the Anglo-Saxon world, some elements inherent in it have also played a role in other welfare regimes. This is obviously the case for Nordic welfare states, but also, as will be explained below, for those classified by the comparative literature as "corporatist" (or "conservative").

True, there have been many questions concerning Marshall's concept as exposed in his book on "citizenship and social class" (1965). The concept has been criticized for being overly Anglo-Saxon, gender-blind, or neglecting the role of civic participation, which is the interplay of political and social citizenship (Johansson & Hvinden, 2007; Lister, 2003; Mead, 1997; Turner, 2001). In addition, there were complaints that Marshall was not clear enough about the extent to which the realization of social citizenship required fiscal redistribution, minimum welfare provision, and a high degree of collectivism (Powell, 2002).

Moreover, critics have pointed to the fact that the concept was ambiguous in that it did not address the tensions between the idea of social citizenship and the market order in which it was (meant to be) embedded (Dean, 2008).

Nonetheless, Marshall's approach to citizenship helps make sense of the development of the welfare settlement throughout western Europe (Rees, 1996). Marshall set out how civil, political, and social citizenship emerged as a normative framework, first for smaller sections of the population and then extending to larger parts of it, with the three types of citizenship mutually reinforcing each other. Moreover, he understood citizenship "as a status bestowed upon those who are full members of a community" and "are equal with respect to the rights and duties with which that status is endowed" (Marshall, 1965, 18). With these cornerstones, the concept not only illuminates the intrinsic connection between social and universal political rights but serves as a key analytical tool to assess both the character of welfare state entitlements and changes in this character.

Social citizenship, in Marshall's sense, addresses a configuration in which individuals belonging to a national community enjoy inalienable rights to social welfare provision in cash and/or in kind. At the same time, it embodies a set of institutionalized ties between members of a political collectivity that are grounded in common rights and duties. This holds true regardless of the fact that democratic participation in the provision of social welfare, or "welfare democracy" (Fitzpatrick, 2002), was widely neglected in this approach. Concerning the nexus between social and political citizenship, it is important to see that the former appears as a prerequisite to the fulfillment of the latter. This is, at least, the prevailing interpretation of the concept. Individuals, so this interpretation goes, can only be full and equal members of a (political) community if fundamental needs concerning their physical and social reproduction are met. Hence, welfare regimes endorse citizenship at large to the extent that they bestow individuals with entitlements that cover those needs, irrespective of the citizens' relative economic status and regardless of their propensity to comply with the (other than constitutional) rules imposed by political majorities. It is common to assume that this implies a level of social welfare provision exceeding the poverty line.

A particular interpretation of Marshall's model, suggested by Esping-Andersen (1990) in his seminal book on the foundations of Western welfare regimes, should also be taken into account. Drawing on the concept of "de-commodification," Esping-Andersen applied Marshall's approach to the regulation of waged labor. De-commodification, he posited, was achieved when citizens could "freely, and without potential loss of job, income or social well-being, opt out of work" (Esping-Andersen, 1990, 23). While Esping-Andersen's concept is not fully congruent with Marshall's perspective (Powell, 2002, 236), it makes clear that in modern Western society, the realization of social citizenship is widely based on the right to make life choices independently of market pressures.

A crucial question is how far it makes sense to draw on this Anglo-Saxon concept for the analysis of welfare regimes outside the Anglo-Saxon countries.

While this does not pose any problem for Nordic welfare states, those labeled *conservative* or *corporatist* are rarely discussed in the terms of this concept. True, at first glance, corporatist welfare states exhibit features alien to the concept, including a strong link between salaried employment and welfare entitlements and a more marginal role for social rights associated with the basic citizenship status, such as flat-rate universal basic pensions and means-tested benefits for the unemployed.

It is obvious, however, that corporatist welfare states have been—more or less—inspired by ideas related to social citizenship. True, perfect de-commodification remained a fiction in all "real" types of Western welfare states. Yet in corporatist countries, ordinary (breadwinning) employees enjoyed considerable latitude when it came to choices concerning labor market participation during the postwar decades. Such latitude was the foundation of what Turner (2001) has labeled the status of the "worker-citizen." This status materialized, *inter alia*, through unemployment benefits that protected the social status of jobseekers over a longer period, and furthermore unconditional income support (in case of personal hardship), pensions exceeding the poverty line, and access to social and healthcare services free of charge. Granted—and this was not a particularity of corporatist welfare states—the level of entitlements corresponded to a given record of (previous) labor market participation. From the 1960s until the 1980s, however, labor market participation was almost guaranteed to (male) citizens, together with the prospect of employment standards approaching the average of the wage-dependent population. In any case, the conditionality of social protection was limited when compared to both early industrialism and the recent "workfare era."

The story is of course different for women, as these were often dependent on derived entitlements, with this restriction creating problems for those unable, or unwilling, to rely on the achievements of a breadwinning husband. As female labor market participation was rising (more or less rapidly) across corporatist (and other) Western welfare states during the second half of the 20th century, however, the status of "worker-citizen" status became ever more universalistic. In a nutshell, while the concept of social citizenship was always a rationale that informs political agendas rather than empirical reality, it *de facto* became increasingly relevant.

Meanwhile, however, a good deal of the contemporary literature on Western welfare states suggests that this movement has come to an end. This conjecture addresses corporatist varieties as well. All welfare regimes have witnessed the spread of market values (Baldock, 2003; Bode, 2008; Frericks, 2011; Gilbert, 2002, 99–135) as well as a far-reaching overhaul of basic benefit schemes, including through what are commonly referred to as workfare policies (Ellison, 2005; Handler, 2003). At discourse level, the emphasis has been placed on individual duty, self-responsibility, free choice, and self-governance (Kemshall, 2002)—all notions at odds with the universalistic momentum of the Marshallian concept. Charges were made to the—apparently—unconditional character of many welfare state rights, which was assumed to contribute to passivity, social exclusion, and a declining work ethic.

There is, however, a paradox. While major social programs have been subject to privatization and retrenchment, many Western welfare states, including the corporatist regimes, have seen the propagation of a new kind of universalism, centering on ideas such as broader access to childcare or user rights granted to disabled people (Chan & Bowpitt, 2005; Cowden & Singh, 2007; Dean, 2008; Ellis, 2004; Lister, 2004; Mabbett, 2005). As social policies in Europe have effectively drawn on this agenda, there seems to be more to welfare state reform than mere retrenchment. Against this background, the actual development of social citizenship-related elements inhabiting Western welfare regimes, in general, and corporatist welfare states, in particular, deserves closer inspection. This is the rationale underlying the subsequent analysis of the case of Germany, which is generally viewed as the corporatist welfare regime *par excellence*.

REAL SOCIAL CITIZENSHIP IN GERMANY—PAST AND PRESENT

The Concept of Social Citizenship in Germany and its Functional Equivalents

In Germany, the notion of social citizenship as such is almost a non-issue in both the institutional architecture of the welfare state and the public debate referring to this architecture (but see Steinert, 2007). Having said that, citizenship-related issues have recently been discussed with respect to the living conditions of immigrants and ethnic minorities. In this vein, political citizenship (*Staatsbürgerschaft*) and its preconditions were also addressed with an eye on social welfare provision, for instance regarding the exclusion of illegal immigrants from basic welfare entitlements. Yet, even in this debate, the notion of social citizenship has seldom been addressed. On the whole, it has not become part of what might be termed the official "welfare culture" of Germany.

However, basic ideas inherent to it do play a role in this culture—in other words, it does contain functional equivalents. For instance, social citizenship has *de facto* been addressed by German scholars dealing with "social justice" issues (Nullmeier & Vobruba, 1995). This pertains firstly to "participative justice" (*Teilhabegerechtigkeit*), understood as a fundamental social value to be brought to fruition by distinctive welfare state institutions (Leisering, 2004). Secondly, those dealing with the social doctrine of German Catholicism, fundamental to the institutions of the German welfare state (van Kersbergen 1995), have referred to "needs-oriented (social) justice" (*Bedarfsgerechtigkeit*) as a further essential cornerstone of the German social model. Moreover, welfare state entitlements have often been dealt with as social rights, in a sense similar to those put forward by Marshall (1965). For example, the debate on constitutional norms stipulating inalienable basic rights has touched upon social welfare issues in various respects. Moreover, social rights have been a key topic in German "social policy thinking" ever since the 19th century (Kaufmann, 2003).

Finally, following the early discussions of the "green movement" in the 1980s, the enactment of a universal and unconditional minimum income benefit into social law has repeatedly been the subject of academic debate (see, e.g., Grözinger et al., 2006). This suggestion has sometimes embraced the idea of upgrading unpaid work by granting volunteers monetary rewards. Overall, however, such ideas have found only a limited echo, not least because they have obviously gone against the tide of the dominant approach to labor market policy in Germany. This approach has emphasized the extension of salaried work and pressures to make citizens accept jobs regardless of their personal circumstances and the charac-teristics of these jobs (see below). Altogether, when exploring the role that social citizenship has actually played in the German welfare state, one has to dig deeper and look at institutions not (directly) associated with the concept as such.

Traces of Social Citizenship in the Postwar Settlement

Certainly, the German welfare state is (still) heavily infused with its Bismarckian heritage. In the Bismarckian tradition, welfare (and healthcare) entitlements are closely linked to the status of the salaried employee. Compared to liberal welfare regimes, entitlements are generous, particularly unemployment benefits (during the first year of unemployment) and public retirement provisions (as regards current pensioners in particular). Conversely, guaranteed flat-rate entitlements, emblematic of universalistic welfare policies, appear rather alien to this tradition. As we shall see, however, the German welfare regime, as it has taken shape over the course of the 20th century and especially after the Second World War, exhib-its a number of elements that have instilled a *de facto* social citizenship rationale in its structural design.

This is not the place for a detailed description of the German welfare sys-tem (overviews are provided by Bleses & Seeleib-Kaiser, 2004; Clasen, 2005; and Jochem, 2009). A quick foray into its architecture illustrates that the sys-tem depends largely on social insurance institutions and is strongly infused with employment-related entitlements, mainly in the area of social pension and unem-ployment insurance. The "worker-centeredness" of the welfare system is obvious, then. At the same time, however, the current German welfare system (still) com-prises elements that, in all but name, conform to the idea of social citizenship, often within the confines of social insurance schemes. Major citizenship-related entitlements in the current welfare regime are highlighted by italics in Table 9.1. These include minimum benefits as retirement provision, the reimbursement of healthcare expenses, a basic bundle of long-term care services, income support in case of unemployment, child allowances (plus options for subsidized parental leave), as well as a wide range of social support services in case of evidenced need (for neglected children, battered women, indebted individuals, and so on).

Table 9.1. Main Elements of the German Welfare Regime

Program	Benefit	Funding	Membership
Old-age pensions	Payments mainly dependent on prior contributions (*yet with minimum benefits*)	Payroll contributions (employee/employer)	Mandatory for employees
	Subsidies to individuals purchasing private pension plans	General taxation	Voluntary
Health insurance	*Expenses for medical care* (with co-payments) Income replacement according to prior contributions	Payroll contributions (employee/employer)† Minor input of tax revenue	Social insurance mandatory for employees up to ceiling* (*private insurance option beyond this*)
Long-term care insurance	Proportion of expenses incurred for care services Long-term care allowance	Payroll contributions (employee/employer)†	Mandatory for employees
Unemployment insurance	Income replacement according to prior contributions	Payroll contributions (employee/employer)	Mandatory for employees
Long-term jobseeker allowance	*Flat rate with means-testing*	General taxation	Universal access
Social assistance	*Flat rate with means-testing*	General taxation	Universal access
Social services	*Benefits in kind* (mostly means-tested)	General taxation Social insurance funds Minor input from voluntary agencies	Partially universal access
Child benefits	*Per capita flat-rate benefits*	General taxation	Universal access
Parental leave	*Flat rate* & benefits depending on earnings (partially means-tested)	General taxation	

* The self-employed and employees with an income exceeding €4237 (2012) can opt out into private insurance.
† Employers pay a slightly lower rate than employees.

It is noteworthy that social assistance (*Sozialhilfe*), introduced in the 1960s, and a number of social services have always (more or less) been subject to means-testing and "pedagogical" interventions under the responsibility of welfare bureaucracies and social workers. In reality, however, social assistance came as an unconditional right to basic social well-being, irrespective of the propensity of benefit recipients to take up salaried work. In the past, healthcare provision, too, was (widely) available to (almost) all citizens free of charge just as pension schemes embraced minimum benefits above the level of social assistance for those having worked as a salaried employee for a longer period. Unemployment benefits were granted on a permanent basis to citizens with a short work record if they could not find a job that corresponded to their qualifications (including in terms of salary) and if the total revenue of the recipient's household was below a certain level. One can conclude, then, that, given the aforementioned panoply of quasi-universalistic entitlements, the German welfare regime as established during the 20th century exhibited a particular, corporatist, version of social citizenship.

Corporatist Social Citizenship Under Stress

Over the past two decades, the German welfare regime has undergone substantial change. This change was path-breaking in many respects but also fraught with considerable ambiguity. In the following sections, major welfare programs are reviewed with particular reference to what has happened to the corporatist variety of universalistic social welfare provision with those reforms that have been enacted since the 1990s. The review covers three basic areas: unemployment protection, pensions, and healthcare.

Concerning unemployment benefits, Germany has witnessed a sea change over the past years, with the Hartz reforms entailing a partial overhaul of the former, mainly status-oriented, protection scheme (Clasen & Goerne, 2011). This scheme had granted lifelong (if degressive) benefits to the large majority of (male) citizens with some years of work experience, in correspondence with previous earnings and mainly above the poverty line. The reforms enacted in 2004 have reduced income-related unemployment benefits to a maximum length of 12 months for those under 50. As for workers approaching retirement, this has increased up to 24 months, following amendments to these reforms. In addition, long-term jobseekers have been shifted onto a flat-rate allowance labeled "Unemployment Benefit II" (in 2012, €374 per month for a single adult, to which a housing allowance is added). The former social assistance scheme (*Sozialhilfe*) is now confined to those unable to work longer than three hours a day.

Furthermore, the definition of what was previously considered "suitable" employment for those receiving unemployment benefits was significantly modified. Jobseekers now must accept any employment available in their area (defined as within two hours travel distance), provided that the wage offered does not fall below a certain level (after 6 months of unemployment, below the benefit itself; prior to this, 70% to 80% of the previous salary). Unlike in the past, formal skills or the type of profession prior to unemployment are not taken into account. Those on Unemployment Benefit II have to accept any reasonable employment. Moreover, long-term jobseekers can be compelled to take a "One-Euro-Job" offered by public or nonprofit employers on a fixed-term basis (six to nine months). These jobs, held by some 670,000 citizens in 2010, are paid at the rate of one euro per hour over Unemployment Benefit II in most cases.

According to the advocates of these reforms (which include the social democrats), the Hartz reforms were meant to benefit recipients of the (former) social assistance scheme by offering them new gateways to job placement services. Reorganizing the job service agencies was indeed viewed as a cornerstone of the reforms. While, as with developments in other countries, labor offices were pressured to ensure that jobseekers were "market-ready," the unemployed were now to be handled as individual "customers." In the new discourse, there was an emphasis on the right to individually tailored service provision (Rauch & Dornette, 2010). This was meant to remedy the previous bureaucratic welfare culture in which jobseekers were treated as "mass clients." That said, this change in the overall philosophy of labor market-related public services was paradoxically accompanied by a substantial contraction in the scope for individual self-determination concerning where to work, and under which conditions. Those who do not conform to the rules (in terms of registration, applications, participation in preparatory programs, etc.) now face severe sanctions.

Altogether, it is evident that, in the area of unemployment protection, the corporatist social citizenship that once embraced quasi-universalistic entitlements for all those with some work experience has become subject to a profound shift towards re-commodification (marketization). At the same time, a new kind of universal right has been created: that of individualized placement services that are open to everyone—although the potential to exercise this right has proved limited in practice (Mayerhofer et al., 2009). Moreover, the reforms brought a promise to move former recipients of social assistance from a paternalistic poor relief scheme into a job placement system in which they were treated like other jobseekers. This could be seen as an attempt to extend the "worker citizen" rationale of the postwar settlement, even though the aforementioned re-commodification has, on the whole, undermined this rationale. Hence, the transition from a passive to an "enabling" welfare state was a political promise rather than reality.

In the field of pensions, Germany has witnessed a similar paradigmatic change (Schmähl, 2007). The postwar pensions system granted pay-as-you-go and earnings-related retirement provisions to the great majority of the German population. In the wider literature, the German approach to retirement provision was often seen, therefore, as emblematic of corporatist welfare. The system provided comprehensive work-related (defined-benefit) pensions, ensuring wage replacement rates of up to 70% of gross average earnings. Its principal aim was to guarantee that workers could continue to enjoy a comparable standard of living after they retired to that they had enjoyed previously. It proved less generous to (the small number of) self-employed workers on low incomes and to citizens who had taken longer career breaks or been in part-time employment. Women were (and remain) a case in point. What is commonly referred to as the "breadwinner model" created derived pension rights for married partners, yet numerous women with poor employment records were forced into the social assistance system, which granted more modest (means-tested) income support. By the end of the last century, however, the number of citizens who depended on this benefit had decreased markedly.

We should note that prior to the 1990s, low-income years were upgraded through a specific provision in the pension calculation formula. Moreover, during the postwar decades, social insurance coverage was successively extended to further stages of a citizen's life course, including periods of education and family care (only the latter survived the reforms of the 1990s and 2000s). Minimum pensions, the major beneficiaries of which were women, had long been provided within the legal framework of social assistance but were fraught with the take-up problems familiar in other countries. In 2003, minimum pensions were institutionally decoupled from social assistance in order to improve take-up rates. Private and occupational retirement provision long played a marginal role (less than a tenth of pension benefits originated from this source at the turn of the millennium).

Implicitly, at least, the development of the social insurance-based pension scheme(s) during the postwar settlement infused the pension system as a whole with elements of social citizenship. Granted, a longer-term record of employment was indispensable, so that many women and self-employed were excluded from (generous) benefits. But since salaried work was (and still is) the predominant pattern in the lives of male citizens, and since women too were increasingly taking up salaried work from the 1970s onwards, the pensions system developed towards quasi-universalism—not least because work interruptions or low-pay episodes were smoothed out to a considerable extent by the system even though a means-tested retirement provision was easily available.

However, pension reforms enacted between 2001 and 2005 have curtailed (future) standard wage replacement rates substantially. Those now aged 40 or below will enjoy little more than 55% of real wages after retirement age. Citizens without a history of full employment will be even worse off. Since unemployment among senior citizens is fairly high, incomplete contribution records are likely to occur. Certainly, cuts in public pensions were meant to be offset by state-sponsored private savings. The pensions reforms of the 2000s brought in a new kind of funded pension plan (Bode, 2008, 37–40, 60–69). Today, holders of personal savings accounts receive direct flat-rate subsidies to top up their own contributions, with public support approaching 30% of the capital saved in the first years. For those whose earnings exceed a certain threshold, generous tax breaks kick in. Subsidies or tax exemptions are also awarded to workers enrolling in funded corporate schemes, which resemble personal plans in most respects (although they enjoy the particular advantage of investments being exempt from social security levies). As for regulation, private pension plans must protect the nominal value of the capital invested. Many guarantee a minimum rate of interest (1.75% in 2012). Most suppliers have to reinsure themselves against insolvency. However, there is an increasingly used option to put money into investment funds, which do *not* offer such guarantees.

Importantly, the objective of the pension reforms was more than to prevent further increases in contribution rates, which was assumed to be problematic for private businesses. The political elite (including the social democrats) defended pension reforms, *inter alia*, by contending that they enabled citizens to find individually tailored solutions to their personal situation. It was thought that women, in particular, would benefit from the option to build their own pension account in the absence of a (comfortable) contribution record with social insurance. One should also note the change in the administration of minimum pensions, which, in 2003, became detached from the social assistance framework in which they had been embedded during the 20th century. Because this reform relieved relatives of their obligation to support (poor) parents, this helped to consolidate the social right to receive a guaranteed minimum notwithstanding modest contribution records in the social insurance scheme. This guaranteed minimum for "pensioner-citizens" may be seen as an extension of the corporatist approach to social citizenship that was instilled in the postwar pension regime, with an impact on take-up rates but *not* on the regime's overall generosity.

Again, the overall outcome has been paradoxical: while the public promotion of private retirement saving is infused with universalistic norms—not least because it deliberately attempts to empower low-income savers—the eventual level of pension provision depends on individual thrift and the fate of a given pension plan on the financial markets. Both the phasing-out of redistributive mechanisms within the public pension scheme and recent cuts in benefits create particular risks for those unable or unwilling to invest in private pension schemes (Lamping & Tepe, 2009). Hence, while individual choice was extended, retirement provision became (partially) marketized and less secure overall, with low-income workers the main victims. Overall, the new "responsibility mix" that Germany adopted from the liberal model of providing public support for individual self-protection (see Chapter 15) has brought greater social inequality, notwithstanding novel attempts to contain old-age poverty.

Similar contradictions can be observed in the field of healthcare provision. German healthcare insurance, currently operated by approximately 150 nonprofit sickness funds, is widely considered as a further core pillar of the Bismarckian welfare regime. Enrollment was long directly linked to salaried employment, with sickness benefits largely dependent on prior earnings. Subsequently, the bulk of benefits awarded were increasingly in kind, just as many other groups became covered by the sickness funds. The system thus adopted a quasi-universalistic character. It is important to note, however, that private insurance companies are permitted to offer full coverage, but only to citizens whose earnings exceed a certain threshold (Thomson & Mossialos, 2006). This private opt-out clause provides around 10% of the German population with more generous, and sometimes less expensive, access to medical care.

Today, social insurance contributions are (still) earnings-related while benefits are granted on the basis of need. Service supply is left to independent providers, which are remunerated by a multipayer system made up of nonprofit sickness funds and the private insurance sector. The sickness funds are subject to a unified legal framework that stipulates the list of reimbursable medical services and the level of additional public subsidy to be injected into the system. While the funds are economically independent, differences between the risk structures of their enrollees are broadly (but not completely) balanced out by a redistributive compensation scheme. The latest healthcare reform made enrollment in a healthcare insurance scheme mandatory (Lisac et al., 2010). Previous years had seen a rapidly growing number of uninsured (mostly self-employed) citizens. Private insurers were compelled to accept any claimant within the confines of a basic service package. In this particular respect, then, a further step towards universalization was taken. To some extent, universalism has also been strengthened through the contract policies of the sickness funds. Since 2007, the discounts negotiated between the sickness funds and suppliers of generics have brought reductions in the patients' co-payment bill, which advantages the chronically ill and low-income households. Since the late 1990s, the sickness funds have been given greater leeway to grant discounts to enrollees who participate in programs for special treatments (Busse, 2004). From this perspective, universalism has proved a lasting feature of the German healthcare system.

That said, with the healthcare reforms of the 1990s and 2000s, more has been left to the market. For those covered by social insurance, out-of-pocket payments have markedly risen over the past 20 years, although individual caps apply. In 2008, co-payments amounted to 13% of total expenses, up from 9.5% in 1995. This implies a rising burden on households with modest earnings, including the classic "worker-citizen." Moreover, while the healthcare reform enacted in 2008 established a standard contribution rate (15% of the payroll, roughly shared by employers and workers), it also stipulated that sickness funds can levy additional flat-rate contributions from their enrollees should they run into deficit (which has meanwhile happened with some of the funds). A number of sickness funds used this opportunity thereafter. Hence personal (market) income now makes a difference to citizens' access to healthcare. From this perspective, corporatist social citizenship has been reduced in scope, while conditions for accessing healthcare provision have become more unequal.

Change is under way in another respect, too. Since the mid-1990s, the German healthcare system has exhibited a particular version of the internal market (Bode, 2010a). Sickness funds now compete for enrollees. To some extent, they can offer distinctive insurance conditions and some (contracted) services (gatekeeper GPs, inexpensive drugs, integrated care, etc.). In a similar way, the funds can grant bonuses to attract particular groups of enrollees. There is, then, a tendency to differentiate the range and the conditions of services—a trend that is consistent with the advent of a new "consumer agenda" in healthcare internationally (Newman & Kuhlmann, 2007).

Regarding the foundations of the healthcare system built up from the late 19th century onwards, these developments are again indicative of (slow) paradigmatic change. The least one can say is that while corporatist quasi-universalism has been consolidated in some respects, it has been weakened in others. Accordingly, consumer rights have been strengthened in that individuals are invited (indeed, encouraged) to make choices as to how use their entitlements. In this area, too, new universalistic elements have appeared that stress individual rights within a more marketized environment, creating greater social inequality.

REASONS FOR CHANGE

A key challenge in the debate on changes in the welfare state is understanding the reasons behind these changes—which, as illustrated above, in the case of Germany essentially meant a shift away from collectivistic welfare towards greater individual choice. Concentrating on non-economic explanations, as the proper domain of the social sciences, one influential body of literature that has addressed the aforementioned challenge focuses on (allegedly) new risks that are proliferating in contemporary Western societies (Armingeon & Bonoli, 2006; Kemshall, 2002; Powell et al., 2007; Schustereder, 2010; Taylor-Gooby, 2004). Drawing on a body of sociological theories around the theme of the "risk society" (for an overview, see Ekberg, 2007), the new risk narrative suggests that pressures on the modern welfare state have come about because of institutions that have remained unchanged since the aforementioned "golden age" and no longer fit into the social structure of contemporary society. These pressures are viewed to challenge existing elements of social citizenship and imply that collective social citizenship is ever less likely to be realized. In other words, the new social risk narrative insinuates that changes in the institutional setup of contemporary welfare states are, or will be, a logical consequence of the changing sociostructural settlement of Western society.

When we examine the three major social risks to which this narrative refers, however, serious doubts can be raised about its claims. The first observation alludes to demographic change, which is expected to undermine the foundations of long-established social protection schemes and create a perception of "age as risky and uncertain" (Powell et al., 2007, 70). In Germany, this is currently a prominent issue, with the German population aging more quickly than in many other Western welfare states (Höhn et al., 2008). The number of childless couples in particular seems to be growing, which is tending to narrow the options for informal care. However, the extension of formal care arrangements, which is required to cope with this demographic evolution, is a long-established tendency in Germany (Dammert, 2009, 19–28). It is largely based on quasi-corporatist institutions (long-term care insurance) that, with an add-on from social assistance, cover expanding needs. In light of this, the challenge posed by current demographic developments consists of little more than extending (and improving) existing personal care and nursing services—building on the efforts already initiated during the (late) "golden age" of the welfare state. It is hard to see why a quantitative increase in long-term care needs as such should be incompatible with the arrangements adopted (incrementally) during this "golden age." Likewise, the increase in the relative proportion of societal resources devoted to pensioners has proved to be a secular trend, particularly under the institutional framework of the postwar settlement. There is thus no "technical" reason why, with a steeper rise in what is referred to as the old-age dependency ratio, demographic change should become incompatible with this framework. It should also be noted that other institutional frameworks (those based on funded pension schemes), which were long deemed to be more compatible with demographic change, have been severely hit by the recent financial crisis.

The second class of (allegedly) new problems referred to in the "new risk" literature has its origins in the development of Western labor markets. Salaried work is viewed as becoming insecure across the board—that is, unstable and subject to permanent shifts concerning status and income issues. This popular interpretation has, however, not been left unchallenged internationally (see, e.g., Febre, 2007, or Mythen, 2005). As for Germany, job tenure remained relatively constant in the 1990s and even grew by one tenth between 1995 and 2005, as in other European societies (OECD, 2007). Taking men in Western Germany as a point of reference, the "survival rate" in a given occupation has not changed between cohorts entering the labor market in the 1950s and 1960s and those starting in the 1980s and 1990s. In the 2000s, this tendency was maintained (Mayer et al., 2010). East Germany shows a different pattern but may exhibit an exceptional case in the long term.

It is true, however, that part-time and temporary work has risen sharply. Part-time work has become a typical pattern of female labor market participation in Germany. That said, its expansion began long before the end of the "golden age" of the welfare state. What is new is that part-time employment tends to be ever less covered by social security, a situation that originates, to some extent at least, in social policies enacted during the past two decades. The same is true of temporary work, which has been a very dynamic sector in recent years, with the share of workers contracted by personal leasing agencies exceeding 3% (in 2012) of the total workforce (0.5% at the beginning of the 1990s). Importantly, however, when better opportunities come up, workers seek to change to permanent employment. The same is true for fixed-term employment, which has almost doubled over the past 10 years—as a result, it should be noted, of new legal provisions. In 2008, it affected one in eleven employees; yet again, the majority of these employees (mostly youngsters) sooner or later end up as permanent workers. Therefore, although transition periods have become longer overall, the work-related pillars of the modern life course, as established throughout the 20th century, persist both empirically and culturally for the great majority of the German population. Hence, in this country, too, "labor market insecurity is universal in a strictly hypothetical sense" (Mythen, 2005, 139). Even though it has grown over the past years, unstable employment is anything but a collective and permanent social risk that the classical unemployment protection (or pension) schemes are (or would have been) unable to cope with. One should note as well that current poverty risks linked to atypical jobs are by and large a result of social policies, more precisely an intentional dismantling of postwar social protection schemes. In Germany, it was this institutional change that created new risks—and then provoked new policies such as tax credits granted to those on a low-salary job.

Germany has also seen persistent long-term unemployment and the emergence of the (flexible) "working poor." Long-term employment doubled between 1990 and 2005 and has proven quite stable since then, despite a slight recovery of the German labor market more recently. As with temporary work, it affects the lower classes in the first instance. Regarding the working poor, in 2007, one in five employees were paid less than €9.50 per hour in the West and €6.87 in the East, with this concerning ever more breadwinners (see Bosch, 2009); it has grown markedly over recent years (by more than 20% since 2004). This is certainly one indication that corporatist social citizenship, based on a relatively egalitarian wage distribution and higher-skilled professional work, is on the retreat.

However, while both phenomena—long-term unemployment and the (flexible) working poor—are a novelty in the postwar era, it would be overly simplistic to view them as new risks that (have) challenge(d) corporatist welfare state institutions in the first instance. It has long been argued by those sympathetic with the new social risk narrative that institutions such as status-conserving unemployment benefit schemes endorse labor market segmentation. While it is true that Germany did see the exclusion of low-skilled, often elderly, workers from (decent) employment from the 1980s onwards, this segmentation persisted after those labor market reforms that markedly reduced the status-conserving character of the unemployment benefit scheme. Furthermore, the recent financial crisis has shown that liberal regimes equally may see both labor market segmentation *and* robust unemployment.

A third issue under debate, and maybe the one most often referred to in the new risk literature, pertains to the rise of new family models. The increased incidence of family breakups poses a particular problem to the German welfare regime insofar as it was based largely on a breadwinner model. In this model, lone parents face considerable economic risks unless they are entitled to alimony payments or if they are prevented, or refrain, from taking up employment. Indeed, as full-time work is not very widespread among German women with children, the prevalence of poverty is particularly high among lone mothers. Again, however, the new social risk narrative proves at least incomplete. First of all, institutions protecting parents following a family split-up (rights to receive alimony from the ex-partner) have been constrained in Germany by political decisions, with this, once again, creating new poverty risks. While those institutions that were emblematic of the "old" German welfare state, such as a tax regime that privileges married couples or a relatively poor childcare infrastructure, sit uneasily with the living conditions of contemporary German women, the association between social change and institutional (social policy) change proves rather loosely coupled. Secondly, while late-modern family life in Germany is more turbulent than in previous eras, disorganized patterns of female labor market participation, as well as women forced into complex childcare arrangements, are by no means new historically. Reconciling motherhood and salaried work has *always* been an issue for German women. While normatively, female labor market participation was deemed transitional in postwar Germany, it often proved a stable arrangement empirically, with many women having "to handle a complex double role of both being responsible for reproductive work and care in the family and for contributing to the family income" (Naumann, 2007, 7). What is more, women's labor market participation began to rise as early as in the 1950s, alongside welfare entitlements that extended beyond the (breadwinning) worker status. Given the fact that German women managed to increase their labor market participation in parallel to the invigoration of institutional norms related to corporatist social citizenship, it is hard to see why growing rates of separation should undermine or endanger these norms in the new millennium.

In view of this evidence, the "new risks narrative" sheds hardly any light at all on the background to changes in the current German welfare regime, nor on the shortcomings of those changes. One thus has to search further for an explanation. First of all, developments in the political economy matter (Peters, 2011). Despite the recent economic crisis, current Western societies have certainly become no less affluent since the end of the "golden age." Yet they have seen changes in the redistribution of national wealth across social classes. In Germany, the share of national income awarded to capital owners (including the upper middle classes) has grown markedly over the past two decades. Between 1994 and 2008, the GDP/wage ratio fell from 72% in 1994 to 65% in 2008 (note that in 2009 there was a reversal of this tendency, due to the financial crisis). Average workers have seen an erosion of their net earnings (by approximately 10% over the aforementioned period). The number of those citizens living on less than 60% of the average income, which includes many salaried workers, has risen significantly (by almost 50% over the same period, with one in six Germans in this situation at present). This has triggered (additional) pressure on social welfare provision, given both the shrinking sources of social security contributions and the simultaneous reduction of levies on capital income enacted by successive governments.

Overall, if the reference point is the individual citizen, Germany has seen welfare retrenchment in many instances in that the material needs of those who are the "victims" of the market economy are met less generously than in the past. To a considerable extent, it was the welfare reforms of the 1990s and 2000s that left those with little economic (and cultural) capital with the higher burden that they face today. Labor market policies that force unemployed citizens to accept low-paid jobs have helped reduce wage levels for those whose "employ-ability" is limited. Pension reforms have laid the onus of coping with demo-graphic change on workers, while employers have been alleviated and the "big players" in the financial market invited into a new business. Conversely, the recasting of the welfare state has enhanced the economic position of capital owners. Many have seen this as inevitable, given the pressure of economic glob-alization. Whether or not this is the case, the economic elites have been suc-cessful in enhancing their societal power, which, in turn, has created space for redistributive welfare policies. This is one major, if banal, piece of background information to the overhaul of social citizenship-related welfare programs, and not only in Germany.

But is not just the economy (… stupid); popular ideas and cultural attitudes are crucial as well. As far as Germany is concerned, it is obvious that new pat-terns of welfare-related sense-making have pervaded the political establishment, including the social democrats, over the past years (Seeleib-Kaiser & Fleckstein, 2007). One development merits particular attention in the context of this vol-ume. The advent of the welfare market and choice agenda as outlined in the preceding section is indicative of a new user model—which Clarke et al. (2007) refer to as "citizen-consumer"—taking center stage. An important factor in the popularity of this model is the marked rise of the new middle classes over the past decades (Crouch, 2004). Although these do not represent the majority of the population, they have become a key player in contemporary civil society. At the same time, more collectivistic forces (especially trade unions) have been los-ing ground (concerning Germany, see Bode, 2010b; Brömme & Strasser, 2001). One expression of this shift is the marked upswing of the Green Party, which was actively involved in those paradigmatic welfare reforms enacted between 1998 and 2006. While consumer identity has spread across the entire society (Bauman, 1998; Prisching, 2006), it is the values set of the new (better-educated) middle classes that is one driving, or trend-setting, force behind the growing appetite for markets and greater choice with regard to welfare programs (Walter, 2010). This implies both a normative emphasis on (new) rights to self-deter-mination *and* tendencies towards social closure in the process of risk-pooling, since active choice is predominantly exercised by citizens endowed with a certain cultural capital.

In Germany, it seems that proponents of "choice rights" and those interested in containing social protection programs (against the prospect of rising needs) have struck a bargain over the partial marketization of welfare state provision. A "dominant coalition" in the polity has adopted the new mantra of fostering consumer rights, associated with the chance to opt out of collectivistic modes of social and healthcare provision, as a new version of citizenship-related univer-salism that promises all citizens mastery of their own social protection. This is an important, if not the essential, aspect of the societal background of the growing fuzziness of (corporatist) social citizenship in Germany.

CONCLUSION

This chapter has argued that the idea of social citizenship was enshrined, albeit incompletely, in the corporatist (German) welfare regime under the postwar settlement. While this occurred within a framework reserving the most generous entitlements to highly skilled sections of the waged workforce, basic welfare rights were granted to a large majority of the population and a number of quasi-universal benefits were integrated into social insurance schemes. It would therefore be misleading to view social citizenship as a concept that only fits into the Anglo-Saxon (and maybe Nordic) "worlds of welfare." Rather, the nexus of social and political citizenship, as postulated by many scholars working with the Marshallian concept, also inhabited the corporatist German world of welfare.

With the decline of corporatism as a regulatory model, however, the German welfare state has entered a new phase. Recent welfare reforms have entailed the partial curtailment of social citizenship and the stronger influence of market forces on the life course of citizens. The scaling back of classical social entitlements and the proliferation of new consumer rights appear to be two sides of one coin—not only in Germany, but also in other welfare regimes (see Blomqvist, 2004; Gilbert, 2002; Newman & Kuhlmann, 2007)—namely, a twofold process of re-commodification or the creeping marketization of citizenship (see Crouch, 2004, 78, with a similar observation). On the one hand, citizens are increasingly exposed to the requirements of financial, labor, or health markets. Drawing on the argument of (the early) Esping-Andersen, social citizenship is scaled back as protection from market forces becomes weaker. On the other hand, the new citizenship-related "welfare consumer rights," as ambiguous they may appear, confer a market logic upon the use of social welfare provision. With the advent of the "citizen-consumer" as a major reference point for welfare reform, we can make out a new philosophy here—one that associates welfare state citizenship with a universal right to personally tailored services and income-protection plans.

Both the increasing risk of poverty for those at the bottom end of the social ladder and the diversification of service-related entitlements (for instance in the healthcare sector) are indicative of new limitations to quasi-universalism in what can be coined the *postcorporatist era*. In this era, the nexus between social and political citizenship is endangered for those who depend the most on social welfare entitlements. While the new "consumer rights" are, ultimately, of limited use to these groups, the threat of social exclusion is a reality for them (Steinert, 2007). However, if the German welfare regime has become less universal overall, the country has also seen reforms infusing more universalism into certain sections of this regime, apart from consumer rights issues. This is the case for healthcare, where the universalistic rationale has been strengthened, mandatory coverage has been extended, and the chronically ill have been targeted by extensive treatment programs. The repercussions of the collectivistic tradition inherent to the "old" German welfare regime can also be perceived in the way that the private pension market is regulated. In contrast to most other contemporary welfare states, direct support is provided to those with lower incomes embarking on a private pension plan. It should also be mentioned that Germany has recently seen considerable efforts to make public or publicly administrated childcare provision accessible to greater sections of the population (Evers et al., 2005), which may be interpreted as a further indicator of growing universalism.

As for the fate of social citizenship in Germany, a fuzzy picture emerges with three major dimensions. First of all, ideas related to social citizenship have persisted in some areas, while in others they seem to be on the retreat. This has led to the fragmentation of social citizenship insofar as there remains considerable basic universalism (or quasi-universalism) in the key reproductive spheres of society (health, family life), while provisions that affect the more productive spheres (work, income replacement) exhibit a plain tendency towards re-commodification.

Secondly, fuzziness is also an issue regarding the "choice agenda" as an expression of citizenship-related rights to individually tailored social welfare. This is most obvious in the field of unemployment protection and labor market integration, where individualization often chimes with authoritarian pressure on benefit recipients who are expected to comply with the duties imposed on them. Elsewhere, choice options are constrained considerably by poor market transparency (in the private pension market and regarding public health insurance coverage). Finally, even where the universalistic promise is maintained normatively, the rise of market (or quasi-market) governance via regulated commercial provision or internal markets generates uneven outcomes in terms of coverage and quality, simply because in a (provider) market, there are always winners *and* losers (Bode, 2010a).

Thirdly, the fuzziness of the current configuration in Germany is also due to a frozen status quo following the recent path-breaking welfare reforms, since these have not been uncontested (particularly on the political left). At present, the country has made an uneasy compromise between paradigmatic change and pragmatic conservatism. This compromise was embodied by both the "grand coalition" government in office between 2005 and 2009 and the center-right government succeeding it. With the financial crisis, this fuzzy situation persisted, materializing most obviously in labor market policies that draw massively on publicly subsidized reduction of working hours, which is an instrument emblematic of the corporatist era. Thus, Germany has recently seen ideologically mixed policies—that is, inconsistent regulatory movements that some have deemed an expression of a "neo-Bismarckian" approach to welfare reform (Hassenteufel & Palier, 2007) and that bear witness of the "hybrid nature" of contemporary welfare policies in this country (and elsewhere; see Chapter 15).

More generally, the agenda of marketization remains controversial in wider society and the subject of a "cultural battle" (Bode 2008). But what will happen in the near future? It has been argued in this chapter that the driving forces behind recent welfare reforms are not, or are only to a limited extent, associated with what social scientists exploring welfare state change have referred to as "new risks"—that is, developments that surface in the sociostructural settlement of Western societies. Rather, both the increasing societal power of capital owners and the cultural dynamics resulting from the rise of the new middle classes have provoked the dissemination of a different reading of citizenship rights. This reflects a new "cult of the individual" as well as the spread of market and consumer values in wider society, but particularly among the trend-setting social classes. Against this background, a key factor for the future will be the degree to which these social classes will cope and deal with the fuzziness of the consumer choice model mentioned previously. This model may turn out to be an illusion for many or even a threat to those who make "wrong" decisions in the newly created welfare markets. In the current fuzzy and fragmented landscape of the German welfare state, there indeed is room for both a re-actualization of (corporatist) social citizenship and further marketization.

REFERENCES

Armingeon, K., & G. Bonoli (Eds.) (2006). *The politics of post-industrial welfare states. Adapting post-war social policies to new social risks*. London/New York: Routledge.

Baldock, J. (2003). On being a welfare consumer in a consuming society. *Social Policy & Society* (2) 1, 65–71.

Bauman, Z. (1998). *Work, consumerism and the new poor*. Buckingham: Open University Press.

Bleses, P., & M. Seeleib-Kaiser (2004). *The dual transformation of the German welfare state*. Houndmills Basingstoke: Palgrave Macmillan.

Blomqvist, P. (2004). The choice revolution: Privatization in Swedish welfare services in the 1990s. *Social Policy & Administration* (38) 2, 139–155.

Bode, I. (2008). *The culture of welfare markets. The international recasting of care and pension systems*. New York/London: Routledge.

Bode, I. (2010a). Towards disorganised governance in public service provision? The case of German sickness funds. *International Journal of Public Administration* (33) 2, 61–72.

Bode, I. (2010b). Thinking beyond borderlines. A German gaze on a changing interface between society and the voluntary sector. *Voluntary Sector Review* (1) 2, 139–161.

Bosch, G. (2009). Low-wage work in five European countries and in the United States. *International Labour Review* (148) 4, 337–356.

Brömme, N., & H. Strasser (2001). Gespaltene Bürgergesellschaft. Die ungleichen Folgen des Strukturwandels von Engagement und Partizipation. *Aus Politik und Zeitgeschichte* (B25–26), 6–14.

Busse, R. (2004). Disease management programs in Germany's statutory health insurance system. *Health Affairs* (23) 3, 56–67.

Chan, C. K., & G. Bowpitt (2005). *Human dignity and welfare systems*. Bristol: Policy Press.

Clarke, J., J. Newman, N. Smith, E. Vidler, & L. Westmarland (2007). *Creating citizen-consumers: Changing publics and changing public services*. London: Sage.

Clasen, J. (2005). *Reforming European welfare states. Germany and the United Kingdom compared*. Oxford: Oxford University Press.

Clasen, J., & A. Goerne (2011). Exit Bismarck, enter dualism? Assessing contemporary German labour market policy. *Journal of Social Policy* (40) 4, 795–810.

Cowden, S., & G. Singh (2007). The "user": Friend, foe or fetish? A critical exploration of user involvement in health and social care. *Critical Social Policy* (27) 5, 5–23.

Crouch, C. (2004). *Post-democracy*. Oxford: Oxford University Press.

Dammert, M. (2009). *Angehörige im Visier der Pflegepolitik. Wie zukunftsfähig ist die subsidiäre Logik der deutschen Pflegeversicherung?* Wiesbaden: Verlag für Sozialwissenschaften.

Dean, H. (2008). Social policy and human rights: Re-thinking the engagement. *Social Policy & Society* (7) 1, 1–12.

Dwyer, P. (2004). *Understanding social citizenship. Themes and perspectives for policy-practice*. Bristol: Policy Press.

Ekberg, M. (2007). The parameters of risk society. A review and exploration. *Current Sociology* (55) 3, 343–366.

Ellis, K. (2004). Promoting rights or avoiding litigation? The introduction of the Human Rights Act 1998 into adult social care in England. *European Journal of Social Work* (7) 3, 321–340.

Ellison, N. (2005). *The transformation of welfare states*. London: Routledge.

Esping-Andersen, G. (1990). *Three worlds of welfare capitalism*. Cambridge: Polity.

Esping-Andersen, G. (1996). After the Golden Age? Welfare state dilemmas in a global economy. In G. Esping-Andersen (Ed.), *Welfare states in transition. National adaptations in global economies* (pp. 1–31). London: Sage.

Evers, A., J. Lewis, & B. Riedel (2005). Developing child-care provision in England and Germany: Problems of governance. *Journal of European Social Policy* (15) 3, 195–209.

Fevre, R. (2007). Employment insecurity and social theory: The power of nightmares. *Work, Employment & Society* (21) 3, 517–535.

Fitzpatrick, T. (2002). In search of welfare democracy. *Social Policy & Society* (1) 1, 1–20.

Frericks, P. (2011). Marketising social protection in Europe: Two distinct paths and their impact on social inequalities. *International Journal of Sociology and Social Policy* (31) 5–6, 319–443.

Gilbert, N. (2002). *Transformation of the welfare state. The silent surrender of public responsibility.* Oxford: Oxford University Press.

Grözinger, G., M. Maschke, & C. Offe (2006). *Die Teilhabegesellschaft. Modell eines neuen Wohlfahrtsstaats.* Frankfurt/Main: Campus.

Handler, J. F. (2003). Social citizenship and workfare in the US and Western Europe: From status to contract. *Journal of European Social Policy* (13) 3, 229–243.

Hassenteufel, P., & B. Palier (2007). Towards neo-Bismarckian health care states? Comparing health insurance reforms in Bismarckian welfare systems. *Social Policy & Administration* (41) 6, 574–596.

Höhn, C., R. Mai, & F. Michael (2008). Demographic change in Germany. In I. Hamm, H. Seitz, & M. Werding (Eds.), *Demographic change in Germany. The economic and fiscal consequences* (pp. 9–33). Berlin, Heidelberg: Springer.

Jochem, S. (2009). *Reformpolitik im Wohlfahrtsstaat. Deutschland im internationalen Vergleich.* Münster: Lit.

Johansson, H., & B. Hvinden. (2007). Opening citizenship: Why do we need a new understanding of social citizenship? In H. Johansson & B. Hvinden (Eds.), *Citizenship in Nordic welfare states. Dynamics of choice, duties and participation in a changing Europe* (pp. 3–17). London/New York: Routledge.

Kaufmann, F.-X. (2003). *Sozialpolitisches Denken—die deutsche Tradition.* Frankfurt/Main: Suhrkamp.

Kemshall, H. (2002). *Risk, social policy and welfare.* Buckingham: Open University Press.

Lamping, W., & M. Tepe (2009). Vom Können und Wollen der privaten Altersvorsorge. Eine empirische Analyse zur Inanspruchnahme der Riester-Rente auf Basis des Sozio-oekonomischen Panels. *Zeitschrift für Sozialreform* (55) 4, 409–430.

Leisering, L. (2004). Paradigmen sozialer Gerechtigkeit. Normative Diskurse im Umbau des Sozialstaats. In S. Liebig, H. Lengfeld, & S. Mau (Eds.), *Verteilungsprobleme und Gerechtigkeit in modernen Gesellschaften* (pp. 29–68). Frankfurt/New York: Campus,

Lisac, M., L. Reimers, K.-D. Henke, & S. Schlette (2010). Access and choice. Competition under the roof of solidarity in German health care—an analysis of health policy reforms since 2004. *Health Economics, Policy and Law* (5) 1, 31–52.

Lister, R. (2003). *Citizenship. Feminist perspectives* (2nd ed.). Basingstoke: Palgrave Macmillan.

Lister, R. (2004). The Third Way's social investment state. In J. Lewis & R. Surrender (Eds.), *Welfare state change: Towards a Third Way?* (pp. 157–182). Oxford: Oxford University Press.

Mabbett, D. (2005). The development of rights-based social policy in the European Union: The example of disability rights. *Journal of Common Market Studies* (43) 1, 97–120.

Marshall, T. H. (1965). Citizenship and social class (first published 1950). In T. H. Marshall, *Class, citizenship, and social development.* New York: Anchor Books.

Mayer, K. U., D. Grunow, & N. Nitsche (2010). Mythos Flexibilisierung? Wie instabil sind Berufsbiografien wirklich und als wie instabil werden sie wahrgenommen? *Kölner Zeitschrift für Soziologie und Sozialpsychologie* (62) 3, 369–402.

Mayerhofer, W.-L., O. Behrend, & A. Sondermann (2009). *Auf der Suche nach der verlorenen Arbeit. Arbeitslose und Arbeitsvermittler im neuen Arbeitsmarktregime.* Konstanz: UVK.

Mead, L. M. (1997). *The new paternalism.* Washington, DC: Brookings Institution Press.

Mythen, G. (2005). Employment, individualization and insecurity: Rethinking the risk society perspective. *Sociological Review* (53) 1, 129–147.

Naumann, I. (2007). *From the "Women's Question" to "New Social Risks." One hundred years of social policy discourse on the reconciliation of motherhood and work.* Paper presented at the 5th ESPAnet Conference (Vienna, September 2007).

Newman, J., & E. Kuhlmann (2007). Consumers enter the political stage? The modernization of health care in Britain and Germany. *Journal of European Social Policy* (17) 2, 99–111.

Nullmeier, F., & G. Vobruba (1995). Gerechtigkeit im sozialpolitischen Diskurs. In D. Döring (Ed.), *Gerechtigkeit im Wohlfahrtsstaat* (pp. 9–53). Marburg: Schüren.

OECD (2007). *Economic Outlook 2007—1* (No. 81). Paris.

Peters, J. (2011). The rise of finance and the decline of organised labour in the advanced capitalist countries. *New Political Economy* (16) 1, 73–99.

Powell, J. L., A. Wahidin, & J. Zinn (2007). Understanding risk and old age in Western society. *International Journal of Sociology and Social Policy* (27) 1–2, 66–76.

Powell, M. (2002). The hidden history of social citizenship. *Citizenship Studies* (6) 3, 229–244.

Prisching, M. (2006). *Die zweidimensionale Gesellschaft. Ein Essay zur neokonsumistischen Geisteshaltung.* Wiesbaden: Verlag für Sozialwissenschaften.

Rauch, A., & J. Dornette (2010). Equal rights and equal duties? Activating labour market policy and the participation of long-term unemployed people with disabilities after the reform of the German welfare state. *Journal of Social Policy* 39 (1), 53–70.

Rees, A. M. (1996). T. H. Marshall and the progress of citizenship. In A. M. Rees & M. Bulmer (Eds.), *Citizenship today. The contemporary relevance of T.H. Marshall* (pp. 1–23). London: UCL Press.

Seeleib-Kaiser, M., & T. Fleckenstein (2007). Discourse, learning and welfare state change: The case of German labour market reforms. *Social Policy and Administration* (41) 5, 427–448.

Schmähl, W. (2007). Dismantling an earnings-related social pension scheme: Germany's new pension policies. *Journal of Social Policy* (36) 2, 319–340.

Schustereder, I. J. (2010). *Welfare state change in leading OECD countries. The influence of post-industrial and global developments*. Berlin: Springer.

Steinert, J. (2007). Sozialstaat und soziale Ausschließung. In J. Mackert & H.-P. Müller (Eds.), *Moderne (Staats)Bürgerschaft. Nationale Staatsbürgerschaft und die Debatten der Citizenship Studies* (pp. 147–166). Wiesbaden: Verlag für Sozialwissenschaften.

Taylor-Gooby, P. (2004). New risks and social change. In P. Taylor-Gooby (Ed.), *New risks, new welfare. The transformation of the European welfare state* (pp. 1–28). Oxford: Oxford University Press.

Thomson, S., & E. Mossialos (2006). Choice of public and private health insurance: Learning from the experience of Germany and the Netherlands. *Journal of European Social Policy* (16) 4, 315–327.

Turner, B. S. (2001). The erosion of citizenship. *British Journal of Sociology* (52) 2, 189–209.

van Kersbergen, K. (1995). *Social capitalism. A study of Christian democracy and the welfare state*. London: Routledge.

Walter, F. (2010). *Gelb oder grün? Kleine Parteiengeschichte der besser verdienenden Mitte*. Bielefeld, Transcript.

10

THE IRON LAW OF RIGHTS: CITIZENSHIP AND INDIVIDUAL EMPOWERMENT IN MODERN SWEDEN

Lars Trägårdh and Lars Svedberg

The modern Swedish welfare state can plausibly be regarded as a fulfillment of T. H. Marshall's (1950) vision that broad social rights would come to complement civil and political rights, completing a historical process that entailed an evolution from civil citizenship, characteristic of the 18th century, through political citizenship, starting in the 19th century, to social citizenship, culminating in the 20th century. Indeed, the Swedish—or Nordic—"model" has been characterized precisely by the way in which fundamental entitlements, such as education, healthcare, childcare, and pensions, have been granted universally to individuals on the basis of citizenship. However, even as Sweden is often celebrated for its generous and universal social rights, a darker underside has, from time to time, come into focus, one that concerns the rights of individuals—especially in situations when they come into conflict with the welfare state.

Given these preliminary observations, this chapter has two aims, the first empirical, the other theoretical. Empirically our subject concerns the relationship between individual and state in Sweden as it is expressed in social policy—that is, the domain where social citizenship and social rights find concrete expression. Here we will engage with some of the crucial challenges cited by Evers and Guillemard in Chapter 1, particularly the question of whether individual empowerment and agency is—or is not—accommodated in social policy. While we will consider the broad trends regarding conceptions of citizenship and the character of rights, we will focus on few policy areas that, we contend, are well suited to illuminate fundamental questions of power in the relations between state and individual. First we will consider the position of children, since so many of the welfare state policies and social rights have from the very beginning been aimed towards and justified by the state's special interest in the well-being of children, mothers, and families. Second, we will consider the rights of the disabled, which are especially significant in the Swedish context since they are, uniquely and controversially, constituted as *bona fide* individual rights, claimable in a court of law. Third, we will discuss the compulsory care of substance abusers and HIV-positive individuals, policy areas in which the lack of protection of individual rights is particularly striking. Finally, we will broaden the perspective—already touched upon in the previous sections—to include healthcare in general, the policy area that perhaps more than any is sure to touch all citizens, bringing to the fore fundamental questions of citizenship and rights, and how to balance community interest with individual empowerment.

At the theoretical level we will, in keeping with the theoretical agenda set out by Evers and Guillemard in Chapter 1, engage with Marshall's observations concerning citizenship and rights, as well as Isaiah Berlin's (1958) classic distinction between positive and negative liberty. Marshall emphasized the continuity and coherence, theoretically, between civil and political rights, on the one hand, and social rights, on the other, arguing that both should be individual rights guaranteed by law. However, in keeping with his vaguely socialist perspective,[1] he also noted tensions and contradictions and posed the question of how the rights of individuals were to be balanced against the legitimate duty of the modern, democratic state to safeguard community interest and to promote social equality as well as to guarantee justice and fairness for individuals. Berlin, on the other hand, coming from a more liberal point of view, noted that in modern society the idea of "freedom" tended to be used in a confusing and contradictory fashion that, in our view, parallels some of the tensions between civil and social rights that Marshall noted, and that we will pinpoint in our analysis of the Swedish case. Thus Berlin contended that there existed a fundamental difference between negative freedoms and rights, which protected the individual from state coercion, and positive freedom, which to the contrary relied on the exercise of state power to provide individuals with resources that in turn enabled them to develop and prosper. To a great extent, we argue, one can think of civil rights as forms of negative freedom, while social rights are concrete expressions of positive freedom.

Our own contribution, beyond the empirical exposé, will be to interrogate the idea that the progression from civic and political rights to social rights constitutes a straightforward improvement from the individual's point of view. Instead we will consider both losses and gains in this historical movement; on one side the extraordinary breadth of social rights in the Swedish welfare state, on the other the equally stunning (but perhaps less commonly noted) lack of individual rights. We will also seek to understand the historical roots of this relative strength of social rights and the corresponding weakness of individual rights in Sweden; the prominence of positive rights and freedoms and the lack of negative rights and freedoms; and how the primary focus on community interest, both nationally (for example, in healthcare) and locally (for example, in compulsory care), is balanced with a concern for individual integrity and interest. This analysis will center on how the relationship between the state and the citizen is culturally embedded in past practices and how it then is (re)-institutionalized in the modern welfare state. Going beyond Sweden as an empirical case, we will conclude on a theoretical note by posing what we call "the iron law of rights," suggesting that the advancement of collective social rights necessarily entails a corresponding loss of individual legal rights.

THE HISTORICAL ROOTS OF SOCIAL INSURANCE AND SOCIAL RIGHTS IN SWEDEN

Swedish welfare policies have a long history. Since the prohibition of the Catholic Church in the 16th century, local communities were, under the provisions of the Poor Laws, responsible for their own poor, old, and sick. These laws were designed to distinguish between the "deserving" or "honest" poor and those considered to be lazy vagabonds: the aid was to be given only those who were both "deserving" and who actually came from the local community. However, the rapid increase of landless rural laborers during the first part of the 19th century, associated with land reform, incipient industrialization, and accelerated population growth, rendered the old system of Poor Relief progressively less able to answer the budding "social question." In the work of the Poor Relief Commissions set up in 1839 and again in 1870, one can note the gradual realization that a new category of poverty was emerging: unemployment. The 1870 Commission's work resulted in legislation that made employers responsible for laid-off workers they had brought into the community—anticipating a Bismarckian approach to the social question.[2]

Due to the extraordinary extent of Swedish emigration to the United States during the last decades of the 19th century, the unemployment issue was, however, overshadowed by the fear that Sweden's national strength was being depleted and that the greatest danger to Swedish society, and its rapidly growing industry, was a labor shortage. Furthermore, the emigrants were often peasants or farm laborers, rather than industrial workers, as poverty and famine tended to strike hardest in rural areas. These facts shifted the debate away from proposals for Bismarckian-style worker's insurance towards universal pension plans, taxation reforms, universal suffrage, and homestead acts that affected the entire, still predominantly rural population.

At the political level, the landed elites, including the land-owning peasantry, still dominated the parliament, where they were facing an increasingly powerful alliance of Liberals and the Social Democrats. The Swedish peasants, who historically had played a political role unheard of in the rest of Europe, opposed any version of a Bismarckian solution on the simple grounds that they were not workers but property-owning businesspeople, albeit often just as poor with regards to disposable income as any worker. To satisfy the peasants' demands, a plan was devised that included not only the wage-earning workers but also the property-owning peasants. (The rich and the urban middle class were largely non-players in the debate over the reforms, which were aimed primarily towards the toiling classes who constituted the potential "social problem," raising the specter of a divisive class struggle or even a revolutionary threat.) The result was the precedent-setting universal[3] *Folkpension* (people's pension) legislation of 1913, the first major entitlement reform in Sweden.

These early developments, predating Social Democratic hegemony, set a pattern that became typical for the Swedish and Nordic social security systems. As Bent Rold Andersen has pointed out, while "most countries on the continent adopted the principles of Bismarck's 'workingmen's insurance' as their basic model of cash benefits," this never became the case in Scandinavia (Andersen, 1983, 16). Instead of an insurance system based on contributions and risk calculations, inspired by voluntary private insurance schemes, the Nordic system is "characterized by being run by nationalized agencies, integrated in the governmental public sector, financed primarily through general taxation, and providing benefits conditioned on citizenship, not on previous occupation, income and contributions" (Andersen, 1983, 17). This system Andersen called "people's insurance" as opposed to the Bismarckian "workingmen's insurance" schemes.[4]

Historically, then, it is important to note that the Swedish preference for citizenship as the condition for entitlements originated not in a principled and explicit embrace of the idea of citizenship but rather in a classic political compromise over the design of a particular reform against the backdrop of the peculiar character of the Swedish political geography. Indeed, one may well question the extent to which Sweden differs from the Bismarckian model: many of benefits have in fact over time become tied to current or past income, for example unemployment insurance, sick pay, and additional pension plans. Thus, while a specific social right may in general be granted on the basis of citizenship or legal residence, the level of the cash benefit is in many cases determined by the level of income and status as worker. This puts a finger on the interesting relationship between the central political categories of "people" and "worker," and the way in which both tend to trump the notion of "citizen."

CLASS, WORKER, PEOPLE, AND CITIZEN: CLASHING KEY CONCEPTS

As the Social Democrats during the 1930s rose to political dominance, they gradually left the Marxist language of "class" and "class struggle" behind in favor of a more inclusive discourse centered on the idea of the *folk*, the people. The organizing concept and key political slogan became *folkhemmet*, the people's home, an idea that at heart celebrated on the one hand the democratic primacy of the masses (people as *demos*)—first and foremost the workers and the peasants, but over time also the broader working middle class, over time known simply as wage-earners (*löntagare*)—and on the other national community and cross-class solidarity (people as *ethnos* or nation) (Trägårdh, 1990, 1993, 2002).

The shift from speaking in the name of one group (the working class) to speaking on behalf of another one (the people) underscores the collectivist mindset of the Social Democrats, one rather foreign to the ultimately liberal and individual-centered idea of the citizen. However, the concept of citizenship did in fact play a role during the formative years of the 1920s and 1930s—for example, in the much-quoted speech from 1928 in the Swedish *Riksdag* in which the Social Democratic leader, Per Albin Hansson, first launched the term *folkhemmet* as a key concept for the Social Democrats. In the speech he actually referred not only to *folkhemmet* but also to *medborgarhemmet* (the home of citizens). However, the potency of the *folkhem* concept, with its nationalist, romantic, and communitarian overtones, completely overshadowed the cooler, more liberal and individualist notion of a country of citizens, foreshadowing the primacy of community interest over individual rights that would come to characterize much of later Social Democratic social policy.

Neither the political debate nor academic research has either before or after been characterized by a pronounced or lasting interest in probing the notion of citizenship in a deeper sense.[5] One possible reason for this is that the Social Democrats and the workers' movement have tended to associate the language of citizenship with a liberal, individualist and "bourgeois" tradition that historically had excluded those with no property and little income or wealth.[6] Another reason is that for the Social Democrats the notions of "worker," "class," and "people" were far more natural given their ideological program at large, rooted as it was in Marxist ideology and nationalist discourse, on the one hand, and the legacy of the mass movements, on the other.

SOCIAL POLICY, THE WHOLESOME WORKER, AND THE UNDESERVING POOR

Far more crucial than the concept of citizenship has been the ideal of the well-behaved and wholesome worker (*den skötsamme arbetaren*) as the privileged protagonist in the Swedish *folkhem* (Ambjörnsson, 1988). While the Swedish public and political discourse only rarely is explicitly focused on duties and responsibilities, it is nonetheless well understood that the (social) rights have to be earned, and earned through hard work and good behavior according to the prevailing moral codes of the social contract. As Lundberg and Åmark (2001, 176) argue from a historical perspective, the Swedish welfare state effectively demands that the citizens satisfy three demands: "the obligation of labour-market participation—everyone must work; the obligation of social respectability, or social good behaviour—everyone has to behave well; the obligation of social responsibility—everyone has to take responsibility for him/herself and one's family."[7] Those who do not live up to those moral principles, who stand outside the social contract, are deemed unworthy and undeserving and as such often become subject to harsh and unsentimental treatment at the hands of the state and its many agents, including the professions (see Åmark, 2004; Björkman; 2001; Larsson, 2008).

Indeed, this distinction between deserving and undeserving came to the fore already in the pension reform of 1913 cited above. While the basic benefit was universal and unconditional, it was also so limited that one could not subsist solely on it. For this reason a supplementary benefit was added, which, however, was conditional on the recipient being both poor and an honorable citizen, excluding for example individuals with alcohol abuse problems (Berge, 1995; Sejerstedt, 2005).[8] It was not until the 1950s that these conditions regarding economic and moral status were removed.

The separation of the worthy and ordinary citizens and those who are unfit and in fact not qualifying as full citizens is reflected in the distinction between laws, policies, and rights associated with universal welfare aimed at the wholesome majority and the laws and services pertaining to "welfare cases," with its historical roots in the old stigmatizing Poor Laws.

The kinds of norms described here were later incorporated into the emerging system of public welfare provisions. Behind the talk of general welfare for all, in Swedish social policy there has always existed a view of the poor and disadvantaged that has continued to bear traces of the old poor relief attitudes, where it is important to investigate whether or not the problem in question is self-inflicted (Johansson, 2001). If, on account of his or her own acts, a person is not able to fully contribute to the common good, but instead causes the society costs for care and support or is a nuisance to the environment, then it is easier to question this person's right to make decisions about his or her own property and lifestyle than in the case of a congenital disability.

The most infamous and blatant case is that of the forced sterilizations that took place during the 1940s, which—as the historian and journalist Henrik Berggren (1998) notes—can be seen as an expression of a "central and disturbing notion that characterizes Swedish welfare ideology," namely that the social rights of the universalist welfare state presuppose a people composed of healthy, strong, and economically productive individuals. Those who do not live up to these criteria "can be denied their citizenship rights."[9]

The preoccupation with the well-behaved worker has deep historical roots. Indeed, the struggle on the part of the liberal bourgeoisie and the Social Democrats to gain the right to vote for their constituencies went hand in hand with a general moral improvement project (see Esiasson, 2010; Stenius, 2009). Equally important was (and still is) the close collaboration with the various popular movements and the corporatist structures set in place to connect these to the state. The undeserving tended to have only a tenuous relation to the labor market and little access to the increasingly powerful social/popular movements and thus no entryway into the corporatist structures. Thus, the emphasis on solidarity among Swedish citizens has primarily been aimed at those considered deserving—that is, the industrious and hard-working, to which category the less fortunate—the undeserving—were not counted.

Hernes (1988) underlines that the reforms not only focused on creating good welfare and greater equality ("for all") but also nursed the ambition to involve the citizenry in the decision-making process with the aim of reducing—as she expresses it—the potential for paternalism that exists in all welfare systems. The problem is that the marginalized and the drug-dependent have been accorded little real chance of participation and co-determination. However, it should be noted that in the mid-1960s, a so-called client movement developed in Sweden. This movement emerged at the same time as the general radicalization of the Left in the wake of the events of 1968. The focus was on organizing alcohol and drug abusers, prison inmates, and the mentally ill. Meeuwisse (1997) writes that Sweden indeed was one of the few countries where the client movement early on was relatively well organized.

There is little doubt that this movement, in alliance with certain government officials, lawyers, and healthcare professionals, was important in launching a critique of the paternalist tradition and for bringing attention to the need for reform measures aimed at these vulnerable groups, including the humanization of care and punishment in Sweden (Modig, 2004; Nestius, 2004). Yet we must agree with Evers (2009, 249–250) that this movement: "though culturally important, often remained politically weak. Some built new nationwide interest groups and NGOs, but these were mostly weaker than long-established organizations."

A further difficulty—from the perspective of the "undeserving" person—has been a lack of concern with the rights of the individual, the emphasis being placed instead on collective needs and collective measures. This of course is not a matter only of principle but highly concrete measures proposed for and against them. The possibilities of taking a point of departure in individual rights, individual needs, or expectations of individually designed measures have been limited, not to say nonexistent.

It has been difficult for members of marginalized groups such as substance abusers to have their interests taken note of and their basic needs satisfied through the major collectives. Those who did not/do not live up to the demands imposed came to be second-class citizens who did not equally share the social rights. The general, expansive welfare model has, as Johansson (2001) points out, been complemented with a restrictive attitude to marginalized groups. This is an aspect that has been largely ignored, not least in comparative Nordic and international welfare research.[10]

SOCIAL RIGHTS VERSUS INDIVIDUAL RIGHTS

While the implementation of universal social rights and entitlements based on citizenship constitutes the core project of the Swedish welfare state, this expansion of social insurance schemes has not been accompanied by a similarly rich theoretical or political discussion of the nature of rights any more than it has provoked a searching debate over citizenship. This is especially true for any concern that social rights might be achieved without being constituted as legally binding individual rights claimable in a court of law, as in the case of civil and political rights, to engage Marshall's categories. Indeed, what is characteristic is that social rights in Sweden have primarily taken the form of what we will call "collective social rights"—that is, "rights" that are in a strictly juridical sense (individual, claimable, enforceable in a court of law) not rights at all, even if they are often seen and spoken about as such.

To appreciate the Swedish context for the way in which the crucial distinction between individual and collective social rights has found concrete expression in politics and law, it is, however, necessary to consider not only the centrality of the idea of the wholesome worker when it comes to social policy but also the character of the Swedish social contract at large and the relationship between state and individual in particular. As one of us has argued at length elsewhere, the hallmark of the Swedish welfare state is an alliance between individual and state that has, relatively speaking, emancipated relatively powerless individuals—workers, women, children, the elderly, the disabled, the sick, the unemployed—from traditional hierarchical and patriarchal institutions and social structures, including the family, churches, charities, and the various neo-feudal arrangements that characterized early industrial Sweden (Berggren & Trägårdh, 2006, 2010; Trägårdh, 1997).

In particular, the historical struggle to establish social rights based on citizenship and a system of universal rather than need-based social insurance has been linked to a deep and abiding revulsion against charity, a word that to this day has strong negative connotations in Sweden (Svedberg, 2005). The positive view of charity that one today can encounter in the Anglo-American world and elsewhere is in a way the logical opposite to the moral logic that underlies the Swedish welfare state. It can also be noted that this negative view of charity is linked not only to a dislike of unequal power relations in personal relationship and a collective memory of a time when poorer women served as maids to the rich and poor workers toiled in feudal-like arrangements in company towns (*brukssamhällen*), but also to certain contempt for weakness and the weak. In Sweden, like other Nordic countries, independence and stoic endurance of even harsh conditions are seen as virtues, and dependency and weakness is conversely seen as a personal moral failing as much as something rooted in social causes (Björkman, 2001; Larsson, 2008).

Without doubt, the gains associated with this social contract have been considerable for the dispossessed and disempowered, but notably the social and family policies have also emancipated everyone else, including middle-class men, from the constraints of family and community, turning Sweden into one of the most individualistic societies in the world. Indeed, in this regard the moral logic that underpins the statist individualism of the welfare state and the supposedly quasi-socialist Sweden has a great deal of affinity with the fundamental tenets of classical liberal ideas: the basic unit of society is the individual, not the family or any community or association mediating between individual and state (Berggren & Trägårdh, 2006, 2010; Trägårdh, 1997).

This individualistic aspect is all the more important to underline, since it is common to describe Sweden as a (neo)corporatist state where individuals derive their social identity, political power, and sense of community from "corporations" and, in some accounts, barely exist socially and politically outside such communities, such as unions and a plethora of other interest and identity organizations (Heckscher, 1946; Rothstein, 1992; Soysal, 1994). This is not to say that corporatist structures do not exist, but these matter more on the input side of the political system (i.e., the governance structure) than on the output side (i.e., social and family policy, where corporate membership is less of an issue). It is here that on the contrary the individualist character of Swedish society is most visible. Arguably, it is also this aspect that is most meaningful to the majority of individual citizens in their day-to-day life, not least in their relationship to the state and its agents. Here laws and policies are felt that ensure the autonomy of women from men, the lack of dependence of the old on their children, the relatively strong rights of children in relation to their own parents, the universal and individual access to healthcare, daycare, education, elderly care, and pensions.

However, as we shall see below in our discussion of drunks, drug addicts, HIV-positive individuals, and other social outcasts, the potency of corporatist organizations does matter a great deal to those who are members of weak and embattled minorities, who do not have the political muscle to ensure passage of laws and programs that cater to their special needs, as has been the case for other, more powerful groups, especially the working-class union members. Soysal (1994) among others has described the type of corporatist model that characterizes Sweden as one where membership is organized around corporate groups (defined by occupation, ethnicity, religion, or gender) and their functions as sources of action and authority. This is in contrast to the liberal model, where it is the individual rather than the group who is considered the source of action and authority, and people living in a corporate system "gain legitimacy and access to rights by subscribing to the wider collective groups" (Soysal, 1994, 38). Again, and it deserves repeating, in such a tradition and such a system it becomes extremely difficult to assert and uphold marginal, not quite morally legitimate, individual interests.

Finally, the alliance with the state comes with a price even for the morally correct majority. To begin, it is linked to a strong dependency of the individual on the state with respect to fundamental social insurance and social services.

Secondly, and most crucially, individual citizens have little power in relation to the state. That is, Swedes have strong collective rights to various entitlements but weak individual rights (Delli-Carpini & Trägårdh, 2004; Trägårdh, 1999a,b). As Urban Lundberg and Mattias Tydén (2010, 36) have pointed out in an overview of the literature on the "Swedish model," this is a perspective that can be viewed as a critical counterpoint to the conventional and more celebratory account of a "success story." They argue that while "the traditional approach" centers on how the welfare state freed the individual "as his social rights, or social citizenship to use TH Marshall's famous concept, was being fulfilled," the critical approach "claims that the fundamental right of the individual to govern his or her own life was lost during the very same process."[11]

This tension between collective and individual rights, as well as a general preference of the former over the latter, is expressed in many policy areas. On good days, and for the well-behaved, well-employed, and healthy, this distinction has little practical import. However, for those citizens at the margins, for whom welfare means not the universal access to basic education, healthcare, pensions, etc., but rather targeted benefits and special care, it does matter greatly. The same is also true for those minorities and individuals who do not have access to, and/or are represented by, powerful corporatist interest groups. Sweden lacks the type of civil rights tradition that has battled discrimination and secured rights of individuals and minorities in other countries, most famously the United States. The absence of a bill of rights protecting individuals against the state is a telling fact, and it was not until recently that anti-discrimination laws have been put in place, and even now the effectiveness of these laws from the individual's point of view is debated.

The preference for politically constituted social rights over legally binding individual rights is also related to the strong anti-juridical tradition that characterizes Sweden. For Swedish Social Democrats, even as they left Marxist ideology behind, juridically and constitutionally constructed rights came to be associated with individualism and "bourgeois" privileges that stood in the way of reforms that would benefit "the people." As the influential Swedish jurist Gustaf Petrén pithily put it: "all constitutionally embedded rights make it more difficult for the government to at will, and at any given moment, do the right thing for society at large." Furthermore, he writes, ironically, "such protections, it is argued, are unnecessary for ordinary citizens since the Social Democrats would never do them any harm."[12] In fairness to the Social Democrats, it should however be added that there are no signs that the center-right parties that have ruled Sweden since 2006 in any way are diverging from this position. Indeed, if anything they appear to have adopted this statist and paternalist position with enthusiasm.

Add to this the lack of a constitutional separation of powers that translates into an extreme form of parliamentary and majoritarian rule, and the picture emerges of an individual citizen who is simultaneously autonomous from other citizens and fundamentally disempowered in relation to the state. Again, while there has been some limited debate in media and among academics about the pros and cons of a bill of individual rights, an independent judiciary, judicial review of laws, the separation of powers, and related issues, it has not resulted in any significant changes in laws and institutions (Delli-Carpini & Trägårdh, 2004; Holmström, 1998; Nergelius, 1996; Nergelius & Holmström, 2000). Those supporting such reforms constitute a distinct minority (Nergelius, 2006).

BEST INTEREST OF THE CHILD—THE LINCHPIN OF THE SWEDISH WELFARE STATE

Both foreign and domestic critics have at times been quite dramatic in denouncing Sweden's love affair with the state, in the case of Roland Huntford (1971) going so far as to claim that Swedes "worship the state," "love their servitude," "do not have democracy in their hearts," and "exhibit a preference for government by the bureaucrat rather than by politician." However, before we turn to the dark underside of the Swedish social contract, let us emphasize its more positive side. For one, there is no evidence that Swedes, fully equipped with their political rights and constantly subject to surveys, in general dislike the welfare state. On the contrary, using their votes they have time and time again affirmed their support for this system. This is the result of the considerable gains that have *de facto* emancipated many of the weaker members of society and turned the members of the middle class into more fully autonomous citizens equipped with generous social rights (Svallfors, 1999).

In this regard, the child occupies a special position. What we can think of as a state/child alliance serves as the linchpin in the edifice we call the welfare state (Berggren & Trägårdh, 2006; Sandin, 2003). While the political compromise that led to the pension reform of 1913 was the first major social rights legislation in Sweden, it was only with a plethora of policies directed towards children that the interventionist state truly came into its own. The child occupies a special place since it is innocent and defenseless, yet also a citizen-in-becoming. Unlike the old, sick, and disabled, for whom we may feel compassion and pity, but with whom we also would rather not identify but generally try to avoid thinking about, the child is associated with feelings of love, joy, and hope for a better future. Indeed, the will to provide for the well-being of children is possibly the closest we get to a universally shared value.

For this reason, to speak in the name of the best interest of the child is a potent rhetoric for a state that seeks to extend its reach into the private domain, with the aim of providing first education, later healthcare, followed by a number of rights and protections that included rights of children in relation to more or less delinquent and incompetent parents (Lundström, 1993; Vinterhed, 1977). The state–child alliance, and the relative ease by which policies aimed at protecting the rights of children were defended, served as a door opener for other social and family policies, for example those concerned with the pre- and postnatal care of mothers, women's rights, individual taxation, high-quality daycare, parental leave insurance, laws against physical punishment of children, changes in family law to shift responsibility for the elderly from the family to the state, and so on, even including the child's right to an actively involved father.

Indeed, much of the legislation concerning children was from the outset concerned with the specter of failed fathers. One of the most important changes in family law in Sweden during the first decades of the 20th century concerned the very idea of the illegitimate child, a legal category that was eliminated. No child should have to sufferer a lower status simply because his or her father was an absent or "deadbeat dad." Here we see how yet again the concern with the ideal of the honorable worker and father informs social policy. This was followed by the first child allowances that were given to mothers to ensure that fathers did not spend the money on alcohol (they are still paid to the mother, not the father) (Bergman, 2003).

One central notion here was the idea of individual autonomy, the child as a proto-citizen whose dignity and fundamental equality with other individuals was guaranteed by the state, an idea that over time was to be extended in a variety of policies and laws, covering not only the defenseless child but also women, the elderly, the sick, the disabled, and so on. However, equally important was the rather different—even opposite—principle of "saving" the child from a number of threats, ranging from bad parents and a culture of poverty to the personal failings of the child or youth himself or herself. Indeed, as many historians and other social scientists have shown, the modern state's interest in youth and children has been intimately bound up with an anxiety over youth as a social problem (Berggren, 1995; Olsson, 1992; Svedberg & Trägårdh, 2007, 2008).

And as Marshall points out, one of the first instances of a modern social right, namely universal primary education, is not simply a right, to be freely chosen (or not), but rather takes the form of a compulsory duty under national law, enforceable by fines. Neither parent nor child has the right to say "no thanks" to this right, since schooling is made compulsory. The argument is that the child, to cite Rousseau, must be "forced to be free" if necessary against his or her will, since the collective need to educate and socialize the young into a fully formed citizen trumps any individual will in this regard. Presumably the child will as an adult be grateful for this instance of compulsion, since it allows him or her to fully realize the potential for full civil, political, social, and economic citizenship (see also Sejerstedt, 2005).

However, while few people would argue against compulsory education, there can be little question that this coercion on the part of the state is not simply a gesture of care and compassion, but also an expression of anxiety and the urge towards social control. While it is true that children sometimes learn useful things in school, including social skills not necessarily part of the curriculum, much of the effort constitutes a poorly veiled attempt to pacify and store youthful energies that might otherwise find a more anarchic and even destructive outlet. This suspicion of the child was, however, in character with a much broader distrust of the citizen on the part of the agents of the state. If we stay close to laws and policies that concern children and their well-being, it is worthwhile to note that one of the first encounters that new parents have with the state is the routine home visit by a nurse or social worker connected with the local childcare facility (*Barnavårdscentral*, or BVC). While such visits tend to be friendly and sometimes informative, the element of inspection, supervision, and surveillance, to invoke Foucault, is always there as well.

In Sweden, then, the principle of the people's insurance, as opposed to the working man's insurance, was closely linked to the idea of the state as the natural ally of not only the elderly (basic pensions), but also the innocent and worthy child (education, healthcare, daycare), which in turn implicated the mother (prenatal care, healthcare for women). By extension, healthcare, like pensions, came to be seen as a natural universal social right. These were programs and entitlements that by and large were provided equally to all on the basis of citizenship, as distinct to those social rights that were conditional and tied to the performance (pay) as a good worker (sick pay, unemployment insurance, etc.), and finally those inferior rights rooted in the old Poor Laws that were offered to those who failed to live up to that ideal altogether (social assistance).

In recent decades, Sweden has stood in the forefront in the campaign to establish "children's rights," playing an important role in designing and pushing for the signing and acceptance of the UN Convention on the Rights of the Child and being the first country to abolish physical punishment of children.[13] The rights and interests of the child are championed by many actors in Sweden, ranging from Swedish Save the Children to the Office of the Children's Ombudsman. And by most international comparative ratings, Sweden and the other Nordic countries rank at the very top when it comes to measures of child well-being, just as they do with respect to gender equality.[14]

This emphasis on the autonomy of the child, as opposed to a more common and traditional view of the child as an object of care and protection, has found expression in the notion of the "child as a rights-bearing citizen," just as the enduring emphasis on gender equality and women's rights has resulted a broadly accepted ideal of equal representation of women in all areas of work and private life.[15] However, even as we emphasize this emancipatory and egalitarian aspect, the notion of the empowered child, or "child-as-citizen," the reversal of this motto also resonates in the Swedish context, namely the "citizen-as-child," subject to the care and protection at the hands of the all-powerful "nanny state." It is indicative of the limits of the (children's) rights perspective that Sweden has so far elected not to fully incorporate the Convention of the Rights of the Child into Swedish law in such a way as to make it directly accessible to children and their representatives.

DISABILITY RIGHTS IN SWEDEN: BETWEEN SOCIAL AND INDIVIDUAL RIGHTS

In Sweden the disabled occupy a special place in the overall landscape of citizenship and rights. Historically they had been treated in a way not dissimilar to the poor, the old, and the sick, as objects of pity and the recipients of charity. During the early phase of the welfare state this legacy was still present, as they were subjected to a paternalism that centered on the strategy of separating the disabled from the community of "normal" citizens and institutionalizing them in special facilities where they could receive the care and attention of professional experts (Förhammar, 2004; Lindberg, 2006, Lindberg & Grönvik, 2011).

A reaction against this paternalist tradition began to emerge in the 1970s, starting with more traditional disability rights organizations like DHR and HSO, but it was only under the influence of the American disability community and their fight for equal status with other citizens that Swedish disability rights activists, especially the Independent Living movement, began to fight this traditional treatment from a radical rights perspective (Berg, 2007, 2008; Grünewald, 2009; Jeppsson Grassman, & Svedberg, 1993; Lindberg, 1996; Ratzka, 1998). The American movement was modeled on the civil rights movement, and was at heart an anti-discrimination movement (Mayerson, 1994; Shapiro, 1993). For the movement activists the "problem" was not disability as such but the various obstacles that filled the landscape of normality that prevented the disabled from gaining access and freely moving around and functioning in society. When the landmark Americans with Disabilities Act (ADA) was passed in 1990, it provided disabled individuals with a powerful weapon, namely the right to sue offending individuals, commercial establishments, government agencies, etc. that did not provide access to roads, pavements and stairs, buildings, shops, schools, and any other facilities. These were, furthermore, rights not specifically directed to those confined to wheelchairs but also covering other disabilities (the deaf, the blind, the mentally disabled, etc.).

In Sweden, Independent Living and other disability rights groups, taking advantage of the brief presence of a center-right government in the early 1990s that included a minister, Bengt Westerberg, who supported the disability rights movement, managed to push through its own version of ADA, in Sweden called LSS (Ratzka, 2003). Significantly and unusually in the Swedish context, this was a law that was designed as a legally binding and claimable individual right. Combining an American-style emphasis on anti-discrimination and right to access with Swedish-style social rights (providing money and resources), LSS did not simply provide the legal basis for anti-discrimination lawsuits, but also provided a right to personal assistance, allowing disabled persons to take care of themselves in their own homes and moving around in society. By comparison, ADA may have provided physical access in a revolutionary way, but it did little to improve the economic hardship that effectively kept many American disabled people confined in a socially marginalized position, for example lacking the kind of access to personal assistants that LSS provided for in Sweden.

This duality of LSS turned out to be not only a strength—in terms of rights provided to the disabled—but also a weakness in a political sense. Whereas ADA tended to spread the cost of providing access to a large number of building owners, businesses, government agencies, etc., the cost for LSS was largely carried by the local governments. This has proven to be very expensive and has led to a backlash, led by the association of local governments in Sweden (SKL), which argued that this individual right was provided by the central state but without the corresponding funding—that is, as an unfunded mandate (Bring, 2004; Petersén, 2005). This meant, SKL argued, that the high cost of carrying out LSS had a negative impact on the rights of other citizens. Thus, the LSS puts in focus the ever-present potential for a collision between an individual right belonging to members of a particular group and the social rights of the citizenry at large. In Sweden the impulse on the part of politicians and professionals tends, not surprisingly, to be to side with social rights that leave power with them rather than individual rights that provide power to individual citizens within a distinct minority.

While the disabled are viewed as deserving and worthy, there exists a considerable political resistance to give them special treatment. This is especially true in the case of claimable individual rights, whose logic is foreign to the Swedish tradition of favoring social rights that legally take the form of the state taking on a broad responsibility while reserving for itself the right to determine when, how, and to what extent it provides those services. The counterargument is that in a majoritarian democracy, with weak individual rights and ineffective anti-discrimination law, such rights, claimable in a court of law, are necessary to ensure that the interests of the disabled, a small minority, are not set aside in the rush to provide resources to the "normal" citizens who are more likely to deliver the larger amount of votes.

COMPULSORY CARE OF SUBSTANCE ABUSERS

The present situation with respect to substance abusers harks back to the long historical tradition from which our current legislation has sprung. A wide-ranging moral improvement project in the early 20th century found expression in—among other things—severe temperance legislation in 1913. The abuse of alcohol was seen as a social problem that threatened or destroyed the ability of the individual to earn his living and was also a threat to society at large, to the abuser's family, and (to a much lesser extent) to the individual himself (Esiasson, 2010; Stenius, 2009). Measures were largely directed towards the poor and the marginalized, and it remains that way today (Rexed, 1977; SOU 1967:36; Storbjörk & Room, 2008).

The focus of the 1913 temperance legislation lay on detention. The strongly paternalistic tradition, which thus marked the original temperance legislation, was taken over and developed by the Social Democrats and integrated into their "people's home" policy with its heavy emphasis on work, national health, and the spirit of industriousness (Ambjörnsson, 1988; Björkman, 2007). The paradoxical coincidence of a "right" and an obligation that we noted in the case of the primary education of the young also prevailed, but in this case the emphasis on compulsion was so strong that no one would speak of these laws as "rights," even though the underlying logic was similar, as we shall see. From the 1950s up to the 1980s, the maximum duration of compulsory treatment was one year, although this could under certain circumstances be extended to two years (Björkman, 2001; Mattsson, 1984).

The Care of Abusers (Special Provisions) Act (LVM) was passed in the early 1980s. This Act allowed compulsory treatment of substance abusers for two months, with the possibility of extending this by another two months under certain circumstances. The conditions for compulsory interventions were attached to different kinds of dangers; first, the health condition of the abusers and other serious dangers to themselves, and second, possible risks related to the security of the abuser's family. During a very short period from the end of the 1970s there was a certain limited debate (see, e.g., Börjeson, 1979; *Nej till vårdtvång*, 1977), connected to the client movement mentioned earlier, that attempted to influence the legislation in a more liberal direction. All in all, however, this movement had little long-term effect on the shaping of policies and legislation regarding abuse. On the contrary, it was the third sector organizations advocating more stringent legislation against abuse that won a stronger foothold during this same time and came to influence the restrictive Social Democratic policy then carried out (Nordegren, 2004; Sannegård, 2004).

In 1989, a revised LVM Act came into effect, in which the word "can" was replaced with the word "shall," underlining the demand for compulsory intervention in order to fulfill the criteria of the law. Compulsory treatment was also then extended to a maximum of six months (Elmér, 1989; Lehto, 1994; Nilssen, 2005; Norström & Thunved, 2006; Palm & Stenius, 2002). The Act does not require that voluntary treatment should be tried before using compulsory measures.

When compulsory treatment was extended from four to six months, the paternalistic compulsion in Swedish care of abusers that has always been there gained an even more central role. During the 2000s, both Social Democratic and center-right governments have pushed further along this line, leading to further entrenchment.

A study by Stenius (2009) shows that care of abusers both in Sweden and in Finland is unusually extensive from an international perspective. Both countries view alcohol abuse as a social problem with measures mainly directed towards the poor, an explicit aim being to help abusers to become capable citizens through treatment and training, echoing the arguments in favor of the compulsory education of children. Compulsion is supposed to function as a deterrent and to have a therapeutic effect. However, Stenius and Runquist (2009, 49) point out a crucial difference today between the Swedish and the Finnish legislation. This difference lies in the aim of the state with regard to compulsory care. In Finland, as in most countries with compulsory care, the law is distinctly intended for handling acute situations, first and foremost when a person is presenting a danger to life, whereas in Sweden it is a law with a much more diffuse therapeutic aim to treat and motivate the delinquent and divergent to become more normal.

How, then, does Sweden fare in a comparative perspective regarding the compulsory care of abusers? Nilssen (2005, 141), writing of Sweden, Denmark, and Norway, provides the following summary. Compared with the other Scandinavian countries, Sweden has constituted the most comprehensive legal rules warranting compulsory interventions towards adult substance abusers. Norway occupies a middle position, accepting compulsory interventions on a more limited scale than in Sweden but on a broader scale than in Denmark. In a comparison of involuntary treatment of adult substance abusers in Sweden, Norway, Denmark, and Finland, Lehto (1994, 16–17) also argues that Sweden stands out in several ways. Sweden allows the longest periods of involuntary institutionalization, has the highest number of involuntary institutionalizations in specialized institutions for substance abusers, and places different demands on authorities with respect to the treatment of substance abusers.

What, then, are the justifications given for compulsory treatment? In the Scandinavian comparison referred to above, Nilssen (2005) argues that measures to tackle substance abuse have mostly been a question of social control, punishment, and behavioral correction. Palm and Stenius (2002, 74) interpret the justification for compulsory treatment in Sweden today slightly differently, as an expression not so much of a desire to protect society from harm as the desire to protect individuals from harming themselves—that is, the paternalistic argument. A study by Wallander and Blomquist (2005) appears to confirm this. Their investigation, which consisted of a survey of social workers' assessments of clients in relation to the Care of Abusers (Special Provisions) Act, found that the respondents regard the special criteria relating to (physical and mental) health as more important than those relating to violence and the client's social situation. They also found that several factors not specified in the legislation, such as the respondents' ideological convictions as well as the organizational structure and prevailing traditions at local workplaces, have an effect on the social workers' ideal judgments of client eligibility for compulsory care. Wallander and Blomqvist (2005, 77) argue that this might reflect some form of "routinized practice" whereby social workers continue making the same type of judgment they are used to making.

Skretting and Järvinen (1994) present findings from a small study where doctors in Sweden, Denmark, Norway, and Finland were asked to give their views on the appropriate care model for a number of hypothetical cases. They found that paternalistic justifications for compulsory care were considered acceptable only among the Swedish doctors. Interestingly, the study found that the Swedish respondents, despite supporting the use of involuntary measures, were not more optimistic about the effectiveness of these methods than the respondents from the other Nordic countries. A number of studies have shown that there is support for the present system both among the general public and within government. Quite a lot of patients themselves in compulsory treatment are also in favor of it (see Ekendahl, 2001).

What explains this strong support for compulsory treatment among Swedes? Palm and Stenius (2002, 74) identify three types of legitimacy that play a part: administrative, medical, and political. In clarifying the concept of administrative legitimacy they write: "While decisions about commitment for alcoholism in the early 20th century in other countries most often seemed to have been taken by civil courts, the Swedish solution was to place the initiative and decision-making within the administration. Only the local social board was regarded as having the necessary intimate knowledge of the drunkards and their lives to be able to make individualised decisions." This, according to Palm and Stenius (2002, 74), implies that the growth of the Swedish welfare system conserved and even expanded the use of compulsion. "Compulsory treatment, being part of the strongly applauded and expanding welfare system, became difficult to criticise" (see also Sejerstedt, 2005).

On medical legitimacy, Björkman (2001) among others refer to the role of the medical doctor in the 19th and first part of the 20th century. The medical profession was the social engineer *par excellence*. Swedish doctors were not only "medical men"; they were politicians as well. Palm and Stenius (2002) argue that another important factor behind the broad support for compulsory treatment in Sweden is the role of the municipal layperson boards and the corporatist welfare system, where religious, temperance, client, or other voluntary organizations systematically have been involved not only in welfare provision but also in policymaking. This system grants the local community the right to make decisions about individual citizens, and it is this that they refer to as political legitimacy.

What perhaps is most striking in the wider perspective is the lack of attention and debate provoked by this type of legislation, but when the current legislation with its intensification of the compulsion component was driven through by the then sitting Social Democratic government, there were surprisingly few objections from the other political camps. What is more, in the textbooks on Swedish social policy and social work, no importance whatsoever is attached to these issues (see, for example, Elmér, Blomberg, Harrysson & Petersson, 2000; Meeuwisse, Sunesson, & Swärd, 2006; Olofsson, 2007).

Finally, in 2009, the Swedish government appointed an investigator to look over the legislation on substance abuse, including compulsory care, and in a discussion memorandum presented by the Enquiry in 2010 it is proposed that in the future compulsion should be allowed to take place only in exceptional cases

(*Missbruksutredningen*, 2010a). The compulsory care of today has weaknesses, it was pointed out, among others deficient treatment methods, uneven application across the country, and difficulty in meeting the needs of persons with comorbidity of mental illness with substance abuse.

There seems to be wide approval for the proposal to strengthen the right of the individual to investigation and treatment (*Missbruksutredningen*, 2010b). Notable is the statement made by the organization responsible for monitoring and following up that different forms of care are carried out according to current laws and regulations (National Board of Health and Welfare) and that the present legislation on compulsory care functions well, when there is little scientific verification that such is the case (Bergmark, 2004; Gerdner & Berglund, 2010). Among voluntary organizations, several are critical of the use of current compulsory measures; for example Rainbow Sweden considers that involuntary measures should be used only in acute situations and then for a maximum of one month only.

In line with the Swedish historians Urban Lundberg and Mattias Tydén (2010), we find that the Swedish history of compulsory care of substance abusers is not a question of humanism *or* social control, with one following the other, but a continuing history of both; whereas in the first phase social control dominated and humanism constituted a thin veneer, in the later (current) period humanism may appear dominant over social control, but beneath the humanist facade the primacy of social control and community interest over individual rights and empowerment remains largely unchallenged.[16] This is not least clear if we consider the treatment of AIDS patients and HIV-positive persons in Sweden, a subject that we now turn to.

AIDS AND THE CLASH BETWEEN INDIVIDUAL RIGHTS AND THE NATIONAL INTEREST

The patterns and tendencies described above are also visible when we turn to the Swedish response to AIDS. In a sweeping comparative analysis of how the industrialized world responded to the AIDS crisis, the historian Peter Baldwin concludes that those who tested positive for HIV in Sweden "were subjected to one of the most draconian regimes of surveillance and control in the Western world" (Baldwin, 2005, 242). He argues further that this approach ultimately was rooted in, on the one hand, an abhorrence of drug use and (excessive) alcohol use, and, on the other, a tendency on the part of officials, experts, and lawmakers to side with perceived interest of society over the rights of individuals.[17]

As Baldwin shows, even as AIDS as a disease was the same everywhere, the response to the epidemic differed substantially. In some countries public authorities reacted immediately; in others they stuck their heads as far into the sand as they could. In some countries the reactions were measured and balanced; in others they appeared panic-stricken. The response was also colored by the fact that those affected appeared to belong to morally dubious groups, at first gays, later drug addicts, a group that over time was extended until it became known in North America as the infamous "H-group" of AIDS victims: Haitians, heroin addicts, homosexuals, and hookers. These all seemed, in varying degrees, to be culpable in some vague way. It was not until additional groups, such as hemophiliacs and eventually heterosexuals from the middle class, were also infected that AIDS began its normalizing journey from moral calamity to ordinary, if deadly, disease.

In this perspective Sweden was extreme in several regards. The authorities reacted earlier than in other countries and resorted to measures that were far more drastic than what became common in other, comparable countries. The public debate quickly turned hysterical, and not only the routinely high-strung tabloids like *Aftonbladet* and *Expressen* turned up the heat: even the normally staid editorial page of *Dagens Nyheter*[18] announced that the threat from AIDS was so serious that one may have to set aside the civil rights of the citizens in order to stop the spread of the disease—and this at a time when not one Swede had yet died of AIDS.

This was a point of view that the parliament and the government were quite happy to agree with. As the first country in Europe, Sweden passed compulsory laws in March 1983, and a campaign ensued where the rights of individuals to liberty and privacy quickly were sacrificed on the altar of "national health" (Baldwin, 2005, 153).[19] When other countries, such as Great Britain, choose a voluntary approach that respected the rights of individuals and trusted their capacity to act rationally on the old principle from 1855 that "every man may be his own quarantine officer," Swedish health officials appeared, according to Baldwin, to subscribe to old maxim "*Vertrauen is gut, Kontrolle ist besser*" (trust is good, control is better).[20]

The reference to principles and quotes from the past is not gratuitous; in fact, Baldwin is able to show that the treatment of HIV-positive persons has a long history, going back to 19th-century cholera epidemics and the response to them. Back then, Sweden also stood out as the "most drastic interventionist" country, imposing harsh measures such as "inspecting travellers, disinfecting goods, isolating the ill and fumigating dwellings," and this long after more lenient methods had been introduced elsewhere. Similarly for syphilis, where Sweden had created a "system of sanitary statism," according to which all citizens were subjected "to much the same restrictions as were elsewhere imposed only on prostitutes: medical inspection, compulsory treatment if ill, reporting of diseased to the authorities and to sexual contacts, strictures on potentially transmissive behaviour, and incarceration for recalcitrants" (Baldwin, 2005, 227).

The principle was "better safe than sorry," and the state elites took the position that it was best to "treat all citizens as equally dangerous and culpable," as

Baldwin puts it (Baldwin, 2005, 227). In other words, the great trust that Swedes to this day have for the state was not mutual, but instead the state's systematic distrust of citizens' capacity to take personal responsibility translated into a strategy of robbing them of their basic civil rights in the name of national security and health.

During the AIDS era this pattern was repeated in full force, and Sweden again broke all records when it came to a cold-hearted policy based on the right of the state to compulsion when the general interest clashed with concerns for individual rights. The laws that were passed in 1983 and again in 1985 and 1988 built on earlier legislation: "compulsory examinations, mandatory contact tracing, possibly indefinite quarantine of recalcitrants, as well as extensive monitoring of HIV positives' behaviour by the police and the authorities" (Baldwin, 2005, 154).[21]

Furthermore, it was decided to deny anonymity to those who were tested. In debating the issue with a few protesting liberals and communists, a Swedish Social Democrat argued that granting anonymity would "represent a victory for the interest of the individual," an unfortunate outcome since at stake, he thought, "were the more important and justified concerns of the community" (Baldwin, 2005, 256).

In trying to make sense of this "prophylactic Swedish *Sonderweg*," which was surprising to some foreign observers who associated Sweden with tolerance, democracy, and rights, Baldwin argues that it is not the case that we can explain the harsh approach to AIDS simply by reference to the similar policies chosen in the fight against cholera, syphilis, and other contagious diseases. Although such continuity in laws and institutional responses is indeed crucial, so is the deeply ingrained Puritanism that has long informed Swedish social and health policy. A deep abhorrence of—and lack of tolerance for—alcohol and drug users as well as prostitution and vagrancy has translated into a long history of "zero tolerance" of such deviants from the norm of the healthy and wholesome worker.

Once an individual transgresses the fundamental social contract in this regard, he or she effectively puts himself or herself outside the society of deserving citizens and becomes subject to treatments where his or her individual rights are seen as secondary to the interest of the community and the social rights of the good citizens. In this regard HIV-positive persons occupy a middle ground. At first they were treated like unworthy moral outcasts (libertine homosexuals and wanton drug addicts), later as deserving victims of a disease but still seen as threats (like cholera victims) to the community, and not fully trustworthy to take full responsibility and thus not deserving of their full civil rights, including the right to privacy. Here community interest again trumped any concern with individual rights, in the eyes of the professionals who were the self-appointed guardians of the general will.

RIGHTS TO HEALTHCARE, RIGHTS IN HEALTHCARE

The treatment of HIV-positive persons and AIDS patients can be viewed as a special case within the broader category of healthcare in particular and social rights and obligations in general, with links both to the history of compulsive care of substance and alcohol abusers, the patterns described with respect to children's rights and care, and the tension between paternalism and the struggle for individual rights that characterized the situation of disabled persons in Sweden. In the final empirical section of the chapter we will turn to the question of rights to and in healthcare as it pertains to the "average" or "normal" citizen, for whom the encounter with healthcare is not linked to marginal and extreme afflictions, or to questions of moral turpitude, but to ordinary cases of birth, disease, accident, and aging.

Public healthcare in Sweden certainly qualifies as a classic social right in Marshall's sense. It is linked directly to citizenship (and/or legal residence), including children and youth; it is individual; it is provided and available to all on equal terms; and it is not dependent on employment, age, income, or other limiting conditions. And by many accounts, Swedish citizens appear, on balance, to find the healthcare system to be a good one, even though reported complaints to HSAN (the official board handling such complaints, see below) have risen in recent years from less than 1,500 in 1990 to just under 5,000 in 2009 (HSAN yearly reports). This is very much in harmony with surveys that indicate that a substantial majority of Swedish subjects approve of the welfare state at large (Svallfors, 1996, 2002). The subjective appraisals of Swedish citizens are confirmed by international comparative studies that tend to find that Swedish healthcare is, if not the best in the world, then reasonably good and relatively cost-efficient.[22]

However, the downside of these strong social rights *to* healthcare, in a broad but unspecified sense, is that they come with weak individual rights *in* healthcare. This is the case since the right to healthcare is, in fact, not a right at all in the strict sense, namely a right that is individual as well as claimable and enforceable through a court of law. Instead, Swedish laws that regulate the provision of healthcare constitute first and foremost a declaration that the state takes on the responsibility and obligation to provide all citizens with the best available healthcare in the best fashion possible within the guidelines of the law on healthcare. At the same time, the power to determine exactly what care is provided when and where is ultimately reserved for politicians, professionals, and experts. This means that even though one tends to speak about a "right" to healthcare in Sweden, this is merely what one expert, Lotta Westerhäll (1994), calls a "quasi" or "service" right (Trägårdh, 1999a,b).

Indeed, time and time again the very notion of claimable individual rights in healthcare has been rejected in governmental commissions and subsequent revisions of the law, often in direct response to attempts at introducing a patients' rights perspective, beginning in the late 1970s.[23] Therefore, this system of social insurance differs from, let's say, the insurance one might have for one's car, house, or cat in that it is not a legally biding contract according to ordinary civil law. It is a *social* contract, which ultimately depends on the political will of the parliament rather than on judgments made in a court of law on the basis of a law that specifies the rights of an individual. As an individual, one does therefore not have an individual *legal* right that allows one to claim in a court a service or contest a particular choice of treatment or its timing (Karlsson, 2003; Trägårdh, 1999a,b).

To be sure, some option still exists for individuals to bring cases of claimed medical misadventure. One is a court-like institution, HSAN (*Hälso- och sjukvårdens ansvarsnämnd*), that allows patients to file claims against physicians and other health workers. HSAN was created in 1981, partly as a response to the demands made by patients' rights advocates; however, it has had only a limited impact for several reasons. For one, it has effectively tended to privilege physicians since other physicians, in line with a long tradition of paternalism and expert rule, have tried the cases and made the decisions. Furthermore, it has not provided an opportunity for patients to bring their own counsel and expert witnesses, and thirdly HSAN does not have the authority to award punitive and compensatory damages. To seek some compensation, patients have been able to turn to the system for patients' insurance, which however has been a no-fault insurance scheme, concerned only with straight compensation, not with questions of justice and right and wrong.

The fundamental logic is here the same as the one we have encountered above in discussing compulsory care and the treatment of AIDS. The paramount interest is in safeguarding the health of the population at large, not to provide justice and rights for individual citizens. Throughout, Swedish healthcare is dominated by a concern for the system as a whole, and increasingly with the economic efficiency of healthcare delivery. The context for this is of course the demographic, technological, and financial trends that indicate that as people live longer lives, the population ages, and the capacity to provide care increases, but at an ever-increasing cost, the ability of the state to provide healthcare to all will be limited by the sheer size of the cost. However, the concern for efficiency has been present for some time, reflected in the ideas central to New Public Management, including the effort to bring a market-like dynamic into the system by introducing competition among providers and freer choice for patients, equipped with something like healthcare vouchers.

These trends have culminated recently in a new system that gives citizens a broad freedom of choice between primary care facilities and specialists.[24] In a related move, attempts are made to construct Internet-based systems for information on hospitals and clinics, ultimately types of list and index-like ratings that patients as well as politicians making decisions about funding and contracts can use to pick and choose among providers, from the level of the region, the hospital, down to specialists, clinics, and individual physicians.

These developments can in certain regards be viewed as empowering for individuals, if we think of them as citizen-consumers. However, this type of consumer power is limited in many ways. The information on which to make decisions is far from fully available and complete, and questions about who produces and controls such information very much remain. Such consumer-based power is, furthermore, less relevant to citizens struck by sudden and acute health issues than those with chronic and manageable diseases (such as diabetes). And finally, consumer power in healthcare does little for patients subject to malpractice or abuse of power by healthcare providers.

In this regard the current vogue for "evidence-based medicine" shows ominous signs of introducing a new type of expert-dominated healthcare that borders on neo-paternalism. The most dramatic expression of this is the dismantling of HSAN, which was suggested by a recent governmental commission and in fact took effect as of January 2011.[25] The rationale appears to be that it is, from the point of view of the healthcare system as a whole, not productive to assign blame to particular individuals, since naming and blaming would tend to discourage healthcare workers from bringing attention to problems in the system. Instead, the focus should be on correcting the errors in the healthcare delivery processes that allow for mistakes and malpractice. Therefore, the right of individuals, already weak, to bring up particular cases against actual people is to be effectively eliminated. This is expressed rhetorically in a shift from a language invoking "patients' rights" (albeit in a vague and weak manner) to one promoting "patient safety." The need for individuals to seek and find justice in particular cases, namely those that affect themselves, is in this context seen as secondary from the point of view of those for whom the viability of the system, not the rights of the individual, is the central concern.

The risk that this line of defense of the public healthcare system runs into is that people may vote with their feet and cash and choose the role of market actors with individual rights rather than citizens with social rights. Options along these lines include private insurance, which is now available, as well as "healthcare tourism," whereby Swedes travel abroad to get treatment. And such mobility is also a legal right with the EU, according to rulings in the European Court of Justice that have declared that EU citizens have the right to seek medical treatment within all of the EU.

In this perspective, the fundamental question becomes: is it possible to find a solution that strikes a balance between claims made by the proponents of a national health system perspective and those who champion individual rights? Given the accelerating need to construct a just system not only for choosing where to spend the available healthcare money but also to protect individual integrity, it seems that it is crucial not to invest all the power with the experts speaking for the system and none with the individual at the center of each actual case—for it is precisely when we are forced to prioritize and make choices that individual rights become crucial.

In an earlier period, when healthcare was more primitive and the cost much lower, money was not an issue, but the state could plausibly claim that it would indeed provide all citizens with all the best care available. Today such a claim is much less plausible. Should we fail to find a solution that can balance the rights of the individual with a legitimate concern for the healthcare system and national health, the long-term prospects for the legitimacy of a public system for healthcare, construed as a social right for all citizens, would seem to be bleak indeed.

CONCLUSIONS: "THE IRON LAW OF RIGHTS"

In this chapter we have tried to illuminate the paradoxical character of the Swedish welfare state with respect to the position of the individual in relation to the state. In particular we have emphasized two aspects, one that concerns a tension between universal citizenship and the exclusion of those deemed unworthy, the other an embrace of social rights at the expense of individual rights.

Starting with the first pension reform in 1913, we thus identified a tension between an emphasis on universal benefits based on citizenship and a tendency to limit full rights to such benefits to wholesome workers and the deserving poor. Indeed, this distinction between "deserving" and "undeserving" remains central to the fundamental logic of the welfare system today, in which many benefits are linked to the ability and willingness to work. The current center-right government has, if anything, further increased this stress on the primacy of the work ethic, displaying a willingness to exclude or marginalize further those who fail to live up to this ideal.

Secondly, we have emphasized how the development of modern Sweden can simultaneously be described as the extension of a plethora of social benefits that have raised the physical well-being, individual autonomy, and social equality of its citizens *and* as a project that at heart has built this edifice of social rights at the expense of fundamental, legally claimable individual rights. What these two avenues of analysis have in common is an emphasis on a benevolent state paternalism that simultaneously emancipates and disempowers the individual in the name of equality, work ethic, equal access to fundamental goods, the primacy of national community and the social imperative, and expert knowledge.

Returning to T. H. Marshall, the question then becomes: is the tension or even contradiction between (collective) social and (individual) civil rights a logical necessity, something that is embedded, in a theoretical sense, in the very nature of civil rights that belong to individuals, on the one hand, and social rights that are collectively possessed by the people as a whole, on the other? Or should we think of the trade-off between individual rights, social rights, and the interest of

community and society in more pragmatic terms, as different political imperatives that can at least to some extent be reconciled and balanced through wise
legislation that leaves no one neither fully satisfied, nor entirely dissatisfied?

For Marshall it was clear that social rights were fundamentally different from
civil rights, even if he appears to vacillate between this position and the one suggested at the beginning of this chapter, that social rights were legally constituted
in the same way as civil and political rights—that is, as legally binding and claimable individual rights (Panican, 2007, 59). To appreciate the tension more fully,
one may start by noting that civil rights appeared to Marshall as closely linked to
the emerging market society that perforce created the radical inequalities that he
normatively was committed to curing. As he put it, "civil rights were indispen-
sible to a competitive market economy," and far from alleviating inequality they
tended to legitimize such social ills (Marshall, 1950, 33).

Classic civil rights were in fact concerned with precisely such matters as the
right to property and the right to make contracts, laws, and rules that were central to the functioning of capitalism. Social rights, on the other hand, were rem-
edies whose aims were, to use the language of Esping-Andersen and others, to
"de-commodify" certain goods by removing them from the market logic and
instead making them part of the rationality of the planned society. In this shift
social rights not simply complemented civil rights, but in a deeper sense overwhelmed them. As Marshall put it, the obligation of the democratic socialist state
"is towards society as a whole, whose remedy in case of default lies in parliament
or a local council, instead of to individual citizens, whose remedy lies in a court
of law" (Marshall, 1950, 59). While Marshall alludes to a need to maintain a "fair
balance between these collective and individual elements in social rights," it ultimately follows that "individual rights must be subordinated to national plans"
(Marshall, 1950, 59).

At the time that Marshall wrote, in 1950, in the wake of the World War II and
during the high age of optimism regarding the prospects for building a planned
society based in a commitment to national solidarity, it seemed that taming
capitalism and eradicating inequality were more pressing issues than protecting individual rights and safeguarding the dynamism of the market society.
Today, 60 years later, things appear in a somewhat different light. Enthusiasm
for planned societies and command economies has waned to the point of obliv-
ion, and even erstwhile Social Democrats subscribe to some version of a "third
way" that thinly disguises a new consensus around the market society as the
only way.

Along with this embrace of the logic of the market has come both an increased
acceptance of inequality and a new emphasis on the individual and his or her
rights to pursue property and individual happiness. With this has followed a
decreased acceptance of the paternalism of elites and the subordination of the
individual to the supposed interests of the national community. While relative

social equality and to some extent even economic equality remain strong values, associated with the fundamentals of a good society, these sentiments have to coexist on more equal terms with the individualistic desire for freedom, and not only *through* but also *from* state interference and expert control, to invoke Berlin's distinction between negative freedom from state coercion and positive freedom through the resources of the state.

In this new political situation, what becomes clear is that Berlin's analysis of positive versus negative freedom is as relevant as ever. If we bring this analysis to bear on Marshall's distinction between civil and social rights, we end up with what we will call the "iron law of rights:" where social rights grow in the name of positive freedom, individual rights and negative freedom diminish—and vice versa. In entering a social contract, the individual perforce relinquishes his or her sovereignty. This is to some extent true for any society. There is, however, a crucial difference between a system of social insurance typical of a modern welfare state, where the ultimate power lies with politicians and experts, and a system of private insurance where the relations of power is regulated in civil law with the individual as a named party to the contract. At the aggregate level the former may well be superior in terms of social outcomes and economic rationality, but at the necessary cost of reducing the power of and justice for the individual.

This bring us back, then, to the question posed above and also alluded to by Marshall: can we at least pragmatically find a way to negotiate between the imperatives of national interest, social solidarity, and the rights of the individual? In the Swedish context one possible way to handle the dilemma would be to develop further the system of vouchers, now used for education and healthcare. By converting vouchers from politically determined social rights into *bona fide* legally constituted individual contracts with the chosen provider (which could be for-profit, nonprofit, or public), the principle of citizenship-based social rights guaranteed by the state and funded through taxes could be joined to the idea of legally claimable, individual rights.

Clearly, insofar as social rights are, as the iron law of rights would suggest, and as Marshall himself noted, linked to an increase in power on the part of the state and its agents over individual citizens, a shift in favor of individual rights must entail some kind of partial retreat of the state and the primacy of the social. This returns us to the crucial question posed by Evers and Guillemard in Chapter 1, namely the extent to which the shift from a traditional focus on social security to the contemporary language of "social investment" also constitutes a concerted attempt to ensure individual agency and empowerment. Certainly one can imagine that this transition *could* entail a move away from paternalism and a primary focus on social control and integration towards an embrace of individual agency and individual rights. But at least in the Swedish case it is clear that concrete institutional reforms in this direction still have to be realized. Until then, the iron law of rights will continue to present us with a fundamental choice—or trade-off—between individual empowerment and paternalistic social rights.

ACKNOWLEDGMENTS

We wish to thank Karin Gavelin for her thorough research and insightful commentary as well as the following for reading various drafts and making many valuable suggestions and comments: Peter Baldwin, Adalbert Evers, Håkan Johansson, Alexandru Panican, Johanna Schiratzki, and Kerstin Stenius. Also thanks to Johan von Essen and the other members of the Institute for Civil Society Studies seminar at Ersta Sköndal University College, where we presented an early draft in the fall of 2010.

NOTES

1 For example, Halsey (1996) calls him an "ethical socialist"; see also Giddens, 1996.

2 There exists an enormous literature on Swedish social insurance and the historical development of the Swedish welfare state. In this section we are simply aiming to provide the big picture and will refrain from providing detailed references; however, the account is based on Trägårdh (1990).

3 In fact, it initially excluded a small group of individuals, but this was of less practical significance and did not affect the vast majority of the population, including the poor.

4 The difference in logic between the Nordic and the Bismarckian system, noted by Bent Rold Andersen already in 1983, was later systematized further by Gösta Esping-Andersen (1990) into his well-known "regime" typology.

5 In Sweden, the question of citizenship has been discussed primarily in the context of the politics of immigration. In this debate the focus has been less on citizenship *per se* and more on the more pressing matter of how to integrate immigrants.

6 It didn't help that the Swedish word for citizen (*medborgare*) was simply a variation on the word for bourgeois (*borgare*), a linguistic point that is even more true for German, where *Bürger* means both citizen and bourgeois and the term *Mitbürger* is just a rhetorical affectation rarely used by anyone other than politicians and propagandists.

7 The third obligation that Lundberg and Åmark list is, as we argue in this chapter, more questionable. While an obligation to care for underage children remains, this is no longer true for the care of the elderly parents or adult children.

8 This point is still ignored by some Nordic scholars—for example, see Lundberg & Åmark (2001, 158), claiming "all persons above the age of 67, who had no incomes, were granted the supplements."

9 The quote is from Berggren (1998); on the history of forced sterilizations see also Broberg & Hansen, 1996; Broberg & Tydén, 1991; Runcis, 1998; and Sejerstedt, 2005.

10 See, however, Lödemel (1997), who has discussed this contradiction, using the term "the welfare paradox."

11 Lundberg and Tydén provide a useful summary of both the tractional and the critical approach, including references to key texts.

12 Gustav Petrén quoted in Zaremba (1992, 75) (our translation).

13 On the Convention and its legal status in Sweden, as well as children's legal rights more broadly, see Schiratzki (2010).

14 See, for example, UNICEF (2007).

15 Indeed, children's rights and gender equality are profoundly interlinked, both normatively and in concrete social and family policies.

16 However, Printz et al.'s remarks (2003, 258–259) strike us as important, namely that the rights perspective more often is emphasized when it comes to the functionally disabled than, for example, substance abusers and social assistance recipients. They write: "The question of how we evaluate the importance of rights for exerting influence can therefore be seen as connected in some degree with how we view different groups—their status in the society and what moral values we use as points of departure for our reasoning."

17 Baldwin also argues, similarly to Berggren (1998) cited earlier, that this harsh reaction was also part and parcel of the same mentality that informed "compulsory sterilizations on a scale rivalled only in the Third Reich" (Baldwin, 2005, 242).

18 These are the three largest newspapers in Sweden.

19 In Swedish the key concept is *folkhälsa* (i.e., the health of the people)—a longstanding concern that still today, long after the vogue of the 1930s regarding eugenics and social Darwinism, is represented in Swedish policy and government institutions such as *Statens folkhälsoinstitut* (Swedish National Institute of Public Health).

20 The maxim is usually credited to Lenin, though written evidence that Lenin actually said this appears to be missing.

21 By the mid 1990s this law had been used around 60 times, and those who fell victims to the law were incarcerated on average a year but in some case several years.

22 In the latest (2000) World Health Organization (WHO) rankings, Sweden was listed as 23rd overall in terms of healthcare and as 7th when it came to expenditure per capita.

23 For example, see SOU 1997:154 (Patienten har rätt), SOU 2008:117 (Patientsäkerhet), SOU 2008:127 (Patientens rätt).

24 See the governmental commission SOU 2008:37 (Vårdval i Sverige) and the subsequent law that is now providing for a right to choose between different producers of primary healthcare in Sweden.

25 SOU 2008:117 (Patientsäkerhet).

REFERENCES

Ambjörnsson, R. (1988). *Den skötsamme arbetaren.* Stockholm: Carlsson.

Andersen, B. R. (1983). Rationality and irrationality in the Nordic welfare state. In B. R. Andersen, *Two essays on the Nordic welfare state.* Copenhagen: AKF.

Åmark, K. (2004). Trygghet och tvång—två teman i aktuell nordisk välfärdsstatshistorisk forskning. In *Arkiv för studier i arbetarrrörelsens historia,* no 91, 1–19.

Baldwin, P. (2005). *Disease and democracy: The industrialized world faces AIDS.* Berkeley: University of California Press.

Berg, S. (2007). *DHR: 80 år av rörelse.* Stockholm: De handikappades Riksförbund.

Berg, S. (2008). *25 år: Independent Living i Sverige.* Johanneshov: STIL.

Berge, A. (1995). *Medborgarrätt och egenansvar.* Lund: Arkiv.

Berggren, H. (1995). *Seklets ungdom: retorik, politik och modernitet 1900–1939.* Stockholm: Tiden.

Berggren, H., & L. Trägårdh (2006). *Är svensken människa: Gemenskap och oberoende i det moderna Sverige.* Stockholm: Norstedts.

Berggren, H., & L. Trägårdh (2010). The autonomous child and the moral logic of the Swedish welfare state. In H. Mattsson & S.-O. Wallenstein, *Swedish modernism: Architecture, consumption and the welfare state.* London: Black Dog Publishing.

Bergman, H. (2003). *Att fostra till föräldraskap.* Stockholm: Stockholms Universitet.

Bergmark, A. (2004). Tvångsvårdens utfall: en uppföljning av missbrukare vårdade med stöd av LVM. In *SOU 2004:3 LVM-utredningen: forskningsrapporter: bilagedel.*

Berlin, I. (1958). *Two concepts of liberty.* Oxford: Clarendon Press.

Björkman, J. (2001). *Vård för samhällets bästa.* Stockholm: Carlssons Bokförlag.

Björkman, J. (2007). Rätten till det goda hemmet. Om rätten till bostadsinspektion i 1930-talets Stockholm. In K. Florin, E. Elgán, & G. Hagemann (Eds.), *Den självstyrande medborgaren? Ny historia om rättvisa, demokrati och välfärd.* Stockholm: Institutet för framtidsstudier.

Börjeson, B. (1979). *Inre och yttre tvång.* Stockholm: Tiden.

Bring, S. (2004). *Medborgare eller målsägare: sociala rättigheter och välfärdspolitiska dilemman.* Stockholm: Svenska Kommunförbundet and Landstingsförbundet.

Broberg, G., & M. Tydén (1991). *Oönskade i folkhemmet: Rashygien och sterilisering i Sverige.* Stockholm: Gidlund.

Broberg, G., & N. R. Hansen (Eds.) (1996). *Eugenics and the welfare state: Sterilization policy in Denmark, Sweden, Norway, and Finland.* East Lansing: Michigan State University Press.

Delli-Carpini, M., & L. Trägårdh (2004). The juridification of politics in the United States and Europe: Historical roots, contemporary debates and future prospects. In L. Trägårdh (Ed.), *After national democracy: Rights, law and power in America and the New Europe*. Oxford: Hart Publishing.

Ekendahl, M. (2001). *Tvingad till vård. Missbrukares syn på LVM, motivation och egna möjligheter*. Rapport i socialt arbete 100, Institutionen för socialt arbete, Stockholms Universitet.

Elmér, Å. (1989). *Svensk socialpolitik*. Stockholm: Liber.

Elmér, Å, S. Blomberg, L. Harrysson & J. Petersson (2000). *Svensk socialpolitik*. Lund: Studentlitteratur.

Esiasson, P. (2010). *Karl Staff*. Stockholm: Bonniers.

Esping-Andersen, G. (1990). *The three worlds of welfare capitalism*. Cambridge: Polity.

Evers, A. (2009). Civicness and civility: Their meanings for social services. In *Voluntas 10, 2*, 239–259.

Förhammar, S. (2007). *Från tärande till närande: funktionshinder, utbildning och socialpolitik i Sverige*. Lund: Studentlitteratur.

Gerdner, A., & M. Berglund (2010). *Översikt om tvångsvård vid missbruk—effekt och kvalitet*. Stencil till Missbruksutredningen.

Giddens, A. (1996). T. H. Marshall, the state and democracy. In M. Bulmer & A. Rees (Eds.), *Citizenship today*. London: UCL Press.

Grünewald, K. (2009). *Från idiot till medborgare: de utvecklingsstördas historia*. Stockholm: Gothia.

Halsey, A. H. (1996). T. H. Marshall and ethical socialism. In M. Bulmer & A. Rees (Eds.), *Citizenship today*. London: UCL Press.

Heckscher, G. (1946). *Staten och organisationena*. Stockholm: Kooperativa förbundets bokförlag.

Hernes, H. (1988). Scandinavian citizenship. *Acta Sociologica, 31*(3), 199–215.

Holmström, B. (1998). *Domstolar och demokrati: den tredje statsmaktens politiska roll i England, Frankrike och Tyskland*. Uppsala: Acta Universitatis Upsaliensis.

Huntford, R. (1971). *The new totalitarians*. London: Allen Lane.

Jeppsson Grassman, E., & L. Svedberg (1993). Frivillig verksamhet på fältet—En närstudie av sju organisationer. In *SOU 1993: 82*.

Johansson, H. (2001). *I det sociala medborgarskapets skugga*. Lund: Arkiv.

Karlsson, L. (2003). *Konflikt eller harmoni: Individuella rättigheter och ansvarsutkrävande i svensk och brittisk sjukvård*. Göteborg: CEFOS.

Larsson, J. (2008). *Folkhemmet och det europeiska huset*. Stockholm:Hjalmarson & Högberg.

Lehto, J. (1994). Involuntary treatment of people with substance related problems in the Nordic countries. In M. Järvinen & A. Skretting (Eds.), *Missbruk och tvångsvård*. Nad-publikation no. 27.

Lindberg, L. (1996). *Den amerikanska lösningen*. Stockholm: HSO.

Lindberg, L. (2006). Handikappolitikens utveckling—från institutioner till sektorsansvar. In P. Brusén & A. Printz (Eds.), *Handikappolitiken i praktiken. Om den nationella handlingsplanen*. Stockholm: Gothia.

Lindberg, L., & L. Grönvik (2011). *Funktionshinderspolitik—en introduktion*. Stockholm: Studentlitteratur.

Lödemel, I. (1997) *The welfare paradox: Income maintenance and personal social services in Norway and Britain, 1946–1966*. Oslo: Scandinavian University Press.

Lundberg, U., & K. Åmark (2001). Social rights and social security: The Swedish welfare state, 1900–200. *Scandinavian Journal of Social History, 26*, 157–176.

Lundberg, U., & M. Tydén (2010). In search of the Swedish model: Contested historiography. In H. Mattsson & S.-O. Wallenstein (Eds.), *Swedish modernism: Architecture, consumption and the welfare state*. London: Black Dog Publishing.

Lundström, T. (1993). *Tvångsomhändertagande av barn*. (Dissertation). Rapport i socialt arbete no 61, Institutionen för socialt arbete, Stockholms Universitet.

Marshall, T. H. (1950). Citizenship and social class. In *Citizenship and social class and other essays*. Cambridge: Cambridge University Press.

Mattsson, H. (1984). *Den goda förmyndaren*. Stockholm: Liber.

Mayerson, A. B. (1994). *The history of the ADA: "Of the people, by the people, for the people."* Berkeley: Disability Rights Education & Defense Fund.

Meeuwisse, A. (1997). *Vänskap och organisering*. Dissertation. Lund: Arkiv förag.

Meeuwisse, A., S. Sunesson, & H. Swärd (Eds.) (2006). *Socialt arbete: en grundbok*. Stockholm: Natur och Kultur.

Missbruksutredningen (2010a). *Bättre vård och stöd för individen. Om ansvar och tvång i den svenska missbruks- och beroendevården. En diskussionspromemoria av Missbruksutredningen*. Statens offentliga utredningar.

Missbruksutredningen (2010b). *Remisssammanställning av Missbruksutredningens Diskusionspromemoria bättre vård och stöd för individen. Om ansvar och tvång i den svenskaissbruks- och beroendevården*. Statens offentliga utredningar.

Modig, C. (2004). Vänstervinden, R-förbunden och samtidshistorien. In M. Adamson et al. (Eds.), *När botten stack upp. Om de utslagnas kamp för frihet och människovärde*. Hedemora: Gidlunds förlag.

Nej till vårdtvång: En debattbok om socialarbetarnas roll i den framtida socialvården (1997). Stockholm: Sveriges socionomförbund/Tidens förlag.

Nergelius, J. (1996). *Konstitutionellt rättighetsskydd: svensk rätt i ett komparativt perspektiv*. Stockholm: Fritzes förlag.

Nergelius, J. (2006). Situationen kring sociala rättigheter i Sverige—för bostadslösa och andra. *Nordisk Alkohol & Narkotikatidskrift, 2–3*, 64–68.

Nergelius, J., & B. Holmström (2000). Mer makt krävs till domstolarna. *R&D, no 2*, 28 January.

Nestius, H. (2004). Varför i helvete har vi ingenting att säga till om. In M. Adamson et al. (Eds.), *När botten stack upp. Om de utslagnas kamp för frihet och människovärde*. Hedemora: Gidlunds förlag.

Nilssen, E. (2005). Coercion and justice: A critical analysis of compulsory intervention towards adult substance abusers in Scandinavian social law. *International Journal of Social Welfare, 14*(2), 134–144.

Nordegren, T. (2004). De utslagnas befrielserörelse. In M. Adamson et al. (Eds.), *När botten stack upp. Om de utslagnas kamp för frihet och människovärde.* Hedemora: Gidlunds förlag

Norström, C., & A.s Thunved (2006). *Nya sociallagarna: med kommentarer, lagar och förordningar som de lyder den 1 januari 2006.* Stockholm:Norstedts Juridik.

Olofsson, J. (2007). *Socialpolitik. Varför, hur och till vilken nytta?* Stockholm: SNS Förlag.

Olson, H.-E. (1992). *Staten och ungdomens fritid.* (Dissertation) Lund: Arkiv.

Palm, J., & K. Stenius (2002). Sweden: Integrated compulsory treatment. *European Addiction Research, 8*(2), 69–77.

Panican, A. (2007). *Rättighet och rättvisa: användbarhet av rättigheter och rättvisa i sociala projekt.* (Dissertation) Lund: Lunds Universitet.

Petersén, L. (2005). *Alternativ till rättighetslagstiftning inom kommunal vård och omsorg: vad behöver ändras och varför?* Stockholm: Sveriges Kommuner och Landsting.

Printz, A., et al (2003). Den enskildes ställning—några utvecklingslinjer under 1990-talet. In *Socialtjänsten i Sverige. En översikt 2003.* The National Board of Health and Welfare.

Ratzka, A. (1998). I kläm mellan laissez faire och den sociala ingenjörskonsten. *Socialpolitik, no 2.*

Ratzka, A. (2003). "Independent living in Sweden." www.independentliving.org/docs6/ratzka200302b.html

Rexed, B. (1977). Paneldebatt—diskussion och utfrågning. In *Nej till vårdtvång.* Stockholm: Sveriges socionomförbund/Tidens förlag

Rothstein, B. (1992). *Den korporativa staten.* Stockholm: Norstedts.

Runcis, M. (1998). *Steriliseringar i folkhemmet.* Stockholm: Ordfront.

Sandin, B. (2003). Barndomens omvandling—från särart till likart. In B. Sandin & G. Halldén (Eds.), *Barnets bästa: en antologi om barndomens innebörder och välfärdens organisering.* Stockholm/Stehag: Symposium.

Sannegård, W. (2004). När mormor blev knarkare. In M. Adamson et al. (Eds.), *När botten stack upp. Om de utslagnas kamp för frihet och människovärde.* Hedemora: Gidlunds förlag.

Schiratzki, J. (2010). *Barnrättens grunder* (4:e upplagan). Lund: Studentlitteratur.

Sejerstedt, F. (2005). *Socialdemokratins tidsålder.* Nora: Nya Doxa.

Shapiro, J. P. (1993). *No pity. People with disabilities forging a new civil rights movement.* New York: Times Books.

Skretting, A., & M. Järvinen (1994). Symbolpolitikk og paternalisme? In *NAD-publikation no 27.*

SOU 1967:36. *Nykterhetsvårdens läge Del I.* Stockholm: Esselte.

SOU 1997:154. *Patienten har rätt.* Stockholm: Fritzes.

SOU 1998:103. *Bemäktiga individerna—Om domstolarna, lagen och de individuella rättigheterna i Sverige.* Stockholm: Fritzes.

SOU 2008:37. *Vårdval i Sverige.* Stockholm: Fritzes.

SOU 2008:117. *Patientsäkerhet.* Stockholm: Fritzes.

SOU 2008:127. *Patientens rätt.* Stockholm: Fritzes.

Soysal, Y. (1994). *Limits of citizenship: Migrants and postnational membership in Europe.* Chicago: Chicago University Press.

Stenius, K. (2009) Missbrukarna och lokalsamhället: En introduktion till boken. In K. Stenius & L. Johansson (Eds.), *Socialt medborgarskap och lokal missbrukarvård.* Sorad forskningsrapport no 55, Stockholm University.

Stenius, K., & W. Runquist (2009). Lokala definitioner av missbruksproblemen. Paternalistiska helhetslösningar och liberalare alternative. In K. Stenius & L. Johansson (Eds.),*Socialt medborgarskap och lokal missbrukarvård.* Sorad forskningsrapport no 55, Stockholm University.

Storbjörk, J., & R. Room (2008). The two worlds of alcohol problems: Who is in treatment and who is not? *Addiction Research and Theory, 16*(1), 67–84.

Svallfors, S. (1996). *Välfärdsstatens moraliska ekonomi. Välfärdsopinioner i 90-talets Sverige.* Umeå: Boéa bokförlag.

Svallfors, S. (1999). *Mellan risk och tilltro: Opinionsstödet för en kollektiv välfärdspolitik* Umeå Studies in Sociology, no 114, Department of Sociology, Umeå University.

Svallfors, S. (2002). Political trust and support for the welfare state: Unpacking a supposed relationship. In B. Rothstein & S. Steinmo (Eds.), *Restructuring the welfare state: Political institutions and policy change.* New York: Palgrave.

Svedberg, L. (2005). Det civila samhället och välfärden—ideologiska önskedrömmar och sociala realiteter. In E. Amnå (Ed.), *Civilsamhället Några forskningsfrågor.* Stockholm: Riksbankens Jubileumsfond i samarbete med Gidlunds förlag.

Svedberg, L., & L. Trägårdh (2007). Unga, civilsamhälle och välfärd. In *Fokus En analys av ungas hälsa och utsatthet.* Ungdomsstyrelsens skrifter 2007:14.

Svedberg, L., & L. Trägårdh (2008). Det civila samhället, ungdomarna och välfärden. In *Konsten att bry sig om. Föreningslivets betydelse för unga, kommunerna och staten.* Ungdomsstyrelsens skrifter 2008:7.

Trägårdh, L. (1990). Swedish model or Swedish culture. *Critical Review, 4*(4).

Trägårdh, L. (1993). *The concept of the people and the construction of popular political culture in Germany and Sweden 1848–1933.* Dissertation. Dept of History, UC Berkeley.

Trägårdh, L. (1997). Statist individualism. In O. Sorensen & B. Stråth (Eds.), *The cultural construction of Norden.* Oslo: Scandinavian University Press.

Trägårdh, L. (1999a). Bemäktiga individerna: om domstolarna, lagen och de individuella rättigheterna. In *SOU 1998:103.* Stockholm: Fritzes.

Trägårdh, L. (1999b). *Patientmakt i Sverige, USA och Holland*. Stockholm: Spri.

Trägårdh, L. (2002). Crisis and the politics of national community: Germany and Sweden, 1933–2000. In L. Trägårdh & N. Witoszek (Eds.), *Culture and crisis: The case of Germany and Sweden*. London and New York: Berghahn Books.

UNICEF (2007). *Report Card 7, Child poverty in perspective: An overview of child well-being in rich countries*. UNICEF: Innocenti Research Centre.

Vinterhed, K. (1977). *Gustav Jonsson på Skå*. Stockholm: Tidens förlag.

Wallander, L., & J. Blomquist. (2005). Who "needs" compulsoratory care? *Nordisk alcohol- & narkotikatidskrift, 22 (supplement)*, 63–85.

Westerhäll, L. (1994). *Patienträttigheter*. Stockholm: Nerenius & Santéns förlag.

WHO (2000). *WHO World Health Report*. http://www.photius.com/rankings/healthranks.html

Zaremba, M. (1992). *Minken i folkhemmet*. Stockholm: Timbro.

PART III

COUNTRY CASES: EASTERN EUROPE

11

THE POLICY OF ACTIVATION IN THE CZECH REPUBLIC AND CITIZENSHIP RIGHTS

Tomáš Sirovátka

INTRODUCTION

Changes in (post)modern society[1] are challenging the nature of welfare state provisions, as well as the forms of governance used in public policy. At the level of principles, ongoing reforms touch the very essence of social citizenship: the scope of the rights of the citizen and the balance between rights and obligations is being reconsidered, and rights are becoming increasingly conditional (see Chapter 1). As for the measures being implemented, these are emphasizing employment-centered and activation policies.[2] Shifts in public governance include the decentralization and localization of policies, the pluralization of actors, the dominance of new forms that accentuate indirect methods of influence, cooperation, and partnership, contractualization between the state and other agents as well as between institutions and clients, and the individualization of the services provided (cf. Giddens, 1998; Mosley & Sol, 2001; Serrano Pascual, 2004; Valkenburg & van Berkel, 2007; van Berkel & Møller, 2002).

The welfare states of countries undergoing a market transition can be seen as "unfinished, emergency welfare states" (Inglot, 2008), which are layering these new elements onto other elements that remain from the former communist system; however, these reforms involve a deeper paradigmatic shift than elsewhere in Europe, especially at the level of the goals and principles that guide public policies (cf. particularly Offe, 1996; Ferge, 1997; and others). Although the activation policies, which are the central element of the current welfare state reforms, are influenced by intervention from the European level (Open Coordination

Method and resources of the European Structural Funds), they are designed and implemented within the context of national policies. Since the reform measures taken are largely a product of established forms of governance and specific implementation conditions, the results of reform in postcommunist countries are distinctive and, in many respects, different to the EU-15 countries.

This chapter examines the link between the activation policies implemented at the national and local levels and their impact on (social) citizenship in the Czech Republic. Our findings are based on cross-sectional and institutional analysis, and implementation studies of selected activation policies carried out at several local employment offices in the Czech Republic.

The chapter is divided into four sections. The first section sets out our theoretical assumptions: we explain our understanding of the link between citizenship and activation policies and how the governance framework for public policies influences their implementation. In the second section, we clarify the wider policy context and approach: the perceptions of the issue of social rights, the corresponding policy discourse, and the legitimacy of the policies. In the third section, we examine the emerging activation strategy that is being shaped at the national and local levels (where relevant) in three areas: (1) regulations concerning entitlement conditions and incentives to work; (2) active labor market policies (ALMPs); and (3) individual counseling for the unemployed on the basis of individual contracts. In the conclusion, we discuss the wider consequences of the activation policies, as designed at the national level and implemented at the local level, in terms of their effect on citizenship.

THEORETICAL BACKGROUND

Citizenship consists of rights and duties, of participation, and of identities (Lister, 1998; Marshall, 1964). These three dimensions are mutually interlinked and interdependent. This is especially clear when we focus on the social dimension of citizenship: "the right to live the life of a civilized being according to the standards prevailing in society" (Marshall, 1950, 172, in Andersen & Jensen, 2002, 6) finds expression in the welfare states of Europe in, among other things, the guarantee of an adequate living standard, including the minimum subsistence income, and is traditionally associated with participation in paid work. It is also expressed in the establishment of social insurance rights and in the sharing of moral obligations to society (identity), namely to work in order to earn one's own living or to search actively for a job when one is unemployed.

The dynamic changes in the economy and labor markets, global economic competition, and economic pressures on the welfare state would require the mutual link among these three dimensions to remain strong in order to maintain the existing level of social citizenship. However, participation in paid work becomes the weakest element in this chain of mutual interdependence. Under these circumstances the welfare states are being pushed to reconsider the essence of social citizenship in terms of the residualization of social rights and of redefinition of the relationship between social rights and obligations (Lister, 2002).

From whatever perspective it is reconsidered, the core issue is to increase labor market participation as a condition for guaranteeing the social rights, as well as for the possibility of identifying with the moral order. In this way, the new understanding of citizenship "rights" is greatly expanding: for example, Dahrendorf (1988) and Bauman (1998) believe—irrespective of their doubts about the availability of paid work for a major part of the population of a postmodern society—that people's curtailed participation in the labor market and in systems of production, and the related limitations on their levels and patterns of consumption, are major sources of social exclusion, since in the society of "producers" or "consumers" (Bauman, 1998) such limitations deny them the chance of social inclusion. For Giddens (1998, 102), social inclusion "refers in its broadest sense to citizenship, to the civil and political rights and obligations that all members of a society should have, not just formally, but as a reality of their lives. It also refers to opportunities and to involvement in public space. In a society where work remains central to self-esteem and standard of living, access to work is one main context of opportunity." This way of thinking is directly associated with the idea of developing the "social investment state" (see discussion in Chapter 4 and Evers and Guillemard in Chapters 1 and 15).

Although the role of economic activity in realizing full citizenship has become centrally important, the global market economy has meant that a "full right to work" is impossible to guarantee. There may not be enough meaningful jobs available, or people may lack the skills to do the jobs. This is why Marshall interprets citizenship as a social status that is based on mutually linked sets of rights (civil, political, and social) and is thus not necessarily linked to paid employment: to use Esping-Andersen's terminology, these social rights may be understood as the "right to decommodification." Nevertheless, Marshall did not overlook the issue of work obligations when he referred to the "duty … to put one's heart into one's job and to work hard" (Marshall, 1950, 79–80 in Lister, 2002, 41). In a broader sense, social rights were grounded in the assumptions of "responsibilities towards welfare of community" (Marshall in Chapter 1). Given the environment of the structural changes in postmodern society and the changes in the political discourse and strategies (compare Gilbert, Chapter 4), the discussion of "active citizenship" has intensified, opening the opportunity to reshape the link between social rights and obligations, particularly in terms of the right to economic participation and the obligation to carry out paid work.

Although the full guarantee of work is not explicitly included in the citizenship rights, the commonly shared view is that the citizenship rights should provide some guarantee of support for jobseekers, the development of skills and the protection of the standard of living in return for the obligation to work.[3] The focal point of the debate is, then, the balance between the "right to decommodification" and support of jobseekers on the one hand, and the obligation to work on the other hand (for the idea of "balance" compare Giddens, 1998; and Chapters 1 and 4).

In line with the assumptions made by Marshall and Giddens, and in various chapters in this volume, we will focus on the following aspects of the citizenship that are related to the right to work:

- Civil/personal rights (balance in the labor contracts, the right to determine one's own life course and to the respect of privacy)
- Political rights (representation in collective bargaining)
- Social rights (the right to fair treatment, open and equal access to the labor market, and the right to adequate social protection in case of unemployment).

We must note that in the contemporary "postindustrial" context, which is demanding ever more responsibility and flexibility on the part of the individual, with the rise of "active citizenship," personal/civil rights (or human rights from the broader perspective of "global citizenship") in various forms have become crucially important, whether embodied in anti-discrimination measures, empowerment, or the balance of the client–public services relationship. It is precisely these personal/civil rights that appear to have been suppressed in postcommunist countries (mainly through the procedures for treating clients) due to the legacy of communism and the slow advance of civil society.

In the conditions of changing labor markets, activation strategies that aim to integrate the highest possible number of those fit for work into the system of paid employment use a broader set of social policy and employment policy measures. Here, we adopt the typology of the approaches to activation policies that is (with some minor reservations) shared among the researchers both in western and eastern Europe and outside, while relating these approaches to the aspects of citizenship discussed above.

The literature on activation policy has traditionally identified two stylized "model approaches" to activation. Of course, these approaches represent "ideal types," while in reality activation strategies usually include elements of both these approaches. These approaches are known as the workfare model and the social inclusion model (Nicaise, 2002); they represent the liberal approach versus the universalistic approach (Barbier, 2004)[4] or the employability versus the capability approach (Bonvin & Farvaque, 2007). If we view the activation strategies from the perspective of their goals and principles, we see that what differentiates them is the choice between emphasizing the goal of enforced labor market participation based on the strategy of nominal and wage flexibility of labor on the one hand, and emphasizing the goal of social inclusion and the strategy of functional flexibility (or capability) on the other hand. A differing interpretation of the right to (quality) employment, understood as a citizens' right, is the central distinction

(Standing, 1999).[5] The social inclusion approach emphasizes finding (and keeping) a suitable and meaningful job. The strategy of workfare or work-first strategy, by contrast, recognizes the necessity of accepting any job or work program, irrespective of its quality or suitability.

The basic features of these strategies are summarized in Table 11.1.

The policy of activation concerns the nature of citizenship rights. Although the core issue here is the balance between rights and responsibilities, and hence the increased conditionality of social provisions, the redefinition of social rights that emerges from activation strategies is complex. We seek to identify at least four elements in tackling rights that correspond to the understanding of the

Table 11.1. Two Modes of Activation

Dimensions	Work-First/Workfare Approach	Social Inclusion Approach
Policy discourse	Dependency, incentives, welfare expenditure cuts Individual responsibility, citizens' duties	Social exclusion, social inclusion, social cohesion Collective responsibility, citizens' rights (and duties)
Objectives of activation	Labor force flexibility (nominal and wage) Activated people	Functional labor flexibility Active people
Principles of activation strategies	Work-first, workfare, enforcement	Human resource development, employability (capabilities)
Measures	Administrative pressures, conditionality Incentives, making work pay	Complex measures: individual support, income, training, access to work, empowerment
Typical target groups	Long-term social welfare recipients, young people	Universal coverage (citizens) and preferential treatment of the disadvantaged
Status of clients	Exposed to pressures in order to meet conditions and duties Subordination	Expectation of responsible citizenship, possess rights Partnership, reciprocity
Choices available	Limited choice Mainly low-paid market jobs	Broader range of choices Good-quality training/jobs available
Treatment of clients by street-level bureaucracy	Individualized screening Discretion used for effective enforcement	Recognition of needs, individualized approach Mutual negotiation
Consequences for citizenship rights	Residualized citizens' rights Duty to accept any job (re-commodification, flexibilization)	Citizens' rights remain broad and strong "Right to work" balanced with obligation to work, work ethic as citizen's participation

Note: Author, based on Barbier (2004), Serrano Pascual (2004), Standing (1999), van Berkel & Møller (2002).

"right to work" outlined above. These elements may be applied either universally or selectively since they are often associated with specific target groups within the unemployed:

1. Conditioning rights—this means imposing greater obligations and requirements on those who are granted rights (a typical requirement is proving that one is intensively seeking employment and/or participation in activation measures; these become conditions for safeguarding or retaining the right to the protection of income)

2. Curtailing rights—reducing rights, granting fewer rights (typically, providing lower levels of benefit, for shorter periods of time in the case of inactivity)

3. Extending rights—providing a wider set of rights, although these may often involve greater conditionality (for example, providing new "making-work-pay" benefits to those who accept low-paid jobs, providing the right to counseling, or job offers based on a jobseeker's contract, improving benefits to the unemployed). The right to the support of capabilities is the central right here: this may take any form that promotes human and/or social capital development (the provision of the right to individual treatment and support in job-search, work-practice or training, voice in the process of determining the adopted measures, etc.).

In theory, while the work-first (enforcement) approach curtails individual rights, the inclusive (participation) approach expands them; both approaches may condition citizenship rights with corresponding obligations.

POLICY DISCOURSE AND GOALS OF THE ACTIVATION STRATEGY IN THE CZECH REPUBLIC

The public policy discourse in postcommunist countries is marked by a peculiar combination of the legacies of the past and the new realities of the market: a low level of social capital in the dimension of trust, a paradigm shift in policy discourse towards individualism, and limited consideration of solidarity and social rights in general.[6]

Research into social capital in postcommunist countries has brought to light one crucial element of the legacy of the communist past: the specific pattern when informal networks (bonding social capital) were recognized as the crucial form of social capital, with limited bridging capital between the higher and the lower social strata, and a generally lower level of trust in institutions and general trust was evidenced (see Rose, 2001; Rose et al., 1998). Pichler and Wallace (2007) distinguished four social capital regimes: one of these patterns is the East-Central/Baltic/Balkan pattern, in which informal social capital clearly substitutes for formal social capital and, more importantly, general trust is low—in the Czech Republic, for example, it is only 17%, compared to 33% in the EU-15 on average (Pichler and Wallace 2007).[7]

Ferge (2009) and similarly Evers and Guillemard (Chapter 1) assert that a weak civil society is incapable of defending social rights adequately, while Howard (2002) states that three main factors can explain why a weak civil society and low general trust are apparent in postcommunist societies: the legacy of the mistrust of institutions that prevailed during the communist era; the persistence of friendship networks and close circles of trusted friends and family that developed during the communist era; and a certain degree of disillusion on the part of citizens who feel disappointed or cheated by the new system.

Most importantly, the legacy of the communist past has completely broken the consistency of citizenship rights. Civic/personal and political rights were suppressed by the regime while social rights were established not as the result of a democratic political process, but rather as a "gift" (or a "political bribe"), bestowed by a state that required a great deal of political loyalty from its citizens in return. For example, since poverty was not officially recognized as a "status" for ideological reasons, the poor had no right to social benefit entitlements. However, at the discretion of the state administration, benefits and social services could sometimes be provided (compare Mareš & Možný, 1995). Civil, political, and social rights were therefore not interdependent or mutually reinforcing, as Marshall assumed; rather, they were separated.

During the process of market transition, the reconstruction of civil and political rights dominated, while issues of solidarity and social rights were nearly absent from the public and policy discourse.[8] Czech Prime Minister Václav Klaus (of the center-right party of Civic Democrats) expressed this new orthodoxy in the principles of social policy as a set of "responsibilities": the first responsibility being that of the state to taxpayers to use their money effectively; the second responsibility being that of the recipients of welfare benefits to other citizens, as expressed in their effort to improve their own situation, since assistance from other citizens is not unconditional; and the third responsibility being that of the state to the recipients of welfare in the sense of not undermining their family ties and solidarity through wasteful support from state (Klaus, 1995). These considerations emphasize obligations, while rights are understood to be highly conditional. In a more detailed discussion on discourses of social rights in the Czech Republic, Potůček (Chapter 14) concludes that social rights issues did not receive substantially more attention between 1992 and 2010 and that discourses typically took place in isolated parallel epistemic communities. He also argues that the national policy documents from 2006 and subsequent years did not use the concept of social rights, and neither did the orienting political documents from 2007.

Another feature of the transformation discourse is a continuity of the deformed understanding of social rights associated now with a widely shared assumption that citizens are granted too many social rights as "provisions" by the state, when they are neither required nor prepared to take full responsibility for their welfare. This assumption is reinforced by the widespread shadow economy, where the unemployed take a part that destroys the legitimacy of social rights and also by the fact that in the Czech Republic the replacement ratio of the aggregate of available social benefits (in addition to unemployment benefits, these include social assistance and other income-tested family-related benefits) was relatively high until the first years of this century.[9] The replacement rate of social assistance benefits for a two-parent household with two children and one long-term unemployed member (a one-earner household) on earnings of about two thirds of the average wage was 91% in 2002, and for a lone parent it was about 80%. This was higher than in Germany, France, the UK, or the Netherlands, and comparable with most EU-15 countries (for detail see OECD, 2009).

In comparison with other European nations, the Czechs (along with the Danes) emphasized the individual causes of poverty most strongly (56%) and the social causes least strongly (44%) in 2007 (see Table 11.2).[10] The Czechs seem to share an assumption about a significant proportion of "artificial unemployment" (represented by passive claimants or people active in the shadow economy), and opportunities in the informal economy are seen as common because the public administration has failed to eliminate it effectively. In September 2007, 37.5% of Czechs agreed that social assistance benefits were being misused, 36% did not know, and 21% disagreed with this statement[11] (compare Sirovátka & Rákoczyová, 2009).

It was striking that the policy discourse emphasized the lack of willingness to work and adverse incentives generated by the system of social benefits. In mid-2003, we conducted an exhaustive inquiry among 344 employees in senior management positions in all 77 local employment offices in the country. An absolute majority of the executives agreed with the notion that entitlements to benefits should be conditional on the obligation to accept any employment (or participate in an activation program) after a certain period of time: 41% agreed completely, while 43% agreed to some extent (Sirovátka et al., 2003).

It follows that political and economic elites in the Czech Republic have devoted a great deal of attention to improving incentives to work in the formal labor market

Table 11.2. Potential Causes of Poverty in Czech Society, 1999 and 2007

	1999 (% of respondents)	**2007 (% of respondents)**
Why are there people living in poverty in Czech society? There are four possible causes: Which of them do you find most important?		
They have had bad luck.	15%	22%
They are lazy and lack willpower.	42%	34%
There is injustice in our society.	19%	21%
Poverty is an unavoidable part of progress.	18%	23%

Source: European Values Study, Czech Republic 1999, Eurobarometer 2007.

and promoting the flexibility in the workforce, especially wage flexibility. However, the first policy documents that were adopted in the Czech Republic in 2004 after the country's accession to the EU (in line with the Lisbon strategy, the National Action Plan for Employment in 2004 and the National Action Plan on Social Inclusion 2004–06) took a fairly balanced approach to the strategy of activation. These policy documents respected fundamental citizenship rights and conformed to the general principles of the EU Social Model and Social Inclusion agenda. These principles were explicitly formulated in the election program of Social Democrats in 1998 and 2002 as well as in government declarations from the same period.

The National Action Plan for Employment was launched by the Czech government in 2004 and recognized not only a lack of motivation to work but also structural problems in the economy and inadequate qualifications as the main causes of long-term unemployment. Not only did it strongly emphasize Guideline 8 of the European Employment Strategy (making work pay), but it also included preventive measures, improving the capacity and quality of individualized assistance for the unemployed, the scope of the ALMP, the participation of the long-term unemployed in ALMP measures, life-long learning, and so on. Similarly, the National Action Plan on Social Inclusion of 2004–06 promised to "support and stimulate the long-term unemployed to actively seek employment," to create new jobs for those with disabilities and the long-term unemployed, to increase the minimum wage, and to adjust the subsistence minimum in line with standards of adequate protection on a regular basis, while creating incentives to work. All these objectives were formulated rather vaguely, however, and the documents lacked clear objectives. Neither were adequate facilities and resources allocated with which to achieve these objectives.

Further policy documents (the National Reform Programme 2005–08 and the National Action Plan on Social Inclusion 2006–08[12]) formulated a fairly marked preference for measures that increased conditionality and curtailed benefits, with the objective of improving the incentives to work in various policy fields. They adopted the approach of individualizing the problem of unemployment and social exclusion. This meant that economic incentives and/or the support of individual preferences and skills in job-seeking were given a central position, while the commitment to increasing the capacity for individual counselling and increasing the scope and improving the targeting of the active labor market measures (job creation and vocational training) remained inadequate. We will examine how the implementation of the activation strategy affected citizenship rights.

THE ACTIVATION STRATEGY AND CITIZENSHIP RIGHTS

The Right to Social Protection (Benefit Schemes)

The most consistently applied activation measures implemented since 2004 have been those aimed at improving the incentives to work. These measures have involved a combination of strategies: they have increased the conditionality of benefits (by widening the definition of "suitable employment," for example); they have introduced "negative incentives" by curtailing rights (such as delaying the revaluation of the subsistence minimum, or introducing the notion of the "existence minimum," which is set at a level below the subsistence minimum); and finally they have introduced "positive incentives," by improving the minimum wage, tax bonuses, and back-to-work and in-work benefits/tax credits. Overall, the measures curtailing citizens' rights (or the increasing conditionality of those rights) have clearly outweighed those that have expanded those rights.

Most of the changes introduced in the new Employment Act of September 2004 (Act no. 435/2004) took a "work-first" approach (enforced participation), increasing conditionality through strict job-search incentives: the definition of "suitable employment" was widened to include temporary work in the case of the long-term unemployed, irrespective of qualifications, accommodation, and accessibility by transport (under the new legislation, only the citizen's health status has to be considered). The refusal to accept temporary employment (including subsidized jobs such as public works) or the refusal to undergo a medical examination may result in sanctions (the complete loss of benefit entitlements for a period of six months, rather than three). Secondly, school graduates lost their entitlement to unemployment benefits unless and until they met the employment record condition (i.e., 12 months within the past three years).

A few elements that extended and enhanced rights were also introduced: the law establishes individualized contracts—Individual Action Plans (IAPs)—as a standard tool for working with the unemployed, and it obliges the employment offices to offer an IAP to all jobseekers under 25 years of age. Although participation was voluntary at first, failure to comply with the commitments detailed in the IAP could result in sanctions—the loss of unemployment benefit. Secondly, the Act also allows the unemployed to retain their entitlement to unemployment benefit while engaging in temporary part-time employment, provided their earnings do not exceed half the minimum wage.

Similarly, important changes in the social assistance scheme were adopted by the Czech Parliament in the first half of 2006 and came into effect in January 2007.[13] Again, these consisted mainly of increasing conditionality and curtailing rights. These measures targeted long-term unemployed social assistance claimants specifically. Firstly, the "existence minimum" was introduced. This amounted to around two thirds of the living minimum for a single person, and was to be applied in cases where an individual had been assessed as unwilling to work or cooperate in improving his or her income. At the time of implementation, it was, in fact, an expansion of social rights, since previously these "non-cooperative claimants" could have been excluded from entitlements entirely. However, as we will explain later, in the context of other measures, the introduction of this new status effectively brought about a curtailment of rights.

Secondly, adult children and parents sharing accommodation came to be considered as a single household when testing for the means of subsistence. This excluded most young people from entitlements. Thirdly, the possibility of in-kind benefits or benefits to a "substitute" recipient was made possible in cases of misconduct. Lastly, an activation plan was required for those who were welfare dependent for over six months, and a plan of individual motivation for those whose situation required immediate assistance.[14]

Additionally, some new elements that strengthened rights were implemented, but had no significant impact in practice. A disregard on earnings was applied: to improve the incentive to work, only 70% of earnings and 80% of income from sickness and unemployment benefits were taken into account when assessing the means of subsistence. However, since the living minimum after the deduction of housing costs was too low (about 10% of the average wage) while the minimum wage was much higher (almost 40%), this measure had little effect, except for those in part-time low-wage employment or in the case of large families (where the living minimum for all members of the family increases) who live from one wage.

It must also be noted that in past years, the revaluation of the subsistence minimum occurred with a lag, which meant that, for example, the replacement rates of the living minimum dropped for all categories of households (Table 11.3). In August 2007, as a part of the new right-center government's austerity package, which aimed to reduce the budget deficit, the automatic revaluation of the living and existence minimums was abolished and from that point on, revaluation would take place at the discretion of the government. Finally and most importantly, in 2008 a workfare programme that curtailed the rights of recipients of social assistance was introduced under which, after six months of receiving social assistance benefit, the unemployed would be entitled only to the "existence minimum" rather than the "living minimum." Under this new benefit regime, claimants are only entitled to the living minimum if they participate in "public service" (between 20 and 30 hours per week), and if they work over 30 hours per week, they receive a bonus of half the difference between the living and existence minimums. These rules are applied even to those who cannot work due to health problems/disabilities.

As a consequence of this strategy of curtailing rights, the level of social assistance benefits has been allowed to drop by delaying their revaluation after 2000: the replacement rates of benefits to wages in long-term unemployment fell considerably in 2008 (Table 11.3), and this excludes those who receive support corresponding to the level of the existence minimum.

To summarize, pressures for activation by making rights more conditional have been the dominant theme of all these measures: positive incentives have

Table 11.3. Changes in the Net Replacement Rate of Social Benefits Addressed to the Long-Term Unemployed (60th month of benefit receipt) in Czech Republic

	67% of AW						100% of AW					
	No children			2 children			No children			2 children		
	S	CE	CEE	LP	CE	CEE	S	CE	CEE	LP	CE	CEE
2001	53	80	56	75	92	70	36	60	45	65	74	59
2002	50	77	55	74	88	68	35	57	45	63	73	58
2003	48	75	54	72	85	69	33	54	44	62	71	58
2004	44	70	53	70	81	65	30	50	43	57	68	55
2005	45	71	53	67	76	70	31	51	44	57	65	59
2006	42	62	53	68	76	68	29	48	43	54	63	57
2007	47	71	53	69	80	62	29	52	44	55	62	52
2008	42	66	56	67	77	61	30	47	47	53	57	52

Notes: S = single person, LP = lone parent, CE = couple, one earner, CEE = couple, two earners. AW = average wage

Source: OECD, 2009 (Benefits and Wages: tax-benefit OECD model)

been relatively feeble, while negative incentives have been strong. We explain this approach to activation by the high legitimacy of an enforcement strategy. This legitimacy stems from the widespread feeling that it is necessary to increase the pressure on the unemployed and give them greater incentives to work. A second factor in explaining this approach to activation, however, can be found in the attitude of the state administration, which tends to neglect the rights of citizens—a legacy of the communist era. The principle of voluntary participation, which was applied temporarily in the IAP and is inconsistent with the current work-first approach, may be attributed to the lack of personnel and financial resources available to screen individual job searches and/or involve the unemployed in ALMP schemes.[15]

Overall, the strategy of income protection has focused on improving the incentives of unemployed people to work by combining curtailments of rights (lower benefits) with increased conditionality (the widening of the definition of "suitable employment," the introduction of the existence minimum), plus some weaker positive incentives that have extended rights (in-work benefits and bonuses). The issue of incentives has formed the core of the activation strategy, with a prevailing emphasis on enforcement (the introduction of the existence minimum and the scrapping of the subsistence minimum).

Right to Open Access and Support of Capabilities (ALMPs)

Traditionally, ALMP measures have been among the least-developed public policies in the Czech Republic. This stems from the common assumption that disincentives to work are the principal problem. In response to a threefold rise in registered unemployment in the late 1990s (from 3% to 4% to 9% to 10%, according to data from the Public Employment Services [PES] register), and with the proportion of the long-term unemployed exceeding 40%, the Czech Republic did increase its spending on ALMPs slightly, although this still failed to match the levels of spending common in other EU countries. This expenditure amounted to only around 0.12% to 0.13% of GDP, and only around 1% of the labor force have participated in the ALMP measures in recent years. This participation rate is less than in other countries with similar unemployment rates, which are compared with the Czech Republic (see OECD, 2008, data for 2004–05). The Czech Republic's expenditure in this area as a percentage of GDP is about nine times less than that of Sweden and about half that of Portugal and is at a similar level to spending in Hungary. Correspondingly, the participation rate for ALMP measures as a percentage of the labor force is four times lower than that of Sweden and less than half of the rates in Portugal and Hungary. The Czech Republic seems to be a particular laggard in vocational training: the difference with other countries is even larger in this field (expenditure only 0.02% of GDP, number of participants only 0.15% of the total labor force). The public finance reforms implemented in 2003 reduced the social insurance allocation for labor market policies from 3.6% to 1.6% of the payroll, prioritizing the inadequate pension fund instead and thus fixing this pattern of fairly low expenditure.

The new Employment Act implemented in 2004 made provision for several new instruments: subsidies for employers to provide on-the-job training (for selected target groups of the unemployed)[16] and compensation of travel expenses. Existing job-creation subsidies, particularly for unemployed people with disabilities, were increased slightly, and the right of disabled people to a place on a work rehabilitation program was established. Finally, the law also made it possible to finance targeted (local) employment projects. An important objective of the NAPE 2004–06 was to improve the range of active employment policy measures by increasing the funding allocated to this sector (Ministry of Labor and Social Affairs [MLSA], 2004, 41). Although a new Employment Act introduced some new instruments for an ALMP, these new instruments had a negligible impact after 2004 (MLSA, 2006; MPSV, 2007, 2008, 2009).

However, beginning in 2005, new opportunities presented themselves for activation policies and a more individualized approach to tackling unemployment at the local and regional level through measures and projects financed by EU structural funds. During 2006 and 2007, the EU structural funds (mainly the European Social Fund [ESF]) enabled an increase in the number of the ALMP participants to over 39% of the unemployed (which represented a doubling from previous numbers).[17]

However, in 2008, the scope of active labor market measures, including the ESF projects, was reduced. It has become clear that measures financed through the structural funds have tended to replace the existing national ALMP measures rather than complement them (for example, the scope of labor market training

Table 11.4. Active Policy Measures and Unemployment (Czech Republic), PES Data

	2004	2005	2006	2007	2008
Unemployed	*541,700*	*510.416*	*448.545*	*354.878*	*352.250*
Total ALMP participants	105,959	97,797	141,210	136,649	85,284
as % of unemployment stock	19.6	19.2	31.5	38.5	24.2
from which ESF in %			30.8	53.7	34.5
Expenditure in thousands CZK	3,937,882	4,027,853	5,300,675	5,673,321	6,131,729
from which ESF	:	:	*1,277,664*	*2,100,517*	*2,678,729*

Note: Expenditure includes also investment stimuli.

Source: MLSA, 2004, MLSA, 2006, MPSV, 2007, MPSV, 2009 web portal http://portal.mpsv.cz/sz/politikazamest/trh_prace/

dropped between 2006 and 2008) (see Table 11.4). The limited scope of ALMP measures has meant that it has not been possible to guarantee open access to the labor market for vulnerable groups. Another limitation of "open access" has been its failure to target labor market training on disadvantaged groups: according to our analysis based on data by the PES, the proportion of the participants within specific groups of the unemployed remained significantly lower in 2008: 7.3% for the disabled, 6.1% for the low-skilled, 7.6% for those over 50 years old, 10.1% for those under 25 years old, and 9.1% for the long-term unemployed. The average figure for all those unemployed was 15%.[18] It is interesting that vocational training/requalification programs financed under the ESF scheme did not improve the targeting of the programs on disadvantaged groups, even though these ESF projects were designed primarily to facilitate the integration of disadvantaged groups into the labor market (compare Horáková et al., 2010).

Similarly, there are some indications that vulnerable groups are also under-represented in job-creation measures: it is only in sheltered jobs and public work that groups such as the disabled, the unskilled, and older workers are represented proportionately. Meanwhile, for job-creation measures in the private sector, the proportion of unskilled and older workers is clearly lower than the overall proportion of the unemployed that they represent (Kulhavý & Sirovátka, 2008).

Thanks to rapid economic growth (during 2005–07, this was at around 6%), the number of registered unemployed rate fell from 7.7% in December 2006 to 6.0% in December 2007 and 2008. This improvement extended to all categories of the unemployed. The proportion of long-term unemployed, however, remained stubbornly high until the end of 2007 (about 39%) and only dropped to about 29% in 2008. It seems that this was mainly due to the curtailment of the social rights of this group and more frequent sanctions (the exclusion of the long-term unemployed from the registers of employment offices). The number of these cases increased between 2004 and 2008, from 11% to 26% of all those whose status as unemployed came to an end (our own calculations based on data from the MLSA). However, the proportion of the low-skilled in the official figures only dropped from 32% to 30%, while the proportion of disabled people grew from 15.8% to 17.4%, and that of unemployed people aged over 50 grew from 27.1% to 29.3%.[19]

Personal Rights: Self-Determination, Balanced Contracts

Welfare dependency and the lack of motivation on the part of unemployed individuals to find employment were considered to be the main causes of the high proportion of long-term unemployed. PES therefore felt a strong need to increase the pressure on the unemployed. With preparations for EU membership well under way (which was to occur on May 1, 2004), guidelines on how to address the issue of long-term unemployment came from the European Employment Strategy, specifically its Guideline 1 "prevention and early activation," which promotes the implementation of IAPs. These individual contracts appeared to be an inexpensive tool for eliminating benefit dependency or abuse. Besides this, they were intended as an extension of the rights of unemployed people to individual support while seeking employment, and an increase in the conditionality of their rights to social protection. The National Action Plan for Employment 2004–06 therefore stipulated that all employment offices should, from 2004 onwards, introduce IAPs (First Opportunity) for unemployed people under 25 years of age, with the prospect of extending this to all unemployed people from 2006 (New Start). The Ministry of Labor and Social Affairs therefore embedded this instrument within the new Employment Act and within the National Action Plan for Employment, and obliged all employment offices to implement it by offering an IAP to every unemployed individual below 25 years of age.

However, no significant institutional reforms, such as those undertaken by other countries (Germany, Austria, the Netherlands, or the UK), were introduced to support the managerial and implementation capacity of the Czech Republic's PES and to individualized contracts to be implemented effectively on the front line. As a result, the problem of inadequate counseling facilities had to be addressed by introducing the principle of voluntary participation and allowing the outsourcing of the individual diagnostics or individual counseling to the unemployed to the external agencies (both profit or nonprofit).

We have observed that since the pilot stage (2003) of the program, when the objectives of IAPs were being formulated, employment offices stressed greater responsibility, independence, and pro-activity for jobseekers, in line with the original idea of the IAPs, which had been to mobilize the unemployed. Similarly, the original aim was to invite high numbers of the unemployed to participate in IAPs. However, employment offices in areas of high unemployment, where this goal was simply too ambitious for the capacity of the available staff, could never hope to achieve this aim. One important contradiction that arose through the implementation of IAPs was that local employment offices were, even in the pilot phase, aware of their inadequate resources (in terms of time and personnel) and

accepted the strategy of allocating resources in a way that favored the more motivated and cooperative unemployed individuals (cf. Lipsky, 1980). This selective
recruitment for the IAP program (and the very low number of participants in the
IAP program that resulted) was more apparent firstly at those employment offices
that had a higher workload per mediator, and secondly at those that sought to
take a genuinely professional and individual approach to counseling, proceeding
in accordance with the IAP's methodological guidelines, collecting and processing case information, and evaluating and developing the IAP regularly.

The aims of the program were not achieved due to limited numbers of participants and the largely formal approach of the employment offices (which limited the program to signing the contract and undergoing a somewhat truncated
job-mediation process[20]). In 2004, when IAPs were first rolled out at all employment offices, the proportion of the young unemployed who were newly registered at employment offices and who signed an IAP was 49%. In 2006, this had
fallen to a mere 18% (MLSA, 2005; MPSV, 2007; own computations). The target
of 25,000 IAPs promised for 2006 in the National Reform Programme of 2005–
07 was not met: in fact, only 7,000 were signed.

However, in spite of downsizing the IAP program, we have observed that it
has produced some minor innovations concerning an individualized approach to
the unemployed and some positive results in terms of extending personal rights
in some local settings. Although the resources devoted to activation, in terms of
both personnel and funding, remained limited even after the new Employment
Act was implemented at the beginning of 2004, the possibility of carrying out ESF
projects under the Operational Programme for Human Resources Development
presented better opportunities for activation at the local level. First of all, it broad-
ened the range of programs suitable for activating unemployed people with several overlapping handicaps in the labor market. In practice, the scope of applying
these projects varied a great deal according to local conditions. Secondly, these
new opportunities prepared the ground for more individualized intervention
and the enlargement of the range of options available—both of which favor the
unemployed by enhancing their human and social capital. Among other things,
the newly available resources of ESF enable the expansion of the capacity of PES
through outsourcing measures such as individual diagnostics, counseling, vocational training, work experience, or even subsidized employment with private
agencies or NGOs.

There is also evidence of another positive innovation in the counseling process as a result of the shift away from using the IAPs as a mass enforcement tool
and towards "selective support" for cooperative clients. One of the employment
offices we surveyed came close to the ideal method of implementation for IAPs
(which best corresponds to the prescribed method of a professional individual working with the client). In this case, the dominant approach was professional, solution-oriented, and individualized treatment based on expertise and

discretion. In similar, though rather rare cases, local discretion over implementation enabled a strengthening of the right to self-determination, which took the form of offering individual counseling, which was followed by genuine individual casework and support.

The particular coincidence of policy objectives, design, and implementation described above means that IAPs have resulted in a strengthening of the right to individual support for only a small minority of the unemployed. However, they have meant a restriction of privacy and self-determination through the threat of losing the right to income protection for the majority of those who have signed. But for the great majority of the unemployed, IAPs have had no impact at all. Recently (2008/9), IAPs have taken a rather different direction: legislation has made the instrument obligatory, with an explicit threat of sanctions. Parliament has approved the proposal that employment offices must develop an IAP with each unemployed person after five months of unemployment. Failure to sign or to meet the obligations of this individual contract will result in the unemployed person's removal from the unemployment register and the loss of any entitlement to unemployment benefits or social assistance. Given that due to the implementation conditions the formal bureaucratic approach to IAPs prevails, this measure implies a substantial curtailment of both personal and social rights for a considerable proportion of the unemployed.

CONCLUSIONS: INCOMPLETE CITIZENSHIP?

The Czech Republic initiated its activation strategy in 2004. Although policy documents designed along the lines of the Open Coordination Method (the National Action Plan for Employment 2004 and the National Action Plan on Social Inclusion 2004–06) promised a complex approach, and the new Employment Act from 2004 provided for some supportive regulations that appeared to extend social rights related to work and enhance their capabilities and employability,[21] no concerted effort was made to follow up such an approach in practice. The activation strategy implemented at the national and local levels can be seen as an inconsistent version of the work-first model of activation, which also relies on "workfare" measures. Overall, the measures taken aim to increase conditionality and curtail the rights in two spheres: personal rights (the right to self-determination and the right to privacy) and social rights (the right to protection of income, open access to the labor market, and the support of skills). The policy is only marginally supplemented by measures that strengthen or extend rights by making work pay and supporting skills and access to employment. This approach is rooted in the strong belief, shared by the public and policymakers alike, that the principal causes of long-term unemployment are a lack of self-reliance and individual responsibility, and a preference for welfare dependency.

Various measures have been implemented during 2004–09 that include restricting rights and increasing conditionality, as well as minor (and conditional) extensions of social rights (such as an offer of better benefit entitlements for those who accept low-paid jobs). The principal focus is on reducing the social right to income protection (lower social benefits, either in general or in special cases; the delayed indexation of the living and existence minimum; the exclusion of the young people from entitlements to unemployment benefits and social assistance) in combination with an increase in the conditionality of social rights (a stricter definition of "suitable employment"). On the other hand, the support provided to the most disadvantaged people to enhance their capabilities and employability has not increased in its scope, targeting, or intensity.

Similarly, individualized contracts (IAPs), which were originally expected to become a core measure by which to mobilize a high proportion of the least-motivated unemployed but also as a means of extending rights by providing individualized support in the search for employment, have lacked the scope and quality required to have a significant effect. The currently prevailing approach is essentially a simple formalized arrangement between the client and the employment office, and efforts are being made to develop IAPs as a tool of enforcement and discipline.

The changes in activation policies have also affected social citizenship in a second way. The rights provided have become more selective: different groups of unemployed people and welfare benefits claimants now enjoy different rights, and this is apparent in both legal and practical terms. The latter trend represents a change in the quality of the social citizenship created by activation policies and is a kind of selective residualization of citizens' "rights" or dualization in social rights. In concrete terms, some categories of the unemployed are provided with higher benefits, tax relief/bonuses, and assistance to improve their skills and level of labor market participation. Some other categories, such as younger unemployed people or the long-term unemployed (often disabled, older workers), have seen a curtailment of their right to income protection, while their formal rights to access the labor market and receive assistance to enhance their employability is, in practice, being curtailed. Instead, social rights are being made more conditional in the name of greater flexibility of labor,[22] implying a deterioration of the overall quality of citizenship rights.

We may ask, then, why activation policies in the Czech Republic have tended to move towards the work-first/workfare approach, thereby endangering a number of citizenship rights. The restriction of social rights seems to correspond to trends in the development of the Czech welfare state as a whole. This development is underpinned by a policy discourse that emphasizes the responsibilities of the individual (through a neoliberal discourse, see Chapter 12), although neither personal nor civil rights are given a central place. This paradox may be attributed to the persisting legacy of communism, which has obstructed awareness of citizenship rights, meaning that institutions are not expected to fully respect and support the rights of citizens in certain life situations, such as unemployment, seeking employment, and negotiating individual contracts between jobseekers and PES.

Lastly, institutional shortcomings also play a role, such as weak governance and inadequate preparedness for implementation. This constellation has meant that a simple form of activation has come to dominate, based on enforcement (which curtails civil rights) and the reduction of social rights (lower levels of benefit and greater conditionality). This is because the state administration lacks the ability to implement measures that are more demanding in terms of time, professionalism, financial resources, and effective management and coordination.

However, thanks to the weak and inconsistent implementation of the enforcement strategy, which otherwise would result in a significant curtailment of citizenship rights, there has been a certain room for policy innovation in the area of individual support and in the bottom-up process that has emerged spontaneously when favorable internal conditions (such as cooperative actors and experienced professionals) have coincided with favorable external conditions (such as the resources made available through the ESF). Additionally, institutional regionalization in the form of the establishment of administrative structures that implement the measures of the structural EU funds, and the emergence of the ESF's projects, have brought about further decentralization and pluralization of the parties involved, strengthening the bottom-up process of policymaking.

Consequently, the activation strategy has to some extent been shaped and influenced more by the second line of policymaking (bottom-up), which has emerged chiefly through the involvement of local actors and has brought some innovations in terms of the support of social rights implied by improved access to the labor market and enhancing the employability of disadvantaged people.

An interesting point is that this second line of policymaking is to a greater extent influenced by the principles of the inclusive participation (human capital) approach, because it has been carried out by local partners financed by European funding under predetermined conditions. However, mainstream national policy priorities, and methods of governance and implementation, have not allowed for any substantial impact on the enlargement of rights in the sense of developing skills, supporting access to labor market, or the self-determination of life course. Neither are large-scale innovations likely where there is a lack of personnel and suitable ALMP measures to assist the unemployed. For example, the IAPs, as implemented via the top-down mechanisms of policymaking in legislation as a routine standard tool, and without the necessary facilities, have curtailed personal rights rather than strengthening them.

There are two general problems that are jeopardizing citizenship rights. Firstly, while the importance of civil/personal rights is increasing in contemporary post-industrial societies with a greater emphasis on self-responsibility (Chapter 1), the legacy of the communist past implies that these rights are neglected in the policy practice. Secondly, the "neoliberal attack" on social rights has been strong and effective, since these rights became largely discredited during communist times (when they were perceived as "political bribery" by the regime) and associated with "passive citizenship" (the notion is borrowed from Chapter 1). An "incomplete citizenship" seems to emerge: if civil/personal rights are not being safeguarded sufficiently and the concept of social rights is discredited, "full citizenship" (all three dimensions mutually reinforcing) is unlikely to emerge. The question is whether and how fast social actors will reflect the key importance of civil/personal rights and social rights and their mutual interdependence within "full citizenship."

ACKNOWLEDGMENTS

This study was written with the support of the Czech Grant Agency (Project no. P404/11/0086), *Modernization of the Czech Social Policy*.

NOTES

1 We emphasize here the economic pressures on the welfare state emerging from globalization, demographic changes, and the aging of the population on the one hand, and labor market dynamics and the uncertainties of labor market status, and processes of social differentiation and individualization on the other hand.

2 Activation policy, as referred to in this chapter, is the dynamic linkage introduced into public policy between social welfare, employment, and labor market programs, which involves a critical redesigning of previous income support, assistance, and social protection policies in terms of efficiency and equity, as well as enhancing the various social functions of paid work and labor force participation (Barbier, 2004).

3 This is how the legislation deals with the "right to work": for example, in the Czech Employment Act no. 435/2004 Coll., par. 10, right to work is defined as the right to job mediation and other different kinds of support by Public Employment Services in the case of unemployment (both benefits and active measures).

4 Or liberal versus social democratic approach (see Chapter 1).

5 Identity, in the sense of sharing the common work ethic, is one of the citizens' responsibilities and qualities that cannot be enforced by external pressures.

6 See excellent discussion in Ferge (1997).

7 Data by Eurobarometer 2004; general trust indicated by the question of whether most of people can be trusted or one can't be too careful in dealing with people.

8 It is illustrative that the notion of social rights seems to be absent from the public discourse and policy documents, although in the Strategy of Social Reform by the first post-Communist Czechoslovak government from 1990, a reference to the Charter of Human Rights and to the EU Social Charter appears.

9 Although the replacement rate of unemployment benefits to wages was only 50% in the first three months and 45% in the following three months (another three/six months for the unemployed over 50/55 years).

10 In the EU-15 countries, responses as to the causes of poverty were on average as follows: individual causes (39%; lack of luck 21%, laziness 18%) and social causes (49%; injustice in society 36%, inevitable because of progress in society 13%). In the 12 new member states the responses were as follows: individual causes (40%; lack of luck 14%, laziness 26%) and social causes (52%; injustice in society 42%, inevitable because of progress in society 10%).

11 Missing answers to 100%—those who did not respond. The survey "Social inclusion and social policy" conducted by Sirovátka and Mareš (agency FOCUS, random sampling, N = 1,300).

12 This is Part 2 of the National Report on Social Protection and Social Inclusion 2006–08.

13 Act on the Existence Minimum and Subsistence Minimum, Act on Assistance in Material Need—Act no. 110/2006, Act no. 111/2006.

14 This measure was not realized in practice due to insufficient staffing in the social departments of municipalities, and in 2008 it was removed from legislation.

15 It is worth noting that in discussing the Employment Act in 2004, the local employment offices strongly resisted the original intention of the PES central authority to make IAPs obligatory for all unemployed under 25; the center had to respect their position, being aware of their inadequate personnel resources. As we will explain, however, in 2009 IAPs were made obligatory for people unemployed longer than five months.

16 These subsidies are, however, quite low—half the level of the minimum wage (i.e., 20% of average wage) and provided for three months only.

17 This is, however, still significantly less than the resources promised. An analysis carried out by the Ministry of Labour and Social Affairs attributes this fact to insufficient personnel and a lack of professional skills within the state administration (MLSA, 2006).

18 Own computations based on data by the MLSA (http://portal.mpsv.cz/sz).

19 Own computations based on data by the MLSA (http://portal.mpsv.cz/sz). Data mirror the situation before the economic crisis in 2008–09.

20 Some of the counselors-mediators said, "There was hardly anything to write down."

21 In line with "the activating social investment agenda" (see Chapter 15).

22 The broader definition of "suitable employment" in the first place and then the other procedures associated with means-testing.

REFERENCES

Andersen, J. G., & P. H. Jensen (Eds.) (2002). *Changing labour markets, welfare policies and citizenship.* Bristol: The Policy Press.

Barbier, J.-C. (2004). Activation policies: a comparative perspective. In A. Serrano Pascual (ed.) *Are activation policies converging in Europe? The European employment strategy for young people* (pp. 47–84). Brussels: ETUI.

Bauman, Z. (1998). *Work, consumerism and the new poor.* Philadelphia: Open University Press.

Bonvin, J.-M, & N. Farvaque (2007). A capability approach to individualized and tailor-made activation. In R. Van Berkel & B. Valkenburg (Eds.), *Making it personal. Individualising activation services in the EU* (pp. 67–85). Bristol: The Policy Press.

Dahrendorf, R. (1988). *The modern social conflict: An essay on the politics of liberty.* London: George Weidenfeld and Nicolson.

Ferge, Z. (1997). The changed welfare paradigm: the individualization of the social. *Social Policy and Administration, 31*(1), 20–44.

Ferge, Z. (2009). Social citizenship in the new democracies, the difficulties in reviving citizens' rights in Hungary. *International Journal of Urban and Regional Research, 20*(1), 99–115.

Giddens, A. (1998). *The Third Way: The renewal of social democracy.* Cambridge: Polity Press.

Horáková, M., H. Tomešová-Bartáková, & J. Vyhlídal (2010). *Opatření aktivní politiky zaměstnanosti financované z prostředků ESF [Labour market policies financed from the ESF resources].* Prague: Research Institute of Labour and Social Affairs.

Howard, M. M. (2002). The weakness of postcommunist civil society. *Journal of Democracy, 13*(1), 157–169.

Inglot, T. (2008). *Welfare States in East Central Europe, 1919–2004.* Cambridge, New York: Cambridge University Press.

Klaus, V. (1995). Principy zdravé sociální politiky. *SONDY* 31, 14 August: 1.

Kulhavý, V., & T. Sirovátka (2008). *Efektivnost opatření aktivní politiky zaměstnanosti [Effectiveness of active labour market policies].* Prague: Research Institute of Labour and Social Affairs.

Lipsky, M. (1980). *Street level bureaucracy. Dilemmas of the individual in public services.* New York: Russell Sage Foundation.

Lister, R. (1998). Vocabularies of citizenship and gender: the UK. *Critical Social Policy, 8*(3), 61–77.

Lister, R. (2002). Citizenship and changing welfare states. In J. G. Andersen & P. H. Jensen (Eds.), *Changing labour markets, welfare policies and citizenship* (pp. 39–58). Bristol: The Policy Press.

Mareš, P., & I. Možný (1995). Status for the poor. *Occasional Papers in European Studies* 7, Centre for European Studies, University of Essex.

Marshall, T. H. (1950). *Citizenship and social class and other essays*. Cambridge: Cambridge University Press.

Marshall, T. H. (Ed.) (1964). *Class, citizenship and social development*. Garden City, New York: Anchor Books.

MLSA (MPSV)—Ministry of Labour and Social Affairs Czech Republic (2004). *Národní akční plan zaměstnanosti 2004–2006 [National Action Employment Plan 2004–2006]*. Prague: MPSV.

MLSA (MPSV)—Ministry of Labour and Social Affairs Czech Republic (2005). *Analýza vývoje zaměstnanosti a nezaměstnanosti v roce 2005 [Analysis of employment and unemployment dynamics in 2004]*. Prague: MPSV.

MLSA (MPSV)—Ministry of Labour and Social Affairs Czech Republic (2006). *Analýza vývoje zaměstnanosti a nezaměstnanosti v roce 2005 [Analysis of employment and unemployment dynamics in 2005]*. Prague: MPSV.

Mosley, H., & E. Sol (2001). Process evaluation of active labour market policies and trends in implementation regimes. In J. De Koning & H. Mosley (Eds.), *Labour market policy and unemployment* (pp. 163–177). Cheltenham: Edward Edgar.

MPSV (MPSV)—Ministry of Labour and Social Affairs Czech Republic (2007). *Analýza vývoje zaměstnanosti a nezaměstnanosti v roce 2006. [Analysis of the development of employment and unemployment in 2006]*. Prague: MPSV.

MPSV (MPSV)—Ministry of Labour and Social Affairs Czech Republic (2008). *Analýza vývoje zaměstnanosti a nezaměstnanosti v roce 2007 [Analysis of the development of employment and unemployment in 2006]*. Prague: MPSV.

MPSV (MPSV)—Ministry of Labour and Social Affairs Czech Republic (2009). *Analýza vývoje zaměstnanosti a nezaměstnanosti v roce 2008 [Analysis of the development of employment and unemployment in 2006]*. Prague: MPSV.

Nicaise, I. (2002). *The active welfare state: The response to social exclusion?* Leuven: HIVA.

OECD (2008). *Employment outlook*. OECD: Paris.

OECD (2009). *Tax-Benefit Model*—www.oecd.org/els/social/workincentives

Offe, C. (1996). *Modernity and the state: East, West*. Cambridge: Polity Press.

Pichler F. & C. Wallace (2007). Patterns of formal and informal social capital in Europe. *European Sociological Review, 23*(4), 423–435.

Rose, R. (2001). How people view democracy: A diverging Europe. *Journal of Democracy, 12* (January), 93–106.

Rose, R., W. Mishler, & C. Haerpfner (1998). *Democracy and its alternatives: Understanding post-communist societies*. Baltimore: Johns Hopkins University Press.

Serrano Pascual, A. (Ed.) (2004). *Are activation policies converging in Europe? The European employment strategy for young people*. Brussels: ETUI.

Sirovátka, T., et al. (2003). *Problémy trhu práce a politiky zaměstnanosti [The problems of labour market and employment policy, Czech Republic]*. Brno: Masarykova univerzita.

Sirovátka, T., & M. Rákoczyová (2009). The impact of the EU social inclusion strategy: The Czech case. In A. Cerami & P. Vanhuysse (Eds.), *Post-communist welfare pathways: Theorizing social policy transformations in Central and Eastern Europe.* Basingstoke: Palgrave Macmillan.

Standing, G. (1999). *Global labour flexibility. Seeking redistributive justice.* Houndmills, Basingstoke, Hampshire and London: Macmillan Press Ltd.

Valkenburg, B., & R. van Berkel (Eds.) (2007). *Making it personal. Individualising activation services in the EU.* Bristol: The Policy Press.

van Berkel, R., & I. H. Møller (2002). The concept of activation. In R. van Berkel & I. H. Møller (Eds.), *Active social policies in the EU. Inclusion through participation?* (pp. 15–44). Bristol: The Policy Press.

12

FRAGMENTED SOCIAL RIGHTS IN HUNGARY'S POSTCOMMUNIST WELFARE STATE

Julia Szalaï

CONCEPTS AND FRAMEWORKS

This chapter takes departure from two important strands of thought that both conceive of social citizenship as the ultimate foundation and the most essential normative concept of the modern welfare state but that follow different paths when it comes to elaborating on the actual content of this concept. The first is T. H. Marshall's classic work on the historical evolution of the trinity of civil, political, and social rights (Marshall & Bottomore, 1992). Two of his arguments are of key importance for us when applying his theory to conceptualize the postcommunist welfare state. Firstly, Marshall's emphasis on *gradualism* has to be taken into account. He argues that the sequence of the three sets of rights cannot be altered at will: it is the enrichment of the institutions and practices of civil and political rights that prepare the ground for the institutionalization of social rights. In other words, legal arrangements and the daily practicing of universal rights of political participation precondition claims on universal social rights that can only be perceived and exercised under the conditions of liberal democracy. Secondly, social rights—as much their institutions as the daily social perceptions of them—are the product of a lengthy *social dialogue* rooted in the powerful movements and struggles for recognition of social groups that have been excluded in the past. In other words, social rights cannot be "constructed" in a top-down fashion simply through legislation. Instead, these rights assume a widespread politicization of the affairs of everyday life, and are pushed forward by the large-scale contestation of the prevailing order of the distribution of income, wealth, and opportunities.

Marshall's two important arguments are further developed by Will Kymlicka, who reconceptualizes the notion of the trinity of rights in light of the important historical changes that have been brought about by mass immigration from the global South toward the global North (Kymlicka, 1995). As Kymlicka stresses, a high degree of *cultural heterogeneity* has become a decisive feature of European societies in the past three decades: thus, once-applicable liberal concepts of citizenship have to be revisited accordingly. In this vein, he outlines a genuinely multicultural arrangement for practicing rights of ethnic and national minorities in a way equal to those of the majority of the nation-state. The struggles for recognition on the part of these minorities are vitally important here: again, the daily understanding of citizens' rights is seen as the result of continual movements and their claims to reshape the scope and content of public discourse. Kymlicka's approach will be of utmost importance for us when looking at the actual content of social rights of ethnic minorities—particularly those of the Roma citizenry—in postcommunist Hungary. As will be shown, inequalities of rights have a clear ethnic substance here that provides the basis for institutional discrimination in welfare distribution, which then results, in turn, in the social exclusion of Roma *en masse*. An absence of political institutions through which to exercise their rights in a meaningful way is just part of the story. A built-in dualism in welfare arrangements based on two distinct concepts of social rights has played a perhaps even more significant part in the process: while failing to meet claims on distributional justice, a sharp segmentation of the provisions according to the principles of "contribution" versus "neediness" has contributed to the exacerbation of social exclusion on ethnic grounds.

In the discussion that follows, I will apply the two conceptualizations of social rights briefly outlined above to analyze the performance of Hungary's postcommunist welfare state. As I will attempt to show, it was a meaningful conversion of earlier gradually elaborated paths of covert marketization under state-socialism that provided the socio-historical foundation of postcommunist transformation. At the same time, it has been that very same gradual process that, gaining rapid institutionalization in the service of majority interests after the collapse of the old regime, has led to the sharp fragmentation of social rights with the concomitant massive social exclusion of the country's largest ethnic minority: its dramatically impoverished and marginalized Roma community.

THEORIES AND POLICIES GOVERNING HUNGARY'S POSTCOMMUNIST WELFARE STATE

Although neither of the theories described above has had wide resonance within Hungary's political discourse, a pragmatic interpretation of social rights has guided decision making since the very start of the period of transition. Two strands of thoughts have played a significant role: the "social market" theory and neoliberalism.

Notions of the social market strongly influenced the orientation of systemic change. Despite some rather important differences in ideas about how marketization should be accomplished in the early 1990s, there was a broad consensus among competing political actors when it came to outlining the role of the state. The shared claim was a speedy disentanglement of the political structures that had facilitated the earlier unquestioned overpower of the state above the citizenry, and the simultaneous construction of institutions to safeguard individual freedoms and the rights to knowledge, a healthy life, and a minimum of standard of living. In other words, unlimited freedom was never on the agenda: access to healthcare, provisions for quality schooling, guaranteed minima in housing, and the maintenance of public social security were seen as the constitutionally ascribed responsibilities of the new state. At the same time, it was the new system of democratic political institutions that was perceived as providing the means for exercising the necessary control over the actual accomplishment of the state's duties. Surely, such a control presupposed a strong and well-organized civil society that was hoped to spontaneously come into being upon "liberation from the state's oppression." In its initial consensual interpretation during the first years of the transition period, the "social market" theory reflected ideas and hopes about a strong representative democracy and ongoing, meaningful dialogue between the state (the envisioned agent of "social" momentum) and the citizen (as an agent integrated into the market). In other words, it was thought that the state would be deprived of its economic role, while the market would become the powerful agent of a new social integration.

In this latter respect, ideas on developing a "social market" seemed to be in perfect harmony with those neoliberal claims that gave momentum to one of the most important aspects of the systemic change: the conversion of the old property relations. It was widely believed that rapid privatization would be a primary aspect of both economic advancement and the rise of a strong civil society. In addition to its economic role, marketization was seen as a powerful tool for stripping the "old" state of its oppressive inclinations, and systemic changes in the sphere of production were thus meant to bring about further radical change in the political arena, too.

As these ideas were translated into the actual accomplishment of the privatization process, a number of other neoliberal beliefs came to play a significant role. In the context of this chapter, it is the immediate dismantling of the once-omnipotent communist state that merits our primary attention. In this unprecedented historic process, cardinal reforms in social security and welfare were high on the agenda, being seen as an unquestionable precondition for genuine change. The urgency of radically limiting the role of the central state in these areas was justified by a range of powerful legal and financial considerations. As to the legal aspects, it was a widely shared view among domestic and foreign advisors, economists, and financial experts alike that unless there was a severing of the close bond between the centrally administered schemes of redistribution and individual entitlements to benefits and provisions, the very essence of the systemic transformation would be jeopardized: neither the reallocation of properties, nor the recruitment of labor, nor free entrepreneurship as the fundaments of marketization could be successfully established and ingrained otherwise. As to considering the financial side, the equally widely shared view of the former "premature welfare state" (Kornai, 1996) implied that welfare expenditure had accounted for an excessive share of the state budget during the late 1980s, and the involved imbalances suffocated economic growth and healthy social development. It followed that upon the turnover, such spending should be substantially reduced in order to reallocate funds for the primary purposes of transforming economic management according to the rules of the market, as well as to bring about modernization and economic adjustment.

However, another important neoliberal principle behind advocating revolutionary reforms in the spheres of welfare policy and expenditure was the goal of promoting *social justice* and *efficiency*. A recurring motive in criticisms of the social policy of the late state-socialist period was that—contrary to the declared goals of the communist regime—central redistribution, strictly linked to employment, had in fact served to increase income inequalities, rather than moderate them. Moreover, by deriving entitlements from compulsory full employment, the misconstrued concept of "universalism" had brought about massive social injustice by routinely channeling substantial funds to the relatively prosperous strata of society. Therefore, when laying down the principles of the new welfare system, one of the fundamental goals was eliminating "waste" or, to put it in plain terms, to ensure that only those really in need received supplementary resources through redistribution and only to the level of their neediness. It was hoped that with all this, the new system would not only become more targeted but also more just: public money was only to be spent to meet the needs acknowledged by consensus, and only on those who fell below a commonly agreed level of neediness. At the same time, it was assumed that the fortunate majority who lived above this invisible yet generally acknowledged line of true poverty would follow other paths opened up and regulated by the market (contribution-based provisions of social security, private pension schemes, market-related benefits in healthcare, etc.). The new arrangements were thus expected to automatically keep apart the two purposefully designed subsystems, each with its own clear-cut mechanism of distribution for meeting two distinctively but justly defined sets of demands.

The technical and practical considerations underlying the transformation were linked to the assertion of these new ideas of justice and efficiency. While the universalistic considerations and welfare elements of the centrally distributed provisions were remarkably weakened by the introduction of a sequence of new regulations, the dramatically reshaped division of roles between the central bodies of welfare distribution and the significantly empowered local authorities left the definition of the scope and content of "customarily acknowledged" needs to thousands of autonomous urban and rural communities (Vági, 1991; Horváth 2000). With this, the new regulations implied that in the area of needs, only minimum standards were defined with general applicability, while at the same time it was also made clear that henceforth the central state was not prepared to set down any legal or financial guarantees for their enforcement.

In summary, the welfare reforms of the past two decades took their ideological inspiration from the widely shared notions of the "social market," but their actual implementation has taken a neoliberal path. As will be shown below, the dominance of neoliberalism has led to two simultaneous developments. On the one hand, it has resulted in the abandonment of the notion of universalism and contributed to the concomitant "desertion of the state" (Standing, 1997). On the other hand, neoliberalism has added significantly to the gradual evolution of a bifurcated welfare structure with remarkable divergences in the social rights of the respective welfare clienteles.

REINTERPRETING THE ROLE OF THE CENTRAL STATE[1]

As we have seen, a substantial curtailment of the state's economic power was seen as one of the primary means of bringing about genuine systemic change. Significant cuts in social expenditure, together with deep-going reforms in the areas of social security and welfare assistance, were thought to assist the process. These widely propagated commitments were much in line with the claims of speedy marketization, and also corresponded to the requirements that the global financial institutions (the World Bank and IMF in the first place) and the European Union put forward. It is, then, all the more surprising that for the past two decades, the scale of state spending has in fact remained unchanged: macroeconomic data show that social security expenditure has accounted for a stable 13% of GDP (Central Statistical Office, 1997, 2005). However, remarkable changes have taken place in how this spending is structured. The central state as an agent behind maintaining welfare has practically disappeared: the ratio of governmental provisions to finance unemployment and family benefits dropped from 20% in 1991 to 6% in 2005. Simultaneously, there has been a substantial rise in the share of social security (from 72% to 84% during the same period), while the ratio of local welfare assistance has grown from four to ten percent (Central Statistical Office, 1997, 2005). At first glance, these shifts are in line with the neoliberal ideas outlined above that required the withdrawal of the central state, and claimed to adjust entitlements to performance. One might suppose that the increased dominance of social security reflects the success and achievements of the market, while relative generosity has also risen in meeting the needs of those outside its realm. However, these assumptions are not borne out under closer scrutiny. As I will show, the two welfare arenas do not function—as envisaged—according to the rules of returns by contribution on the one hand, and according to neediness on the other. Instead, they are bringing about diverging levels of social inclusion, and thereby creating two separate categories of social citizenship. An exploration of the mechanisms that have produced these results requires a closer look at the role played by the *central state* in these two subsystems, for it will become clear that it is not the market *per se* but the marketized shares drawn from the state's revenue at the expense of welfare that are at work in the background.

Let me briefly outline how this rather surprising development has come about. The origins are to be found in the social history of the 1980s. By that time, the great invention of "liberalizing" the planned economy through the limited functioning of the so-called second economy had been developed to a relatively advanced stage in Hungary. As a number of studies have demonstrated convincingly, the way of life founded on two pillars (that is, to base livelihood on work in the formal, state-regulated segment of the economy in combination with an intensive participation in family-run micro-level productive endeavors) became a model that was followed by no less than three quarters of households, thereby effectively assisting political stabilization of the post-1956 regime as well as the country's economy (Szelényi, 1988; Laki, 1998). Beyond such immediate advantages, the widespread practice also had numerous lasting benefits such as the acquisition of otherwise inaccessible skills and qualifications, the development of new attitudes toward business, and the adoption of new rules of "fair trade" that later contributed importantly to Hungary's pioneering position among the transitional economies of the 1990s (Farkas & Vajda, 1990; Laki, 1998; Laki & Szalaï, 2004).

However, the enforced and enduring cohabitation of the two economies also had some deeply problematic implications. Given the unquestionable domination of the rules and requirements of the state-controlled first economy over the second order of informality, the scope, time, and energy that people could devote to their productive activities in the private sphere had to be adjusted—or, to put it more accurately, subordinated—to the pulsation of the planned sector. At the same time, a degree of flexibility still had to be maintained: some limited acknowledgement of the productive needs of the second economy also had to be inserted into the daily functioning of the system. Amid the constant efforts to create the necessary balance, it was exactly the field of state-run welfare distribution that turned out to provide the necessary bridge between these perpetually conflicting needs. Innovative new benefit schemes in social security and income support were set up to simultaneously ensure the continuation of the party-state's unrestricted power to compel people to contribute to the formal economy and to grant them a limited degree of freedom to temporarily withdraw from it. This dual system was run by the socialist firms that functioned as gatekeepers. Given that claims for benefits could only be submitted with the prior permission of the employer, granting such requests became a matter of "merit" and "deserve": employees in key positions enjoyed a rather high degree of freedom to leave the arena of socialist production temporarily and focus on their family business in the second economy, while those in marginalized positions were often denied on the grounds of "unreliable behavior" and "lack of discipline." At the same time, the firms, as agents of accomplishing the socialist plan, kept strict control over the needs of the planned economy: if required, they simply suspended providing the "document of consent of the workplace," thereby blocking people's move between the two economies. In this way, social security benefits grew to become an important means by which employers developed a new set of incentives that helped them to find innovative ways for adapting to the market while also fulfilling the requirements laid out in the central commands. Looked upon from the employees' perspective, the same social security benefits provided a legitimate shield for withdrawal from the formal economy that otherwise would have been deemed criminal action, while smart economizing with the additional financial resources, over and above their wages, helped to accommodate their business and accumulate substantial assets in the private domain (Szalaï, 1991). However, the development of such new double-faced programs gradually undermined the classic corrective functions of central income distribution, for it was an ever-increasing portion of the public welfare funds that was channeled into semiprivate production in the second economy: it became common practice to use benefits as "salaries" for unpaid informal work, and/or as extra payments to supplement (otherwise low) earnings in the formal sphere (Szalaï, 2007). In this way, a rapid erosion of the benefit schemes has surfaced to the detriment of those living solely or mainly from such sources, and henceforth the political innovations had their grave contribution to the spread of poverty by the late 1980s (Ferge, 2000; Spéder, 2002).

With the systemic change, inherited poverty has come to mean massive social exclusion. In the eyes of the majority, it seemed justified to blame the poor for their earlier "failure to participate" in the covert market relations of the second economy and to question their right to public support on these historic grounds. This apportioning of blame was reinforced by widespread criticism of the policy of "forced assimilation" that drew Roma under the umbrella of compulsory full employment. Since they had occupied unskilled positions in the least-developed segments of industry and agriculture, Roma became the first victims of marketization: mass unemployment suddenly turned to the general experience of an entire minority. The majority, meanwhile, did not see anything unusual in this: cutting off Roma communities in their totality from access to employment has gradually developed into a self-justifying argument for "minoritization"—that is, for creating "other" schemes of welfare for people who are not "us." These widely shared attitudes have contributed in an important way to the dualization of welfare that has meant continuing to "convert" state funds into support for the businesses of those active in the market while simultaneously squeezing the poor—especially the Roma poor—into a sealed system of strictly controlled welfare assistance away from the market. In this way, the once structurally constructed engagement of the state and the market for the sake of "market success" has been reinforced according to new needs and legitimizing ideologies, while the contrasting concept of "market failure" has been translated into direct dependency on local communities. In light of the shortcomings of the post-1990 transformation process, this will, however, come as no surprise. As I will show below, there is a wide range of interests—old and new, transient and enduring—that ensure that there is still support for maintaining this kind of dual arrangement at all costs.

Let me first consider the interests involved in maintaining the state's continued participation in market relations.

The arguments are, in the first place, based on a number of obvious economic motives. Independent economic activity entirely separated from the state requires stable capital backing and a firmly established market, but neither of these conditions was present in the decades of state-socialism (Voszka, 2003; Laki & Szalaï, 2004). Hence, the mere survival of domestic businesses and with it the country's potential to keep pace with increased competition on the world market have been at permanent risk. This is why the need for the state pillar in the simple material sense has continued to be a constant element of postcommunist transformation and economic adaptation ever since (Báger & Kovács, 2004).[2]

At the same time, the need for the financial presence of the state has been kept alive by the fact that economic restructuring has induced erosion even into those market relationships that had hitherto been regarded as fairly stable and "everlasting." The privatization of state-owned firms disrupted the flow of state orders that had been thought to be secure, while the collapse of the traditional Eastern markets and the rather difficult access to Western markets in replacement have confused and endangered established export relationships. Furthermore, a significant influx of foreign capital and consumer products has resulted in fierce competition on the domestic market, too. All this has greatly increased the risks associated with full commercial independence and increased the need for the state to play a stronger buffer role (Báger & Kovács, 2004; Szalaï, 2007).

In addition to the pressures that are reasoned by the extra burdens and risks of marketization, there are also important cultural and attitude factors at play when claiming the state's long-term protection for establishing independence from it. A wide variety of groups judge that the time has come for "the state" to compensate them for their historical grievances and decades of "lagging behind," to give them open assistance to achieve the advancement that they "deserve"—and they do not cease to outbid each other in submitting claims for compensation that are "legitimate" in their own right. Having the arguments justifying these claims accepted and enacted in legislation, and thereby securing annual financing from the central budget, is a question of political brute force. Access to public funds has primarily been, then, a direct function of the latent bargaining positions established prior to the systemic change (Laky, 2004).

However, it is above all in the realm of employment that the state's presence in welfare has been proclaimed the most loudly. Hungary's opening up to the world market, the increased presence of strong Western multinationals, and low levels of competitive knowledge and skills have combined to produce lasting and widespread insecurity on the labor market that has even endangered the positions of the better-qualified strata of the labor force. Under these conditions, it has again fallen to the state, in its welfare role, to meet the need for preventing and protecting against the risk of poverty. Social security, and within it the public pension scheme, is seen as the proper arena in which to seek compensation and stability. In response to enormous enduring pressure, the purposeful application of the idea of "reward according to contribution" has given rise to no fewer than 103 different forms of entitlements to a public pension: a range of disability schemes, early retirement programs, entitlements to fractional pensions, individually negotiated exceptions from the general rules according to acknowledged "reasonableness," and so on, have all been introduced to provide security under rapidly changing conditions. The outcome is clearly reflected in a pronounced shift in the sources of daily livelihood: for sizeable groups, it is their pension that is considered to substitute both the status and income once derived from employment. A few data show the significance of this strange trade-off very clearly. While the proportion of households with at least one member in employment dropped from 59% in 1992 to 44% in 2005, the ratio of households with at least one pensioner jumped from 43% to 61% in the same period (TÁRKI, 1992, 2005). The same trend is also reflected in macro-level data: while the proportion of pensioners under the age of 60 was relatively low at 12% in 1992, the corresponding figure had jumped to 28% by 2005 (Central Statistical Office, 1997, 2005). The indicated shifts have had a number of consequences. First of all, under conditions of rapidly shrinking employment, social security benefits have provided protection against falling into poverty. Secondly, they have served to reduce financial risks: regardless of success or failure in business, pensions provide a secure livelihood and a base for free experimentation on the market. Thirdly, pensions help to protect families' social status: pensioners are, by definition, fully acknowledged members of society who enjoy the full range of citizens' rights, while those on the dole or those forced to stay at home lose their ties with the community, leaving them severely marginalized. This latter effect is perhaps even more important than the finances. Households' relative loss of income is richly compensated by extended access to the informal market, where pensioners still provide a plentiful source of labor that can be easily mobilized on request (Szívós & Tóth, 2004).

At the same time, it has to be noted that contributions have hardly been able to keep pace with the needs that these shifts imply. Hence, it is the central state that has been left to bridge this gap.[3] However, growing transfers undermine the principle of "reward for contribution" and turn competition for central funds into a matter of fierce power struggles between the relatively better-off and the poor. All this also means that, despite initial expectations of creating a separation between state and civil society, the state has remained an agent in defining the content of social citizenship. The implied notion is bound to participation in the market: it is only those with ties to property or engaged in employment whose access to centrally distributed benefits is secure. The outcome is clearly reflected in data on the prominent role of centrally distributed public welfare in people's daily living. While the benefits in question (pensions, family allowance, childcare benefits) accounted for 44% of the yearly income of households in 1992, their proportion had risen to 49% by 2005. However, the increase is due exclusively to larger claims by the better-off: households in the tenth decile of income distribution derived only 11% of their yearly income from welfare benefits in 1992, while their share had climbed to no less than 24% by 2005. This increase in access has clearly taken place to the detriment of the poor (those in the first decile), for whom the respective data showed a dramatic decline from 54% in 1992 to 41% by 2005. The remarkable shift in shares from the central allocated budgets become even more visible when comparing the actual magnitudes: in 1992, the rich received only 73% of what was being transferred through social security (and/or central benefits) to the poorest households, while the respective index jumped to no less than 177% by 2005 (own calculations, based on Central Statistical Office, 1997, 2005).

As a result of the factors and trends mentioned, attempts at slimming down the state have so far actually meant that it has gotten fatter: the proportion spent by the central state on financing itself as the designated agent of administering the truly complex process of systemic transformation has risen steadily over the past two decades (Central Statistical Office, 1997, 2004). The inseparability of the state and the market and, with it, the tight interlocking of the public and private spheres and resources of living seem profoundly ingrained in Hungary's postcommunist society and economy. Despite strong motives for greater independence from the state, the majority continue to have a deep-rooted interest in maintaining this bond, even though the cost of doing so has skyrocketed to the extent that it has become an impediment to the economic progress of the country as a whole (Kornai, 2005; Central Statistical Office, 2004, 2005).

There has been only one arena where the door has remained open for repeated cuts: welfare assistance for the poor. Here, the state has been able to rely on a broad and enduring political consensus. All its efforts to apply more draconian and uncompromising rules have been met with massive approval by the non-poor majority.

Let us look briefly at how these cuts have worked in daily reality.

THE GHETTO OF POVERTY WITH THICKENING WALLS

As outlined above, the creation of a separate, publicly funded subsystem to provide efficient and just welfare exclusively for those in need was an inherent part of the liberal welfare reforms of the 1990s. While the primary goal certainly was to contribute in this way to the coveted downsizing of the state, some further important considerations were also involved.

First of all, it was widely believed that poverty would wither away of its own accord as economic recovery took hold. The arguments were in line with the neo-liberal doctrines that dominated policymaking: under conditions of continuous growth and the concomitant expansion of the labor market, poverty would shrink to a residual size with successful economic adjustment, and it would hit people only temporarily, if at all. Secondly, it was also believed that improved targeting and the local schemes built on community consensus would ultimately generate support generous enough to help the poor to escape destitution. Thirdly, by swiftly decentralizing a great number of schemes and provisions that had previously been centrally administered, it was assumed that the key decisions on people's daily lives would be taken on the basis of close personal knowledge and acquaintance, hence enhancing the fairness, flexibility, and accuracy of the system.

However, history has proved all these expectations wrong. As amply demonstrated by a number of independently run studies that have repeatedly arrived at the same conclusion, there has not been even the slightest reduction in the degree of poverty, and the extent and depth of social exclusion have actually increased during the past two decades (Ferge, 2000; Havasi, 2002; Spéder, 2002; Szívós & Tóth, 2004, 2008). Welfare assistance has clearly done little to help the poor. The question thus arise: Why has this been the case?

Only part of the answer is to be found by looking at the functioning of the system of local welfare assistance alone. In terms of its principles and constituents, the scheme in Hungary is certainly neither better nor worse than similar arrangements anywhere else (Ferge, 2000; Szalaï, 2007). Having said this, one can then suggest that it is probably more the associated social and cultural implications and the economic and political relationships involved that are responsible for its striking inefficacy than any particular technical details of the scheme as such.

When looked at it from this broader perspective, it seems justified to say that the creation of a separate local system exclusively for the poor has actually served a number of goals other than that of helping the disadvantaged. The primary achievement of Hungary's decentralized assistance scheme has indeed been to perform *the purposeful transformation* of the previous all-embracing system of centralized redistribution that had been exclusively ruled by the party-state (Central Statistical Office, 1997, 2004, 2005, 2009). Together with this, the scheme has accomplished a perhaps even more important mission: the canalization of a significant section of the affected social groups into a sealed subdivision of welfare provisions. True, without the great expansion of welfare assistance as a new, dynamic branch of the economy it would have hardly been possible to break up the former oversized system: while "guiding" large strata of society into the market-regulated field of provisions, it was also essential to "evict" other large groups from the potential use of central funds—and the local schemes reacted to this call with great perfection.

The involved "exchange" not only required applying financial techniques for regrouping, but it also opened the way for important mobility processes. Another important function of the rapidly growing system of welfare assistance was that, by calling thousands of new offices into being, with tens of thousands of decent middle-class jobs on the labor market, it *created a refuge* for many of those made vulnerable to dismissals during the process of economic restructuring (Central Statistical Office, 2005).

An examination of local support in its community context reveals further important functions beyond these macro-level roles. After all, the scheme turned out to be instrumental in *maintaining peacefulness* and assisting with a smooth engaging in the daily life of local communities. Firstly, the system has provided professional machinery and an institutional background to enable the non-poor majority to deal with poverty as a minority problem, separate from its own "normal" affairs. Secondly, it has offered an efficient means of managing fluctuations in local labor markets. Thirdly, by creating a strong bond between public work and entitlements, municipal welfare assistance schemes have guaranteed an enduring supply of the human resources for the least-qualified and least-wanted jobs. In addition, the fragmented, decentralized system of means-tested local provisions to replace the earlier centralized arrangements has successfully masked the selective drive of the welfare reforms to cleanse the contribution-based subsystem of social security of its welfare functions by entrusting care of the poor to the municipalities. The welcome veil of decentralized decision making about those cases that have fallen out of the market has benevolently hidden the potentially arising question of *social responsibility for poverty* and reduced poverty alleviation almost exclusively to a matter of improving the *level of expertise* of a few local welfare workers.

It is important to stress that while the system fulfills the economic and political functions listed here—which at first glance may appear foreign to the spirit of assistance—considerations of fairness and neediness mentioned above lose none of their significance. Quite the contrary: local welfare providers are not being dishonest when they constantly affirm that their work is guided primarily by these very considerations. However, by transforming these guiding principles into hundreds of thousands of decisions on individual cases with all their specificities, a continual "translation" exercise is being carried out in order to draw the line between the justified and unjustified claims—whereby it is not fulfilling the needs of the claimants but providing a politically acceptable disguise for selecting between them that becomes their primary task. In the final analysis, it is thus the *legitimization* of the prevailing deep social divides that is assigned to them as their chief role in the broad division of labor.

As I will show below, this fundamental trait of the assistance scheme continues to be inevitable.

In this new order of localized welfare, the keyword is *distinction,* which, at the same time, has a clear meaning: as said, it is the borderline between accepted and unaccepted forms of need. However, due to the lack of any universal norms for the assessment of need, the new decentralized arrangements leave this assessment process to the discretion of local welfare providers who establish their criteria with exclusive reference to the community in which they operate. This way of assessing the needs of the poor depends on the consent of the non-poor majority whose new authorization has led, in turn, to the reinvention of the centuries-old idea of *deservingness* as the most powerful and "just" basis for selection. The renewed inclusion of behavioral traits in the selection process has led to extraordinary results at the national level: within a decade, the number of those granted by municipal public assistance has dropped by no less than 65% (Ferge, 2000; Havasi, 2002; Szalaï, 2007). In other words, instead of encouraging solidarity and generosity, "deservingness" has provided a means by which to justify the majority's urge to reduce public support for those in need. As recent surveys have shown unequivocally, only a relatively narrow section of the needy can be sure that, once they have been accepted, they can count on unconditional support. But the majority of the poor who apply for assistance do not belong in this group. Local welfare office workers share the view of the majority of the general public that the poor hold a good deal of responsibility for their situation and they can certainly be expected to make at least some attempt to improve their own lot. On the basis of such a widely held conviction, nobody would then question the rightfulness and indeed the necessity of taking into account the degree of the applicant's "faults," "errors," "failures," and "irresponsibility" when gauging applications for welfare assistance from "taxpayers' money."

The errors, shortcomings, and irresponsibility that can be listed when making decisions come in many different forms, but the most serious instance of "one's own fault" is the lack of "proper" employment, which is understood as a "failed" attitude to work—for people can always engage in *some* kind of work if they really *want* to. The vast body of literature produced to refute such views has not managed to dispel this preconception. It is perhaps unnecessary to argue at length that the clear ethnic basis of such attitudes provides convenient confirmation of the tension that is most evident in the everyday life of local communities. Labeling Roma as "idle" is inspired by the tacit race to justify deservingness: it reflects the frustrations over personally felt impoverishment of the non-Roma majority who have suffered relative losses or, at the very least, have lived in a state of constant insecurity during the lengthy process of economic transformation, towards the Roma minority, who live in extreme and lasting poverty. A clear distinction of these two types of poverty and the social statuses that are involved is a widely shared political need. Furthermore, the implied ethnic/racial differentiation entails some beneficent outcome also in the economic sense: it helps to keep claims for local assistance within limits. After all, among the truly needy, there is increasingly fierce rivalry between Roma and non-Roma groups, and it is always the "others" who are to be blamed for "eating up" the scarce municipal funds and lowering the actually delivered sums of assistance while boosting the rates of refusal due to the exhaustion of the local welfare budget.

Of course, in demanding that the cases of "fault" be carefully screened out, no one states (openly) any ethnic or racial implications, but certainly everyone understands what is at stake. The practice of welfare assistance then converts this widely inferred thought into differentially allocated sums. At the same time, it transforms rivalry among the poor and the arising *openly* racialized preselection to the rule-governed cooperation of local welfare providers with their clients under the guise of *covertly* racialized mechanisms of distribution.[4]

Empirical findings show that, regardless of personal attitudes, staff in local welfare offices simply have no means at their disposal to react properly to the current labor market position of the many applicants—for the most part Roma—who were thrown out of regular employment 10 to 15 years ago, and who have since then been able to engage only in casual work or unregistered black labor, if any at all. From the point of view of welfare providers, this labor market situation *does not exist*. They have two possible responses. The first is to try to force the clients into "proper," legal jobs; local staff thus come to regard their official task as being, above all, the prosecution of crime. The second possible response is to acknowledge the reality and become a silent accomplice with the "cheating" clients, in which case they risk their own positions. Either way, continual conflict is unavoidable.

It is this that creates the dynamics of one of the main roles of decentralized welfare in today's Hungary: meeting the local demand for the worst jobs and providing a repository for labor market fluctuations. Survey data show that Roma—and the very poorest non-Roma, who share a similar fate—came to realize this long ago, taught by the pressure of their daily experiences. The first among these experiences is the extreme segmentation of the Hungarian labor market, which dates back to the origins of the post-1990 economic transformation. As a result of gradually intensifying segmentation, the poorest strata of workers (which include a disproportionate number of Roma) are now almost entirely excluded from *any* access to proper jobs (Kertesi, 2005). The second set of lessons that the poor—especially the Roma poor—had to draw is that the emerging market, which has replaced the earlier second economy, has induced unprecedented competition among those in employment to capitalize on all the good jobs that are available in the newly acknowledged small businesses. In this vast process of "marketization from below," access to work is still, at most, only partly regulated by supply and demand, and remains largely a question of trust, networks, and connections, where the former relations of mutual favors play the main role in distributing labor (Kertesi, 2005). The poor have generally not had, and still do not have, anything to offer in exchange, and so the well-paid contracts, commissioned work, or consultancy projects remain beyond their reach. Even if they have the necessary training and experience, they still have little hope of being the ones to learn about any opportunities that exist in time to seize them. The cultural arguments that attribute the lack of employment to "bad" socialization and a subsequent "faulty" attitude to work have to be weighed against the stark reality of sharp segmentation and dramatic exclusion, which is further aggravated by widely applied, though rarely openly admitted, ethnic/racial distinctions.

Under these circumstances, it is taken for granted that if, on rare occasions, the possibility of even the worst kind of paid work arises, it is a *must* for the poor to accept it without hesitation or bargaining. It seems clear, then, that whether the poor have their hands full with work or not does not depend on their attitude. It is the reality, however, that their efforts remain largely invisible—both to themselves, because of the very low remuneration they receive for what is often extremely demanding, hazardous, and humiliating work, and to the outside world, because no written contract is involved to provide any record of the employment, and furthermore, because neither the worker nor the employer paid taxes or social security contributions on this unregistered activity. In addition to the involved obvious defenselessness it is a most tragic irony that such a traceless existence is in the own best interest of the poor themselves. The situation is clear: if they do not have even the chance of a proper occupation, then they should at least be allowed a livelihood; for they simply have no other option than to apply for welfare assistance, which the staff of the welfare office would refuse to provide if they knew about their "illegal" income from unofficial work. At the same time, this income is so low that it makes no real difference to the daily livelihood of even the poorest of the poor. Under such circumstances, welfare assistance is quite literally needed merely to survive—obtaining it is of vital importance. For this reason, it remains also of vital importance that the sharp-eyed welfare providers be reassured: concealing the work that turns up now and then in the gray or black economy is in the *common interest* of both the office and the client.

This common interest has two implications. On the one hand, it guarantees that unregistered employment, enshrouded in the working of local welfare assistance, continues to flourish unchecked and as needed. On the other hand, it ensures that the bargain that is stuck between the provider and the client remains a matter of an internal struggle between the welfare workers, who have little choice but to carry out the public will, and the defenseless poor—predominantly Roma—in the service of demonstrating general "justice" and the wise and thrifty use of public funds (Szalaï, 2007).

In this way a ghetto is being constructed out of the commonality of these constrained interests. All that remains is to safeguard its walls so that the peacefulness of the community can be maintained and the majority can accomplish the huge national task of modernization while enjoying the gifts of democracy, which—for the time being—has implied full citizenship only for them. Persistent "cultural arguments" that explain poverty along the lines of deservingness, with all the ethnic/racial implications that these entail, are crucially important here. Without this powerful means of justification, participation in the market would fail to legitimize the coexistence of two subsystems in a hierarchical order and the two distinctive realms of citizenship on which it is based.

CONCLUSION: THE EMERGENCE OF A BIFURCATED WELFARE STATE

In this chapter, I have sought to describe the complexity of macro- and micro-level interests that have informed the ongoing social struggles around the role of the postcommunist welfare state and its responsibilities towards its citizens. I have argued that the conflicts involved cannot be understood without considering the legacy of the former state-socialist order that has greatly influenced the process of restructuring welfare according to the often-conflicting goals of economic and political transformation. While the deep-going qualitative change of transforming a planned economy into a market-regulated one necessitated the rapid dismantling of the institutional structure inherited from the previous regime, democratization has implied a universalization of civil control over it. The initial idea was to sequence these two huge historical shifts. It was expected that the swift conversion of property relations would give rise to a private market and an independent bourgeoisie, which would act as twin foundations for progress toward the automatic expansion of civil control over the state. Furthermore, and in line with the evolution of the postwar Western welfare states, growing civil control over the state would bring about a universalization of democratic citizenship rooted in undivided civil, political, and social rights. In other words, marketization would facilitate economic adjustment and democratic rule in one fell swoop. The dismantling of the inherited state structures through privatization was thus seen as the obvious first step towards genuine systemic change.

However, such reasoning has not stood the test of history over the past two decades of the postcommunist transformation. The pressure of the severe economic crisis during the 1980s, which manifested itself in extraordinary external and internal state indebtedness, meant that swift privatization at all costs was seen as the only way to recovery. Under such conditions, the conversion of the rundown stock of the planned economy logically led to the unconditional opening up of the domestic market, which has in turn brought about a rapid influx of global capital. However, the unrestricted opening up of the economy concluded in an unexpected devaluation of its marketable value: no less than 40% of the jobs available in the early 1990s were lost in competition with cheap labor in the developing world, while only some 10% have been replaced ever since. Under these circumstances, welfare provisions that had once been designed to assist forced employment in service of the state-socialist project had now to be rapidly retailored to moderate the intensity of competition for secure employment, while simultaneously supporting vast groups in the insecure informal economy.

Most importantly, the successful implementation of the transformation project assumed a marked reduction in the previously excessive power of the central state. However, forceful downsizing quickly turned into the actual *desertion of the state*. The abolition of the all-embracing programs of the old regime produced a lasting vacuum, which led, in turn, to a rapid increase in the number of people without any form of social protection at all. Hence, as well as a steep rise in the ratio of those in poverty, the withering away of centralized welfare schemes contributed significantly to the swift social exclusion of the weakest groups of those who had once been fully engaged in the service of "socialist production" and thus had remained entirely dependent on the provisions of the then ruling communist party-state.

But the process had some further consequences. As demonstrated above, the drastic retrenchment of the centrally distributed resources led to fierce social struggles. The newly available central funds have quickly been absorbed through privatization and economic adaptation from below. At the same time, decentralized municipal welfare programs have proved incapable of keeping pace with the relentless increase in the number of applicants: the poor struggling for mere livelihood and impoverished sections of the middle class seeking compensation unequivocally identified the new local assistance schemes as their only resort. The ruthless competition that has evolved between these two groups has contributed to the sharpening of the deep socioeconomic divides along class and racial/ethnic lines that have come about as an unintended but inevitable consequence of economic restructuring.

By the turn of the millennium, the processes indicated had resulted in the evolution of a bifurcated welfare system with hermetically separated structures of provisions for the well-integrated and the marginalized groups of society. As the country began to thrive economically, the contribution-based services and benefit schemes have produced a remarkable rise in standards and coverage for those who succeed in establishing secure positions in Hungary's already dominant market economy. At the same time, however, the highly segregationist world of local welfare assistance has been left to meet the needs of those who failed on the market and remained terminally excluded—the poorest. The longer they continue to be stuck in poverty, the thicker will grow the walls that lock them into the second-tier arrangements designed "for them alone."

It is worth noting that this dualism of social rights represents a departure from Marshall's ideas on social citizenship in two important ways. Firstly, it is only the first set of rights that are derived from a social dialogue between actors on the market and the state: the principle of "reward according to contribution" seems to be a powerful extension of the notion of the business contract, and also reflects people's desire to preserve or redefine their social status in the new environment. However, the fundamental principle of "neediness" represents the deprivation of any capacity to enter into any negotiations and contracting process, and thus subjugation to the rule of administrative power. Secondly, while

Marshall described gradualism as an ongoing process toward the universalization of formerly restricted rights, nothing similar has occurred in postcommunist Hungary. Universalism has been misconstrued as the concept of enforcement that replaced rights under state-socialism, meaning that a major task of postcommunist welfare policy has been to drive this concept out of the welfare system of the new democracy. In other words, selectivity and separation became the main objectives of the reform process, and claims to maintain universalism were considered as relics of the failed system of the past.[5]

Such a bifurcated system is also a long-term departure from the western European path of social development that had been envisioned. Deeply ingrained into the structure inherited from late socialism, the emergence of a new domestic bourgeoisie has been conditioned by maintaining strong bonds to the provisions of the state. This is clearly reflected in the still-dominant form of living based on two pillars: one of private and semiprivate business, and another involving the acquisition of state resources through welfare distribution to keep the former running. Though this combination may be familiar from the state-socialist past, the function of the two pillars has been altered by the new rules of the market. Given the conditions of steadily shrinking employment, it is entitlements to welfare provisions ruled by anticipated "contributions" that are mobilized to substitute for vanishing labor force participation. In addition, participation in small-scale entrepreneurship is meant to assist material advancement—though without any motivation to break the bonds with the state (Laki, 1998; Laky, 2004). In other words, enduring economic dependence on the state is seen as a precondition for civil independence: the widespread conversion of welfare funds into private business is perceived as a legitimate means of accomplishing the still-unfinished process of *embourgeoisement*, and claims for the maintenance of state provisions are articulated according to the historical arguments of all-societal restoration (Szalaï, 2007). However, such a state of affairs resembles earlier sociopolitical patterns of "catching up," when modernization was confined strictly to the economic sphere, and hence embraced only those sections of society that had been well integrated into mainstream market relations. The danger involved in this is easy to identify: it means that, yet again, modernization plays an active role in weakening social cohesion, leading to the inadequate working of the country's democratic political institutions.[6]

Furthermore, the intense struggle to maintain the fusion of the state and the market results in the poor being crowded out. The construction of a system sealed in decentralized schemes of means-tested assistance in the local communities in exchange for powerfully keeping them away from the domain of guaranteed central provisions can only be seen as the institutionalization of a *second order of citizenship*. Nevertheless, in a country with a democratic constitution and declared citizens' rights, such a differentiation cannot be made openly. When framed, however, in "cultural" terms, it reveals the moral implications of democratic citizenship, that is nothing but a contract between society and the individual to meet certain obligations in return for certain rights. Those who cannot meet the first part of the contract should not expect society to grant them the second. In this vein, claims on creating a separate subsystem of provisions for the needy are purposefully fulfilled and, at the same time, justified by the notion of "cultural otherness."

However, as shown, this construct becomes the basis of *structural disintegration*. After all, the conjugate principles of unlimited competition on the market and expulsion on the grounds of individual failure provide the rationale for maintaining the institutional separation of an entirely closed world—a genuine ghetto—for those to whom the concept of "other" applies: Hungary's highly marginalized long-term poor and, above all, the Roma among them. Given the lack of multicultural political arrangements, their culturally conceived secondary citizenship becomes the base for sheer subordination on ethnic grounds.

In sum, the two coexisting subsystems of welfare—the rather generous public funding of the market and the running of the impoverished quarters of public provisions for those who fall outside of it—reflect and reproduce the outlined strange social contract advancing steadily toward a social structure divided along ever-sharper fault lines with ever-more-pronounced institutional separation that follows a hierarchical order of citizenship. Such structural developments are also behind the gradual weakening of new democratic institutions and the spread of populist anti-Western and anti-market claims. Whether the "new–old" rhetoric that calls for a "strong and protective nation-state" with authoritative power will resonate among those who identify themselves as the ultimate losers from the postcommunist transformation is a matter of great concern for all future reforms in welfare and beyond. The answer to this question will greatly affect the shaping of state–citizen relations that will be of essential importance in determining the quality of Hungarian democracy in the longer run.

NOTES

1   Most of the statistical data in this section represent the period between the early 1990s and the mid-2000s. After Hungary joined the European Union in 2004, the systems of data collection and publication have been adjusted to the prevailing EU regulations and requirements. Due to the profound reorganization, data referring to the years after 2005 cannot be directly compared, for the most part, with those from earlier years.

2   It is hardly a surprise that the global economic crisis has given a new impetus to such claims. Much in accordance with similar developments elsewhere, the reconceptualization of the state as a key actor of the working of the market and as a primary driver of the healthy recovery of society has reflected the actual expansion of the state's role in regulating the economy while providing substantial resources to its daily running (Voszka, 2009).

3   It becomes clear at a closer look at the finances that it is the central state's budget that backs the indicated mass movement of the "marketized reinterpretation" of public social security. As compared to the early 1990s, when cross-financing from the central budget accounted for only 6% of the yearly revenue of the pension fund, the respective rate had risen to 29% by 2004 (Central Statistical Office, 2005). This peak was then followed by a modest decline. However, despite all attempts at halting the "outflow" of the tax revenue toward the pension system, the respective yearly ratios never could be set below the still-high level of 22% to 23% (Central Statistical Office, 2009).

4   In a sense, the year 2008 brought about a breakthrough by turning the covert ethnic/racial contents of local welfare assistance into open "ethno-cultural" principles in a new flagship provision: the scheme that "helps you on the road to work." According to this new workfare program, "able-bodied" adults are no longer entitled to any type of assistance without participating in local public work programs. Such programs are organized and controlled by the municipality, and the administration has the right to set additional requirements ("obligatory home gardening"; "decent housekeeping," etc.). At the same time, the client has practically no rights: any refusal of the (type of) work implies becoming excluded from the entire assistance scheme. The local government can make exceptions in "justified cases" (i.e., save the "deserving poor"). It is no wonder that the new scheme has gained its dubious reputation as a "program to regularize Roma." After all, its primary mission is to further select among the poor by providing some decent work and/or exemption to "ordinary" non-Roma people, and simultaneously by tightening the rules and making their application extremely arbitrary in case of the Roma poor.

5   It goes without saying that the described rejection of universalism does not favor multiculturalism either. After all, rapid territorial segregation, the rise of welfare ghettos, and the lack of parliamentary representation of the Roma minority work strongly against a dialogue that should inform the shaping of the political and legal institutions of a genuinely multicultural society. Instead, the current trends point in the opposite direction: they indicate that ethnic/racial discrimination—both institutional and personal—has grown to set the stage for the conflicting daily reality of multiethnic cohabitation.

6   By pointing to this danger, one does not speak any more about a potential future, but points to the daily reality. For the first time in the history of post-socialist Hungary, the radical right, with its openly racist and anti-Semitic program, gained 16% of the seats in parliament in 2010. In addition to their substantial influence in lawmaking and governance, they have succeeded in mobilizing substantial paramilitary troops that march through the poorest Roma towns and villages and blackmail Roma *en masse*. All this happens without any powerful response on the part of the police or the government.

REFERENCES

Báger, G., & Á. Kovács (2004). A magyarországi privatizáció néhány tanulsága [Some lessons of privatisation in Hungary]. In G. Báger & Á. Kovács (Eds.), *A privatizáció Magyarországon I [Privatisation in Hungary, Vol. 1].* Budapest: ÁSz FEMI.

Central Statistical Office (1997). *Magyar Statisztikai Évkönyv 1996 [Hungarian Statistical Yearbook, 1996].* Budapest: CSO.

Central Statistical Office (2004). *Magyar Statisztikai Évkönyv 2003 [Hungarian Statistical Yearbook, 2003].* Budapest: CSO.

Central Statistical Office (2005). *Szociális Statisztikai Évkönyv 2004 [Statistical Yearbook on Welfare, 2004].* Budapest: CSO.

Central Statistical Office (2009). *Szociális Statisztikai Évkönyv 2008 [Statistical Yearbook on Welfare, 2008].* Budapest: CSO.

Farkas, E. J., & Á. Vajda (1990). Hounsing. In R. Andorka, T. Kolosi, & G. Vukovich (Eds.), *Social report* (pp. 91–113). Budapest: TÁRKI.

Ferge, Z. (2000). *Elszabaduló egyenlőtlenségek [Inequalities getting out of control].* Budapest: HRSZE.

Havasi, É. (2002). Szegénység és társadalmi kirekesztettség a mai Magyarországon [Poverty and social exclusion in Hungary today]. *Szociológiai Szemle, 12*(4), 51–72.

Horváth, T. M. (2000). Directions and differences of local changes. In T. M. Horváth (Ed.), *Decentralization: Experiments and reforms* (pp. 19–61). Budapest: OSI/LGI.

Kertesi, G. (2005). *A társadalom peremén [On the margin of society].* Budapest.

Kornai, J. (1996). *Vergődés és remény. Gondolatok a gazdasági stabilizációról és a jóléti állam reformjáról [Floundering and hope. Thoughts on stabilization of the economy and reform of the welfare state]* (pp. 175–205). Budapest: KJK.

Kornai, J. (2005). Közép-Kelet-Európa nagy átalakulása—siker és csalódás [The great transformation of Central and Eastern Europe: Success and disappointment]. *Közgazdasági Szemle, 52*(12), 907–936.

Kymlicka, W. (1995). *Multicultural citizenship. A liberal theory of minority rights.* Oxford: Clarendon Press.

Laki, M. (1998). *Kisvállalkozás a szocializmus után [Small entrepreneurs after socialism].* Budapest: KSZA.

Laki, M., & J. Szalaï (2004). *Vállalkozók vagy polgárok? [Entrepreneurs or citoyens?]* Budapest: Osiris.

Laky, T. (2004). *A magyarországi munkaerőpiac 2004 [The Hungarian labour market, 2004].* Budapest: Foglalkoztatási Hivatal.

Marshall, T. H., & T. Bottomore (1992). *Citizenship and social class.* London: Pluto Press.

Spéder, Z. (2002). *A szegénység változó arcai [Changing faces of poverty].* Budapest: ARTT—Századvég.

Standing, G. (1997). The folly of social safety nets: Why basic income is needed in Eastern Europe. *Social Research, 64*(4), 1339–1381.

Szalaï, J. (1991). Hungary: Exit from the state economy. In M. Kohli et al. (Eds.), *Time for retirement* (pp. 324–362). Cambridge: Cambridge University Press.

Szalaï, J. (2007). *Nincs két ország ... ? [Is it still one nation ... ?]* Budapest: Osiris.

Szelényi, I. (1988). *Socialist entrepreneurs.* Madison: University of Wisconsin Press.

Szívós, P., & I. G. Tóth (Eds.) (2004). *Stabilizálódó társadalomszerkezet [Stabilising social structure].* Budapest: TÁRKI.

Szívós, P., & I. G. Tóth (Eds.) (2008). *Köz, teher, elosztás [The public shere, financial burdens and the specificities of income redistribution].* Budapest: TÁRKI.

TÁRKI (1992–2005). *Household Panel and Monitor Surveys.* Budapest: TÁRKI.

Vági, G. (1991). *Magunk, uraim: Település, tanács, önkormányzat [It's us, sirs: settlements, local councils, local governments].* Budapest: Gondolat.

Voszka, É. (2003). *Versenyteremtés—alkuval [Competition in the making—through bargains].* Budapest: Akadémiai.

Voszka, É. (2009). Versenybarát és versenyteremtő állam—válság előtt, válság közben [The market-friendly and competition-generating state—prior to the crisis and during the crisis]. *Közgazdasági Szemle, 56*(10), 913–932.

13

THE TWO DECADES OF SOCIAL POLICY IN POLAND: FROM PROTECTION TO ACTIVATION OF CITIZENS

Marek Rymsza

POLISH SOCIAL REFORMS AFTER 1989 AND THE IDEA OF SOCIAL CITIZENSHIP

During the communist period in Poland, as in other central and eastern Europe countries, one of the main problems was a lack of the material components of citizenship and about the apparent (unenforceable) character of the rights theoretically extending to the citizens. As those times fade into history, is the institution of citizenship being renewed in accordance with T. H. Marshall's vision, or with some other scenario? Does this process include social citizenship, and if so, to what extent? And what is the role of social policy in shaping and implementing the notion of citizenship? This chapter seeks to answer these questions.

One of the distinguishing features of the communist regimes of central and eastern Europe lay in the deep chasm between the official public order and realities on the ground. The constitution of the Polish People's Republic of 1952, for instance, guaranteed freedom of association to citizens. And, sure enough, citizens were free to join associations, but in order to apply to the courts to register an association, they first had to obtain permission from the Ministry of the Interior. Such permission was granted (or, at least as often, refused) on a fully discretionary basis, with no formal right of appeal. Such examples of theoretical civic rights with little to back them up in practice were myriad, and the rule of thumb was that the further east one traveled, the more constitutions were "civic" and the more the citizenry was deprived of even basic rights. Thus, one of the tasks of the transformation period lay in restoring institutions to guarantee the enforceability of civic rights—in short, in restoring the rule of law (Kurczewski, 2009). In the case of Poland, such institutions were duly created, to mention the independent courts, the Constitutional Tribunal, or the Civic Rights Ombudsman (the latter office was actually instituted in the final years of the Polish People's Republic). But if we look at guaranteeing the enforceability of social rights, the situation is much less straightforward. Why?

In the sequence of realizing civic rights posited by T. H. Marshall, civil rights precede political rights, which in turn precede social rights. Viewed in this way, the extension (or, to be more accurate, the discovery) of social rights constitutes a complement to other rights already enjoyed by citizens (Marshall, 1950). In the communist countries of central and eastern Europe, meanwhile, social rights were basically a form of compensation for the lack of other rights. The state curtailed civic freedoms and imposed dependency on its citizens; in return, it guaranteed to them a certain level of social security, or tried to guarantee it—although the socialist state was not always capable of meeting the obligations it had assumed. At least it made an earnest effort, though, unlike with its activities in the sphere of civil and political rights, which it deliberately suppressed, meeting any dissent with suppression. Thus, the systemic transformation was based on the restoration of freedom of speech, freedom of association, the right to strike, the right to private property, and the right to engage in business activity. Filling the "space of freedom" was by no means an easy task (Tichner, 1993, 2005).

Rejection of the communist order, logically enough, entailed rejection of its quasi-rights and unrealistic social guarantees. True to the sequence posited by Marshall, the transformation implied casting the old system off and restoring to the citizens first their basic freedoms (i.e., their civil and political rights), which might then provide a foundation for building up social rights. Any attempt to retain the nominal social rights formulated by the socialist state was bound to fail because it would mean clinging to the old, discredited institutions and blocking development. There was no way that the basic freedoms could somehow be grafted onto the previous social rights because social rights in their socialist form had been derived from the omnipotence of the state.

So what really happened to Poland during the last two decades of change? How did the state social policy shape the sphere of citizens' entitlements? This chapter gives a short description of the evolution of social policy in Poland after 1989 based on the concept of three waves of social reforms. From a more theoretical perspective, the chapter examines T. H. Marshall's concept of three-dimensional citizenship, according to which implementation needs to follow a sequence: from civil, through political, to social entitlements. The chapter gives some additional arguments and new data to assess to what extent the Marshall study is only an explanation of a historical process of shaping welfare states in the most developed (western) part of Europe that has only limited usefulness in explaining processes of building democracy in other spaces and times. It also deals with the question of the extent to which Marshall was able to discover and formulate a more universal concept of a "logic of democracy".

The Polish case shows that suggesting democratic frames of public order like Marshall's concept of citizenship requires first of all the discovery (or rediscovery in the case of central and eastern Europe) of the impact of history—here, the impact of a half-century of communism on citizens' civil and political rights. One decade of systemic transformation was quite enough to do that in Poland. On the other hand, two decades were not enough to clarify what kind of social entitlements must be provided to citizens. And who is responsible for that "provision": the state and its institutions/services or civil society and its mediating structures? (see the discussion on this point in Chapter 1). May we treat this as evidence of the weakness of Poland's newly rebuilt democracy, or does it only show that the transformation from communism to democracy has not been finished yet? In my opinion, the second explanation is much more useful for comparative research as it touches on the dynamic nature of transformation itself.

Even if T. H. Marshall's explanation of the step-by-step implementation of multidimensional citizenship is historically correct, history never ends. The implementation of social rights, even if this achieves a significant reduction of class divisions in democratic societies, does not finish the story of societies-in-progress. As I will show below, the next (and current) phase of Western democracies evolution is reshaping social rights of citizens from a "passive" formula to an "active" one. The concept of active social citizenship is a way of striking a balance between the three classic components of Marshall's citizens' rights. The "dynamic dimension" of transformation in central and eastern Europe is a consequence of the phenomenon that in fact this process has an obvious starting point (the rejection of a communist regime) but no clear finishing post. "Western democracy" patterns cannot serve as a stable point of reference because they are also undergoing a permanent process of reshaping.[1] The idea of social citizenship is a good example.

Conditions and Environment of Polish Social Policy at the Turn of the 21st Century

Since 1989, social policy in Poland has been influenced by three key factors: (1) the inner "logic of transformation," (2) ideological conditions connected with the newly emerging political scene, and (3) external structural circumstances.

The logic of transformation was associated with the rejection of the communist system and the swift turn towards a democratic polity, a market economy, and civil society. Researchers have since endeavored to reconstruct the post-socialist model of social policy that took root in Poland (and, indeed, in other countries in central and eastern Europe) during the first decade of these political, economic, and social transformations; as a point worth noting, none of these states seemed to question that this was anything more than an interim model

(Deacon, 1993). The "target" model, meanwhile, remained unknown for both decision-makers and researchers.

Even though the transformative processes of the late 20th and early 21st centuries in central and eastern Europe are generally regarded as having no precedent in European history, there are many similarities between the social policies of the postcommunist states (especially in the first stage of the transformation process) and the compensatory policies of western European countries (especially those influenced by the Bismarckian tradition) pursued in the late 19th and early 20th centuries, before the emergence of the modern welfare states. At the same time, however, the conditions of transformation mean that the social policies of the countries in central and eastern Europe were distinct from those now being pursued by the older member states of the European Union ("old EU-15"), since they are policies tailored to a different stage of development (Arts & Gelissen, 2010; Haggard & Kaufman, 2009).[2]

Second, we cannot disregard the influence of ideological elements. There is much empirical proof, at least in the case of Poland, that ideological factors have played an active role in the transformation process. It may be argued that the considerable popularity gained in the 1990s by the tripartite typology of social policy models put forward by Gøsta Esping-Andersen (Esping-Andersen, 1990) was due not only to the fact that the breakdown of various economic and social indicators from the developed countries cited by the Danish researcher constituted empirical confirmation of the means of grouping national social policies around three model solutions once formulated by Richard Titmuss (Titmuss, 1974). But it also demonstrated that the countries of central and eastern Europe embarking on the path of transformation faced a choice between these three titular worlds of welfare capitalism, and that these basic choices are not so much a matter of political institutions (strict political direction is rather obvious) or even of the economy, but of social policy.

Paradoxically, in contrast to the attitude of Esping-Andersen himself,[3] the decision-makers of the newly free central and eastern European countries saw the social democratic model as less attractive than either the conservative or the liberal models of social policy (see Deacon, 1993, Table 9.3)—it had too much in common with the socialist model that had just been discarded. It was for this reason that the public debate over the preferable social policy model played out in Poland in the late 1990s could be described as a collision between the patterns raised in Continental European social policy tradition (or the "Rhein" model—Albert, 1994) and the neoliberal Anglo-Saxon ones (Rymsza, 1998). The neoliberal concepts were largely "imported" from the United States (via international institutions such as the World Bank or the International Monetary Fund)[4] and the "Continental option," which was connected with the attempt of some decision-makers to reconstruct the social institutions that had operated in Poland in the interwar period in combination with the Bismarckian model.[5] Currently, however, as the basic institutions of the civic freedoms have been restored and constitute a permanent element of the social order, the Nordic social-democratic solutions are becoming ever more appealing to Polish decision-makers.

The third factor shaping social policy in Poland is the aggregation of structural elements leading to far-reaching transformation of the European social model and, thus, to the evolution of social policies pursued by many European countries. This aggregation encompasses factors such as demographic changes, first and foremost the aging of the population of welfare societies (Coleman, 2010; Schulz, 2010), key shifts in the labor markets (Scharpf & Schmidt, 2000), progressing globalization that brings Europe up against new social and economic challenges (Kennett, 2008; Yates & Holden, 2009)[6] while reducing the possibilities of regulation by the state (*The State in a Changing World*, 1997; Staniszkis, 2000), and the legitimization of new social risks that requires changes to social protection systems (Beck, 1992; Bonoli, 2010). It has already become obvious that these transformations do not resemble the neoliberal deregulation called for in the 1980s and its attendant dismantling of basic welfare institutions (see Castles, 2007) but are a reconstruction of European welfare states.[7] One of the key areas of this reconstruction appears to be associated with the concept of active social policy (van Berkel & Møller, 2002). Implementing this concept in Poland will be one of the main topics of this chapter, for it is this current of change in the operation of social programs that exerts the biggest impact on changes to the idea of citizenship, social citizenship included.

In this context, it might be noted that the aggregation of external structural factors shaping European social policies described above has caused the Esping-Andersen typology gradually to lose some of its luster. The ideological social policy models have proved to be lacking in effectiveness as a stable point of reference in defining the directions of social policy reform in the postcommunist countries in that the social policies of the developed countries co-shaping these models were themselves in upheaval.[8] What is more, independently of the systemic transformations under way (and, by now, largely completed), Poland as well as the other countries of the region are European anyway and, as such, are subject to some of the same structural factors and conditions shaping their development, taking an active role in constructing a revised European social model. Some researchers have gone so far as to note that their experiences of transformation actually enable the postcommunist countries to adapt to new challenges more quickly than the "old EU-15" (Szomburg, 2004). For example, jettisoning the doctrine of full employment as a legacy of communism (as was done, for instance, in Poland or in Estonia) is probably easier than giving up on the principle of de-commodification as a benefit of the "golden age" of western European social policy (as suggested by the lack of support for even moderate social reform programs in France or in Germany).

In my opinion, the current revision of the European social model can be described as an "ideological convergence"—so in a similar way as some classic comparative social policy studies explained the birth of the European welfare states a century ago. It might be recalled that welfare states were built up, depending on the political equations of the given country at the given time, by the German conservatives, the British liberals, and the Swedish social democrats (see Flora & Heidenheimer, 1981; Jones, 1985; Marshall, 1975). By analogy, the recent social reforms in central and eastern Europe are the work of political parties hailing from a variety of backgrounds and profiles—Christian democrats, liberals, or leftists (who often trace their political lineage to the pre-1989 order). The latter have adopted and supported neoliberal solutions with surprising eagerness, as we see in Poland or, most of all, Hungary.

But it is also possible to analyze the above-mentioned reconstruction of the European social model as a result of the ideological shift toward an active social policy that is connected with the ongoing process of reshaping the idea of social citizenship (see as well the remarks about links between activation policies and active citizenship in Chapter 1). This means that ideological conditions play (or may play) an active and crucial role in reshaping social policy, but rather on the European, supranational level. At the same time, the new European trends implemented in Poland may be seen by the Polish decision-makers as a kind of quasi-structural, external "objective" conditions for shaping social policy at the national level.

The social policy implemented in Poland after 1989 has been shaped by the three factors briefly discussed above. Each of them has to be taken into account in comparative analysis. Using the logic of transformation perspective, we can explain the certain distinctiveness of the social policies of the countries in central and eastern Europe, Poland included, especially in the first half of the 1990s. Ideological conditions have to be taken into account, especially when we study the social reforms undertaken by Polish decision-makers at the end of the 1990s. The clash of alternative ideological visions of social order was the main reason why decision-makers were not able to implement a cohesive modern social policy model. Taking into account factors of a macro-structural character, meanwhile, enables an understanding of the considerable convergence that we can observe in the evolution of social policies of the "new EU-10" (including Poland) and the older fifteen members, particularly during the past decade.[9]

Over the past 20 years, social policy changes in Poland have proceeded in sudden shifts rather than by way of a steady, linear process, and this owes much to the ideological factors brought about by changes on the political scene. This point and the three sequences, or "waves," of reform will be discussed in greater detail below.

THE THREE "WAVES" OF SOCIAL REFORMS IN POLAND

Looking back at the past 20 years, one can discern three peaks in reforming activity in the social sphere: 1990 to 1993, 1998 to 2000, and 2003 to 2004. Each of these three successive waves of reform had its distinct form and was governed by its own logic.[10] In the 1990s, there were two periods of social reforms, both inspired and implemented by the post-Solidarity parties, and the processes of change slowed markedly during the years when leftist parties with a postcommunist lineage held power. The authors of the first and the second wave of reforms had sufficient strength and determination to initiate systemic change but were unable to limit the side effects and social costs of this change; they also proved unable to parlay the social benefits of these reforms into political gains. In both instances, the result, predictably enough, was electoral losses and political marginalization.

The next decade, however, brought a reversal of the roles: the third wave of social reforms (in 2003–04) was the work of a leftist coalition that, in this way, joined in the current of social reforms undertaken in various European countries by parties of the New Left in search of some "third way" as a means of reinvigorating European social democracy (Giddens, 1998, 2002; Kowalik, 2001). In Poland, the implementation of this concept was limited to the popularization of activation programs—the Democratic Left Alliance party, buffeted by a succession of corruption scandals, was incapable of any real renewal and, soon enough, lost the support of Polish society.

Between 2005 and 2010, by what was the eighth year of rule by various configurations of right-wing Solidarity-rooted parties, no major social reforms were undertaken. The much-touted Fourth Polish Republic program of the conservative Law and Justice Party implemented from 2005 through 2007 fizzled and failed; its successor in power, the liberal Civic Platform, has steered a cautious course, generally avoiding systemic reforms. To some extent, however, since 2005 an activation approach to social policy has been maintained.

THE FIRST WAVE OF REFORMS (1990–93): SAFETY NET PROGRAMS

The first wave of social reform in the early 1990s was associated with the institutionalization of protection measures devised to somehow soften the fall of those social groups that lost out in the process of economic shock therapy (Rymsza, 1998). The preferred approach can best be described by the term a "compensation policy," understood as denoting mitigation of the negative side effects of economic transformation. Niklas Luhmann (Luhmann, 1981) has used the term "compensation policy" to describe the approach developed in Germany towards the end of the 19th century, at a time of accelerating modernization (industrialization and urbanization) driven not by spontaneous economic processes but by intervention of the state, which was seeking to gain the status of a European powerhouse through economic development. The Polish transformation of the 1990s presents a similar instance of "accelerated modernization" that required similar compensation measures (Dziewięcka-Bokun, 2002).[11]

The safety net compensation programs launched in Poland in the early 1990s were taken as the basis of an agreement despite differences, symbolized by the collaboration of Tadeusz Mazowiecki (the Christian democrat and the prime minister), Leszek Balcerowicz (the Minister of Finance, key author of the neo-liberal program of economic overhaul through shock therapy), and Jacek Kuroń (the Minister of Labor and Social Policy, an avowed socialist). The reform program also won the support of the Solidarity trade union.[12] A key issue in this partnership was building a safety net for people losing their jobs as a result of restructuring at the large state-owned enterprises.[13] The government agreed to guarantee social benefits to all Poles without jobs—also to those who had not worked before and who displayed little desire to do so now (Szylko-Skoczny, 2004). Yet the conditions for drawing unemployment benefits have since undergone a gradual elaboration; by the early 2000s, not all unemployed persons, but only around 20% of the registered unemployed could draw benefits (Rymsza, 2005). Thus, the "overprotective" employment regime of the early 1990s morphed into an "underprotective" one. It shows that at the heart of the protective/compensation policy was not a deep interest of decision-makers in building social cohesion during a time of radical changes but a more pragmatic agreement to pay costs for a national journey through the "Red Sea" as a transformation process was defined.

Back in the 1990s, the addressees of protective measures were not expected—or required—to take steps geared at gaining their own economic footing. The idea of the social benefits offered then was to enable those who, for one reason or another, lost out in the economic transformation either to leave the labor market for good (for instance, by way of early retirement) or to cope better with the economic upheavals of that time, assisting them through social welfare benefits and the dense network of municipality social welfare centers (Zalewski, 2005). Against this all-pervasive background of protective social programs, the pro-employment program for disabled persons financed from an earmarked fund was particularly prominent and, as it were, ahead of its time, launched as it was ten years earlier than most other activation programs (Rymsza, 2011b). Yet not all areas of social policy underwent systemic change. For instance, the attempt to implement an inner market in healthcare, modeled on the Thatcherite reforms of the National Health Service in the UK, ended in fiasco,[14] and reform of the social security system was limited to reintroducing some semblance of order to the old age and disability pension schemes, which had been destabilized by inflation in the early 1990s (Rymsza, 1998, 115–129).

The essence of the first wave of social reforms by no means lay in the creation of protective programs as such, but in replacing the all-encompassing social programs (centering mostly on supply of in-kind benefits) inherited from the socialist period by selective programs. Most of these general social programs were connected with employment and with social care benefits from state-owned enterprises (Morecka, 1999). What is more, if one were to adopt a comparative perspective, the actual wages paid to workers in Poland's centrally planned economy may be regarded as having a social benefit aspect. In the Polish People's Republic, with its policy of full employment, jobs were basically a social benefit available to all adults—as were the wages, given the lack of supply-and-demand mechanisms that would enable these jobs' market value to be determined. The economic reform program implemented in the early 1990s was not about "creating" unemployment, but about bringing long-established hidden unemployment into the open, calling the huge accretion of unproductive jobs that characterized the Polish economy in the 1980s by its true name (Kryńska, 2004, 31–32). Accordingly, for many Polish citizens, the economic restructuring of the early 1990s meant a loss of social protection that was only partly compensated by access to unemployment benefits or other forms of social welfare.

What became known as the Balcerowicz Plan provided for the reduction of state regulation of the economy (at the macro level) and scaling back the social functions of the enterprises being restructured (at the micro level). Under these circumstances, it was up to the redistribution programs operating outside the labor market as part of the social security system to take over many of the welfare functions.[15] Thus, the role of the social welfare system was bound to expand, with ever-new groups of not only those immediately affected by the economic reforms, but also those who had hitherto been sustained by the now-dismantled general programs carried over from the socialist era (Hrynkiewicz, 2004). So, the general orientation towards protective measures as well as the search for ways to keep their cost down combined to produce what was very much a "reactive" social policy, clearly focused on day-to-day concerns.

The lack of a long-term social policy strategy becomes strikingly apparent if we consider that in reality the transformation of the 1990s was to a large extent a deferred effect of Solidarity's activities in 1980 and 1981. In December 1981, the communist authorities suppressed the Solidarity trade union and dissident movement by imposing martial law, but it was powerless to stop the progressive erosion of the communist system and, ten years later, sat down at the negotiation table with members of the illegal Solidarity movement to agree to the principles for democratization of the Polish state. But already during the initial upsurge of 1980–81, when the chances of successful political and economic transformation remained slim, Solidarity drew up a program paper, *The Self-Governing Republic*,[16] which proposed quite a cohesive vision for the operation of the state (Gliński, 2006; Holzer, 1990, 280–302). Ten years later, when such a vision could actually be translated into practice, the decision-makers of the Solidarity circle chose to concentrate on the economic sphere and to limit their activities in the social sphere to *ad hoc* measures. To some extent, they seem to have subscribed to the logic of transformation and to the "step-by-step" strategy, but in a way they also dropped the ball, afraid of the citizens.

The uniqueness of the Solidarity movement experience from 1980 to 1981 lay in hands-on discovery of the sheer power of collective action geared towards the common good (Ciżewska, 2010; Szawiel, 2006; Tichner, 2005). In a situation unique in the communist bloc, the public sphere in Poland, for a time, became a civic sphere. Not to be underestimated in terms of its importance in this process of discovering freedom of speech and restoring civic character of the public sphere was the first Polish pilgrimage of Pope John Paul II in 1979. This event laid the groundwork, in societal terms, for the momentous events of August 1980, culminating in legalization of the first free trade union in the eastern bloc (Ciżewska, 2010; Sowiński, 2005; Wnuk-Lipiński, 2006). This "Carnival of Solidarity" did not last long, just over one year, but for ten million members of Solidarity it amounted to a generational experience that left a permanent imprint on the collective consciousness (Hałas, 2010). The Solidarity movement was unmistakably civic in character (Krzemiński, 2006) and—an important point—civil society was spoken of not in terms of opposition to the state, but of responsibility for the state (Gawin, 2006). Hence the program paper mentioned above, *The Self-Governing Republic,* and hence the "solidarity of Solidarity" phenomenon (Ciżewska, 2010, 196–224; Crow, 2002, 90–109). Social rights or employee entitlements were not a central plank in Solidarity's platform. In my opinion, David Ost (Ost, 2005) is incorrect in his interpretation of Solidarity as first and foremost a workers' movement devised to enforce better working conditions or better pay. In fact, the question of social benefits constituted only one among many of its broader appeals of a social nature, and it is the latter that the right to industrial action achieved in the Gdansk shipyard in 1980 was intended to serve, and did serve. Formally, Solidarity was a trade union, but in reality it was a grassroots social and civic movement with broad popular support (Latoszek, 2005).

In 1989, the Round Table agreements brought the renewed legalization of Solidarity as a trade union, but, this time around, the mass social movement was not mobilized. The ensuing transformation was, to a large extent, accomplished by the elite of the Solidarity movement acting, as it were, "over the heads" of the citizenry (Pańkow, 2005). The role envisaged for the mass public essentially came down to keeping calm and staying out of the way of the completion of their mission. "The fall of communism brought [...] an instantaneous disintegration of the entire syndrome of Polish civil society—in every basic meaning of the term—progressing at breakneck speed" (Mokrzycki, 2001, 23). The new authorities feared the reaction of the workers no less than their predecessors in power had done, the difference being that these were now "our" authorities, endorsed with the mandate of democratic elections.[17] The Polish state in its new form created the framework for unfettered civic activism, with the new law regulating associations being one of the key achievements of the Round Table. Yet the assumption was that non-governmental organizations would pursue their operations, as it were, somewhere alongside those of the state; the first stage of political and economic transformations did not envisage any public role for them (Rymsza, 2008).

But does the compensation policy pursued in Poland during the first wave of social reforms (1990–93), as described above, not contradict the thesis concerning the rejection of social rights? In fact, no, it does not. This is because many of the protective measures of the 1990s were not actually associated with granting citizens claims-based social rights; they were more a matter of *ad hoc* measures taken during the transition period, mostly of a discretionary character. It is for this reason that the neoliberally inclined authors of Poland's economic shock therapy agreed to protective measures in the first place; they considered these to be an unavoidable "cost of transition". Various social benefits, the thinking went, amounted to a type of "safety valve" for the economic reforms; those receiving them were to quietly leave the labor market rather than protesting against the changes that were under way (Rymsza, 2004b). Accordingly, the most comprehensive benefits packages were offered to workers of restructured enterprises who were leaving employment as part of the waves of mass redundancies.[18]

To summarize, the social reforms of the first years of transition did not build any visible new social model in Poland. The social protection system served as a tool to compensate for the negative side effects of economic reforms that were put at the very top of the political agenda. Decision-makers tried to minimize social costs of mass unemployment in particular. The Poles were equipped with all basic political rights as well as with new opportunities for economic activity (in practice, only those able to adapt to new conditions). It could be considered paradoxical that the reforms undertaken under the umbrella of the Solidarity civil movement institutionalized social regulations and benefits that cannot be analyzed as social citizenship rights. Solidarity as a trade union consistently pursued the idea of delivering compensation to all losers of the economic transformation. That idea was accepted by the more market-oriented decision-makers as an inevitable cost of the economic shock therapy. But what looked like a consensual, stable social pact at the beginning of systemic changes appeared very controversial only a few years later. The architects of the new economic model withdrew their support for extended social transfers when they understood the "pure" market mechanisms they implemented as irreversible structural fundaments of the new Polish system. From their perspective, the only acceptable way of delivering welfare to people in need were mean-tested programs operating on a lower level than a social welfare safety net that affords clear-cut social rights. Social entitlements, especially as way of helping to strengthen citizenship, were seen as part of the communism legacy and a dead weight for ongoing modernization and economic progress.

THE SECOND WAVE OF REFORMS (1998–2000): BETWEEN DECENTRALIZATION AND MARKETIZATION IN THE SOCIAL SPHERE

The second wave of social reforms was preceded by a period of defensive rule by a coalition of postcommunist parties. In 1993, the parties of the Solidarity-derived right suffered a defeat at the polls and found themselves outside Parliament. The new government, fearing a similar fate, slowed down the reforms significantly. At the end of the 1993–97 parliamentary term, meanwhile, the national assembly (i.e., the two chambers of Polish Parliament sitting in a joint session) enacted a new constitution—an achievement the previous parliaments had not been capable of, tangled up as they were in day-to-day business. This new constitution delineated the social sphere, instituting the general rules under which Poland would follow the social market economy system (as in Germany), the public administration would follow the principles of subsidiarity and of social dialogue, and the state would guarantee social protection to its citizens. The constitution incorporated many pro-social provisions, although their wording tended to be conditional, impeding direct application in practice.[19] In consequence, the influence of the constitution on the social sphere in Poland was and is limited; the values of the constitution seem to have something of a ceremonial function, proudly proclaimed in theory but not necessarily applied in day-to-day practice (Rymsza, 2004b, 254–255).

The policy of refrainment maintained by the Polish government of the years 1993 to 1997 did not stave off an electoral defeat. The new center-right coalition installed after the elections of 1997 duly decided to take a chance on new reforms,[20] making the simultaneous introduction of systemic changes in a number of different areas from January 1999 a key plank of its platform. Their reforms, prepared over the entirety of 1998 (see Kolarska-Bobińska, 2000b), comprised (1) healthcare, (2) social insurance, (3) the operation of the public administration (e.g., continuing decentralization of social services, decentralization of employment services from the national administration to local self-government), and (4) education. Unfortunately, none of these reform programs envisioned an active role for the resurgent third sector organizations—the subsidiarity principle mentioned above enshrined in Poland's constitution has gone without an operational "openness" for civil society (Rymsza, 2008).

The reforms of 1999—unlike those of 1990 to 1993—aimed to create modern institutions in the social sphere (Kolarska-Bobińska, 2000b). Yet, as it turned out, they lacked internal cohesion. In some areas, the emphasis seemed to be on the decentralization of social policy (a good example are changes in social welfare—see Hrynkiewicz, 2001); in others, the focus was on introduction of market mechanisms (such as the pension system reform—see Rymsza, 1999). In other areas still, efforts were made to somehow combine decentralization and marketization, with generally poor results (e.g., healthcare—Dercz & Izdebski, 2004). The years 2000 and 2001 saw extensive amendments of the original legislative instruments that had introduced the reforms in 1999; work on the reform programs had been pursued at breakneck speed, and the results, in terms of quality and cohesion of the statutes, soon became apparent. In this way, day-to-day management of the social sphere by *ad hoc* tinkering with statutory instruments became something of a norm in Poland, leading to the instrumentalization of the law (Rymsza, 2003). To this day, the tendency in the mass media is to discuss not so much the quality of new laws as the number and volume of legal instruments.

Immediately on introducing the four social reforms listed above, participants in the public discourse took to describing them as "the great reforms". This adjective does not appear to have stood the test of time. The longest-lasting effects were achieved by the reform of the self-government system (Frączkiewicz-Wronka, 2002). Reform of the healthcare system was blocked after the next parliamentary election, when—true to what has become an established pattern—power reverted to the postcommunist parties,[21] and the new government replaced the regional health insurance institutions with the National Health Fund (Dercz & Izdebski, 2004). The educational system reform is now criticized as having been implemented in a hurry with significant number of side effects (Zahorska, 2004, 164). The pension system reform—the one with the most serious economic effects, modeled on World Bank proposals (see *Averting the Old Age Crisis*, 1994)— has been, for a decade or so, presented as a flagship product of the neoliberal approach. In 2011, however, the Polish government—facing a worsening public deficit aggravated, among other factors, by the fact that a portion of the pension insurance contributions are being channeled into financial institutions and by the lack of funds for disbursement under the pay-as-you-go formula—decided to temporarily readjust the contributions breakdown so as to direct more money into the public Social Insurance Fund.[22] The second wave of social reforms was a chance to build a modern cohesive system of social protection and an integrated vision of social order. Under that wave, legal instruments for systemic changes in four major areas of the social sphere were prepared. Yet the vision of the new social order was tainted by two material faults—it did not encompass civil society institutions, and it turned out to be substantively incoherent with respect to planning the activities of public entities in that it did not set out a clear direction that the reforms should take. Two basic views clashed here: one called for decentralization of social sphere institution management, and the other for subjecting them to market mechanisms. This controversy was important from the perspective of infusing social policy with a civic element. The decentralization approach may be seen as a form of "socializing" social policy and the inner-markets approach as a way to "commercialize" social policy of the state.

The operational objective of the policy of running social sphere institutions on a market basis was to introduce competition between the service providers and its accompanying mechanism under which, as opposed to the participatory solutions, consumers could vote with their feet. The pension system reform of 1999 might be cited as an example here. This reform provided for limiting of vertical and horizontal distribution through introduction of individual pension accounts and through partly commercializing the system by way of instituting a second pillar (additional pension accounts with private institutions). Participating citizens get an opportunity to vote with their feet by choosing their open pension fund and by transferring their capital from one fund to another (individually, never collectively). This solution is based on the reforms undertaken in Chile in the 1980s, when Chile was still operating under limited democracy and, thus, was—by its very definition—devoid of civic participation. In a similar spirit, in the second pillar of the Polish pension system, "voting with your feet" is not a civic right, but a consumer right. The open pension funds are not self-governing membership entities, but are operated and managed by fully commercial general pension companies; the insured persons thus do not have much possibility of taking collective action in their shared interest (Rymsza, 2007b, 78–79), with their representation taken over by business entities. In my opinion, these short-comings in the area of collective action are one of the reasons why the Chilean model, championed some time ago by the World Bank (see *Averting the Old Age Crisis*, 1994, has met with lukewarm reception among almost all of the fifteen older memberstates of the European Union,[23] where collective representation entities (trade unions, but not only) are active participants of the social protec-tion systems.

The decentralization policy, meanwhile, served to provide a real-terms dimen-sion to the idea of citizenship in that it centered on the social element of the decision-making process, on the creation of institutional conditions conducive to development of social policy at the social level, where citizens can exercise greater control. Unfortunately, this policy only strengthened local self-government insti-tutions, but it ignored civil society entities. None of the four reforms launched in 1999 provided for farming social services or other public tasks out to NGOs—the potential of civil society lay untapped and unused.

The implementation of four social reforms in the years 1999–2000 ended the first decade of transformation during which decision-makers focused on build-ing democratic institutions in the sphere of politics and introducing market mechanisms into the economy. The social policy of that time was fairly reac-tive in nature and served to promote the social acceptance of political and eco-nomic reforms. At the end of the decade, systemic reforms also covered the social sphere and social policy started a new to play a crucial role in politics. Unfortunately, that short period of time under the new regimes was not used effectively either to reinforce and consolidate the new-born civil society infra-structure or to strengthen the idea of social citizenship. The reformers focused first of all on rescheduling and rebuilding the wide range of public institutions operating in the social sphere and not so much on how they had to serve the citizens. If the Poles appeared in the reforming plans, they were treated rather as consumers whose freedom of choice in the field of social services had to be increased than as citizens with rights that had to be secured by the state. If one analyzes the period from 1998 to 2000 from the perspective of developing the idea of citizenship, one must conclude that these two limitations—the failure to appreciate the potential of NGOs and the lack of program cohesion—appear to be a series of missed opportunities. The policy of investment in the third crucial element of the newly (re)built regime beside the market and a democratic state, the civil society, had to wait for better times in Poland.

RENAISSANCE AND REDEFINITION OF THE CIVIC CITIZENSHIP CONCEPT OF T. H. MARSHALL

The years after the implementation of social reforms of the second wave are marked by political polarization with respect to social policy issues. A market-oriented group of decision-makers started to force through the policy of deregulation, the idea of ongoing commercialization in the social sphere, and, above all, the program of significant cuts in social spending. The opponents supported the policy of social protection. Neither of those groups was strong enough to win the battle, which created a space for articulating a policy of a middle way with its mission going beyond this controversy. This third-way social policy focused not on the question of how much to spend on social programs but how to use available resources. It was a shift toward a paradigm of activation that proved acceptable for both polarized groups of decision-makers. The policy of activation stressed the importance of both elements omitted in previous reforms: social citizenship and civil society. What was more, it combined them in a cohesive political project. This was possible because the idea of social citizenship was interpreted in a very modern way according to new European ideas (see the analysis of different aspects of this process in Chapter 1). The paradigm of activation was also legitimized by the EU structures (in 2004 Poland together with other central and eastern European countries became a full member of the EU) and resulted in the third wave of social reforms. To make this trend more understandable, we need to give a short account of the process of reshaping the idea of social citizenship that happened in Europe during the late 20th and early 21st centuries.

The very idea of citizenship is undergoing something of a renaissance in Europe. Beginning in the 1990s, the comparative social policy literature has demonstrated a new interest in the concept of social citizenship, as formulated in the early 1950s by T. H. Marshall (Marshall, 1950) (see Bulmer & Rees, 1996; Turner, 2000). This is coupled with a redefinition of the idea of social citizenship in line with the premises of an active social policy. Instead of "passive" citizenship, defined in terms of the rights of the citizen *vis-à-vis* the state (including social privileges guaranteed by the welfare state), the focus is now on "active" citizenship, defined in terms of membership in a community and entailing, apart from rights (again, including social entitles), also duties *vis-à-vis* this community (van Berkel & Valkenburg, 2007, 8).

It should be noted that associating the idea of citizenship with the state as well as with civil society is equally legitimate. There can be no citizens without a state, but there can also be no full citizenship without civil society. This current shift of emphasis in interpreting citizenship is associated with an increased appreciation of participation in the functioning of democracy. Thus, Marshall's concept of full (multidimensional) citizenship is being associated more with development of civil society than of the state (Janoski, 1998; Turner, 2000).

To fully grasp this interpretation of the social citizenship concept, it is advisable to keep in mind the earlier evolution (which occurred, as it were, in the opposite direction) of the other concept that is central to Marshall's idea—that of de-commodification (Marshall, 1950).[24] Marshall regarded the implementation of the three-dimensional concept of citizenship (viewed as an assemblage of civil, political, and social rights) as a path towards a cohesive but not necessarily egalitarian society (Giddens, 1996, 65). In other words, de-commodification as defined by Marshall was a means towards limiting class divisions, not free market institutions.[25] As noted in Chapter 1, Marshall's citizenship rights should not replace the market but moderate its impact, and it was never Marshall's intention to make people completely independent of the market. This realism was not necessarily shared by the continuators of Marshall's work. The concept of de-commodification that took root in the social democratic social policy model departed significantly from that originally posited by the British sociologist. The architects of the institutional-redistributive welfare state model were generally quite open about their dislike for free-market solutions and tended to treat the de-commodification principle in egalitarian terms, as a formulation of the desire to fully decouple citizens' material living standards from their economic activity.[26] Taken in this way, the principle of de-commodification called into question the economic rationality of activity in the labor market as an exchange devised to result in benefits to both parties in the employment relationship.[27] Accordingly, this version of de-commodification has been challenged by liberal and conservative critics of the welfare state, who point out that social welfare granted unconditionally to citizens who are perfectly capable of engaging in gainful employment demotivates, deactivates, and, in consequence, marginalizes them (see Mead, 1997). The crisis of the European welfare states that began in the 1980s has led to similar criticism of de-commodification also in leftist circles.

These developments coincided with the emergence of the workfare concept in the European discourse, already familiar from the United States (Handler, 2004). The activation and "disciplinary" solutions implemented for American welfare recipients in 1994 as part of reform of the federal social welfare system (Handler & Hasenfeld, 2007; Ziliak, 2009) were eventually replicated in many European countries (Lødemel & Trickey, 2000). That said, there are some basic differences between the original American workfare and the European concept of "social inclusion through work," particularly at the normative level (Karwacki & Rymsza, 2011). While workfare unequivocally refers to the rhetoric of individual self-responsibility and the theory of the underclass in its conservative rendition (see Murray, 1984, 1996), the European policy of social inclusion and its attendant work (re)integration programs bear the hallmarks of Durkheim's concept of organic solidarity based on a functional division of labor in society and work roles (see Glorieux, 1999, 68; van Berkel & Møller, 2002, 4). In this regard, active social policy adheres close to the imponderables of the European social policy tradition, which refers to building social bonds and social cohesion (Rymsza, 2007b).

In the 1990s, European decision-makers—including social democratic politicians—came to realize in growing numbers that paid employment is more than simply a way to earn a living; it also provides a place in a social structure, prestige, contacts, and other intangible assets that cannot be provided by the state and that enable people to fully participate in the life of society. If, then, policies pursued by the state actually discourage people capable of working from seeking jobs and holding them down, the state is promoting social marginalization. In the European version of an active social policy, the assumption is that "inclusive" work ought to fulfill two conditions. First, the dignity of workers ought to be respected at the level of employment conditions, so that the work itself does not become a factor of alienation. Second, the work must be useful to society, for only then can it draw workers into the mutual exchanges around which society is constructed. The work may be subsidized, performed less efficiently, at a higher cost, but—to put it in the language of economics—there must be real demand for the results of such work. Europeans came to realize once again that, as taught by Émile Durkheim (Durkheim, 1999), permanent rootedness in the social system requires that specific individuals are assigned specific functions in the labor market, producing—in turn—unavoidable social stratification, which reflects the inequalities perpetuated by the market. As viewed by Durkheim, social stratification is the consequence of the social rootedness of individuals (Kaczmarczyk, 2005, 14–15). From the perspective of Durkheim (also adopted by Marshall), social policy can, and should, limit social stratification—but not at the price of vocational deactivation that leads to uprooting or marginalization of entire social groups, in that this would weaken social cohesion, an overriding value for both sociologists.

One could say that a policy of inclusion through work amounts to the de-legitimization of the de-commodification principle "from within"—not by opponents of state involvement in the social sphere, but by its proponents (Rymsza, 2003). The European proponents of the activation approach are not out to deconstruct the welfare state, but to reconstruct it; they are not seeking to reject, but to extrapolate Marshall's idea of citizenship by associating it with actual participation of citizens in all aspects of civic life.

To summarize, Marshall is being discovered anew. This time, however, he is not being interpreted as an apologist for an ever-expanding welfare state, but as a social researcher and a propagator of a civic vision of social order. Contemporary debates over how to implement the idea of citizenship in the established welfare states of Europe are a manifestation of the search for a new balance between different aspects of citizenship—between its passive and active components, between the rights carried by citizenship and the duties it entails, between state-based elements of social citizenship and those that are rooted in society. The reinterpretation of the idea of citizenship also flows from the observation that, contrary to Marshall's intuitive feeling, political and civic "achievements" do not naturally accrete over into consecutive spheres of social rights, but are altogether in need of continuous recreation and legitimation by the community of citizens. In consequence, each single aspect of the multidimensionally construed citizenship coexists in a field of tension, where the realization of some may possibly impede the realization of others.

THE THIRD WAVE OF REFORMS (2003–04): TOWARDS AN ACTIVATION APPROACH

The obvious fault of the protective approach to social policy that was favored during the first decade of political and economic transformations in Poland lay in the fact that the beneficiaries of social support were prone to the temptation of deactivation. The accepted wisdom, proved wrong by later events, was that if people driven out of the job market could somehow survive the period of restructuring, the market economy would be capable of absorbing these surplus workers later of its own accord. According to some projections, employment would begin increasing again once jobless Poles came to number between 1 and 1.5 million. In reality, joblessness peaked at well past 3 million, and the labor market seemed in no hurry to take up this surplus labor (Kryńska, 1999). It became painfully obvious that the Polish state had to put active labor market programs (Kryńska, 2004) and active social policy in place (Kaźmierczak & Rymsza, 2003). Beginning in 2002 (i.e., in the immediate lead-up to Poland's accession to the EU), a new theme appeared in Polish social policy, namely the implementation of EU priorities, also with respect to active labor market programs, counteracting social exclusion, and the operation of activation services. Thus, increased interest in the concept of active social policy resulted from the conjunction of two factors: (1) Poland's nationally specific experiences of economic and political transformation, one of the corollaries of which is the conviction that protective social policy measures have largely outlived their usefulness; and (2) the implementation of EU priorities in the field of active labor market policy and active social policy.

Official recognition of the active role that public services may play in counteracting unemployment and social exclusion came in 2002 with the policy document *Strategia Polityki Społecznej 2002–2005* ("Social Policy Strategy 2002–2005"). In its wake, four legislative acts were adopted in the period 2003 through 2004, combining into a package of legal regulations geared towards the popularization of activating measures (Rymsza, 2007a). These included (1) legislation on public benefit activity and volunteer work in 2003, (2) legislation on social employment in 2003, (3) legislation on employment promotion and labor market institutions in 2004, and (4) legislation on social welfare in 2004.

Sometime later, this raft of legislative instruments was supplemented by (5) legislation on social cooperatives in 2006.

The legislation regarding public benefit activity and volunteer work amounted to a practical implementation of the constitutional principle of subsidiarity, obliging public services to work together with the third-sector entities (Rymsza, Hryniewicka & Derwich, 2004). It instituted a framework for cooperation between public institutions and non-governmental nonprofit organizations (third-sector organizations), of which many are involved in activation services. The legislation on social employment gave the local self-government institutions and third-sector organizations the possibility of operating social integration centers. Eight years down the line, about 50 rather cost-intensive and moderately effective social integration centers are in operation (Karwacki, 2010). The basic objective of the legislation on employment promotion and labor market institutions lay in the professionalization of the public employment services. The idea was that services of this sort should be provided first of all by qualified personnel with mediating and career advisory skills. This Act also accorded the status of an accredited labor market service institution to job agencies operating on a nonprofit basis within the third sector; in Poland, such non-governmental agencies constitute the basic recourse for disabled jobseekers, who are generally marginalized in the state-public system (Bartkowski & Giermanowska, 2007). The adoption of the legislative act on social welfare brought about introduction of social contracts to the practice of social welfare centers. On the other hand, Polish social welfare still follows a strategy where social work is combined with the disbursement of financial assistance. This strategy, however, is becoming the target of growing criticism, also from social workers—handling of benefit disbursements is seen as producing hypertrophied bureaucratic structures within the social welfare centers (Rymsza, 2011a). Social cooperatives created under the regulations of the 2006 act are a kind of legal hybrid (something between social enterprises and NGOs—see Izdebski, 2006). The tribulations of the approximately 240 social cooperatives registered in Poland demonstrate that, in general, these are weak institutions that find it difficult to operate on the market (Juros, 2008). The Act transposes to Polish ground solutions familiar from Italy (see Loss, 2008). The Act was amended in 2009 to strengthen the social cooperatives in their economic and institutional aspects (Brzozowska, 2010).

The legal regulations mentioned above were rather puzzling. In 2005 the government put the project of a "frame" act on active social policy before Parliament, but it was not passed. Thus, the future of activation policy in Poland remains undecided. Nevertheless, the social reforms of the third wave (2003–04 and subsequently) were an effort to include Poland in the mainstream of European social policies. A new concept is now taking shape in Europe, generally referred to as active social policy (van Berkel & Møller, 2002). "Active" social policy basically represents an alternative to "passive" policy (one that restricts its activities basically to handing over social transfers). According to the traditional take on social issues, the main goal of state intervention lies in guaranteeing social security for all citizens. The activation approach, meanwhile, places more emphasis on guaranteeing participation in social life, especially participation in the labor market by members of marginalized communities and groups—even at the expense of weakening their social safety net (this is known as conditional support).[28]

At the same time, the reforms of the third wave are a rather half-hearted and inconsistent attempt on the part of the state to rectify the errors and address the limitations of the previous reform projects. The policy of activation and social inclusion through work is a response to the mass unemployment that constitutes the most pressing of the unresolved problems of the social transformation (Tarkowska, 2006). As it turned out, contrary to the expectations of some, the restructured economy has been slow to absorb excess labor. Accordingly, the view has prevailed that the unemployed, especially those who—for instance due to disability—are less capable of fending for themselves, should receive help from the public services in gaining their footing on the job market. In other words, social benefits should, as far as possible, activate clients and improve their employability.

Some 15 years after the launch of political and economic reforms in Poland, decision-makers in the political sphere began to develop an appreciation for the potential of NGOs with respect to vocational and social activation and for the role they can play as mediating structures improving the empowerment of citizens.[29] During the first years, third-sector organizations, much like the public services, focused primarily on protective measures but, soon enough, their focus shifted to activating their clients. But Polish nonprofit organizations remain economically weak; when they enter into cooperation with the state, they tend to develop a dependency on public funding, to the detriment of their civic character. Public social services, meanwhile, do not seem to be adopting an empowerment orientation. Social contracts and other activation instruments are applied on a routine basis more as a form of managing the nascent underclass (Racław, 2012) than as citizenship-based social work in the modern sense of the term (van Ewijk, 2010). Those social reintegration programs that are in operation now put a premium not on social entrepreneurship, but on social employment with low productivity and high costs. This is not conducive to the eventual independence of the clients, neither is it helpful when it comes to building a good image of work-integrated social enterprises. Social enterprises operating in rural areas stand a better chance of taking root in local markets, but, so far, these are few in number (Kaźmierczak & Rymsza, 2008). Despite all this, the social activation approach has considerable potential for growth.

CONCLUSION

After 1989, Polish social policy was for approximately 15 years dominated by protective measures designed to counteract the negative side effects of the economic reforms. The scope of social support for those who lost out on these reforms was considerable, especially in the initial years. This was due to fear among decision-makers about the level of social acceptance for the rapid transformations they set in motion. The intended role of these social programs was to appease suffering citizens and maintain social order, rather than to activate citizens as independent entities. There followed a tendency whereby social spending was gradually scaled back and the circle of clients reduced, with the income criterion becoming an ever-more-widespread tool for defining entitlement. This tendency arose due to budgetary constraints, but also because of a growing conviction that the systemic changes were now a permanent, well-entrenched achievement no longer at risk of abandonment or reversal. The dispute between proponents of protective policies and those who favored radical social cuts escalated. The activation policy, however, went above and beyond this dispute, concentrating not on the level of spending on social programs, but on their allocation. T. H. Marshall has emphasized (Marshall, 1975, 206) that the social rights of the citizens should be guaranteed not only by the state, but also by broad social legitimation for the transfers of resources effectuated via the social protection system. It is my conviction that the activation orientation as a "middle way" presents a real opportunity for building such legitimation, and that this is the most important single argument in favor of the continuation of the activation approach in Poland (and beyond).

On the other hand, Poland needs to strike a balance between the "passive" and "active" components of social citizenship. One of the main goals of social policy implemented in Poland during the second decade of the transformation was the shift towards an activation paradigm. The problem of that policy is connected with the fact that according to "sequence-based logic" described by Marshall, step number four (implementing active social citizenship, which goes beyond Marshall's triple sequence) has to be preceded by Marshall's step three: establishing "passive" social rights of citizens. As I have argued, step number four is in fact much more than just reshaping the result of the former phase; it is an effort to balance the entitlements discovered under all earlier phases, and a way to implement "whole" multidimensional citizenship. It seems that Polish decision-makers have somehow tried to reach phase four without going through phase three. This means that the active citizenship organized by civil society structures is defined by decision-makers as an alternative to passive social entitlements guaranteed by the state. Such active citizenship without state guarantees may end up rather weak and unsatisfactory for the citizens.

It must also be added that the European civil tradition is based on Hegel's vision of the union between the state and civil society (see Fink, 1981; Reichardt, 2004, 48), which allows space for different kinds of cooperation between public administration and third-sector entities and rather limited opportunities for definite shifts of obligation from structures of one kind to another. It seems that social policy in Poland in the coming years will need a new kind of synthesis.

Poland must travel a road together with other European countries to surpass the limits put on the idea of citizenship in Marshall's vision. But more "homework" connected with the implementation of Marshall's phase three has to be done as well.

NOTES

1 The term "transformation" was coined just to give a distinctive name for structural changes in central and eastern European countries. But the "convergences" of the "old EU-15"—although implemented in much less radical ways—has in fact a similar nature.

2 Haggard and Kaufmann consider the political and economic transformations in central and eastern Europe to be a process parallel to democratization of certain countries in South America and in Southeast Asia, regarding these three regions as "developing"—as opposed to the "developed" countries of western Europe or North America. Similarly, Arts and Gelissen classify the countries of central and eastern Europe as emerging welfare states that are at a different stage of development than established welfare states.

3 Insufficient interest in the social democratic model has been criticized by Esping-Andersen himself, whose successive works brought a gradual shift in perspective from that of an impartial researcher comparing the relative merits of three different social policy models to that of an expert propagating the social democratic model (see Esping-Andersen, 2002).

4 See the analysis of the process of Americanization of social policy in Europe in Jordan (1996).

5 At the time of establishment of the Bismarckian social security institutions, Poland was not an independent state, having been partitioned by Germany, the Hapsburg Empire, and Russia in the late 18th century and remaining that way until 1918. At the turn of the 19th and 20th centuries, Germany followed by the Hapsburg Empire adopted the Bismarckian solutions, with the result that they were also implemented in the western and southern parts of what would become Poland. Russia (and the eastern Polish reaches), meanwhile, only had simple social institutions at a very modest scale. After the regaining of Poland's independence in 1918, the Polish authorities worked to forge the various social solutions "inherited" from the partitioning powers into new institutions, although the Bismarckian influence prevailed (see Auleytner, 1994). In this way, during the two world wars, Poland contributed to the continental tradition of social policy, or to what Titmuss terms the achievement-performance model (Titmuss, 1974) or Esping-Andersen calls the conservative model (Esping-Andersen, 1990).

6 These factors would also include the impact of the global economic crisis from 2008 on the social policy of European countries (Jordan, 2010).

7 Please refer to the clear and lucid differentiation between welfare state retrenchment and welfare state reconstruction offered by Clasen (2007, 13–19).

8 New characteristics of the ideological social policy models after one decade have been presented by Robert Goodin and his colleagues (Goodin et al., 2001), and with respect to Europe only by Maurizio Ferrera and Martin Rhodes (Ferrera & Rhodes, 2000).

9 As far as the social sphere is concerned, operation of purely administrative EU bodies and institutions on the member-states should not be overestimated (see Kvist & Saari, 2007).

10 The concept of waves of reform has been formulated in the context of research by the Institute of Public Affairs (Kolarska-Bobińska, 2000a, b; Rymsza, 2004a). The sequence of distinguished three waves of Polish reforms is described in Polish in Rymsza (2004b).

11 With the reservation that, in this case, we were looking at restructuring of traditional industry, not at industrialization.

12 Employer organizations did not support this program for the simple reason that they were not in operation yet.

13 During the socialist period, the problem of unemployment also existed, although it was a hidden one. Its visible manifestation lay in over-employment (nonproductive employment in jobs created out of ideological rather than economic considerations), which led to chronic nonprofitability of state-owned enterprises and of the economy as a whole.

14 Here the real issue was an uncontrolled commercialization of healthcare (see Golinowska, 2000, 82–84), a process that is ongoing.

15 The exception was the mechanisms enabling early retirement. The policy of according pension benefits on favorable terms (taken up by more than one million Poles) translated, in the long term, into a significant strain on public finances; it is a case in point as regards the fears harbored by the liberal decision-makers concerning social reactions to unemployment.

16 Originally it was a name of the most important chapter of the document.

17 This is a simplification of sorts. The elections held in Poland in 1989 were democratic only in part, and the Solidarity government installed in its wake had to negotiate the reform program with representatives of the former communist elite; this may well have been one of the underlying causes of the elitism of the reformers, who feared that, should the citizenry at large become too active, the compromises they achieved may not stand. The first entirely free election in Poland was held in 1991, and it was only then that Poland joined the Council of Europe.

18 The exact terms of the group redundancies varied from industry to industry, the rule being that the better organized (and more capable of mounting protests) the given sector, the higher the severance benefits. Accordingly, the most valuable benefits went to coal miners, and the lowest to employees of defunct textile mills.

19 For instance, the constitution does not name social insurance as a specific social security institution, so implementation of radical pension system reforms modeled after World Bank recommendations was possible.

20 At this point, the prime minister was Prof. Jerzy Buzek, later President of the European Parliament.

21 Over the past 20 years, not a single ruling party has succeeded in retaining power after the next parliamentary elections in Poland.

22 Such a solution is typical of countries that have opted for introducing some commercial elements to their pension systems (e.g., nationalization of pension funds in Argentina and freezing of the contributions). The World Bank has likewise abandoned wide propagation of capital-based pension funds to the exclusion of other mechanisms.

23 The World Bank ideas were reflected to some extend by the Swedish reform of pension system implemented in 1999.

24 It would appear that what we are dealing with here is an "action–reaction" system often described by political scientists in reference to the pendulum analogy: an excessive conceptual or ideological swing in one direction produces an equally pronounced reaction in the opposite direction.

25 As emphasized in the very title of Marshall's essay, "Citizenship and social class" (Marshall 1950).

26 It is in this version that de-commodification is cited by Esping-Andersen as a key trait of the social democratic model of social policy (Esping-Andersen, 1990, 16).

27 In classical economics, a win–win situation obtains when there is an equilibrium between labor demand and supply.

28 Conditional support, by the way, is the element of this entire concept that engenders the greatest controversies as well as different understandings—see the remarks on conditionality under policies of activating citizens in Chapter 1.

29 The ideal of empowerment as currently used in European social inclusion strategies is too much simplified and linked to public administration programs. In fact, empowerment is a result of accumulation of social capital within the civil society structures. See the classic concept of empowerment as a "product" of nonprofit mediating structures activities in Berger & Neuhaus (1977).

REFERENCES

Albert, M. (1994). *Kapitalizm kontra kapitalizm*. Kraków: Znak.

Arts, W. A., & J. Gelissen. (2010). Models of welfare state. In F. Castles et al. (Eds.), *The Oxford handbook of the welfare state*. Oxford: Oxford University Press.

Auleytner, J. (1994). *Polityka społeczna. Pomiędzy ideą a działaniem*. Warszawa: Instytut Polityki Społecznej Uniwersytetu Warszawskiego.

Averting the Old Age Crisis (1994). Oxford: Oxford University Press.

Bartkowski, J., & E. Giermanowska (2007). *Urzędy pracy wobec problemu bezrobocia młodych osób niepełnosprawnych*, "Analizy i Opinie" No 70, Warszawa: Instytut Spraw Publicznych.

Beck, U. (1992). *Risk society: Towards a new modernity.* New Delhi: Sage.

Berger, P., & R. Neuhaus (1977). *To empower people: The role of mediating structures in public policy.* Washington, D.C.: American Enterprise Institute.

Bonoli, G. (2010). The politics of new social policies: Providing coverage against new social risks in mature welfare states. In C. Pierson & F. Castles (Eds.), *The welfare state reader.* Cambridge: Polity Press.

Brzozowska, J. (2010). *Rozwój spółdzielni socjalnych w Polsce na tle nowelizacji Ustawy o spółdzielniach socjalnych*, Trzeci Sektor, No 21.

Bulmer, M., & A. M. Rees (Eds.) (1996). *Citizenship today. The contemporary relevance of T.H. Marshall.* London: UCL Press.

Castles, F. (Ed.) (2007). *The disappearing state? Retremchment realities in an age of globalisation.* Cheltenhem and Northampton, MA: Edward Elgar.

Ciżewska, E. (2010). *Filozofia publiczna Solidarności.* Warszawa: Narodowe Centrum Kultury.

Clasen, J. (2007). *Reforming European welfare states. Germany and the United Kingdom compared.* Oxford: Oxford University Press.

Coleman, D. (2010). Population ageing: An unavoidable future. In C. Pierson & F. Castles (Eds.), *The welfare state reader.* Cambridge: Polity Press.

Crow, G. (2002). *Social solidarities. Theories, identities and social change.* Buckingham and Philadelphia: Open University Press.

Deacon, B. (1993). Developments in east European social policy. In: C. Jones (Ed.), *New perspectives in the welfare state in Europe.* London: Routledge.

Dercz, M., & H. Izdebski (2004). Zmian w ochronie zdrowia: permanentna reforma systemu. In M. Rymsza (Ed.), *Reformy społeczne. Bilans dekady.* Warszawa: Instytut Spraw Publicznych.

Durkheim, D. (1999). *The division of labor in society.* New York: The Free Press.

Dziewięcka-Bokun, L. (2002). *Rola państwa w realizacji polityki społecznej okresie transformacji ustrojowej w Polsce.* "Problemy Polityki Społecznej. Studia i Dyskusje, No 2.

Esping-Andersen, G. (1990). *The three worlds of welfare capitalism.* Cambridge: Cambridge University Press.

Esping-Andersen, G. (2002). Towards the good society, once again. In: G. Esping-Andersen with D. Gallie, A. Hemerijck, J. Myles, *Why we need a new welfare state.* Oxford: Oxford University Press.

Ferrera, M., & M. Rhodes (Eds.) (2000). *Recasting European welfare states.* London: Frank Cass.

Fink, F. (1981). *Social philosophy.* London: Methuen.

Flora, P., & A. Heidenheimer (Eds.) (1981). *The development of welfare states in Europe and America.* Brunswick: Transition Books.

Frączkiewicz-Wronka, A. (Ed.) (2002). *Samorządowa polityka społeczna*. Warszawa: Wyższa Szkoła Pedagogiczna TWP w Warszawie.

Gawin, D. (2006). Sierpień 1980 w świetle tradycji republikańskiej. In A. Sułek (Ed.), *Solidarność. Wydarzenia, sekwencji, pamięć*. Warszawa: Wydawnictwo IFiS PAN.

Giddens, A. (1996). T. H. Marshall, the state and democracy. In M. Bulmer & A. M. Rees (Eds.), *Citizenship today. The contemporary relevance of T.H. Marshall*. London: UCL Press.

Giddens, A. (1998). *The third way. The renewal of social democracy*. Oxford: Blackewell Publishers.

Giddens, A. (2002). *Where now for New Labour*. Cambridge: Polity Press.

Gliński, P. (2006). Samorządna Rzeczpospolita w Trzeciej Rzeczpospolitej. In A. Sułek (Ed.), *Solidarność. Wydarzenia, sekwencji, pamięć*. Warszawa: Wydawnictwo IFiS PAN.

Glorieux, I. (1999). *Paid work: A crucial link between individuals and society? Some conclusions on the meaning of work for social integration*. In P. Lettlewood with I. Glorieux, S. Herkommer, I. Jönsson (Eds.), *Social exclusion in Europe. Problems and paradigms*. Aldershot: Ashgate.

Golinowska, S. (2000). *Polityka społeczna. Koncepcje—instytucje—koszty*. Warszawa: Poltext.

Goodin, R., B. Headey, R. Muffels, & H. J. Dirven (2001). *The real worlds of welfare capitalism*. Cambridge: Cambridge University Press.

Haggard, K., & R. Kaufman. (2009). The eastern European welfare state in comparative perspective. In A. Cerami & P. Vanhuysse (Eds.), *Post-communist welfare pathways. Theorizing social policy transformations in central and eastern Europe*. Basingstoke & New York: Palgrave Macmillan.

Hałas, E. (2010*). Symbolic construction of Solidarity: The conflict of interpretations and the politics of memory.* "Polish Sociological Review", 2.

Handler, J. F. (2004). *Social citizenship and workfare in the United States and western Europe. The paradox of inclusion*. Cambridge: Cambridge University Press.

Handler, J. F., & Y. Hasenfeld (2007). *Blame welfare, ignore poverty and inequality*. Cambridge: Cambridge University Press.

Holzer. J. (1990). *Solidarność 1980–1981. Geneza i historia*. Warszawa: Agencja Omnipress.

Hrynkiewicz, J. (Ed.) (2001). *Decentralizacja funkcji społecznej państwa*. Warszawa: Instytut Spraw Publicznych.

Hrynkiewicz, J. (2004). Zakres i kierunki zmian w pomocy społecznej. In M. Rymsza (Ed.), *Reformy społeczne. Bilans dekady*. Warszawa: Instytut Spraw Publicznych.

Izdebski, H. (2006). *Spółdzielnie socjalne a organizacje pozarządowe—przewidywane skutki Ustawy o spółdzielniach socjalnych*, "Trzeci Sektor" No 7.

Janoski, T. (1998). *Citizenship and civil society*. Cambridge: Cambridge University Press.

Jones, C. (1985). *Patterns of social policy. An introduction to comparative analysis*. London and New York: Tavistock Publications.

Jordan, B. (1996). *A theory of poverty and social exclusion*. Cambridge: Polity Press.

Jordan, B. (2010). *What is wrong with social policy and how to fix it*. Cambridge: Polity Press.

Juros, A. (2008). *Social co-operatives and the third sector*. "Trzeci Sektor"—special English edition.

Kaczmarczyk, M. (2005). Pojęcie Solidarności w teorii socjologicznej. In M. Latoszek (Ed.), *Solidarność w imieniu narodu i obywateli*. Kraków: Wydawnictwo ARCANA.

Karwacki, A. (2010). *Centra integracji społecznej w świetle badań—problemy i wyzwania badawcze*. Trzeci Sektor, No 21.

Karwacki, A., & M. Rymsza (2011). Meandry upowszechniania koncepcji aktywnej polityki społecznej w Polsce. In M. Grewiński & M. Rymsza (Eds.), *Polityka aktywizacji w Polsce. Usługi reintegracji w sektorze gospodarki społecznej*. Warszawa: Elipsa and Wydawnictwo WSP TWP W Warszawie.

Kaźmierczak, T., & M. Rymsza (Eds.) (2003). *W stronę aktywnej polityki społecznej*. Warszawa: Instytut Spraw Publicznych.

Kaźmierczak, T., & M. Rymsza (2008). Social entrepreneurship and development of neglected rural communities. In J. Giza-Poleczczuk & J. Hausner (Eds.), *The social economy in Poland: Achievements, barriers to growth, and potential in light of research results*. Warsaw: Foundation of Social and Economic Activities (available at: www.rci.org.pl).

Kennett, P. (2008). *Comparative social policy*. Maidenhead and New York: Open University Press.

Kolarska-Bobińska, L. (Ed.). (2000a). *Cztery reformy. Od koncepcji do realizacji*. Warszawa: Instytut Spraw Publicznych.

Kolarska-Bobińska, L. (Ed.). (2000b). *The second wave of Polish reforms*. Warsaw: Institute of Public Affairs.

Kowalik, T. (Ed.) (2001). *Spory wokół Nowej Trzeciej Drogi*. Warszawa: Fundacja Eberta.

Kryńska, E. (1999). *Socjalne skutki zmian w zatrudnieniu i dochodach z pracy w okresie przebudowy*. Warszawa: Instytut Pracy i Spraw Socjalnych.

Kryńska, E. (2004). Zmiany w obszarze zatrudnienia i przeciwdziałania bezrobociu: w kierunku równowagi na rynku pracy. In M. Rymsza (Ed.), *Reformy społeczne. Bilans dekady*. Warszawa: Instytut Spraw Publicznych.

Krzemiński, I. (2006). Solidarność—organizacja polskich nadziei. In: A. Sułek (Ed.), *Solidarność. Wydarzenia, sekwencji, pamięć*. Warszawa: Wydawnictwo IFiS PAN.

Kurczewski, J. (2009). *Ścieżki emancypacji. Osobista teoria transformacji ustrojowej w Polsce*, Warszawa: TRIO.

Kvist, J., & J. Saari (Ed.) (2007). *The Europeanisation of social welfare protection*. Bristol: The Policy Press.

Latoszek, M. (2005). Solidarność: ruch społeczny, rewolucja czy powstanie? In M. Latoszek (Ed.), *Solidarność w imieniu narodu i obywateli*. Kraków: Wydawnictwo ARCANA.

Lødemel, I., & H. Trickey (Eds.) (2000). *An offer you can't refuse*. Bristol: The Polity Press.

Loss, M. (2008). *Social cooperatives in Italy,* "Third Sector" – special English Edition.

Luhmann, N. (1981). *Politische Theorie im Wohlfahrsstaat*. München: Günter Olzog Verlag GmbH.

Marshall, T. H. (1950). *Citizenship and social class and other essays,* Cambridge: Cambridge University Press.

Marshall, T. H. (1975). *Social policy in the twentieth century*. London: Hutchinson.

Mead, L. M. (1997). From welfare to work. Lessons from America. In L. M. Mead et al., *From welfare to work. Lessons from America*. London: IEA Health and Welfare Unit.

Mokrzycki, E. (2001). Jaką mamy demokrację? In H. Domański, A. Ostrowska, & A. Rychard (Eds.), *Jak żyją Polacy?* Warszawa: Wydawnictwo IFiS PAN.

Morecka, Z. (Ed.) (1999). *Skutki likwidacji i ograniczenia działalności socjalnej i kulturalnej zakładów pracy*. Warszawa: Instytut Pracy i Spraw Socjalnych.

Murray, C. (1984). *Losing ground. American social policy 1950–1980*. New York: Basic Books.

Murray, C. (1996). The emerging of British underclass. In: *Charles Murray and the underclass. The developing debate*. London: IEA Health and Welfare Unit.

Ost, D. (2005). *The defeat of Solidarity. Anger and politics in postcommunist Europe*. London: Cornell University Press.

Pańkow, I. (2005). Tożsamość członków elit politycznych a tradycja solidarnościowa: konfuzja i iluzja. In M. Latoszek (Ed.), *Solidarność w imieniu narodu i obywateli*. Kraków: Wydawnictwo ARCANA.

Racław, M. (2012). Zmiany w pracy socjalnej z rodzina: w kierunku kontroli stylu zycia i zarzadzania marginalizacja. In: M. Rymsza (Ed.), *Pracownicy socjalni i praca socjalna w Polsce. Miedzy sluzba spoleczna a urzedem*. Warszawa: Instytut Spraw Publicznych.

Reichardt, S. (2004). Civil society—A concept for comparative historical research. In A. Zimmer & E. Priller (Eds.), *Future of civil society. Making central European nonprofit organizations work*. Wiesbaden: VS Verlag für Sozialwissenschaften.

Rymsza, M. (1998). *Urynkowienie państwa czy uspołecznienie rynku*. Warszawa: Tepis.

Rymsza, M. (1999). *The sociotechnics of the reform of national insurance system in Poland*. "Prace ISNS" No 2, Warsaw: Institute of Applied Social Sciences, Warsaw University.

Rymsza, M. (2003). *Instrumentalizacja prawa. Reformowanie sfery socjalnej w Polsce w perspektywie socjologii legislacji.* "Prace ISNS" No 5.

Rymsza, M. (Ed.) (2004a). *Reformy społeczne. Bilans dekady.* Warszawa: Instytut Spraw Publicznych.

Rymsza, M. (2004b). *Reformy społeczne lat dziewięćdziesiątych: próba podsumowania.* In M. Rymsza (Ed.), *Reformy społeczne. Bilans dekady.* Warszawa: Instytut Spraw Publicznych.

Rymsza, M. (2005). W poszukiwaniu równowagi między elastycznością rynku pracy i bezpieczeństwem socjalnym. Polska w drodze do flexicurity. In M. Rymsza (Ed.), *Elastyczny rynek pracy i bezpieczeństwo socjalne. Flexicurity po polsku?* Warszawa: Instytut Spraw Publicznych.

Rymsza, M. (2007a). Rola służb społecznych w upowszechnaniu aktywnej polityki społecznej. In M. Grewiński & J. Tyrowicz (Eds.), *Aktywizacjam, partnerstwo, partycypacja—o odpowiedzialnej polityce społecznej.* Warszawa: Mazowieckie Centrum Polityki Społecznej.

Rymsza, M. (2007b). *Sozialpolitik und soziale Bindungen.* Transit No 32, Vienna: Institute for Human Sciences.

Rymsza, M. (2008). *State policy towards the civic sector in Poland in the years 1989–2007.* "Trzeci Sektor"—special English edition.

Rymsza, M. (Ed.) (2011a). *Czy podejście aktywizujące ma szansę? Pracownicy socjalni i praca socjalna w Polsce 20 lat po reformie systemu pomocy społeczne.* Warszawa: Instytut Spraw Publicznych.

Rymsza, M. (2011b). Rehabilitacja zawodowa osób niepełnosprawnych a zatrudnienie socjalne w sektorze gospodarki społecznej: problem dualności systemów wsparcia. In M. Grewiński & M. Rymsza (Eds.), *Polityka aktywizacji w Polsce. Usługi reintegracyjne w sektorze gospodarki społecznej.* Warszawa: Elipsa & Wydawnictwo WSP TWP w Warszawie.

Rymsza, M., A. Hryniewicka, & P. Derwich (2004). Zasada pomocniczości państwa w Ustawie o działalności pożytku publicznego i o wolontariacie. In M. Rymsza (Ed.), *Współpraca sektora obywatelskiego z administracją publiczną.* Warszawa: Instytut Spraw Publicznych.

Scharpf, F., & V. Schmidt (Eds.) (2000). *Welfare and work in the open economy. From vulnerability to competitiveness.* Oxford: Oxford University Press (vol. 1–2).

Schulz, J. (2010). The evolving concept of "retirement": Looking forward to the year 2050. In C. Pierson & F. Castles (Eds.), *The welfare state reader.* Cambridge: Polity Press.

Sowiński, S. (2005). *Jan Paweł II solidarny,* "Więź" No 7.

Staniszkis, J. (2000). *Postkomunistyczne państwo: w poszukiwaniu tożsamości.* Warszawa: Instytut Spraw Publicznych.

The State in a Changing World (1997). Washington, D.C.: World Bank.

Strategia polityki społecznej. Praca i zabezpieczenie społeczne 2002–2005 (2002). Warszawa: Ministerstwo Pracy i Polityki Społecznej.

Szawiel, T. (2006). Solidarność jako wydarzenie i jako trwanie. In A. Sułek (Ed.), *Solidarność. Wydarzenia, sekwencji, pamięć.* Warszawa: Wydawnictwo IFiS PAN.

Szomburg, J. (2004). *Unia potrzebuje transformacji,* "Rzeczpospolita," 26th May.

Szylko-Skoczny, M. (2004). *Polityka społeczna wobec bezrobocia w Trzeciej Rzeczypospolitej.* Warszawa: Oficyna Wydawnicza ASPRA-JR.

Tarkowska, E. (2006). Życie bez pracy. In A. Sułek (Ed.), *Solidarność. Wydarzenia, sekwencji, pamięć.* Warszawa: Wydawnictwo IFiS PAN.

Tichner, J. (1993). *Nieszczęsny dar wolności.* Kraków: Znak.

Tichner, J. (2005). *Etyka Solidarności oraz Homo sovieticus.* Kraków: Znak.

Titmuss, R. (1974). *Introduction to social policy.* London: Allan and Unwin.

Turner, B. S. (Ed.) (2000). *Citizenship and social theory.* London: SAGE.

Wnuk-Lipiński, E. (2006). Solidarność—na fali procesów globalnych. In A. Sułek (Ed.), *Solidarność. Wydarzenia, sekwencji, pamięć.* Warszawa: Wydawnictwo IFiS PAN.

van Berkel, R. & I. H. Møller. (2002). Introduction. In: R. van Berkel & I. H. Møller (Eds.), *Active social policies in the EU. Inclusion through participation?* Bristol: The Policy Press.

van Berkel, R., & I. H. Møller (Eds.). (2002). *Active social policies in the EU. Inclusion through participation?* Bristol: The Policy Press.

van Ewijk, H. (2010). *European social policy and social work. Citizenship-based social work.* New York: Routledge.

van Berkel, R., & B. Valkenburg (2007). Introduction. In R. van Berkel & B. Valkenburg (Eds.), *Making it personal. Individualising activation services in the EU.* Bristol: Policy Press.

Yates, N., & C. Holden (Eds.) (2009). *The global social policy reader.* Bristol: The Policy Press.

Zahorska, M. (2004). Edukacja: od prób uspołecznienia do prób komercjalizacji. In M. Rymsza (Ed.), *Reformy społeczne. Bilans dekady.* Warszawa: Instytut Spraw Publicznych.

Zalewski, D. (2005). *Opieka i pomoc społeczna. Dynamika instytucji.* Warszawa: Wydawnictwo Uniwersytetu Warszawskiego.

Ziliak, J. P. (Ed.) (2009). *Welfare reform and its long-term consequences for America's poor.* Cambridge: Cambridge University Press.

14

DISCOURSES ON SOCIAL RIGHTS IN THE CZECH REPUBLIC[1]

Martin Potůček

CONCEPTUAL CONSIDERATIONS

Public discourses and social rights (within the broader concept of citizenship rights) are the two core concepts I would like to apply in my attempt to analyze the nature of social policymaking in the Czech Republic. I have been inspired here both by the more general concepts of the sociology of knowledge (Mannheim, 1936), by how Habermas understood the role of communicative mediation in contemporary societies, and by the discursive branch of institutionalism (Novotna, 2008; Schmidt, 2006, 2008).

Public Discourses

The sociology of knowledge studies how actors use ideas and ideologies in political battles. Schmidt, inspired by Habermas, developed the notion of discursive institutionalism and argued that discourse "encompasses not only the substantive content of ideas but also the interactive processes through which ideas are conveyed. Discourse, in other words, refers not just to what is said (ideas), but also to who said what to whom, where, when, how, and why (discursive interaction)" (Schmidt, 2008, 2, quoted in Novotna, 2008, 78).

Kusá (2008) made a comprehensive attempt to apply this perspective to the development of Slovak social policymaking—namely the political processes of retrenching social citizenship rights. Inspired by Foucault and others, she applied her critical discourse analysis to show how the Slovak welfare reforms were backed up by borrowed phrasal idioms and exploited metaphors. "Certain interpretation of societal phenomena can become influential only as a part of discourse and through it. It takes the form of prioritization of words and meanings" (Kusá, 2008, 11). According to Fairclough (1989), discourse is a component of social process, a social activity, and as such, on one hand, it is conditioned by social structures, and, on the other, it contributes to the reproduction of power relations; it can support, challenge, change, or even destroy them. Fairclough respects the parallel existence of divergent and relatively autonomous discourses, which, to some extent, interfere with one other. Public discourses unfold in concrete settings, they have a processual character, they involve identifiable actors, and they eventually result in decisions being taken. The term *discourse failure* refers to situations where attempts to find a common language and explanation for a given situation fail (Pincione-Tesón, 2006). I will use the term *public discourse* as a core term for the empirical part of this chapter.

Social Rights

I do not intend to dwell too long on the concept of social rights. Rather, I will limit myself to an overview of documents that provide the legal and political foundation for the usage of social citizenship rights as a criterion for policymaking in the life of European societies. I would like to characterize recent developments that have affected and sometimes endangered this process—as extensively discussed in Chapter 1.

The precursors of the EU's activities in the field of human rights were the United Nations (with its Declaration of Universal Human Rights, passed in 1948) and the Council of Europe (with its European Convention on Human Rights, adopted in 1950). In both cases, social rights were defined in a universal manner; all human beings should enjoy the same rights—the right to live in dignity and the right to develop their human potential to the full.

The milestone EU documents are listed in Table 14.1.

Evers and Guillemard in Chapter 1 sum up the recent societal trends, which demonstrate that universal social rights, as envisaged by international as well as EU documents, are under threat. At the center of such changes is a shift in the definition of predominantly public and private affairs, influenced by the neoliberal discourse of the period from the 1980s until the beginning of the 21st century. We have witnessed a process of re-commodification of previously universally delivered public social services in most EU member-states (with exceptions in specific policy fields in particular countries). In most of the affluent Western democracies, this is a long-term, incremental process. In all the postcommunist member-states, this process has been in some cases been incremental, but in all cases more rapid than in the West, and sometimes even abrupt. In some instances, especially in the 1990s, this process was even referred to as "shock therapy," embodied in the large-scale privatization of the national economy, including an increasing share of public services (Potůček, 2008). At the end of this chapter, I will illustrate this political shift by referring to the fact that the

Table 14.1. Core EU Agreements Concerning Social Rights

Year	Document
1989	Community Charter of the Fundamental Social Rights of Workers
1992	Maastricht Treaty with its Annex—Agreement on Social Policy
1997	Amsterdam Treaty incorporated Agreement on Social Policy into its main body
2000	Lisbon Strategy
2005	Recalibrated Lisbon Strategy
2009	Treaty of Lisbon with the Charter of Fundamental Rights and Basic Freedoms

Source: Author.

Czech President, Václav Klaus, demanded and achieved an exemption from the Chapter on Fundamental Rights and Basic Freedoms of the Lisbon Treaty as the precondition for its ratification by the Czech Republic at the end of 2009.

METHODOLOGICAL CONSIDERATIONS

Inspired by Kusá's (2008) approach associating the nature of the public discourses in Slovakia with the social policy reforms implemented since 1989, I will apply critical discourse analysis, which "analyzes the ways, by which the political power, dominance and inequalities are created, reproduced and misused by means of texts and speeches in social and political context—and how they are opposed" (van Dijk, 2003, quoted by Kusá, 2008, 12). I will focus this analysis predominantly on the content of political and programmatic documents and the way they are prepared, discussed, and, eventually, implemented.

DISCOURSES ON SOCIAL RIGHTS IN THE CZECH REPUBLIC

Esmark (2006, 14) believes that "a substantial part of the political communication within public spheres is devoted to questions about the formal organization of the political system, institutional competencies, basic rights of citizens etc." In this section, I intend to analyze the various discourses on social rights, and the effect that these discourses have had in the Czech Republic. The reason for making this choice is simple: respect for social rights is the prerequisite for taking seriously the concept of social citizenship as a component of the European political tradition and its main instrument, the European social model (Golinowska, Hengstenberg, & Zukowski, 2009).

Kusá (2008) identifies two public discourses in Slovakia: academic and political. I believe that it may be useful to elaborate on this division by including the administrative and civic discourses. For the sake of this analysis, four main arenas (sectors) have been defined in which discourses take place at the national level: academic, administrative, political, and civic. They overlap in the public sphere. At the same time, they connect and overlap with the discourses of leading political ideologies in contemporary European societies, including the traditional ones (liberalism, socialism, and conservatism) and the more recent ideology of environmentalism (Potůček, Musil, & Mašková, 2008). All of them are influenced by the EU level of decision making. The media also plays a role, generating stimuli for discourse, and sometimes raising specific agendas.[2]

The legal framework for these discourses at the national level was created by the Constitution of the Czech Republic, comprising the List of Basic Rights and Liberties, as passed at the end of 1992, a few days before the final breakup of Czechoslovakia (Table 14.2).

The Academic Discourse

In the Czech Republic, as in other postcommunist countries, the academic world was widely politicized by the breakdown of the communist regime and subsequent events. In this context, *The Social Doctrine of the Czech Republic* (Sociální, 2002; Social Doctrine, 2002) was an interesting example of an original "national initiative." Its original aim was to build a broad academic, and later presumably also national, consensus on the orientation, goals, priorities, and corresponding instruments of Czech social policy. Five preparatory conferences in 1998–2000 constituted a "joint venture" involving the academic, epistemic community gathered around the Socioklub nonprofit advisory association. This group of experts from various social policy fields, disciplines, and political affiliations had decided to seek to develop a common long-term vision, based on a discourse on the future orientation of Czech social policy, in order to make this more programmatic and sensitive to the long-term consequences of the decisions made:

> The work on this program document lasted for almost three years and dozens of specialists representing different institutions, scientific disciplines and schools of thought took part in it. All of them shared a unifying conviction that the current social and political practice was suffering considerably from the absence of a guideline of a long-range orientation. We suppose that this document may serve as a minimum common program basis for the makers and the executors of social policy of the Czech State in the period to come. So we submit it [for] discussion, critical consideration and maybe adoption by the whole political and administrative representation of the Czech Republic regardless of this or that party affiliation, the Ministry of the Government, the level of State administration or membership in any association. We believe that the document will become a starting point for long-range conceptual efforts aimed at the future Czech social policy being able to cope with the changing demands of the time and, also, the expectations of the citizens. (Social Doctrine, 2002, 1)

Table 14.2. Characteristics of Fundamental Social Rights, as Guaranteed by the Charter of Fundamental Rights and Basic Freedoms, Part of the Constitution of the Czech Republic[3]

Article (paragraph) of Part 4	Characteristics of the Social Right
26(3)	Everybody has the right to acquire the means of his or her livelihood by work. The state shall provide an adequate level of material security to those citizens who are unable, through no fault of their own, to exercise this right; conditions shall be provided for by law.
27(1)	Everyone has the right to associate freely with others for the protection of his economic and social interests.
27(4)	The right to strike is guaranteed.
28	Employees have the right to fair remuneration for their work and to satisfactory work conditions. Detailed provisions shall be set by law.
29(1)	Women, adolescents, and persons with health problems have the right to increased protection of their health at work and to special work conditions.
29(2)	Adolescents and persons with health problems have the right to special protection in labor relations and to assistance in vocational training.
30(1)	Citizens have the right to adequate material security in old age and during periods of work incapacity, as well as in the case of the loss of their provider.
30(2)	Everyone who suffers from material need has the right to such assistance as is necessary to ensure a basic living standard.
31	Everyone has the right to the protection of his or her health. Citizens shall have the right, on the basis of public insurance, to free medical care and to medical aids under conditions provided for by law.
32(1)	Parenthood and the family are under the protection of the law. Special protection is guaranteed to children and adolescents.
32(2)	Pregnant women are guaranteed special care, protection in labor relations, and suitable work conditions.
32(3)	Children, whether born in or out of wedlock, enjoy equal rights.
32(4)	It is the parents' right to care for and raise their children; children have the right to upbringing and care from their parents.
32(5)	Parents who are raising children have the right to assistance from the state.
33(1)	Everyone has the right to education.

Source: Charter (1993).

After difficult and protracted discussions, the scholars were able to agree on a single document. This envisaged five functions: an orientation function, the function of building and maintaining a national consensus, a stabilization function, the function of social mobilization, and the function of a guarantee to maintain a permanent orientation towards alleviating social injustice.

The Czech social doctrine proceeds from the civil rights as declared in the Charter of Fundamental Rights and Basic Freedoms of citizens. The inalienable human rights include, for example, the right to life, human dignity, equal treatment without discrimination, and freedom. These rights, formulated in such a general way, are a kind of a social minimum of any social doctrine.

The inalienable social rights were the backbone of this document. They involved the following rights (including the principles and methods of fulfillment):

- to work
- to satisfactory working conditions
- to a reasonable subsistence level
- to health
- to family
- to social security
- to free association
- to education

The document clustered the social rights enlisted by the constitutional Charter of Fundamental Rights and Basic Liberties in a way that could smooth their political implementation.[4]

However, quite different voices came to be heard much more clearly in the academic debate surrounding the formation and implementation of Czech social policy after 1989. Inspired above all by the neoliberal orthodoxy of the Washington Consensus and mainstream economics, they accused the Czech social state of excessive spending, jeopardizing the public finances, following in the steps of the communist heritage, and undermining the responsibility of the individual for his or her own fate. They also attacked the state itself and, in accordance with Milton Friedman's principles, called for minimal government and, in turn, maximum use of the market's regulatory functions.

While the EU interfered little with the academic discourse, other international actors had more influence. In particular, the World Bank and the International Monetary Fund played important roles during this period (not only in the Czech Republic but in all the postcommunist countries that were aspiring to EU membership).

The Administrative Discourse

The Czech civil servants typically did not act independently in the development of the public discourse on social rights. Civil servants in the area under investigation were primarily officials from the Ministry of Labor and Social Affairs. Following the new millennium, the policy area of human rights was, after many years of setbacks, finally acknowledged at the level of central public administration by the establishment of the Ombudsman's Office. However, the ombudsman was given no executive competences.

Generally speaking, civil servants obeyed the instructions of Czech politicians with little resistance. However, politicians were anxious to finalize the pre-accession preparations successfully and subsequently join the EU. This was a path that led the country to apply some previously unknown and unused discursive procedures, even at the national level. Most notably, those included implementing the goals of the Lisbon Strategy and the ensuing documents, and procedures such as the Open Method of Coordination.

Adopted by the then 15 member-states of the EU in 2000, the Lisbon Strategy formulated several ambitious goals that were to be attained by 2010. These goals included transforming the European economy into the most competitive and dynamic in the world, able to create more and better jobs by supporting education, research, and development and, at the same time, strengthening the social cohesion of European societies.[5] The main documents drafted within the framework of the Lisbon Strategy and applied in order to fulfill its social goals included National Action Plans on Social Inclusion and National Reports on Strategies for Social Protection and Social Inclusion.

The first National Action Plan on Social Inclusion 2004–2006 (National, 2005a) followed from the Joint Memorandum on Social Inclusion of the Czech Republic (2004), which was authored jointly by the Czech government and the European Commission and adopted in December 2003. In accordance with this Memorandum, the National Action Plan on Social Inclusion would translate the common goals in fighting poverty and social exclusion into national policies and programs. The document sums up other valid and prepared policies, action plans, strategies, programs, and governmental decrees that have some relevance to the issue of social inclusion. The document's weak point is its lack of explicit goals, its poor definition of responsibility for implementation, and missing links in the budgetary process. Significantly, the Ministry of Finance did not participate in the preparation of this document.

The document posed as a national strategy, "the aim of which [...] is to canvass due publicity to the problems of social exclusion and to help solve them" (National, 2005a, 8). The only explicit, and very significant, reference to the other development goals was: "The important condition of the success of the strategy of social inclusion is its close relationship with the economic policy of the state. The economic situation is characterized, on one hand, by economic growth and virtually zero inflation but, on the other, by a growing public finance deficit. Improvement is therefore perceived as the main political priority" (ibid.).

The EU's Lisbon Strategy was recalibrated in 2005. This recalibration was due to the inadequate implementation in most member-states and also due to the new composition of the European Commission, which reflected the outcome of the 2005 European Parliament elections and the stronger position of the right. Economic priorities came to the fore. This shift coincided, in the Czech Republic, with the appointment of a new Deputy Prime Minister for

Economic Affairs in 2004, who was charged with formulating comprehensive strategic documents—a Strategy for Economic Growth (Strategy, 2005), and the National Lisbon Program 2008 (National, 2005b). The latter document, a basic guide for the country's strategic orientation over the coming few years, came in three parts: macroeconomic (with an emphasis on continued public finance reform equal to squeezing social expenditure associated with the continued relative decrease in tax revenues), microeconomic (with measures to further increase economic competitiveness), and employment (flexibility and openness of labor market and education). Although the Czech Republic's Strategy for Sustainable Development (2004) was approved as the umbrella strategic document that would become the binding basis for all subsequent action, the Strategy for Economic Growth, which was passed a couple of months later, paid only lip service to this document and presented itself as the core strategic document that was to be respected in other strategic endeavors. It did not associate itself with the National Action Plan on Social Inclusion 2004–2006 mentioned earlier. This further weakened the actual status of the Czech government's endeavors in the field of sustainable development in general, and one of its three core elements—the goal to strengthen social inclusion by respecting social rights—in particular.

The following national policy documents, required by the European Commission, namely the National Report on Social Strategies for Social Protection and Social Inclusion for 2006–2008 (National, 2006) and the National Report on Social Strategies for Social Protection and Social Inclusion 2008–2010 (National, 2008), did not deviate substantially from the course set out in the previous document. They were characterized primarily by their resignation to the use of the concept of social rights as a key prioritizing criterion; focus on partial and in particular technical aspects of the fight against social exclusion; and the difficulty of measuring the anticipated outcomes. On the other hand, the practice of public consultation with members of the professional public and civil society continued during the preparation, implementation, and evaluation of the documents.

Sirovátka (Chapter 11) offers persuasive empirical evidence about the way the Czech government has steered the country's social administration in the field of social policy:

The principal focus is on reducing the social right to income protection (lower social benefits, either in general or in special cases; the delayed indexation of the living and existence minimum; the exclusion of the young people from entitlements to unemployment benefits and social assistance) in combination with an increase in the conditionality of social rights (a stricter definition of "suitable employment"). On the other hand, the support provided to the most disadvantaged people to enhance their capabilities and employability has not increased in its scope, targeting or intensity.

The Political Discourse

The tone and content of the political discourse were, to a large extent, determined by the fortunes of the key political forces in the country. The period between 1992 and 1997 was dominated by the conservative and liberal political ideologies. After the collapse of Václav Klaus's government in 1997, an era of governments dominated by the Social Democrats started. During this period, the country's preparations for EU membership culminated with accession on May 1, 2004. As early as 2002, the country agreed to implement the objectives of the Lisbon Strategy in its policies, including the creation of more and better jobs and fighting against social exclusion. Throughout this era, the goals of Czech elected representatives generally coincided with those stated in the Lisbon Strategy.

An important shift in the country's political orientation occurred after the elections to the lower chamber of 2006. After many months of difficult political negotiations, a new center-right government was formed and took office in January 2007.

Its two orientating political documents, the coalition agreement between the Civic Democrats, the Christian Democrats, and the Green Party, and the Programme Declaration of the Government, were presented to Parliament. These documents:

- failed to mention social rights, social justice, social cohesion, the welfare state, or even the EU Lisbon Strategy
- included formulations such as the unbelievable increase (even "an explosion") in social expenditure in the past, excessive tax burden, abundant bureaucratic burden, inappropriately high level of regulation, the firm intention to lower or even cancel some social benefits, and reduce social and health insurance contributions (explicitly for employers and entrepreneurs)
- did mention respect for human rights, including those of minorities and vulnerable groups, and the plan to establish "an agency that will secure complex services to prevent social exclusion and its eradication and make the use of social support more effective and free from misuse."

These political documents neglected the relevance of social rights. They emphasized freedom and the responsibility of individuals for their own fate, as well as their civil and political rights. In this sense, it seemed that Marshall's triad describing the development of citizenship rights in Europe (from 18th-century civic rights to 19th-century political rights to 20th-century social rights) had been reversed by 100 years in those documents (Marshall, 1963). There is an apparent paradigmatic proximity with neoliberal ideology.

Czech Social Democracy was narrowly defeated in the 2006 general election and subsequently decided to emphasize the social aspects of its politics to a greater extent, both in its programmatic documents and in political practice. This, together with some controversial measures taken by the new government (such as the introduction of co-payments for healthcare services and drugs, and significant cuts in spending on some social welfare benefits and the narrowing of eligibility criteria), resulted in an overwhelming victory for Social Democratic candidates in the 2008 regional elections. A few months later, in the spring of 2009, the center-right government lost a vote of confidence in the lower chamber of the Czech parliament. The country was led by a government of bureaucrats nominated in line with an agreement between three parliamentary political parties: the Civic Democrats, the Social Democrats, and the Green Party. After the general election of May 2010, there was another right-wing coalition government established, composed of the Civic Democrats and the two newly emerging political parties, TOP 09 and Public Affairs. In the meantime, the global crisis began to affect the small, open Czech economy. Huge rises in unemployment and government deficits occurred, and the political discourse focused on the questions of who should bear the costs of the crisis, and why. The new government started to curtail the Czech welfare state (and, consequently, accessibility of social rights) even more vigorously than the previous ones.

The Civic Discourse

Czechs tend to be unhappy with the state's attitude to their rights, as Table 14.3 shows.

Civic sector organizations are the main, but not the exclusive, initiators of discourse at the level of civil society. After 1989, Czech civil society was able to re-establish historic traditions that can be traced back to the beginnings of the National Revival in the late 1700s. Financial and institutional support from the countries of western Europe and the United States was another important factor, especially at the start of the transformation process. Today, the Czech civic sector runs a vast array of activities in both service provision and advocacy. The voices of environmental groups, human rights organizations, and organizations advocating specific social groups can be heard particularly loudly in the public arena. On the other hand, social rights as such have not been the focus of attention for these groups.

Table 14.4 follows chronologically five attempts to assert the specific agenda of social rights in Czech public discourse.

Table 14.3. Do You Agree that the Czech State Cares About the Rights and Dignity of Every Citizen? (% of responses, May/June 2008)

Strongly Agree	Somewhat Agree	Somewhat Disagree	Strongly Disagree	Don't Know	No Response
7	32	36	20	4	1

Source: Governance and Modernization in the Czech Republic. Public opinion research CESES/Factum Invenio, Prague 2008.

Table 14.4. Attempts to Assert the Social Rights Agenda in Public Discourse by Informal Civic Initiatives

Time Period	Name of Initiative	Description
1992–94	The OMEGA Project—human belonging, civic solidarity	About 60 activists from academia, NGOs, public administration. and politics attempted to put an end to uncritical adoration of the market's regulatory functions in the transformation of the Czech society, and emphasize the protection of citizens' social rights. Several seminars were organized and several documents were published. The initiative had practically no effect on the broader civic community.
1999–2002	Social Doctrine of the Czech Republic	See section on "Academic Discourse" for more details. The civic initiative by ten academics sparked some interest in civil society and among some politicians, but it had little to no effect on political practice.
2007–2008	*Jsme občané* (We are the citizens)	This initiative was unveiled in January 2007 (symbolically exactly 30 years after the release of the first Charter 77[6] document). It called attention to discrepancies between the democratic ideals of the Czech Constitution and practices that are ever more frequently shaped by neoliberal doctrines. Some of the most striking gaps in the social conditions of the citizen versus the criterion of social rights and entitlements:
		• The human rights of ethnic minorities and migrants are neglected.
		• The Czech Republic is the only EU member-state that has not yet incorporated EU Anti-discriminatory Regulation 78/2000 in its labor law.
		• Women, young and handicapped people, and people above 50 suffer discrimination.
		• Many people (e.g., the homeless) live in material deprivation that is beyond the conditions of human dignity secured by the Czech Constitution, and are deprived of appropriate support.
		• There is ever less space for public discourse concerning key societal problems.
		693 citizens signed the document between January 1, 2007, and November 24, 2008. Some information appeared in the print media, but none of it reached the "media highway." The website of the initiative was not in operation in the beginning of 2009. No significant influence of this initiative upon public policy has been observed.
2010	Call for Permanent Force and Effect of the EU Charter of Fundamental Rights in the Czech Republic	The Czech Republic was the last EU member-state to ratify the Lisbon Treaty in November 2009. Czech President Václav Klaus achieved an exemption from the application of the EU Charter of Fundamental Rights for Czech citizens, yet this Charter had been passed by both chambers of the Czech Parliament as part of the Lisbon Treaty. The authors of the Call, primarily civic sector organizations advocating human rights, demanded that the government made sure the exemption was repealed because the President's steps were not in line with the principles of parliamentary democracy and made Czechs second-class citizens in the EU.[7] The Call was signed by the leaders of dozens of organizations.
2010	ProAlt ("For Alternatives")	ProAlt is the civic initiative criticizing the governmental reforms and promoting alternatives. It brings together people of all professions, generations, and opinions who refuse insensitive cuts and reforms in pensions, health, social and family policy, employment law, education, science and culture, as prepared by the current government coalition, and want to actively refuse them. Its short-term goal is to stop or at least mitigate the reforms in these areas. Its long-term goal is to create confident, active, inclusive, and sustainable society.

Source: Author.

Even though one often speaks of civil society in the singular, it is in fact all about plurality, a multitude of voices and orientations that have to learn to live with each other. Initiatives whose activities are rooted in different ideologies have usually relied on their own institutional platforms. Among the most influential were the Civic Institute, which advocated a conservative stance on the country's development priorities, and the CEVRO/Liberal Conservative Academy, which identified with conservatism and liberalism. In contrast, the Masaryk Democratic Academy was located on the left of the political spectrum.[8]

However, the civic discourses initiated and developed by those institutions rarely exceeded the boundaries of their respective ideological frameworks.

Attempts to Overcome Discourse Failures

It became increasingly clear to stakeholders that attempting to develop a demo-cratic dialogue about human rights in general, and social rights in particular, is no trivial matter. Slowly, they ceased focusing exclusively on the dialogue's content and started to pay more attention to the means of conducting this dialogue.

Public Discourses Initiated by Academia and Citizens

The Social Doctrine of the Czech Republic (see above) was presented at two public discussions co-organized by the Ministry of Labor and Social Affairs and the Upper House of the Czech Parliament, the Senate, in 2001–2002. After the 2002 general election, the document was explicitly mentioned—as the starting point for the further development of government social policy and its priorities and approaches until 2006—in the coalition agreement statement between the Social Democrats, Christian Democrats, and a small liberal party (Union of Freedom) as one of the government's programmatic guidelines, and further discussion among coalition parties about it was envisaged. Nevertheless, despite urgent calls from academic circles, this government failed to make any steps forward before its resignation in 2004: its social policy decisions were taken mainly in response to urgent problems or the demands of various pressure groups. Hitherto, three consecutive governments have failed to take the Social Doctrine as a serious offer by the academic community for a more intensive collaboration in the field of strategic social policymaking. No government office or official took the other three informal civic initiatives (see Table 14.3) as serious partners for further discussion. Pincione-Tesón (2006) would call all cases a cross-border discourse failure.

Public Discourse on Social Inclusion Mediated by the Government, Initiated by the EU

The Czech government adopted the decision to establish a Committee for the Preparation of a Joint Memorandum on Social Inclusion and a National Action Program on Social Inclusion (NAPSI 2004–2006—see above). The appropriate committee was established by the Ministry of Labor and Social Affairs in September 2003. Its 40 members represented:

- selected government ministries (labor and social affairs; education, youth and physical education; health, regional development; the interior; transport; industry and trade; information; the environment; and agriculture)
- other public administration institutions (Government Committee for the Handicapped; Government Council for Roma Affairs; Czech Statistical Office; Ombudsman's Office; Association of Regions of the Czech Republic; and the Association of Cities and Municipalities of the Czech Republic)
- civic sector organizations including social partners (Czech-Moravian Confederation of Trade Unions; Industry and Transport Union; Czech and Moravian Production Cooperative Union; Czech Catholic Charity Association; People in Need; National Council of Handicapped Persons)
- academic community (Charles University Faculty of Social Sciences; Sociological Institute of the Academy of Sciences of the Czech Republic)

This committee was given the task of supervising coordination between the various ministries and ensuring that all the relevant institutions share in inter-ministerial coordination in processing the Joint Inclusion Memorandum (2004) and NAPSI 2004–2006 (National, 2005a). This committee was also asked to implement a comprehensive policy to fight poverty and social exclusion.

As indicated by the list of actors directly involved in the preparation of the NAPSI 2004–2006, due respect was given to the traditional position of social partners in the social dialogue, the representatives of employees and employers as partners to the government, in the regular meetings of the tripartite body—the Council of Economic and Social Agreement. The National Council of Disabled Persons had retained its traditionally strong status *vis-à-vis* the Ministry of Labour and Social Affairs even on this agenda. As indicated by the authors of the NAPSI 2004–2006, its preparation involved also the participation of other partners, notably representatives of the nongovernmental not-for-profit organizations focusing on homeless people and seniors (National, 2005a, 62). There was thus a balanced representation of civic organizations representing various group interests.

The fourth chapter of the NAPSI 2004–2006, entitled "Institutional Support," states that structures for participation in the field of social inclusion have been established not only at the central level (e.g., the Council of Economic and Social Agreement, the Government Council for Non-State Non-Profit Organizations, the Government Council for Roma Affairs, the Government Committee for

Disabled Citizens, the Government Council for Ethnic Minorities, and cooperation with the Association of Cities and Municipalities and the Association of Czech Regions), but also at the regional and municipal level (namely social committees and committees for disabled citizens).

In an effort to involve the wider public in the preparation of the National Action Plan of Social Inclusion, its various chapters have been posted on the Ministry of Labor and Social Affairs' website and other associated websites (National, 2005a, 62). Several conferences have also been organized for the actors involved.

The document NAPSI 2004–2006 encapsulated fundamental citizenship rights and displayed compliance with the general principles of the European social model and social inclusion agenda. The subsequent document, the National Report on Social Strategies for Social Protection and Social Inclusion for 2006–2008 (National, 2006), deviated from this orientation by curtailing social citizenship rights (see Chapter 11). This was also true of the third document, the National Report on Social Strategies for Social Protection and Social Inclusion 2008–2010 (National, 2008). This development reflected the political shift from the government dominated by Social Democrats (2002–2006) to the center-right government dominated by the Civic Democratic Party (2007–2009).

EUROPEANIZING THE CONTENTS AND METHODS OF PUBLIC DISCOURSES

In all European countries, national discourses have had to accommodate the EU and its programs and actions. While this may play a minor role in larger countries with a long history of EU membership (such as Germany), the situation is different for the new EU member-states. EU doctrines and recommendations are a very important point of reference within the national discourses described here.

Many people expect the public dissemination of the EU social inclusion's core ideas, principles, and policies to have a positive effect, but mainly as a sort of public enlightenment whose benefits are diffuse and long term. With respect to the systematic collaboration between the government and NGOs, a more reserved view is appropriate. There is overarching EU-wide empirical evidence that the open method of coordination is a "potentially valuable, but weak instrument" since it will always be dependent on the political will of the national government (*Back to the Future?* 2005) "Without a connection to Brussels, national NGOs struggle to get involved in the OMC" (Fazi & Smith, 2006, 61). The negligible impact of all the endeavors of Czech NGOs to influence government policies in the Czech Republic confirms this general experience. Consulting with NGOs is still felt to be "not in the culture" (Fazi & Smith, 2006, 73). Recently, EU structural funds (and particularly the European Social Fund) have been increasingly tapped to support this public discourse that transcends sectoral as well as—to some extent—ideological boundaries. One may expect this to bring about positive effects in terms of coping better with various technical, organizational, and substantial issues that arise while preparing and realizing such a discourse.

There is one important stream in Europeanization studies that interprets discourse as an instrument or vector of Europeanization (Schmidt, 2002). Domestic actors use the EU instrumentally to support domestic policies by creating a discourse—and, consequently, strengthening their position in the power structure (Hay, 2002; Kallestrup, 2002; Roe, 1994; Saurugger & Radaelli, 2008).

There are two prevailing political positions in the EU policymaking process: one that understands the European project as essentially deregulatory, and another that sees the market as the first step in the process of institution-building at the European level (Taylor-Gooby, 2004a, 184): "Pressures for both liberalism and for a stronger interventionist role exist, and whether the balance between the two will shift in the future is at present unclear" (Taylor-Gooby, 2004b). Thus, the EU does not speak to its members with one voice. As mentioned above, one of its two Janus faces speaks of the need to make the European economy the most competitive in the world, and to pursue market liberalization further (including the broadly defined services of general interest), about fiscal discipline and the flexible labor market. The EU's other Janus face declares its adherence to the principles of social justice, social rights, and the fight against poverty and social exclusion, and nurtures its own aspiration—the European social model. This programmatic schizophrenia, which creates space for a neoliberal as well as an institutional/social democratic interpretation of European polity, has been a serious puzzle for the less experienced national political classes and the public of the first prospective and now new EU member-states, such as the Czech Republic. This split is underlined by the daily experience of many people who were promised economic prosperity along with the country's EU membership, while they contend with difficult access to the labor market and low employability in everyday life, with tightening social provisions, insufficient public services, and so forth.

The EU has not developed strong, clear-cut requirements in the field of social policymaking toward its candidate countries (Horibayashi, 2006; Potůček, 2004), even though Orenstein and Haas (2003) could identify its positive effect on the postcommunist new member-states compared to the postcommunist countries with no immediate prospect of EU membership. There is an obvious discrepancy between the Copenhagen Criteria of accession, which covered a very limited part of the social welfare agenda and was installed in 1993, and the Lisbon Strategy, which was presented as an explicit and balanced public policy program for the candidate countries as late as 2002 and was politically and administratively implemented only since 2004. This discrepancy created a considerable opportunity for other, more active and influential international actors, namely the World Bank and International Monetary Fund, which were dominated at that time by the Washington Consensus' neoliberal ideology (Potůček, 2004).

SUMMARY

The following generalization of the development of social rights discourses in the Czech Republic between 1992 and 2010 can be formulated: in this time period, the attention devoted to social rights issues did not grow substantially. Discourses typically took place in isolated, parallel epistemic communities (Haas, 1992), whether defined sectorally or ideologically. An effective overcoming of barriers was rarely seen between sectors, and never between the different ideological streams. The only institutional platform that offered more systematic support to minimize discourse failures was the EU's programmatic platform, which resulted in the repeated formulation of strategic documents on social inclusion between 2004 and 2010. Recently, the EU also contributed financially to disseminate this issue and support public discourse in the national public space. The agenda of social citizenship has evolved slowly and incrementally, mainly in the civic stream of discourse, inspired by political ideologies of the center-left.

The findings of the chapter are summarized in Table 14.5.

CHALLENGES OF THE FUTURE

A serious problem for European governance is how to build and encourage the conditions for effective, cross-border public discourses about social rights (and other relevant societal issues) at both the national and EU levels—in the face of differentiated, often sharply conflicting economic, social, institutional, and national interests, as well as varying modes of communication within the academic, administrative, political, and civic discourses.

The main questions that need to be answered to overcome discourse failure can be specified as follows:

- How can the boundaries between particular discourses be transcended (e.g., between the "economic competitiveness" and the "social rights" discourse at the EU and national levels)?
- How can "twin" discourses be encouraged (i.e., political–administrative; academic–political; political–civic, academic–civic, etc.)?
- What are the appropriate languages and modes of communication for cross-border discourses?
- How can the political system at large (including the involvement of media) be made better able to facilitate the realization of the above tasks to achieve at least some degree of success?

To address these questions, one must be aware of the nature of the obstacles that lie ahead. Three serious barriers, in my view, add significantly to the difficulty of effectively engaging us, scholars, in the effort to make the European

Table 14.5. Social Rights Discourses in the Post-1989 Czech Republic

Discourses	Initiatives, Periods	Cross-Sectoral Collaboration	Impact on Social Policymaking	Influence of the EU
Academic	Social Doctrine of the Czech Republic 1999–2002	Sporadic enlightenment of political class	Extremely limited	Indirect, very limited
Administrative	National Action Plan and National reports on strategies of social inclusion 2004–10	Organized by civil servants from top to bottom; both academic elites and organizations from the civic sector have been included	Slow diffusion of concepts, norms, methods, and approaches to a socially inclusive society	Considerable direct influence of the programmatic effort of the EU applying the agenda of social inclusion
Political	Left-wing parties apply the concept of social rights in their programmatic documents; conservative and liberal parties neglect it. 1992–2010	The political discourse on social rights going across different political camps is nonexistent. Political parties are not motivated to involve other actors in such a discourse.	Limited, and only on the left of the political spectrum	Left-wing political parties make use of the concept of social rights whereas right-wing ones bet exclusively on the concept of common European market.
Civic	The OMEGA Project—human belonging, civic solidarity Social Doctrine of the Czech Republic *Jsme ob ané* (We are the citizens) Call for Permanent Force and Effect of the EU Charter of Fundamental Rights in the Czech Republic 1992–2010 ProAlt—the civic initiative criticizing the governmental reforms and promoting alternatives	Informal civic gatherings and civic sector organizations are trying to involve the political class in the agenda of social rights. Civic activists and academics collaborate; politicians behave rather indifferently.	Very limited	Only indirect influence by setting the agenda of social rights as a legitimate issue

Source: Author.

public sphere more sensitive to dialogic discourses and voices from the civil society:

1. The coexistence of a dialogic form of communication and a nondialogic form, transmitted by the media, and independent of physical location
2. The reduction of the complex task of communicating effectively to a merely technical problem of the transmission of information ("e-Europe")
3. The ignorance, low political culture, and vested interests of actors involved in the communication processes

The first barrier is associated with the coexistence of a dialogic form with an (increasingly relevant) nondialogic form of communication, transmitted via the media, and independent of physical location (Thompson, 1995). Thompson calls the nondialogic form of communication *mediated publicness*. This indirect and mostly one-way form of communication is crucial, since it shapes the content and quality of communication in the public sphere. It is enormously relevant, but the receivers are hard to identify, and the impact on them is very difficult to evaluate. In addition, it can hardly be defined as a "discourse" as such, since it lacks any active exchange of views or channels for feedback. It is also difficult to make this form of communication equal in terms of the power of the public *vis-à-vis* the media: which interests can influence "the rules of the communication game" most? This has important implications for the ability to find the correct balance between checks between media and other political actors—and, consequently, the democratic legitimacy of the media.

The second barrier stems from the application of a narrow concept of communication, in which this is understood simply as a technical problem of transmitting information (e.g., the concept of e-government as the remedy to problems of public administration). Nevertheless, effective communication is closely associated with the interests that are pursued and compete with other interests. In other words, it is impossible to nurture communication as "art for art's sake," since governance in general, political conflicts, and especially diverse social and economic interests are battlefields in which communication is a means and a weapon at the same time (Golding, 2007a, 2007b). It is in this sense that the social rights agenda constitutes an integral part of the broader domain of human rights (let us once more recall the above-mentioned triad of civil, political, and social rights) as well as the status of citizenship itself.

The third barrier to consider is the low political culture that frames communication processes. The Czech Republic may serve as *pars pro toto*. As has been shown, scholars, civil servants, politicians, and civic activists pursue different agendas, speak different languages, and are not prepared to compare their approaches to social rights, to understand each other, and to follow them as criteria in the ongoing discourses, processes of matching partial interests, negotiating compromises, decision making, and policy implementation. Lack of trust among the actors and inadequate communication skills adversely affect the overall efficiency of public discourses. In the Czech Republic, this is reflected particularly in the ideological gap between the political parties that represent the liberal, conservative, and social democratic worldviews.

Nevertheless, the absence of direct EU influence on welfare state transformation should not obscure the less visible streams of cultural changes associated with the processes of European integration, which have influenced domestic discourses on social policymaking and set up new notions, agendas, approaches, and policy instruments. Call it mutual learning, cognitive Europeanization, or enculturation; it has been changing the cognitive framework of social policymaking—with both EU's Janus faces influential to the extent that was acceptable and/or instrumental for different domestic policy actors. The EU has had a noticeable, and at the same time controversial, impact on the content and outcome of this stream of discourses on the social citizenship rights in the Czech Republic.

According to Dahrendorf (1985), the viability of contemporary capitalist societies at the national level depends on three pillars: market economy, political democracy, and a properly functioning welfare state. Let us try to apply this concept at the EU-wide level as well. In general, it is the common political and material experiences and arrangements encountered by citizens in their national and everyday lives that represent a necessary precondition for the emergence of a European social citizenship as an effective tool for strengthening cohesion within and between the nations and citizens of the EU. The European social model will play a similar role in creating the third pillar of European society's stability to that played by the welfare state, along with the market economy and political democracy, at the national level. Anthony Atkinson's project of a European minimum income, co-financed from the EU budget, is, among other innovative ideas, a proposal to be considered seriously in this respect. Yet with the EU budget representing only a little over 1% of the public resources, with the remaining nearly 99% in the hands of national governments, it seems reasonable to assume that such a project can be allocated to the realm of wishful thinking for the foreseeable future.

The development of public discourses will be vitally dependent on sound and socially just public policies—no matter whether they are European, national, issue-specific, regional, or municipal. And *vice versa*: sound and socially just public policies cannot be created and implemented without effective cross-border public discourses.

NOTES

1 This chapter was prepared as part of the Research Intent of the Faculties of Social Sciences and Philosophy and Arts, Charles University in Prague,

research task "Visions and Strategies of the Czech Republic's Development in the EU."

2 Analysis of the role of the media in public discourses exceeds the extent of this paper.

3 Part 4 of the Charter of Fundamental Rights and Basic Freedoms defines other rights as well (economic rights, intellectual property rights, right of access to cultural heritage, right for a favorable environment). It also specifies some of the social rights mentioned below and defines the instances where further details are prescribed by laws.

4 Kusá (2008) explains why similar academic discourse was absent in Slovakia.

5 Compare *Lisbon strategy* (2010) for evaluation of the Lisbon Strategy.

6 Charter 77 was a Czechoslovak dissent human rights political movement. Václav Havel was one of the first leaders and spokesmen of Charter 77.

7 The Charter has been valid for the Czech Republic since the Lisbon Treaty came to power in December 2009. Nevertheless, according to the protocol, it should become invalid for this country with the first amendment of the Lisbon Treaty (which is expected to happen with the next EU enlargement in 2011 or 2012).

8 See http://www.obcinst.cz/en/, http://www.cevro.cz/cs/, http://www.masaryk ovaakademie.cz/.

REFERENCES

Back to the Future? The Implementation Reports on the National Action Plans on Social Inclusion—An EAPN Assessment. (2005). Brussels: European Anti-Poverty Network.

Charter of Fundamental Rights and Basic Freedoms. (1993). Available at http://www.psp.cz/cgi-bin/eng/docs/laws/1993/2.html

Dahrendorf, R. (1985) *Law and order.* London: Stevens and Sons.

Esmark, A. (2006). *Polity, policy and politics in the European public sphere—Modes of transnational resonance.* Paper presented at the IPSA World Conference in Fukuoka.

Fairclough, N. (1989), *Language and Power.* New York: Longman.

Fazi, E., & J. Smith (2006). *Civil dialogue: making it work better.* Brussels: Civil Society Contact Group.

Golding, P. (2007a). Introduction to special issue of European Societies. *European Societies, 9*(3), 681–684.

Golding, P. (2007b). Eurocrats, technocrats, and democrats. *European Societies, 9*(3), 719–734.

Golinowska, S., P. Hengstenberg, & M. Zukowski (Eds.) (2009). *Diversity and commonality in European social policies. The forging of a European social model.* Warsaw: Wydawnictwo Naukowe Scholar.

Governance and Modernization in the Czech Republic. (2008). *Results of the public opinion research.* Prague: Center for Social and Economic Strategies, Charles University and Factum Invenio.

Haas, P. (1992). Introduction: Epistemic communities and international policy coordination. *International Organization, 46*(1), 1–35.

Hay, C. (2002). *Political analysis.* Hampshire: Palgrave.

Horibayashi, T. (2006). *Central European welfare system: The present characteristics.*   http://project.iss.u-tokyo.ac.jp/nakagawa/members/papers/4(4) Horibayashi.final.pdf

Joint Inclusion Memorandum. (2004). Prague: Ministry of Labour and Social Affairs.

Jsme občané (We are Citizens) (2007).

Kallestrup, M. (2002). Europeanisation as a discourse: domestic policy legitimization through the articulation of a "need for adaptation." *Public Policy and Administration, 17*(2), 110–124.

Kusá, Z. (2008). Diskurz a zmeny sociálneho štátu. (Discourse and Changes of the Welfare State, in Slovak.) *Sociológia, 40*(1), 5–34.

Lisbon Strategy Evaluation Document. (2010). *SEC (2010) 114 final.* Brussels: European Commission. http://ec.europa.eu/europe2020/pdf/lisbon_ strategy_evaluation_en.pdf.

Mannheim, K. (1936), *Ideology and Utopia: An Introduction to the Sociology of Knowledge.* London: Routledge & Kegan Paul.

Marshall, T. H. (1963). *Sociology at the crossroads.* London: Heinemann.

National Action Plan on Social Inclusion 2004–06. (2005a). Prague: Ministry of Labour and Social Affairs. http://www.mpsv.cz/files/clanky/1103/NAPSI_eng. pdf

National Lisbon Programme 2005–2008. (2005b). Prague: Office of the Government of the Czech Republic.

National Report on Social Strategies for Social Protection and Social Inclusion for 2006–2008. Czech Republic. (2006). Prague: Ministry of Labour and Social Affairs http://epolis.cz/download/pdf/materialsEN_15_1.pdf

National Report on Social Strategies for Social Protection and Social Inclusion 2008–2010. Czech Republic. (2008). Prague: Ministry of Labour and Social Affairs. http://www.mpsv.cz/files/clanky/5830/zprava_aj.pdf

Novotna, T. (2008). The European Union in the Czech and Slovak pre-accession public discourses. In T. Cahlík et al. (Eds.), *European Union governance— Challenges and opportunities* (pp. 77–88). Prague: Matfyzpress.

Orenstein, M. A., & M. R. Haas (2003). *Globalization and the development of welfare states in postcommunist Europe.* Belfer Center for Science and International Affairs, John F. Kennedy School of Government, Harvard University.

Pincione, G., & F. R. Tesón (2006). *Rational choice and democratic deliberation. A theory of discourse failure.* Cambridge: Cambridge University Press.

Potůček, M. (2004). Accession and social policy: the case of the Czech Republic. *Journal of European Social Policy, 14*(3), 253–266.

Potůček, M. (2008). Metamorphoses of welfare states in central and eastern Europe. In: M. Seeleib-Kaiser (Ed.), Welfare state transformations (pp. 79–95). Basingstoke: Palgrave.

Potůček, M., J. Musil, & M. Mašková (Eds.) (2008). *Strategické volby pro Českou republiku. Teoretická východiska. (Strategic Choices for the Czech Republic. Theoretical Considerations)* [In Czech]. Praha: Sociologické nakladatelství.

ProAlt ("For Alternatives") (2011). http://www.proalt.cz/?page_id=411

Roe, E. (1994), *Narrative Policy Analysis.* Duke University Press: Durham.

Saurugger, S., & C. M. Radaelli (2008). The Europeanization of public policies: Introduction. *Journal of Comparative Policy Analysis, 10*(3), 213–219.

Schmidt, V. A. (2002). Does discourse matter in the politics of welfare state adjustment? *Comparative Political Studies, 35*, pp. 168–193.

Schmidt, V. A. (2006). *Democracy in Europe: The EU and national polities.* Oxford: Oxford University Press.

Schmidt, V. A. (2008). Discursive institutionalism: The explanatory power of ideas and discourse. *Annual Review of Political Science*, 11 (June), 303–326.

Social Doctrine of the Czech Republic. (2002). Sociální doktrína České republiky. (2002). *Sociální politika*, 1–2, 7–11. The powerpoint presentation available at http://www.martinpotucek.cz/download/esp/social_doctrine.pdf

Strategy of economic growth. (2005). Prague: Office of the Government.

Taylor-Gooby, P. F. (Ed.) (2004a). *New risks, new welfare. The transformation of the European welfare state.* Oxford: Oxford University Press.

Taylor-Gooby, P. F. (2004b). Open markets versus welfare citizenship: conflicting approaches to policy convergence in Europe. In P. F. Taylor-Gooby (Ed.), *Making a European welfare state? Convergences and conflicts over European social policy.* Broadening Perspectives in Social Policy. Oxford: Blackwell Publishing.

The Czech Republic Strategy for Sustainable Development. (2004). Prague: Office of the Government of the Czech Republic. http://www.mzp.cz/C125750E003B698B/en/czech_republic_strategy_sd/$FILE/KM-CR_SDS_eng-20041208.pdf

Thompson, J. B. (1995). *The media and modernity. A social theory of the media.* Oxford: Polity Press and Blackwell.

van Dijk, T. A. (2003). Critical discourse analysis. In D. Schiffrin, D. Tannen, & H. E. Hamilton (Eds.), *The handbook of discourse analysis* (pp. 352–371). Blackwell Publishing.

Výzva k trvalé platnosti a účinnosti Listiny základních práv Evropské unie v České republice. [Call for permanent force and effect of the Charter of Fundamental Rights of the European Union in the Czech Republic] [In Czech]. (2010). Praha: Otevřená společnost.

PART IV

CONCLUSIONS

15

RECONFIGURING WELFARE AND RESHAPING CITIZENSHIP

Adalbert Evers and Anne-Marie Guillemard

The purpose of this book has been to inquire into the changes affecting welfare during the past 20 years and the implication of these changes for social rights and citizenship. There is no consensus in the academic community about the meaning of these changes. Some analysts detect a tendency, in pursuit of a "neo-liberal logic," towards the dismantlement of the whole of the postwar welfare state. Others see reforms that are modernizing welfare, to enable it to respond better to the need for welfare and security in the 21st century.

Our starting point was the concept of citizenship as it was defined by T. H. Marshall after the Second World War. How relevant is this concept when interpreting the meaning of the welfare reforms conducted in Europe over the past two decades? How have these reforms affected the scope and nature of social rights and, as a consequence, modified or altered social citizenship, the feeling of belonging to a community and the recognition of this belonging?

The first conclusion to draw from several chapters in this volume is that citizenship is still a relevant, vital concept for understanding the changes being made in welfare. As Johansson and Hvinden showed in Chapter 2, we are witnessing the "hybridization" of what Marshall considered to be the three basic aspects (civil, political, and social) of citizenship. These two authors propose a grid for interpreting the changes currently under way, which were empirically described and analyzed in the chapters devoted to national cases. For instance, the new emphasis placed on obligations as a counterpart to rights could be evidence that the original "socio-liberal model" of citizenship proposed by Marshall is being reinterpreted. However, we also detect a "libertarian" strain of citizenship in the values attached to responsibility and the degree of choice for individuals, while the efforts undertaken in favor of empowerment and the call for individuals to "participate" reflect the republican dimension of citizenship. Given the apparent presence of many facets of citizenship, it certainly seems necessary to acknowledge the complexity of deciphering the meaning of the changes that are occurring in welfare and social policy in relation to citizenship in all its dimensions.

A second major conclusion is that the welfare reforms under way in Europe cannot be uniformly interpreted as reductions to benefits and entitlements; nor can we detect a trans-European trend toward some kind of "downgrade" to citizenship. The picture drawn in the chapters devoted to national cases is much more complicated than that. One cannot make one single interpretation that reads these developments solely in terms of the "re-commodification" of welfare in line with a "liberal logic," whereby governments are withdrawing from the social sphere and handing it over to the marketplace. Nonetheless, the authors in this volume do agree on the need to be alert to the convergence of qualitative changes that are occurring in the postwar welfare state. Regardless of the phrases used—the "social investment perspective" (Jenson in Chapter 3), "the enabling state" (Gilbert in Chapter 4), or "the active welfare state" (Lister in Chapter 6)—the welfare state is being remolded and the founding principles of the postwar arrangement are being transformed. The chapters in the first part of this book have described the various aspects of this reconfiguration and their implications for social citizenship.

This reconfiguration reflects a change in the paradigms underlying the postwar welfare state. This implies new ways of understanding, designing, and providing welfare, in terms of both the objectives and the instruments used. We will deal with this in the first section of this conclusion, while the second part focuses on the quite different ways that countries have implemented reforms at the national level, with contrasting consequences for individuals and citizenship.

CONVERGENCE ON AN ACTIVATING SOCIAL INVESTMENT AGENDA

From the 1980s onwards, welfare states faced new, demographic, economic, and social challenges. The adjustment policies conducted in response to these challenges also had to address the "pathologies" bred by the institutional arrangements that characterized the postwar welfare state. While seeking to rectify significant dysfunctions in welfare, new routes were opened toward social welfare. This new orientation involved not only cutbacks in social expenditure and reducing the state's responsibility for welfare. The response to the problems of funding the welfare state was not restricted to the purely quantitative targets set as part of cost-containment policies. In fact, it was, above all, a qualitative approach that sought to invent a new way of providing welfare arrangements that would both be suited to the post-industrial era and bring about greater efficiency. In this sense, this new strategy for public intervention in the social sphere signaled a fundamental change in the prevailing paradigm.

Let us borrow Peter Hall's (1993) useful distinction for analyzing the three levels of changes introduced by public policy reforms. The first level includes changes made in the instruments used. Reforms at this level simply play with the parameters of these instruments alone. The many plans for rescuing pension systems that have modified the retirement age or the duration of contributions are examples of changes at this level. Governments have mostly undertaken such "parametric" reforms.

The second level refers to changes in the instruments used, which neverthe-less retain the same objectives. Reforms of this type might include innovative methods of helping balance social service budgets. An illustration of this is the invention in France of a new tax on general revenues, *la contribution sociale généralisée*, which draws funding for social protection not only from wage-earn-ers' and employers' contributions but also from other sources like yield from capital or patrimony.

The third level of change concerns both the objectives and the instruments of interventions. The paradigms that prevailed in the postwar welfare state are undergoing profound change, as a new notion of the aims of social intervention and of the means of achieving it is developed. The new paradigms correspond to a homogeneous, refurbished set of conceptions for thinking differently about how to respond to social risks and ensure that individuals can cope with them in a global, knowledge-based society. The new "activating social investment agenda" entails a fundamental change on this third level. It is activating in that it is not only about protecting people but also claims to enhance their capacity to deal with risky environments; it is about social investment in that it seeks the payoff of such an approach in political, social, but also economic terms. This new conception of the objectives and instruments of social policies helps us analyze the system's anomalies and failures, redefine its values, principles, and objectives, and redesign the route to reforms and the innovations necessary in the instru-ments we use.

Why does this approach known as the "activating social investment agenda" attract our attention? From the perspective of the cognitive analysis of public policies (Muller, 2000), it enables us to describe the normative set of ideas that orient welfare reforms in various countries. As we know, all public policies create frameworks in which interpretation, *Weltanschauung*, is inseparable from nor-mative patterns of action, which have implications about the choice of instru-ments. A public policy cannot be reduced to its operational dimension as a mere response to social problems before providing solutions for them. In this sense, it reflects a way of interpreting the world.

The first section of this conclusion provides a comprehensive review of five major principles that govern the activating social investment agenda: a redefinition of the state's role; the future as the new horizon for interventions; a rebalancing of rights and obligations; a move from the goal of equality towards that of inclusion; and governance that is based on a "mix" of the "pillars" of welfare. The arrangement of these major principles and the weight given to each has led to quite different reforms, depending on the time and country and the way they get interpreted in these contexts, with varying consequences on the scope of individuals' social rights and on citizenship. There is a high degree of ambiguity, since the central signifiers that characterize the activating social investment agenda allow for a considerable degree of choice for interpreting and ranking these principles and for transforming them into operational instruments. However, exactly this kind of openness may account for the rapid diffusion of this new rhetoric and the wide adoption of its basic ideas. Due to the possibility of different interpretations of the activating social investments agenda, a broad consensus on the new global goals of social policies has arisen, but also different strategies for dealing with such an agenda and implementing it. Formulated by an OECD report in 1996, it penetrated the European Union in 2000, as Jenson recalls in Chapter 3.

In the second section of this conclusion, we shall therefore assess, in comparative terms, how the basic paradigms implemented differently have had a varying effect on entitlements and citizenship rights, especially social citizenship.

However, one should begin by mentioning that this new rhetoric seems to have made very little headway in eastern or central Europe compared with western Europe (for key elements of the transition process, shared by these countries see: Ferge, 1997). This is the case even though more than two decades after the breakdown of the communist system, there are now remarkable similarities between these two parts. In the economic sphere, for example, many of these countries have become part of the industrial patterns and networks of the EU, sharing the challenges linked with the transition towards a knowledge-based service society; at the sociocultural level, they have transformed rapidly into societies that are characterized by individualization and consumerism; finally, at the political level, the basic institutional features of liberal democracy have taken root. Moreover, policymaking has to be carried out under much the same international influences and pressures as in the Western European countries. Because the breakdown of the former socialist systems happened at a time when the old welfare consensus that had marked the policies in most western European countries was already rapidly crumbling away, the debate on the kind of welfare systems that should be built was heavily influenced by neoliberal concepts and Western European welfare traditions. In various ways, the contributions from postsocialist countries in this book are written from a "classical" perspective on social policies as sets of rules, benefits, and services that help to provide protection and some degree of security in the face of old and new risks, and that also— by guaranteeing basic social services to all citizens—help to reduce inequalities and strengthen mechanisms of inclusion. From this perspective, social policies are shaped exclusively by social concerns.

However, as stated in the introduction and several chapter of this book (especially Chapter 3), it makes sense to discuss social policies that, by investing in people, help to improve their prospects of coping with risks and inherited inequalities and simultaneously support economic development. Such forms of investment, such as in the central fields of education and training and promoting health, presuppose more personalized, interactive, and pluralist forms of cooperation between institutions and citizens. With respect to the situation in the postsocialist countries, there are proposals that try to develop the potential for social policies in this direction, even if these are stillfew.. One of these is typically drawn from the Western European context—Cerami's concern with what he calls "the need for a new empowering politics of the welfare state" (2008). Looking at those risks and challenges that central and eastern European countries share with Western European countries (the challenges of a knowledge-based service economy, flexible labor markets, and aging populations), he recommends policies that should be based on four pillars: a guaranteed minimum income, a basic income for children, state investment in education and the development of human capital, and guaranteed basic pensions in old age. The fact that these suggestions conceive of the postsocialist countries only in terms of the aspects they share with their Western European counterparts ought to represent (despite the debatable logic of his approach to activating social investment policies) a potential point for further discussions, rather than a reason for abandoning such suggestions immediately due to their apparent rather utopian flavor. In this context, we could also ask why (besides the obvious pressure of difficult circumstances) there is generally so little debate regarding blueprints and designs for future welfare arrangements and what they could mean for citizenship in the postsocialist countries.

Nevertheless, there are exceptions. One remarkable example might be the essay by the prominent Polish intellectuals Bobinska and Rymsza (2007; see as well Chapter 13). In a similar vein to Cerami and other proponents of an investment-oriented and activating welfare state, they claim that a "Social Policy Needed Now" (2007) should combine solidarity with liberalism. They argue that while politics have hitherto concentrated predominantly on building in safety valves for economic reform and on enabling people to cope better with unemployment rather than extending working life, a proactive social policy should in fact increase participation in society and avoid inflexible solutions, cooperate with local government, seek the new integration of social and economic concerns by investing in social enterprises, support both flexibility and security through "flexi-curity," and—in addition to addressing the question of what comes from the state and/or the market—strengthen the third sector and develop appropriate pro-family policies.

Looking to the future, then, we would dare to suggest that despite the significant differences between countries, especially between East and West, a new agenda is taking shape, marked by five basic hallmarks.

Redefining the Role of the State: From a "Providing State" to an "Enabling State" that Activates Beneficiaries

This new orientation redefines the priorities of the welfare state, which should no longer limit its role to curatively providing compensation for events related to insured risks. A protection that distributes a wide range of social benefits as a function of entitlements is no longer enough. The priority is for the state to intervene preventively, not just to provide a cure. The primary objective is not simply to compensate for risks when accidents occur but also to equip people with capacity to cope with risks. The government has to enhance the human capital of individuals and empower them so that they can exercise responsibility and make their own choices. This redefinition of the state's role involves a more positive conception of beneficiaries as autonomous individuals responsible for themselves; and it reinforces the libertarian dimension of citizenship—civil rights that guarantee people their own room to maneuver. However, we sense the dangers that lurk within this redefinition. By criticizing the "protecting state" that provides redistribution and compensation—the activities at the heart of the old industrial welfare state model—and advocating preventive intervention through still-vague entitlements and benefits, the way is open for contrasting reinterpretations, depending on the context of social rights and alterations of them. The least privileged could be deprived of the benefits that were once provided by the old welfare state without being able, in turn, to profit from new forms of investment in human capital. This risk increases if this investment is not targeted to provide disadvantaged beneficiaries with the same level of opportunities as other groups.

The Future as the Horizon for Actions

It is no longer the present but the future that is the horizon for action. The idea of investment clearly entails the expectation of a return on it in the future. This long-term perspective has the advantage of re-legitimizing the welfare state and social expenditure. The latter is no longer seen simply as a financial burden; it is an investment that will yield dividends. Social policies are a factor in production. As an investment in human capital throughout the beneficiary's life course, they contribute to the common wealth. This expenditure is not simply passive; it becomes active through the returns yielded, both economic and social. The social and economic aspects of welfare are thus closely linked. Investing in sectors like education affects not only social well-being, but also economic development.

However, here too one can identify risks and ambiguities. The search for a return on social investment might lead to the selection of the most profitable investment with optimal yield. This strategy could prove to be a double-edged sword, serving as an argument for selecting beneficiaries according to the dividends expected. Investing in healthcare or education during early childhood might be preferred to funding care for the frail elderly, for example. There is also the danger of leaving individuals to themselves when they have to make decisions and plan their lives. Not all individuals have the same ability to think strategically about their options, making rational long-term plans. After all, projecting one's life into the future implies some degree of control over the circumstances of tomorrow, a control that the most deprived lack. The potential limits of the social investment strategy are related to this risk of exacerbating social divisions and thus stigmatizing the weakest, who are deemed incapable of profiting from any investment made in them.

Balancing Rights and Obligations

In Marshall's conception, social rights had a counterpart, namely the citizen's duty to act responsibly in order to preserve the community's welfare. As postwar welfare states developed, the emphasis shifted, however, toward citizens' rights rather than their duties, as evidenced by the importance that Esping-Andersen (1990) placed on the de-commodification of needs as a major function of welfare.

Under the activating social investment agenda, individuals are required to fulfill their responsibilities as autonomous individuals in return for the benefits granted to them. Personal freedom and autonomy lie at the center of this new conception of intervention to enable people to be the authors of their own future. Since work is seen as the best method for ensuring and developing the well-being of individuals, it must be reconciled with welfare, with the latter having to be made "more employment-friendly." This "work first" approach has come out of a diagnosis of the principal anomalies and pathologies of postwar welfare states. Esping-Andersen drew attention to a "welfare state without work," a pathology typical of continental Europe, where social protection has worked counter to employment, creating poverty traps and fostering dependency. To break free from this vicious circle, social entitlements should be made conditional, dependent on recipients' efforts to measure up to their obligations.

As a consequence, social rights are being made ever less universal in nature and ever more conditional. Standard one-size-fits-all programs are being replaced by tailor-made schemes with incentives and disincentives for selected target groups. These schemes incorporate sanctions for beneficiaries who do not fulfill their obligations or who fail to comply with the requirements set in return for the benefits provided. The "work first" approach uses the incentives included in such schemes, in particular those that seek to "make work pay," as "carrots," while the conditions and sanctions serve as "sticks" for "activating" people. A key welfare policy instrument introduced by this approach is "activation." Not only beneficiaries, but also welfare arrangements, are to be activated to promote employment.

The new philosophy of individual responsibility, which forms a central part of all strategies that develop the activating social investment agenda, involves what some French observers have called a "biographical injunction" (Astier, 2007). Accordingly, beneficiaries must prove their willingness to behave as free, responsible persons who are striving to become the "entrepreneurs" of their own lives and live self-sufficiently. Social policies thus become vast programs for making people responsible. This new search for a balance between rights and duties could, in its positive version, stimulate the republican conception of citizenship, which asks citizens to take a fully fledged role in civic affairs. In its narrower version, however—in pursuit of "workfare"—it may render access to benefits dependent on the adoption of required patterns of behavior and thus exert a form of disciplinary pressure on beneficiaries. As we see, notably in Chapter 6 on the United Kingdom, this balancing of obligations and rights could lead—if too much weight is given to the former over the latter—to stigmatization, thus worsening the situation of the underprivileged. We find another illustration of this in Chapters 7 and 11 about the consequences on citizenship of measures for "activating" the long-term unemployed that become especially severe when a marginalized status on the labor market becomes underscored by racial/ethnic discrimination (see Chapter 12).

A Shift from Equality to Inclusion

When redistribution and compensation for risks are no longer the welfare state's core activities, and strategies of activation and social investment are pursued, there is a shift in priority to the detriment of equality, which was a core value in the welfare state during the industrial era. Attention turns to providing equal opportunities to citizens throughout their lives thanks to the investment in human, social, and financial capital made by the new "enabling state" with the aim of empowering the beneficiaries to exercise responsibility and freedom.

The principal aim of intervention thus shifts from equality to "social inclusion," a new category in public policy. The goal of social intervention becomes to prevent, as early as possible, the "exclusion" of the most fragile. The instruments to be used are no longer those of a universal social insurance scheme with its monetary compensation for risks but, instead, programs tailor-made for targeted groups, namely those at the highest risk of exclusion. Social interventions are individualized and personalized with the intention of securing life-course itineraries, which are now flexible and destandardized, by providing the missing resources at the right time. Accordingly, diversified but personalized benefits and services are better suited than social transfers based on standardized, universal eligibility requirements with benefits conditional on the occurrence of the events insured for. The emphasis, everywhere in Europe, placed on early childhood programs for education and care reflects the priority now given to inclusion rather than equality. It is no longer sufficient to provide everyone with equal chances in schooling. The goal is the future well-being and inclusion of everyone. The examination of early childhood programs in Chapters 3 and 6 sheds light on the advantages and dangers of this predominance of inclusion over equality. These programs are fully in line with the activating social investment agenda, since their objective is to develop human capital and fight against poverty by intervening early in the life of the beneficiaries so as to minimize the accumulation of disadvantage and discrimination that could otherwise lead to social exclusion.

Intervention at a young age prevents the perpetuation of disadvantages in the family. The shared goal of the programs for a national preschool curriculum in Sweden and the United Kingdom is to offer very young children the skills they need to succeed at school and thus fight against the failure that the most under-privileged tend to encounter during schooling.

Depending on the implementation of programs and the criteria for selecting beneficiaries, this strategy of inclusion can lead to contradictory results. As a form of affirmative action, it can target the risk of exclusion of the most under-privileged young children. However, the targeting conducted by such programs carries the risk of "dualizing" the system of social protection and thus classify-ing certain categories as second-class citizens, whose access to entitlements and benefits will be conditional. To the extent that they are obliged to undertake pre-scribed complementary actions and show that they "deserve" such special sup-port, such kind of social programs may work to the detriment of personal civil rights. Palier (2010, p. 377), who has observed this in the reforms made within Bismarckian welfare regimes, argues that "the new welfare systems of continen-tal Europe are in fact characterized by a dualized structure, comprised of (less and less) social insurance on the one hand (for the `insiders)' and more devel-oped targeted assistance and activation schemes (for the `outsiders')", who can no longer access contributory benefits. However, we do not share Palier's conclu-sions, which are overly general. Chapter 9, on Germany, for example, shows that there are, similarly, tendencies to create new basic rights for all, albeit through a guaranteed minimum public pension or services such as childcare and eld-erly care. However, Palier has in fact exposed a major risk inherent in a tightly targeted inclusion strategy. Different versions of deviating from the equal treat-ment of all citizens, in western, northern, and eastern Europe, are discussed in Chapters 6, 10, and 12. *And show some trends toward dualization.*

Furthermore, the shift towards issues of inclusion in many countries has to be seen in the context of a background where the distribution of wealth and income within the majority of the "included" has become more and more uneven. The Nordic countries may be the least concerned, while the United States surely takes the lead in this respect. But even in other countries like France and Germany, the gaps between the very rich and the middle classes have increased (OECD, 2008). Given the fact that the activating social investment agenda entails quite a num-ber of challenges for the ordinary citizens and that its most important promise is that they will not fall "over the edge" rather than promising upward mobility throughout, increasing inequalities between the shrinking number of citizens who are still "in" might be an open flank of an agenda that focuses on inclusion strategies without making the "self-exclusion" of a small class from citizenship obligations a subject of discussion.

New Forms of Governance: A "Responsibility Mix" for Welfare and Social Policy

The development of a "proactive social investment state" implies a different form of welfare governance. The state is no longer alone in offering a wide range of benefits and services to citizens. More and more parties are involved. The "pillars" of welfare (or, as the author of Chapter 3 puts it, the "welfare diamond")—namely, the state along with the marketplace, the various organizations that represent the third sector such as civic associations, NGOs, and voluntary agencies, and finally families and communities—are increasingly interconnected through partnerships. Further shifts in the "welfare mix" (Evers, 1993) are triggered. But the state's retreat from the role of "direct provider" does not necessarily mean that it must withdraw from the social sphere. On the contrary, this retreat could reflect a new conception of its role as a "proactive architect" of solidarity and as a coordinator of the various pillars mentioned. The state's role is to mobilize all sources of protection and ensure that "complementarities" are created between state-based and societally based, public and private forms of solidarity. The new policies that aim to reconcile family and work, care for the elderly, supporting volunteer work, or "revitalizing" the participation and involvement of "users" in the services and facilities that are intended for them—all this can be seen as an effort on the part of the state to "reactivate" the different pillars of welfare and create synergy between them in order to provide a closer, more personalized form of services and transfer of funds to the intended beneficiaries.

With regard to citizenship, this new form of governance allows more room for both a libertarian model—with its insistence on the autonomy of individuals and the preservation of their capacity to make their own decisions (i.e., a strengthening of personal civil rights)—and a republican model, with its goal of involving citizens more actively in civic affairs and thereby strengthening democracy through the extension of political democratic rights and responsibilities. In this process of reconfiguring the triad of rights that make up citizenship, the socio-liberal model to which Marshall referred is losing ground. The weight of the role played by the state is being reassessed. The state still guarantees entitlements, but it allows leeway for individuals to make choices about them. Not all the new social policies that aim to increase the involvement of the family, "civil society," and the marketplace along with the state in the creation of "innovative complementarities" have been productive—far from it. Nevertheless, we do not think that they should be cited as evidence of the welfare state's refusal to assume its responsibilities in an effort to transfer them toward the private sector.

The new notion of a "social investment state" may imply a new form of governance based on an "embedded multi-solidarity system" (Paugam, 2007, 970), in which the major sources of protection for individuals are reinforced and closely coordinated. If public authorities are not willing to foster coordination among the parties involved in welfare, the state's retreat from this sector will place a heavier burden on families, civic associations, and, ultimately, individuals. On the other hand, the coexistence of state-based objectives and interventions and its pedagogic aspirations for promoting "good behavior" in all spheres (Newman, 2010) may also pose problems. It may become a process that "tends to draw citizens and social groups into new fields of governmental power" (Barnes et al., 2007, 205) rather than becoming a more civil and civic way of organizing welfare and social services (Evers, 2010).

DIFFERENT STRATEGIES OF IMPLEMENTING AN ACTIVATING SOCIAL INVESTMENT AGENDA AND THEIR IMPLICATIONS FOR CITIZENSHIP

The methodological considerations raised in Chapter 1 focused on the need to recontextualize any analysis of reforms, in order to trace their effects down to the level of beneficiaries. Only in this way can we move beyond theoretical considerations about changes and measure the impact of reforms on citizenship in concrete terms. Our discussion of the major changes in the paradigms of the actions conducted in line with the activating social investment strategy has demonstrated the ambivalence of these new principles: they may have positive effects on citizenship, but equally they have the potential to jeopardize rights. We will now turn to the chapters concerning national cases and analyze how these principles have been applied through the welfare reforms actually carried out. We can then assess the implications for citizenship.

The homogeneous—cognitive and normative—grid of the arrangements of the five principles that underlie the interventions of the social investment state can be used to interpret the reconfiguration of welfare in each country. By examining national reforms using this grid, we can discover the specific arrangement and ranking of these five principles in each particular case. We can then assess the achievements made in the name of this new rhetoric and the impact of these achievements on social entitlements and citizenship.

As pointed out in the first section of this conclusion, the adoption of new paradigms in social investment is leading to an overhaul of the notion of citizenship. This entails more than just the reform of social benefits into measures designed to "activate" entitlements; it also affects the other dimensions of citizenship, namely civil and political rights. As a consequence, implementing the social investment strategy leads to "citizenship regimes" (see Chapter 3) that differ according to the emphasis placed on the freedom and responsibility of individuals, or on the common good, or even on citizen participation. As a function of the scope of the social investment strategy, the priorities established, and the ranking of the five major principles, different versions of citizenship emerge, ranging from the most libertarian to the most republican, from more interactive and democratic styles of governance to making use of the soft power of regulations and attempting to condition the behavior of their addressees. The analytical framework proposed in Chapter 2 encapsulates the repertoire for interpreting how citizenship has been reworked as a function of the new social agenda.

In the pages that follow, we will develop a stylized picture of the way in which the strategy of social investment is being implemented, and the effect of this reconfiguration of citizenship. We shall start by examining those examples where citizenship has not been constructed through the gradual process described by T. H. Marshall. Italy and the postcommunist countries represent cases where the impact of the welfare reforms conducted on citizenship is of a different nature and is perceived quite differently. Secondly, we shall point out three distinct strategies for handling the new activating social investment agenda. Each centers actions around certain of the five principles, with different effects on the scope of entitlements and on citizenship. Each leads to a specific remixing of the Marshallian triad of civil, political, and social rights.

The Presence of the Past: Political and Welfare Legacies that Have Prevented the Realization of the "Marshallian Framework"

The reconfiguration of welfare in different countries over the past 20 years has depended very much on the ways in which political, personal, and social rights were related to each other in the historical quest for welfare and democracy. For the western European countries, Chapter 8, on Italy, illustrates this quite well.

A welfare state that redistributes income through universal entitlements and thus helps develop not only the social but also the political and civil dimensions of citizenship has never existed in Italy. On the contrary, the territorial dualism between northern Italy and southern Italy dominated, from the very start, the construction of the Italian welfare system. Italian citizens do not enjoy uniform, fundamental social rights. These exist for wage-earners in northern industries, but in the south, the population is obligated to local elites and relinquishes its social rights to obtain favors. In Dahrendorf's words, southern Italians have given up entitlements to obtain "provisions."

This "mark of origins" (Merrien, 2002) is still visible in the reforms being made in Italian welfare. The unequal distribution of entitlements, related to the territorial gulf, has been deepened by the generational divide that has marked Italian reforms since the mid-1990s. The Dini pension reforms of 1995 favored wage-earners who already had a steady job and who had contributed to the pension fund for at least 18 years, to the detriment of those, mainly younger people, without a "standard permanent job contract." The reforms will inevitably result in inadequate pensions for the latter. Likewise, the reforms made in unemployment insurance do not provide the same compensation to all wage-earners irrespective of their employment contracts. The young—mostly atypical wage-earners—fall, in the main, outside the scope of these measures and do not enjoy the same protection against unemployment as older wage-earners.

Since these reforms have accentuated the dualism at the heart of the Italian welfare state, they cannot be analyzed as resulting from a change in the paradigms of public intervention. However, we can detect a rearrangement of the basic principles underlying public interventions in Italy in recent reforms, which is in line with the new activating social investment agenda. For instance, the new flavor imparted to healthcare and pensions is reinforcing the part played by private actors and the marketplace. Furthermore, the value attached to individual responsibility and to the family is being used to justify the state's withdrawal from the social sphere.

Turning now to the postcommunist countries in eastern Europe, some will underline the role of the new institutional and political realities of liberal market democracies that have been established and the new social risks that have emerged, while others will give more weight to the impact of the past.

Historical differences have an impact in a number of ways: in economic terms, one can argue that because of the past, the economic pressures are greater in eastern Europe than in western Europe, while the lack of resources is sharper; secondly, half a century of an authoritarian system has left its imprints on citizens, habits, and mentalities, as well as on the conditions for policymaking. Although there is now an almost complete institutional and legal framework for political-democratic, civil, and social citizenship in the postcommunist countries, the complementary practices in politics and everyday life must also be taken account of when one wants to debate the stability and levels of achievement in citizenship. In an often-quoted contribution to the debate on political and economic change in postcommunist eastern Europe, Crawford and Lijphart (1995) enumerate six key elements that linger from the past: (a) a history of backwardness and victimization; (b) the absence of a clearly established successor elite; (c) party systems with weak roots in society; (d) a process of nation building that was interrupted during the communist years; (e) the persistence of institutions established under the old regime, including welfare institutions; and (f) the legacy of a centralized state and command economy. Given that background, which is very different from the one in England but also other Western European countries, social rights do not have the same status with respect to civil and democratic rights.

In any case, when it comes to understanding the opportunities and the challenges of change and rebuilding welfare arrangements—and thereby reconstructing citizenship, especially social citizenship—both elements, the "presence of the past" and the new forces and actors, need to be viewed as inseparable.

One important difficulty stems from the fact that what are today called social rights were for many decades rules and regulations that served to uphold authoritarian leadership in the communist countries. This means, first of all, that it is highly questionable to call them "rights" when they were decrees from the top down that could not be negotiated openly. This concerns first of all the fact that in former socialist states, the public tends not to associate social rights with social negotiations and struggles for better living conditions (as experienced in Western democracies), but rather with attempts to use these "rights" as a means of "passivating" citizens, to bribe sections of the population with special regulations, to use the granting of social entitlements as a substitute for denied personal and political freedoms. Hence, as products of state paternalism and as former socialist achievements, social rights are not perceived as they are in the context of Marshall, where they were to complete and strengthen precisely those democratic and civil freedoms because they could take shape not only from the top down but also from the bottom up, through processes of dialogue and negotiation. Chapter 13 in particular gives an interesting wider perspective on this debate, showing that as well the new social measures taken in the first years after communism were by many politicians seen more as provisional "shock absorbers" and only to a lesser degree as fundamentals for a new postcommunist welfare concept.

In the intellectual debate in the postcommunist countries it has thus often been argued that given the historical differences of former communist countries, the emphasis should now be on rooting civil and democratic rights more deeply in the practices of society. The argument is that only when social legislation is accompanied by corresponding changes in people's expectations, which were shaped largely under the old regime by the protective hand of the state will it be possible to make them contribute positively to building citizenship as a status and a practice rooted in citizens' intercourse. All in all, then, the question is the extent to which a historical sequence of civil, democratic, and social rights that differs from the one that Marshall referred to affects how we must now view their interrelationship—analytically and in political practice.

As history has shown, civil, democratic, and social rights need to be seen as interacting in different ways. There are not only mutually supportive interrelationships but also tensions, and the weakness of one dimension will inevitably affect the nature and status of the others. As a consequence, there is no single route to future concepts of welfare and citizenship.

Reconfiguring Welfare and Reshaping Citizenship

How have the new principles of the activating social investment agenda been applied thus far? The chapters in the second section have shed light on the various strategies of implementation. Let us summarize the major conclusions drawn from them by distinguishing three "stylized pictures" of different strategies, with their own way of reshaping citizenship rights. Each of the three pictures represents a different arrangement and ranking of the five basic principles identified in the first part, as emphasis is given to one or two principles over the others.

The liberal version of the social investment strategy emphasizes the responsibilities of individuals as a corollary to receiving benefits. Accordingly, the state should invest in the future so as to expand individuals' autonomy and develop their capacity for self-sufficiency. In contrast, the social democratic version does not question the welfare state's role in redistribution for the sake of equality. Instead, it seeks to activate the social investment strategy by emphasizing the state's role in making preventive investments in human capital to equip individuals. The third version, a hybrid of these two poles, includes a number of internal contradictions, which are exposed in the chapters devoted to France and Germany in particular.

As for rights and citizenship, these types of implementation of the new agenda lead to contrasting arrangements of Marshall's trio of civil, social, and political rights. These contrasts are evidence of tensions between these three poles.

A Liberal Strategy for Dealing with the New Agenda: Public Support for Private Responsibility

The "third way" was advocated by New Labour in the UK as part of its efforts to break with both the prevailing neoliberalism and the principles of the "old welfare state." This attempt to find a middle way has contributed very much to the rhetoric surrounding social investment. This version bears the hallmark of its origins. The liberty and autonomy of individuals outweigh collective social rights.

The analysis in Chapter 6 of the UK's strategy of implementing policies of activation and social investment sheds light on a special ranking of the five principles of this agenda. The insistence on obligations rather than entitlements has assigned a key place to work, and entitlements, subject to conditions, are granted only if the corresponding obligations are met. This arrangement includes a set of incentives and sanctions that have been incorporated into welfare-to-work schemes. The goal is to accelerate the speed at which individuals return to the labor market, which is deemed the best method for making individuals autonomous and responsible for their own well-being and that of their family.

The second major principle underlying this strategy is that the future trumps the present. Social intervention is legitimate only if it produces a return on the investment made and enhances the self-sufficiency of the beneficiary in the medium term. As a consequence, the government no longer plays the role of a "providing state" that redistributes benefits to compensate for certain risks. The role of the social investment state is to intervene preventively through a "proactive" investment strategy that helps people to remain autonomous and exercise responsibility. The state's withdrawal from its role of "direct provider" of so-called "passive" expenditure is directly attributable to this emphasis on individual responsibility. The optimization of public social expenditure in line with a "prospective investment logic" that is oriented toward the future implies "public support for private responsibility" (see Chapter 4). Social expenditure can thus be said to be "active."

However, this emphasis also shows that New Labour's reforms not only signaled a retreat on rights and citizenship, as suggested by a simplified interpretation in terms of a neoliberal shift in welfare policy. We can draw no single conclusion that fits all cases about whether there has been an advance or a retreat with respect to citizenship. What we can observe is a rearrangement of social, political, and civil rights. The UK's activation and social investment strategy has been designed to reinforce the individual's autonomy to the detriment of collective social rights. The "libertarian element" of citizenship has been reinforced, while collective social rights have been altered.

The assessment of New Labour's welfare reforms in Chapter 6 highlighted alterations in entitlements and social citizenship. Services and benefits based on contributions and social insurance schemes (the mainstay of social entitlements under the postwar welfare regimes) have been restricted in favor of means-tested benefits and tax credits for working. Groups are now targeted with the aim of making recipients active or preparing children to be the "citizen-workers of the future." Unconditional entitlements have become conditional and are being used to change the behavior of beneficiaries. This rise in conditionality also allows room for discretionary decisions by welfare staff and thus reduces the system's transparency. As Lister wrote in Chapter 6, "more personalized forms of delivery spell greater discretion and reduced accountability."

This way of implementing the social investment strategy has, to some extent, brought about an erosion of social entitlements. The poorest, who are the furthest removed from the labor market, may not be able to measure up to the requirements of responsibility or comply with the patterns of behavior expected of them. The inequality between the most able and the least able could widen. The latter may end up being sanctioned for not meeting their obligations and held individually responsible for their failure.

Even with regard to social rights, however, we observe advances and not just a retreat. Some progress has been made toward the universal entitlement to a basic pension and fighting poverty among the elderly. Furthermore, the targeting in New Labour's welfare reforms reaches further into the middle classes than previously (see Chapter 3). Nor has the adoption of a social investment strategy had a purely negative impact on social entitlements and citizenship in the UK. It has led to assistance with childcare and even fostered entitlements in this field that the postwar welfare state never provided. Investing in children helps fight poverty by preventively empowering individuals rather than keeping them in a state of dependency, stuck in the poverty trap of remedial compensation.

A Social Democratic Strategy for Dealing with the New Agenda: Activation of Human Capital in Pursuit of Equality

The social democratic version of an activating social investment strategy combines and ranks the principles that underlie the paradigm in a different way. The welfare state continues to enjoy widespread legitimacy as a redistributor and provider of generous benefits and services. The scope of collective social rights has not been called into question. In Chapter 10, on Sweden, the authors describe a "welfare paradox" that they label "the iron law of rights" whereby "the advancement of collective social rights necessarily entails a corresponding loss of individual legal rights." This remark illustrates the contrast between the liberal and social democratic strategies for activation and social investment. Social citizenship still lies at the center of the new Nordic agenda, although it has been combined to a considerable extent with civil and libertarian elements in the liberal model.

However, the conception of the state's role has been deeply modified and, consequently, so too has the nature of the resources that it redistributes. From a simple "providing state," the welfare state has become a proactive, preventive state, whose priority is to equip individuals with "skills" to achieve in the future and to ensure the well-being and inclusion of everyone. This strategy of strengthening national competitiveness and inclusion does not, however, remove the concern for equality in the social democratic strategy, and especially in the Nordic countries it can build on a long tradition of looking for a "virtuous circle of equality, democracy and growth" (Kettunen, 2011, 31). Today as well efforts are being made to providing equal opportunities to enable beneficiaries to cope with the challenges of the post-industrial era, in particular changes in employment. Reinforcing the work ethic and striking a new balance in social rights by pointing out beneficiaries' obligations are central elements of this model, as in the liberal one. Social rights are now conditional, tied to the individual's efforts to return to employment. However, the two versions do not activate citizens in the same way.

In the social democratic version, incentives predominate over coercion. Making work pay and investing in lifelong education are used to motivate people to remain in, or return to, the labor market. These policies encourage people to adopt the behavior patterns required of them. In turn, it is legitimate to strengthen the rules and regulations to deal with those who do not comply.

There is, however, a further difference between the more social democratic and the more liberal versions of dealing with an activation and investment agenda. Forms of governance also differ, given that each has its own conception of the "responsibility mix." Under the more social democratic version, the state, as pointed out, remains the key player in the new social investment strategy. The state coordinates and orients investment in human capital, and oversees the equality of distribution. The state also regulates the intervention of public and private parties (mainly social services and NGOs) and is the architect of "active forms of solidarity." Not satisfied with investing in human capital and fixing targets, the state also provides services and advice to help individuals make decisions about how to optimize the investment made in them. This type of governance contrasts with the ideal type of practices under the liberal version of "activation." Under the latter, the state makes investment, but instead of a co-responsibility between individuals and social services, the emphasis is firmly on individual responsibility (Barbier, 2005).

What the two approaches have in common is the fact that both operate with a direct link and sharp contrast between state action on the one hand, and individual action on the other hand. Both seem to have trouble utilizing resources that may be forthcoming from social support networks of communities or the associational life of civil society and the third sector. From there, however, joint and collective responsibilities may come into focus differently from pure state collective and individual responsibilities. Obviously, strategies that seek to upgrade the role of community and civil society are met with distrust on the part of those who underline the autonomy of individuals, as well as on the part of those who do not like to see resources upgraded that are difficult to formalize in terms of rights.

Embracing state-based collective social rights, it seems that the social democratic version of the activation and social investment agenda is the one that has the least impact on the triad of political, civil, and social rights as T. H. Marshall defined them. However, one caveat must be added. To the extent to which such rights are made more conditional and thereby conflict with individual rights, a difference can be discerned. While under the old industrial welfare state, the uniform, standardized type of rights and services was in tension with individual rights, the challenge now is to find ways of making the more personal arrangements of today rights-based in order to avoid that respective decisions on service support mirror mainly state and professional power. The degree in which progress can be made in this respect determines the extent to which social and civil rights might be reconciled, although tensions are still prevalent (see Chapter 10, on Sweden).

The Hybrid Nature of Certain National Strategies

The two polar versions of the implementation of the social investment strategy that have been presented reflect conceptions of security for individuals that break with the principles underlying the postwar welfare state. Each version emphasizes certain paradigms on the social investment agenda and ranks them. But each also bears the mark of its original model, which has been mixed and realigned as a function of new paradigms of action. In this sense, we cannot talk of the "path dependency" of these polar models but, instead, of a radical change that nevertheless bears the marks of historical compromises between the values and solutions that favored past arrangements. Besides these two polar versions, with their clearly discernable characteristics (as described in the chapters on the UK and Sweden and, too, in Chapter 3 and 4), the contributors to this volume have brought to light numerous hybrid varieties. Some of them draw from both the versions outlined above, combining them in their effort to orient welfare policy toward activation and social investment. In other issues, trends and concerns become visible that are not at the forefront of either the liberal or the social democratic strategy for activation and social investment. These questions concern the place of civil society in new modes of governance or the role that is attached to social investments that aim at cultivating and upgrading the social capital of community and third-sector associations.

In Chapter 7 Barbier's analysis of France led him to interpret the forms of activation applied in the cases of the unemployed and the poor as hybrid forms of
these polar models. The unemployment insurance reform, which introduced the
PARE in 2001, lies between these two polar versions of activating social investment strategies. When it comes to social rights, relatively generous benefits (in
terms of the level and length of coverage) are still being provided, although less
so than under the Nordic model. Furthermore, minimal emphasis is placed on
the obligation to return to employment as a counterpart for entitlements. The
conditionality of benefits and the system of sanctions have been formally tightened, but implementation has been limited. As a matter of fact, the quality of the
French public employment services (far inferior to those in the Nordic model)
does not enable it to enforce work obligations effectively.

The minimum income scheme for the poor (*revenu minimum d'insertion*
[RMI]), which under its "activated" version (*revenu de solidarité active* [RSA])
was recently renamed, does not include strict obligations for returning to employment that are paired with sanctions. In this case, activation appears to amount
to the objective of inclusion in the medium or long term. Since its goal is to
stimulate social and political "participation," the reform of the minimum income
scheme has, theoretically, produced a universal program for fighting exclusion.
This universal ambition makes it similar to the Nordic version of activation. As
Barbier shows, however, universality has never been achieved. The minimum
income scheme (RMI) represented, in fact, a safety net for the poorest, to whom
it offered limited services and benefits funded through "national solidarity" (i.e.,
public assistance). In this sense, it resembled the liberal version, although it differed from the latter in its weaker emphasis on the obligation to return to work.

In the French reforms, we can detect not so much an alteration of social rights
as their fragmentation, which deepens the existing polarization between the
social insurance system (which covers those who have paid contributions as they
worked) and public assistance (which extends a subject to means-test for all those
not covered by the social insurance system). As a consequence, the new activating
social investment strategy could, in France, deepen the division between these
groups: those who benefit from unemployment insurance, those who benefit
from the unemployment solidarity program (the safety net for the unemployed),
and those who fall into one or more of the three (formerly five) categories of
social minima (the minimum income schemes for the poor). These different categories enjoy neither the same entitlements nor the same services, and in fact the
beneficiaries of the last two entitlements could be called "second-class citizens."
According to Barbier, young people and women are the most at risk of being
eligible only for low-quality benefits and services. As pointed out with regard to
the liberal strategy for activation and social investment, the targeting of social
intervention has the potential to deepen the inequality between those who are
best off and the others. This risk is all the greater in that, in France, the targeting
and individualization of entitlements does not bring any actual empowerment of

the beneficiaries, and does not increase their ability to help themselves. What we observe is a patchwork of measures that borrow from the liberal and the social democratic versions. These reforms bring to mind a "default transformation," a process that, according to Merrien et al. (2005, 352), results from "a fortuitous encounter at a given time between the need to act, the existence of solutions that are already made but might be poorly adapted to goals, and decision-makers with a very limited rationality."

In Chapter 9, Bode gives an account of Germany that highlights changes in citizenship that combine the traditions of a corporatist past with a kind of new universalism of basic social rights and new rules that emphasize the two sides of individualism—the scope for individual choice and the duty of individual self-help. First of all, Bode shows that the need for changes in social citizenship was in large part brought about by the end of full employment, which previously had rendered the difference between the Bismarckian work-related rights and universal rights of all citizens almost insignificant. This put an end to basic arrangements such as unemployment insurance that guaranteed the perpetual right to an unemployment benefit, the level of which was linked to the recipient's status in the occupational system. For decades now, the difference between those who enjoy social rights as "worker-citizens" and those who cannot be included in this category any longer—and are thus deprived of its entitlements—has been growing. However, as Bode shows, this does not mean that a simple process of retrenchment and bifurcation of social rights has taken shape, as Palier (2010) has argued. Rather, with work-based rights becoming ever less universal, and a retrenchment that makes people more dependent on markets, two different elements are gaining importance.

These are activating elements that accentuate individual responsibility but simultaneously open up choices. The level of social pensions is reduced and incentives are given for everyone to select and buy complementary packages on insurance markets. Similarly, reforms in healthcare on the one hand enforce co-payments while at the same time guaranteeing or extending the right to choose a doctor, the type of insurance, the insurance provider, and so on.

This agenda of reducing rights "as we knew them" while strengthening the individual duties of the worker-citizen and individual right to choice of the consumer-citizen is, however, accompanied by a kind of new universalism in basic securities. Where there was once a system for rubberstamping social assistance handouts, one now sees a dense system of advice and guidance for nearly all those outside work: minimum pensions have been removed from the social assistance realm; new arrangements ensure that everyone has access to healthcare, whatever her or his employment status; finally, new services in childcare and elderly care are universally guaranteed, along with individual choice in terms of arrangements and provider.

What we call here "hybrid" concepts, which combine liberal and social democratic versions of activation and social investment (layered over what remains from the long past of welfare), Bode refers to as a "fuzzy configuration in which the work-related social rights that had *de facto* instilled elements of social citizenship in the German welfare regime during the 20th century have been exposed to a shift towards `marketization' (or re-commodification) even though, paradoxically, new universalistic elements have also occurred."

Finally, intriguing mixes can also be found on the road of the postcommunist countries of eastern Europe towards reconfiguring welfare and citizenship. While one can broadly state that basic political democratic and civil rights have been opened up and restored, the evidence for social rights is more mixed. Many of the rules and arrangements of the former systems—such as in social security— now linger on in a new context as "rights" that are open to debate and negotiation. Some of the newly created rights mirror the (re)appearance of formerly unknown risks, which are typically attached to a capitalist economy, such as unemployment. However, while many social rights have been maintained, some have been reduced, and some extended, one has to recognize that the special kind of egalitarianism that accompanied the former authoritarian socialism has been undermined—something that was not equal citizenship but a uniformity in the conditions imposed on those living under those regimes.

At this point, it should already have become clear that the sort of global reasoning that tackles issues of citizenship from the perspective of aggregating levels of social rights does not lead very far. Rights stated—and more specifically social rights—are important to strengthening the status of individuals as citizens, but, as has been argued many times in this book, the two issues should not be equated with one another. Beyond the empirical information given in Chapter 12 (Hungary), Chapter 13 (Poland), and Chapters 11 and 14 (Czech Republic), one can find two important observations concerning the difficult interplay of building social rights and strengthening citizenship.

The first point transcends the debate surrounding the degree to which poorer countries can afford social procurements and rights. Rather, it concerns the impact of an economy that functions differently, rather than one that is less affluent. The critical point of difference stems from the fact that in the postcommunist countries the newly institutionalized market economy is even less inclusive than it is in many Western Europe countries, incorporating a long tradition of working in the informal "black economy" that coexists with and depends upon institutionalized systems of labor, provision, and social networks. Working (simultaneously) in the black market or combining social provisions that are granted on the basis that one is out of work with black labor has, in the postsocialist countries, become a fixed part of daily practices to varying degrees. It cuts across social strata, ranging from badly paid intellectuals who take on extra work, to black labor carried out by those who are officially unemployed (Vagnin, 2000). Under such conditions, as shown in Chapter 12, benefits that are meant to substitute income from employment become a complementary source of income as well as elements that help people to cope better with the enormous insecurity that goes with most black labor. With an eye on the situation in the Czech Republic, Rys, a specialist in the analysis of social security systems in eastern and central Europe, speaks of "a new class of self-employed, financed by the abuse of unemployment benefits," and says that governments have to realize that under such conditions "they are acting in contradiction to their declared policy of moving away from state paternalism" (1995, 201). Obviously, social rights that work in this way may be a blessing for the recipients involved, who have little choice or incentive to act otherwise, but they will not contribute to the strengthening of citizenship. The unspoken link between black labor and social benefits intensifies competition, insecurity, and inequalities, and it forces people to cheat each other and the authorities who ought to represent the political community. In Chapter 12 Szalaï goes further, asking whether there is any collective political will at all to overhaul a system under which income from the informal economy and social benefits take on a complementary role. This may lead to a kind of social appeasement, but it institutionalizes the separation between those citizens who are in the official economy and receive respectable pension entitlements and allowances and those who are "outside," who must depend on combining an income from black labor with what they receive from workfare/social assistance systems. How can social rights and entitlements then escape from being part of a system that undermines the moral foundations of citizenship while reproducing a bifurcated system with two classes of citizens?

The second point concerns the impact of the political culture—social rights when there is a weak civil dialogue. From various angles, all the chapters about the postcommunist countries point to the difficulty of making the quality of social arrangements and concrete social rights into the object of an open public discourse. Chapter 14 concentrates on the difficulty of bringing together representatives from the administration, politicians, and concerned intellectuals, and ensuring a respected place and voice for the latter. As he shows, the Civic Forum has found it difficult to reinforce the concern for social rights and help in bridging the modernization concerns of the EU with the practices of Czech welfare administrations, which are characterized—as shown in Chapter 11—both by old habits and new economic realities.

The weakness of civil society (Howard, 2003) that is evident across the postsocialist countries does not, however, only mean that old and new vested interests and networks can maintain their influence on public policies; it also means, as shown in Chapter 14, that under such circumstances it is all the more difficult to move towards a meaningful notion of the public good, which will provide a basis on which to accept or reject claims for state support and assistance. To the degree that the claims of those stronger groups that are heard in public mirror very partial concerns, the needs of marginalized groups—as shown in Chapter 12—get no advocacy from stronger groups. And a missing capacity of transforming partial claims into collective projects means likewise that under the pressure of coming to workable short-term solutions and to upheld political power,

social policy devices of the ruling parties are used for motives that have nothing to do with strengthening the social rights as parts of citizenship (Kaufmann,
2007, 111, 122). The temptation of using social measures once again as a kind
of group-specific bribe exists in both Eastern and Western Europe, but one may
argue that this temptation is more acute where governments and party systems
are weaker and the problems faced are more difficult and controversial.

Marshall defined the contribution of social rights and policies to citizenship
not simply in terms of equality and inclusion, but also in terms of transforming
inherited and market-based inequalities into a politically shaped stratification
that could be seen as fairer. However, a fairer and more just form of inequality cannot take shape when citizens perceive social entitlements to be the result
of policies that above all serve the political compromises that secure the coalitions in power. Making social rights part of a policy for strengthening citizenship, however, supposes that, to some degrees at least, policies are the result of
a different type of intertwining state policies and bottom-up claims—one where
conceptions of the public good on both sides have a role rather than merely the
concern for survival. In Chapter 12, Szalaï hits the nail on the head when she
argues that the example of her country and, indeed, of current social policies in
the postcommunist countries are a good example of the continuing influence of
two factors that have been essential to Marshall's concept of citizenship: a kind of
gradualism that is aware of the interdependence of the political, civic, and social
culture and the need for a social dialogue that is able to recognize the concerns
of excluded groups in its concepts of the common and public good. Put simply,
there is hardly any chance of good social policy in a "spoiled democracy"—that is
to say, social policy that promotes citizenship in a context where a civic political
culture is lacking.

EU CONTRIBUTIONS TO CITIZENSHIP: A MOVE FROM SOCIAL TO HUMAN RIGHTS AS THE OPTION OF TODAY?

Several authors have drawn attention to the institutional tension between the
construction of the EU and national social policies. Like Scharpf (2009), Barbier
in Chapter 5 observes that the political and legal integration of Europe represents
a threat to public services (the Bolkestein directive) and the social protection that
exists in individual member-states. According to both of these authors, the EU
does not introduce any "new positive rights" apart from legislation on equality and
against discrimination. So far, however, European citizenship, beyond the political right to vote in elections for the European parliament, corresponds chiefly
to the freedom for individuals to move within Europe and the equal treatment
to be granted to all European citizens. It is here that one can find at least a small
window of opportunities for extending citizenship rights through EU actions.
The constitutional basis of the EU, even if it is not much more than a means

for creating an international market, including a corresponding labor market, prohibits discrimination on the grounds of gender, sexual orientation, race, ethnic origin, religion, belief, disability, and age. These fundamental human rights are civil rights for individuals that are included in the Charter of Fundamental Rights of the European Union. In a similar vein, Ferrera (2005) has insisted on the contradiction between the openness, which has inspired European integration, and the territorial closure of policies of solidarity and redistribution, which still fall within the competences of national authorities. Barbier concludes that a European social citizenship does not exist.

These studies show how the building of Europe has reinforced an insistence on human rights to the detriment of social rights. We believe that it is important to raise questions about this shift from social rights toward human rights and to interpret its meaning for social policy and citizenship. The academic community does not unanimously agree on how to do this, however, since any judgment depends on opinions about the current balance between social and individual civil rights. This balance is constantly jeopardized by the tension inherent in democratic societies between the collective need to produce and protect free individuals and the principle of individual freedom. Chapter 10, on Sweden, illustrates this tension clearly. According to the authors, the collective requirements of social solidarity in Sweden are imposed to the detriment of the individual's rights. In this case, the shift from social to human rights could be a positive trend, then. Nonetheless, these authors argue for a new balance between individual and social rights in the Swedish case and, quite clearly, that the former should not be overwhelmed by the latter.

Colette Bec (2007, 191) has worked out the negative consequences of an opposite trend, where "social rights are caught up in human rights." She sees this as a source of concern since it challenges the tension, consubstantial with democratic society, between individual freedom and collective solidarity, which serves as the basis for social rights. Bec sees this irresistible rise of human rights as part of a twofold trend. First of all, there is the neoliberal trend with its attachment to the marketplace and individual freedoms, in opposition to a welfare state that is losing legitimacy. This trend is a potential threat that could reduce the individual's freedom of choice. Secondly, the fight against totalitarianism in eastern Europe has rehabilitated individual rights in countries where authoritarian regimes had long denied human rights.

As a consequence, the specificity of social rights is being sacrificed to other rights. Social rights are constructed out of social relations. They seek to place beneficiaries in the position of being citizens who belong to a community with the ability to use their freedom. They are intended, for the sake of equality and freedom, to regulate inequality, injustice, and domination. This is the perspective from which T. H. Marshall referred to social citizenship as the recognition of the equality of all citizens in an unequal capitalistic society divided into social classes.

The shift from social to human rights obfuscates the relationships that ground rights in a specific society and political community that is able to guarantee these rights to all its member-citizens. Human rights, by contrast, refer to an abstract human being who transcends the special circumstances of history and society and is granted fundamental, inalienable, but also abstract rights in the name of a cosmopolitan human essence. However, as Sen (2002, 112) has rightly remarked, there is no such thing as "world citizenship." Such a shift from social to human rights voids the specific nature of the former. If preserving "dignity" as a new political ambition of social policy is derived from a reference to cosmopolitan human rights taken out of context, this becomes a banal exercise. An examination of the various "rights-to" that are deemed essential, such as the right to equal treatment (directive ML 2000/78 of Nov. 27, 2000) or the rights enumerated in the European Charter of Fundamental Rights, can illustrate this dilemma.

In conclusion, it is necessary to remain vigilant with regard to this shift from social to human rights. On the one hand, it could play out following a gloomy scenario for post-Marshallian citizenship—renegotiating the former prevalence of collective rights and regulations over personal rights as well as restricting the soft power of targeted strategies that promote "healthier" behavior by citizens from the top down. On the other hand, individual human rights can hardly be derived from a cosmopolitan concept of rights that transcend every specific context. The construction of a "social Europe" may be in suspense, but the multiplication of individual human rights cannot make up for this. Nor can it replace the development of a European citizenship. Under the guise of defending and broadening individual freedoms and empowering individuals, we may lose sight of the path towards a society with less exclusion and greater social justice.

POSTSCRIPT: WHAT IS THE FUTURE OF WELFARE AND CITIZENSHIP IN THE MIDST OF THE ECONOMIC AND FINANCIAL CRISIS?

Although the European social model very much depends on the national level and the degree of its realization varies from one member-state to the next (Barbier, Chapter 5), does it have a chance for surviving the current economic and financial crisis, which had made all of Europe quake? The lack of growth and the mountain of debt accumulated by European countries is jeopardizing their commitments to social programs.

What has been argued so far in academic and political debates about the degree the EU has brought additional EU-based rights and/or reduced existing nationally based rights will have to be revised. The international financial crisis—ongoing at the time of this writing—and the forms it has taken with the near-bankruptcy of Greece and a few other EU member-states and the attempts at the EU level to come to the rescue by constructing a joint umbrella of financial guarantees shed new light on the linkage between Europeanization and citizenship.

The public's attention is being turned away from the issue of rights-building under conditions in which the very economic and financial foundations of welfare and democracy are seen as threatened. Given the shortage of public budgets not only in the countries most affected but also in those that have to mobilize enormous sums to create an umbrella of financial aid and security, state-based social rights will have even less room for developing further. The financial crisis of state budgets and of banking systems or, more precisely, the strategies of coping with it are challenging political citizenship. EU member-states are assisted with contracts that narrow the limits of their national sovereignty. Meanwhile, there is no sign that the negotiations between banks, statesmen, and decision-makers on the EU level that carry them out will strengthen an EU-based political power that broadens democratic citizenship. Nowadays, speculations about the future are less focused on increasing democratic EU legitimacy by widening the competence of the European parliament than on creating an EU economic and financial government (or should we say a superagency?) that would clearly limit further the potential realms of decision making for democratic governments at the national level. The impact on national citizenship (rights) could be harmful if, as might happen all too soon, democratic process and political decisions at the national level would be seen as dysfunctional and not be in line with the agenda of such an EU fiscal and economic agency.

Nevertheless, there might be reasons to hope that the current crisis might have positive side effects on the chances for building EU citizenship. Ongoing debates about Europe's financial and economic fate may create a bit of *demos*, a shared concern and interest of people across national borders, that is indispensable for anchoring citizenship as something that is expressed not only in top-down legislation but also through bottom-up actions and identity-building. Despite the gloomy future of the European social model, since the current recession might do away with social rights and citizenship enshrined in law, a more optimistic scenario might be played out whereby our current tribulations would revive a sense of responsibility both in national political cultures and in terms of transnational solidarity within the EU—that is, active and civic components of a culture of citizenship that needs, as T. H. Marshall once argued, both laws and attitudes. Active citizenship and a more civic culture might then help to find new ways for combining social cohesion and economic growth and the respective kind of social investment strategy.

At present, however, the gloomy scenario seems more probable. Cutting social spending, which represents a large percentage of GDP (about 30% in France, for example), has become a major preoccupation of nation-states in a context where it is imperative to reduce the national debt. Many observers are declaring that,

given the tempest in the financial markets now threatening all national economies in Europe, the time is past for concern about the survival of a costly welfare system that was designed during a time of prosperity, so different from the
current age of austerity. This era of belt-tightening tends toward setting limits on
welfare spending. How should we implement policies for redistribution when
state coffers are empty and national governments are heavily in debt? In this
context, we observe a return to the prevalence of an approach that is question-
ing the very foundations of politics, to the degree it is argued that there is a need
for quick decisions and no alternatives given. In this perspective, issues of how
to use and strengthen active citizenship and civic responsibility, dimensions so
important for both democracy and citizenship, become hidden. The peoples of
Europe are given the message to hold out and suffer without a complementary
message about (active) citizenship.

The determination of national governments to center their strategies around
financial preoccupations with key concerns such as the cost-containment of welfare may actualize all the potential risks related to the shift in welfare rhetoric
towards the "activating social investment agenda," risks mentioned earlier in this
chapter.

A main danger results from promoting an "enabling state" in place of a "providing State." In a time of crisis, depreciating a state that provides compensation
opens the way to reducing social benefits and favors new forms of intervention
that, perhaps vague and insignificant, are said to be preventive and to deliver
a better "return on investment." A dual welfare system might develop wherein
public assistance and minimum income guarantees (with obligations related to
"activation") will be offered to the weak and to outsiders on the labor market
while the less disadvantaged and insiders on the labor market will continue to
benefit from the social insurance system, even though benefits will be less generous and supplemented by private insurance systems (see again Palier, 2010). This
would be the threatening face of a kind of social investment state that refuses to
assume likewise the role of a proactive architect that assumes co-responsibility
for welfare at large, regulating the framework both for the public and private sectors and coordinating the different "pillars" of solidarity.

A trend toward a dualization of welfare will however not just deepen inequality between the underprivileged and others. It may also undermine welfare
systems, since, to paraphrase Habermas (1973), it alters their legitimacy and thus
leads to a deeper crisis in the very meaning of these systems. Evidence of this can
be found in a study of recent pension reforms in Europe (Hinrichs & Jessoula,
2011). Public pension systems have become the principal "natural" target of ongoing reforms that seek to reduce public deficits and balance welfare budgets. The
recent reforms, besides postponing the retirement age and increasing the length
of the period of contributions required for a standard pension, have especially
strengthened the link between one's working career and one's level of benefits.

However, such a shift, which is reducing issues of rights and fairness towards the simple question of an adequate link between former individual labor market performance and later entitlements, is threatening a notion of rights that relates to the status of citizenship. A mere orientation to the financial sustainability of pensions instead of their benefit adequacy will threaten especially the younger generations, who, in many European countries, have a hard time finding work or often hold "atypical" jobs that do not allow them to build up the "long contribution records" now necessary for receiving a decent pension in old age. As Hinrichs and Jessoula (2011) have remarked about Germany, "a flexible labour market plus pension reforms makes old age poverty" for future generations. It should be pointed out that it tends as well to undermine the system's legitimacy as a pact of solidarity between generations whose equity becomes questionable.for another scenario? Along with several authors in this volume, we think so. First of all, the current crisis is *de facto* forcing EU member-states toward more solidarity, despite much reluctance. The new interest expressed in more EU "federalism" is evidence of this. Secondly, the social investment strategy has relinked the economic and social spheres. Social policies are no longer understood as being just a cost to be borne by the economy, a cost weighing on employment that pits welfare against jobs, as in the "welfare states without work" of continental Europe that Esping-Andersen has described so well. These policies are to be understood as "investments" with positive effects for both stimulating growth and responding to social needs. The social investment approach could help modernize social interventions by adapting them to the risks generated by the new economy, which entails career trajectories that are more flexible, mobile, and individualized but also, very often, more chaotic (Guillemard, 2005; Morel et al., 2009). The principle is no longer to repair the damage when a risk occurs by providing compensation, but to prevent the deficits and losses of human capital by "equipping" individuals and reinforcing this capital throughout the life course. From this preventive perspective, young people and children receive more attention than the elderly; but this might be a way to reconstruct the pact of intergenerational solidarity, which so many recent pension reforms have altered (see Chapter 8, on Italy).

Finally, this social investment strategy has broken with the neoliberal credo by re-legitimating the state's role for social and economic development. The state is understood in this new perspective as coordinator of a solidarity that aims for a better "welfare mix," relying on several pillars (families, communities, firms, NGOs, not-for-profit organizations, and representatives of state politics). In such a perspective on changing welfare it is obviously important to debate issues of not only social but also democratic and personal rights. And it needs a notion of the subject that includes both, citizenship enshrined in laws and an active citizenship based on a civic culture. This volume has tried to contribute to such a perspective.

REFERENCES

Astier, I. (2007). *Les nouvelles règles du social.* Paris: Presses Universitaires de France.

Barbier, J.-C. (2005). Citizenship and the activation of social protection: a comparative approach. In J. G. Andersen, A.-M. Guillemard, P. Jensen, & B. Pfau-Effinger (Eds.), *The changing face of welfare, consequences and outcomes from a citizenship perspective* (pp. 113–134). Bristol: The Policy Press.

Barnes, M., J. Newman, & H. Sullivan (2007). *Power, participation and political renewal.* Bristol: The Policy Press.

Bec, C. (2007). *De l'état social à l'état des droits de l'homme.* Rennes: Presses universitaires de Rennes

Cerami, A. (2008). New social risks in central and eastern Europe: The need for a new empowering politics of the welfare state. *Czech Sociological Review, 44*(6), 1089–1110.

Crawford, B., & A. Lijphart (1995). Explaining political and economic change in postcommunist eastern Europe: Old legacies, new institutions, hegemonic norms and international pressures. *Comparative Political Studies, 28*(2), 171–199.

Esping-Andersen, G. (1990). *The three worlds of welfare capitalism.* Cambridge: Polity Press.

Evers, A. (1993). The welfare mix approach. Understanding the pluralism of welfare systems. In A. Evers & I. Svetlik (Eds.), *Balancing pluralism. New welfare mixes in care for the elderly* (pp. 3–31). Aldershot: Avebury.

Evers, A. (2010). Civicness, civility and their meanings for social services. In T. Brandsen, P. Dekker, & A. Evers (Eds.), *Civicness in the governance and delivery of social services* (pp. 41–66). Baden-Baden: Nomos.

Fergé, Z. (1997). Social policy challenges and dilemmas in ex-socialist systems. In J. M. Nelson, C. Tilly, & C. Walker (Eds.), *Transforming post-communist political economies.* Washington, DC: National Academic Press.

Ferrera, M. (2005). *The boundaries of welfare, European integration and the new spatial politics of social solidarity.* Oxford University Press

Guillemard, A. M. (2005). The advent of a flexible life course and the reconfigurations of welfare. In J. G. Andersen, A. M. Guillemard, P. Jensen, & B. Pfau-Effinger (Eds.), *The changing face of welfare. Consequences and outcomes from citizenship perspective* (pp. 55–73). Bristol: Policy Press

Habermas, J. (1973). *Legitimation crisis.* London: Heynemann Educational Books.

Hall, P. (1993). Policy paradigms, social learning and the state: The case of economic policy-making in Britain. *Comparative Politics, 25*(3), 275–296.

Hinrichs, K., & M. Jessoula (Eds.) (2011). *Labour market flexibility and pension reforms: Flexible today, secure tomorrow?* Palgrave Macmillan.

Howard, M. M. (2003). *The weakness of civil society in post-communist Europe.* New York: Cambridge University Press.

Kaufmann, R. R. (2007). Market reform and social protection: Lessons from the Czech Republic, Hungary, and Poland.: *East European Politics and Societies, 21*(1), 111–125.

Kettunen, P. (2011) The transnational construction of national challenges: the ambiguous Nordic model of welfare and competitiveness. In P. Kettunen & K. Petersen (Eds.), *Beyond welfare state models. Transnational historical perspectives on social policy.* Cheltenham and Northampton: Edward Elgar.

Kolarska-Bobinska, L., & M. Rymsza (2007). Social policy needed now. *Analyses and Opinions, 5*(73), 1–13

Merrien, F.-X. (2002). États-providence en devenir. Une analyse critique. *Revue française de sociologie, 43–2,* 211–242.

Merrien, F.-X., R. Parchet, & A. Kernen. (2005). *L'etat social. Une perspective internationale.* Paris: Armand Colin.

Morel, N., Palier B., & Palme J. (Eds.), (2009. *What Future for Social Investment ?,* Institute for Future Studies. Research report 2009/2.

Muller, P. (2000). L'analyse cognitive des politiques publiques: vers une sociologie de l'action publique. *Revue française de science politique, 50*(2), 189–207.

Newman, J. (2010). Towards a pedagogical state ? Summoning the "empowered" citizen. *Citizenship Studies, 14*(6), 711–723.

OECD (2008). *Growing unequal? Income distribution and poverty in OECD countries.* Paris : OECD.

Palier, B. (2010). *A long goodbye to Bismarck? The politics of welfare reform in continental Europe.* Amsterdam: Amsterdam University Press.

Paugam, S. (2007). Conclusion. Vers un nouveau contrat social. In S. Paugam (Ed.), *Repenser la solidarité* (pp. 949–980). Paris: Presses Universitaires de France.

Rys, V. (1995). Social security developments in central Europe: A return to reality. *Czech Sociological Review, 3*(2), 197–208.

Sen, A. (2002). Humanity and citizenship. In M. S. Nussbaum, *For Love of Country?* (pp. 111–118). Boston : Beacon Press.

Scharpf, F. (2009). *Legitimacy in the multilevel European polity.* MPIfG Working paper 09/1.

Vagnin, S. (2000). The blessings of the informal economy in central Europe. *Central Europe Review* 2 (4o/41/42).

INDEX

Printed and bound by CPI Group (UK) Ltd, Croydon, CR0 4YY